The Selected Writings of Jan Patočka

Also available from Bloomsbury

Dying for Ideas: The Dangerous Lives of the Philosophers, Costica Bradatan
The Selected Writings of Pierre Hadot: Philosophy as Practice, translated by Federico Testa and Matthew Sharpe
Heraclitus, Martin Heidegger, translated by Julia Goesser Assaiante and S. Montgomery Ewegen
A Philosophy of the Essay: Scepticism, Experience and Style, Erin Plunkett

The Selected Writings of Jan Patočka

Care for the Soul

EDITED BY IVAN CHVATÍK
AND ERIN PLUNKETT

**Translated by Alex Zucker, with
additional translations by Andrea
Rehberg and David Charlston**

BLOOMSBURY ACADEMIC
LONDON • NEW YORK • OXFORD • NEW DELHI • SYDNEY

BLOOMSBURY ACADEMIC
Bloomsbury Publishing Plc
50 Bedford Square, London, WC1B 3DP, UK
1385 Broadway, New York, NY 10018, USA
29 Earlsfort Terrace, Dublin 2, Ireland

BLOOMSBURY, BLOOMSBURY ACADEMIC and the Diana logo are trademarks of
Bloomsbury Publishing Plc

First published in Great Britain 2022

Cover design:
Cover image © LONELY TREE Oil on panel 125 × 85cm 2018 Hervé Constant (artist)
Private collection, Colette Levy, London UK

A catalogue record for this book is available from the British Library.

A catalog record for this book is available from the Library of Congress.

ISBN: HB: 978-1-3501-3910-7
       PB: 978-1-3501-3909-1
       ePDF: 978-1-3501-3911-4
       eBook: 978-1-3501-3912-1

Typeset by RefineCatch Limited, Bungay, Suffolk
Printed and bound in Great Britain

To find out more about our authors and books visit www.bloomsbury.com
and sign up for our newsletters.

Patočka in 1968. Photo by Dagmar Hochová. Copyright Jan Patočka Archive.

Patočka teaches an underground seminar in 1976, with Ivan Chvatík (pictured) and other students. Photo by Jan Endrís. Copyright Jan Patočka Archive.

Patočka with Irena Michňáková and Karel Kosík in 1976. Copyright Jan Patočka Archive.

In Memoriam
Ivan Miloš Havel
(1938–2021)

CONTENTS

PART FOUR Arts and Culture 163

PART FIVE Philosophy of History 261

FOREWORD

Graham Henderson

Chief Executive of The Rimbaud and Verlaine Foundation

I first came across the work of the Czech philosopher Jan Patočka (1907–77) in the early noughties when I read a passing reference to his concept of "putting soul in the city." This struck a chord with me, because my work running an arts charity frequently involves me in arguing for the vital importance of the arts and culture to a successful modern society. I also learned that Patočka had been an important influence on Václav Havel and his concept of "living in truth." In fact, Patočka had been the most famous signatory of Charter 77, the human rights petition that also brought Havel to prominence as someone resisting authoritarian oppression in communist Czechoslovakia, and Patočka's ideas fed into the success of the "Velvet Revolution" and the fall of communism in 1989. It seemed clear that his ideas remain important and intensely relevant to life in the twenty-first century.

Spurred into action, I purchased the best (and effectively only) general introduction to the work of Patočka written in English, by Edward F. Findlay. I was delighted to learn that Patočka's hero was Socrates, and that his ideas were grounded in the idea of the ancient Athenian *polis*, or political community. My work in the arts had already convinced me that I was engaged in a social capital building project, and that championing the arts was inseparable from championing a civil society based on active citizenship. Like Socrates, Patočka places the concept of "care for the soul" at the heart of his philosophical ideas. In fact, this concept is at the heart of the argument he is making for a new more human politics, and he awards the arts a privileged role in accessing the meanings that provide us with a basis for moral action in the world. Here, I thought, was a philosopher whose ideas could help restore the arts to their rightful place at the heart of our democracy.

However, my interest in the philosopher quickly came up against a major obstacle. With the exception of a few pieces in academic publications, none of Patočka's original texts were available in English translation. Outside the British Library Reading Room, it was difficult to get hold of any of his writings. I came to the view that there was a need for a selected edition of some of Patočka's key texts in English translation. This might have remained a pipe dream were it not for the team I was fortunate to be able to bring together for the translation project. In Alex Zucker, the project has benefited from one of the very best translators from Czech into English, someone who has a natural feel for the clarity and precision of Patočka's language. In the Czech Republic, we have received the unstinting support of the Patočka Archive, and in particular of Ivan Chvatík, who has been able to comment on the translations from a position of unrivaled knowledge of Patočka and his texts. It has been a great pleasure working with them both.

In the UK, the project has been delighted to work with Erin Plunkett from the University of Hertfordshire, and to benefit from her academic knowledge. She has been able to ensure that the translations of texts by Patočka recognize this wider context, and she has been able to indicate where terms used by him echo or refer back to the ideas of Husserl and Heidegger, with whose ideas Patočka was deeply engaged. She has brought great energy to the project and has added grace and nuance to the translated texts.

We have also been lucky to be able to work with Bloomsbury in producing this selected edition of texts by Patočka for publication. I am grateful to Liza Thompson, Lucy Russell, and their colleagues at Bloomsbury for ensuring that this bold project has become a reality.

I would also like to express my warmest gratitude to the Czech Ministry of Culture, the Sekyra Foundation in the Czech Republic, and the Jan Michalski Foundation in Switzerland, without whose generous funding we would have been unable to embark on the detailed and time-intensive process of translating Patočka. Among other things, this project has demonstrated a business model by means of which important foreign-language texts can be translated and published for the attention of an English-speaking audience. It is a model I believe will be emulated by other projects in the future.

The publication of this book is undoubtedly a "red letter day" for my charity. Most of the essays it contains are being made available in English for the very first time. It gives me particular pleasure that this edition includes some of Patočka's most important essays about the arts, including "Limping Pilgrim" and "The Writer's Concern." The insights in these inform directly the ongoing work my colleagues and I do in championing the arts. I believe that they have the potential to contribute both to civil society and to the articulation of new understandings and solutions.

I am delighted to note that work on this project has already stimulated a flurry of new academic writing about Patočka's contributions to thinking about the arts and aesthetics, both in the Czech Republic and internationally, notably in a special edition of *Bohemica Litteraria*, volume 23.

My original vision was for this book to be piled high on the "new ideas" table at the front of major bookstores in the UK and North America. It would be great if booksellers give it this kind of billing, which it certainly deserves. Patočka's thought world is rich and subtle, and occasionally dives into complex areas of phenomenology. This does not alter the fact that his ideas are important and topical. Although he does not provide easy answers, his philosophy goes to the heart of our contemporary political, social, ecological, and spiritual crises. The more people engage with his thinking, the better placed we shall be to interrogate our contemporary post-Covid world. In the process, readers may also benefit personally, as I have, from refocusing their attention on "care for the soul."

ACKNOWLEDGMENTS

Our warmest thanks go to all who made this book possible, including the Jan Patočka Archive, the Rimbaud and Verlaine Foundation, the Institute of Philosophy of the Czech Academy of Sciences, the Czech Ministry of Culture, the Jan Michalski Foundation, the Sekyra Foundation the University of Hertfordshire, and the Embassy of the Czech Republic in London. Thank you to Eric Manton, Jozef Majerník, and the late Erazim Kohák for allowing us to edit and publish their translations in this volume. Many thanks to Ludger Hagedorn and the Institut für die Wissenschaften vom Menschen along with the participants of the 2019 IWM Patočka workshop. Thanks also to Francesco Tava, Maria Balaska, and Robert Penney for their insight and generosity. Finally, love and thanks to Eugenio and Luca.

TRANSLATOR'S NOTE

Translating these works was truly a collective effort—more than any project I have worked on to date. Given that I am not a philosopher, Ivan Chvatík and Erin Plunkett's feedback and suggestions were indispensable in terms of both meaning and stylistic considerations. The two of them reviewed every draft of every one of my twelve translations for this volume, and their expertise and understanding of the nuances of translation benefited my work tremendously.

Every translation is an act of interpretation, the translator's personal reading of the text. Still, there are terms in Patočka's writing with established meanings that need to be respected, and even more so when it comes to concepts first formulated in German, which have standard translations in English. Examples of these include *bytí* ("being" or, pace Heidegger, "Being," depending on the context) vs. *jsoucno* ("a being," "existence," or, as it is rendered in some translations of Patočka, "the existent" or "what-is"); and, from Husserl's phenomenology of temporality, *podržování* ("retention") and *anticipace* ("protention").

The questions that arise in the process of translation concern not only the sense of a text, but also its sensibility. A recurring question in terms of sensibility for the essays in this volume was how to translate the word *člověk*, which occurs frequently. Distinct from the word *muž*, most often translated as "man" or "husband," depending on the context, *člověk*, referring to humans collectively, or in the abstract, is typically rendered in English as "person," "human," "man," or "one." (It also appears in the term *Člověk moudrý* or *Člověk rozumný*, what English speakers refer to as *Homo sapiens*.) The Czech language has three genders for nouns: masculine, feminine, and neuter. *Člověk* is masculine in gender but, unlike *muž*, doesn't necessarily call to mind "a man" in the gendered sense. I decided early on that, given the aim of this volume as Graham conceived it, highlighting "a philosopher whose ideas could help restore the arts to their rightful place at the heart of our democracy," with care for the soul his central concern, the language of my translations had to be explicitly inclusive of all people, meaning it had to be gender-nonbinary. Therefore I've used "humans," "human beings," "humanity," and "one" to translate *člověk*, as well as "they"—rather than "he," "she," "s/he," or "he or she"—as the third-person singular personal pronoun.

Although in the popular view, translation is about finding "the right words," in reality it's mainly a matter of style. This isn't to say you don't need the right words for a translation to be convincing. But the right words aren't enough. It also depends on their order, the structure of the sentences, the rhythm and pacing. These are personal elements, even in nonfiction. Patočka adheres to a high-formal style, but five of the essays in this collection were originally delivered as lectures: "Limping Pilgrim Josef Čapek," "Art and Time," "On the Principle of Scientific Conscience," "The Dangers of Technicization in Science," and "The Spiritual Person and the Intellectual." To me this comes through in Patočka's conversational transitions and frequent asides: "Let us now," "I will turn," "it seems to me," "as I see it." At times, I could feel myself wanting to ignore these seemingly superfluous fragments, to pare down the text, keep "only what matters." I never had the opportunity to hear Patočka speak, but these bits surfaced a picture of him in my mind that I found myself drifting off to whenever I was in the midst of his words. Of course, I hope my translations enable readers to engage with the powerful and inspiring ideas and themes of Patočka's work. But beyond that, to me, my translations would be a success if they bring to life not only the ideas of the man but the man himself. Enjoy.

Alex Zucker
Brooklyn, NY

TIMELINE

1907   Born in Turnov, now Czech Republic, then part of the Austro-Hungarian Empire.

1914–18   The First World War leads to the Russian Revolution, the break-up of the Austro-Hungarian Empire, and the birth of new nation states across Eastern Europe.

1918   An independent Czechoslovak Republic is established as a multi-ethnic democracy by Edvard Beneš, Milan R. Štefánik, and philosopher turned statesman Tomáš Masaryk, who served as the country's first president.

1925   Patočka matriculates in Romance studies, Slavonic studies, and Philosophy at Charles University in Prague.

1928–9   Studies at the Sorbonne in Paris.

     First meeting with Husserl, who presented his *Cartesian Meditations* at the Sorbonne in February 1929.

     First published article: "French Philosophy" in the journal *Česká mysl*.

1930   Works as assistant to philosopher J. B. Kozák at Charles University.

1932   Graduates in June from Charles University with a dissertation on Husserl's concept of evidence, supervised by J. B. Kozák: "The Concept of Evidence and its Significance for Noetics."

     Spends winter semester on Humboldt research fellowship in Berlin.

1933   Continuing his Humboldt fellowship, Patočka studies in Freiburg with Husserl and Heidegger.

     Meets and befriends Eugen Fink, Husserl's assistant.

1933   Adolf Hitler becomes German Chancellor, and the Nazis come to power in Germany.

1933–4   Patočka teaches at Hellichova grammar school in Prague.

	Founding member of Czech-German Prague Philosophy Circle (*Cercle philosophique de Prague pour les recherches sur l'entendement humain*); member of Prague Linguistic Circle (led by Vilém Mathesius).
1934–9	Czech secretary of *Cercle philosophique de Prague*. Emil Utitz was the German Chairman.
1935	Organizes Husserl's lectures in Prague, later published as *Crisis of the European Sciences and Transcendental Phenomenology*.
1936	Appointed associate professor at Charles University.
	Habilitation (post-doctoral) thesis: "The Natural World as a Philosophical Problem," responding to Husserl's conception of the natural world.
1937	Marries Helena Matoušková.
	Appointed managing editor of philosophy journal *Česká mysl*.
	Attends Ninth International Congress of Philosophy in Paris.
	On his return, visits the ailing Husserl in Freiburg.
	Daughter Františka born in August.
	Tomáš Masaryk, the founder and first president of Czechoslovakia, dies in September.
1938	The Anschluss – in March Hitler annexes Austria. In September the Munich Agreement between Britain, France, Italy and Germany authorizes Germany to annex several German-speaking areas of Czechoslovakia, effectively dismembering the country.
	Patočka delivers a speech in memory of Edmund Husserl on May 13 at the funeral gathering of Prague Philosophy Circle.
	Elected member of the Institut International de Philosophie in Paris.
1939	In March Germany annexes Bohemia and Moravia, commencing a brutal five-year occupation of the Czech lands.
	Patočka's second daughter Jana born in May.
1939–45	Germany invades and occupies Poland in September 1939, triggering the Second World War in Europe. Patočka is unable to work as a philosopher. Czechs are treated as second-class citizens in their own country by the German Race Laws.

1940	Assassination of Nazi leader Reinhard Heydrich by Czechoslovak resistance fighters leads to reprisals in Czechoslovakia, including the massacres at Lidice and Ležáky.
1944	Patočka assigned by the Nazis to forced labor service building a railway tunnel in Prague.
1945	Son Jan born in February.
	Soviet and Allied troops liberate Czechoslovakia from the Nazi occupation in May.
	Mass-expulsion of German-speaking population of Czechoslovakia as country restored to its pre-1938 frontiers.
1945–9	Patočka works as associate professor in Prague and Brno.
1945–8	Period of relative pluralism in Czechoslovakia as the Communists win the first post-war election in 1946, initially with a genuine popular support.
1947	Patočka participates in the UNESCO conference in Paris.
	On his return, he visits Eugen Fink in Freiburg.
1948	Pro-Moscow communists take power in Czechoslovakia after coup d'état in February.
1949	Dismissed from Charles University after refusing to join the Communist Party. Patočka's transition to the University of Brno is also ruined.
1949–68	Once again a marked man, Patočka is unable to work under the conditions of the Communist dictatorship. He is forced to take a series of archival and research positions in order to pursue academic work at all.
1950–4	Employed as a researcher at T. G. Masaryk Institute in Prague.
1954–7	Employed as a researcher at Pedagogical Institute of the Czechoslovak Academy of Sciences preparing Comenius' collected works.
1957–68	Employed first as a librarian, then as a researcher at the Institute of Philosophy of the Czechoslovak Academy of Sciences.
1960	Publishes translation of Hegel's *Phenomenology of Spirit*.
1964	Defends work for title of Doctor of Science: *Aristotle, his Predecessors and Heirs: A Study of the History of Philosophy from Aristotle to Hegel*.

	Visit to Husserl Archive in Leuven.

Visit to Husserl Archive in Leuven.

Lectures in Aachen, Bonn, and Cologne.

Writes German afterword to Husserl's *Cartesian Meditations*, translated into Czech and published in Prague in 1968.

1965   Visiting professor in Leuven. Works on the elaboration of a new concept of the natural world: "On the Prehistory of the Science of Movement: World, Earth, Heaven and the Movement of Human Life."

1966   Visiting professor in Mainz.

Publishes translation of Hegel's *Lectures on Aesthetics*.

Death of his wife Helena.

1967   Delivers lecture in Cologne.

Guest Professorship in Brno and Prague.

1968   The Prague Spring—a period of expanded freedoms begins in January when reformist Communist Alexander Dubček is elected First Secretary of the Communist Party of Czechoslovakia. Continues until August 1968, when the Soviet Union and other Warsaw Pact members invade the country to suppress the reforms.

Patočka delivers lecture in Freiburg.

Appointed full professor at Charles University and gives courses until his dismissal in 1972.

1969–77   Once again Patočka is increasingly unable to work and publish freely in Czechoslovakia, with his work proscribed and suppressed by the authoritarian Communist regime. He is encouraged by friends to flee abroad but refuses.

1969   Patočka participates in Fourth International Phenomenological Colloquium in Halle.

1970   Delivers lecture in Freiburg.

1971   Receives honorary doctorate from the Technische Hochschule in Aachen, Germany, but is not allowed to travel there. The doctorate is finally presented to him at the residence of the West German ambassador to Prague in 1975.

1972   Forced into early retirement and passport confiscated.

1973   Participates in 15th World Congress of Philosophy in Varna, Bulgaria.

1973–6	Gives underground lectures and seminars in private residences.
	Prohibited from publishing with presses, his works are issued in *samizdat*.
1975	Publication of *Heretical Essays in the Philosophy of History* in *samizdat* (Munich, 1980; Prague, 1990).
1977	Serves along with Jiří Hájek and Václav Havel as one of three initial spokespersons for Charter 77, a major political and human rights initiative with international impact, responded to furiously by the Communist authorities.
1977	Succumbs to a brain haemorrhage after repeated interrogations by secret police (StB).
	Ivan Chvatík and other students act quickly to hide Patočka's unpublished writings from the secret police before they can be confiscated.
	Obituary by Paul Ricoeur in *Le Monde* cements Patočka's international reputation as a philosopher hero.
1977–89	*Samizdat* publication of twenty-seven-volume *Archive Collection of Patočka's Works,* edited by Patočka's students Ivan Chvatík, Pavel Kouba, Miroslav Petříček, Radim Palouš, and Jan Vít.
1977–2021	Immediately after Patočka's death in 1977, Erika Abrams begins translating his works into French. She contacts the clandestine "Jan Patočka Archive" in Prague, led by Ivan Chvatík, and is able to translate directly from Patočka's unpublished manuscripts. Her first translation is the book *Essais hérétiques sur la philosophie de l'histoire* (1975), completed with a foreword by Paul Ricœur and afterword by Roman Jakobson, published by Editions Verdier (Lagrasse, 1981). Today, she has translated and published nearly all Patočka's books, essays, notes, and letters, which has made the Czech philosopher accessible to scholars all over the world. Patočka is now being translated into twenty-five different languages.
1984	Institut für die Wissenschaften vom Menschen in Vienna launches the project *Erforschung und Publikation des philosophischen Werks von Jan Patočka* ("Research and Publication of the Philosophical Work of Jan Patočka").
1987–92	Publication of *Ausgewählte Schriften* I–V ("Selected Writings"), Stuttgart.

1989   The Velvet Revolution in Czechoslovakia ends forty-one
          years of Communist rule. Writer and dissident Václav Havel
          becomes president of the Czech Republic. It is finally
          possible to read and publish Patočka's work in his own
          country.

1990   The Jan Patočka Archive is established by Ivan Chvatík and
          Pavel Kouba as part of the Institute of Philosophy of the
          Czechoslovak Academy of Sciences.

1996   OIKOYMENH press in Prague begins to publish *The
          Collected Writings of Jan Patočka* in Czech (presently
          twenty-one volumes).

2007   International conference "Jan Patočka, 1907–1977" held in
          Prague under the aegis of Charles University and the Czech
          Academy of Sciences, in conjunction with the 37th annual
          meeting of the Husserl Circle. See Ivan Chvatík and Erika
          Abrams, *Jan Patočka and the Heritage of Phenomenology:
          Centenary Papers* (Springer, 2011).

2019   Patočka scholars gather at Senate House in London for a
          seminar and event to launch the project to publish Patočka's
          selected writings in English.

Introduction

Erin Plunkett

The question facing the editors of the present volume is: why Jan Patočka, why now? On the one hand, this is a collection of essays for the specialist, for those working in phenomenology, the philosophy of history, political philosophy, philosophical anthropology, literary theory, and other fields to which Patočka makes valuable contributions—and provocations. Patočka's erudition is remarkable, from his knowledge of Plato and Aristotle,[1] to his rich engagement with Edmund Husserl and Martin Heidegger, to his command of the European history of ideas and his dialogue with contemporaries; there is a wide field of potential impact for his ideas. But perhaps his greatest contribution is the clarity he brings to the question of what is at stake in philosophical inquiry.

For Patočka, philosophy is always an activity oriented toward the urgent question of how to live in the world with others. Given the world in which he lived, in his own words a twentieth century of war,[2] in a Czechoslovakia that endured first Nazi occupation and then decades of Soviet rule, Patočka is alive to the difficulty of this question and to the darkness that hangs over human efforts to live meaningfully. For him, solidarity, justice, truth, and meaning are forged only in the face of radical uncertainty and unease. In this respect, his work has appeal beyond the world of academic specialists; it would be a great loss if a philosopher whose ideas inspired and shaped an entire dissidence movement, and who himself took part in this movement, were to be relegated to an academic footnote. His writings on the movement of human life, on the value of the arts and literature, on the pitfalls of a technoscientific society, on the problems of European identity—these speak to any intellectually curious reader and to any person wrestling with the question of meaningful action. All of us involved in producing this volume share the conviction that the Czech philosopher not only remains relevant but that his ideas are vital for understanding and responding to our contemporary social, political, environmental, and indeed philosophical situation.

The overwhelming majority of writings included here date from Patočka's most creative period, in the 1960s and 1970s. From 1965 to 1972, Patočka was allowed an official university post after many years of being banned from lecturing and publishing; lectures in his characteristically engaging style were delivered to packed auditoriums. After being forced out in 1972 following a shift in government policy, he continued to hold "underground university" seminars in Prague that were attended by keen students, among them my co-editor Ivan Chvatík, who organized many of these sessions. After Patočka's death, Ivan and his fellow students produced and distributed *samizdat* manuscripts of their teacher's work—printed in secret on a Ministry of Finance copy machine—which were eventually smuggled out of the country and made available in Europe. Patočka also published a number of works abroad during his later years, written for German and French audiences. In the texts from this period, readers are presented with a mature vision of Patočka's philosophical thought.

We have chosen to organize this volume around themes for the benefit of the general reader who may be encountering Patočka's ideas for the first time. However, Patočka rarely confines himself to a single theme within a text; readers will find valuable reflections on history in Patočka's writings on arts and culture, or insights into his account of the soul in his writings on history; we hope this volume will offer a sense of the rich interconnections among these themes.

Care for the Soul

Care for the soul is a pervasive theme in Patočka's work and is central to the recent surge of interest in Patočka as a political philosopher.[3] Here, "soul" is not a religious but a philosophical concept, one that pertains to the essential life of the individual yet is inextricably linked to the task of living together in the *polis*. For Patočka, as for Hannah Arendt, care for that element of human being which is not exhausted by mere labor and the maintenance of life is crucial to any genuine politics. The soul forms the counterpart to what Patočka and Michel Foucault call "biologism"[4] or "biopolitics"—a politics that is concerned with optimizing and controlling physical life, but which is in fact hostile to flourishing in a deeper sense.[5]

Patočka offers a portrait of the soul in one of the most eloquent and moving pieces in this collection, "Limping Pilgrim," dedicated to the Czech modernist painter and poet Josef Čapek. The essay was originally a talk delivered on the fifth anniversary of Čapek's disappearance and subsequent death in a Nazi concentration camp, lending poignancy to Patočka's discussion of the soul's struggle as well as presenting a veiled social critique. Patočka obliquely raises the question of what kind of society would allow or actively pursue the death of a person so decent, wise, and humane. And the reader is left to consider what kind of society might result from Čapek's portrait of the soul in contrast to the "titanic" humanism of the nineteenth century.

The arresting image of a pilgrim hobbling along life's way is Čapek's, from his essay of the same title,[6] and through an extended reading of this metaphor, Patočka describes his vision of the path of an authentic human life, moving always towards something that is never specified: a pilgrimage to an unknown region. "The pilgrimage for Čapek truly is a path from the unknown to the unknown, from darkness to darkness. 'I was not—*I am*—I will not be.'"[7] Limping becomes a metaphor for being suspended between two impulses: that which would bind us to the earth and the familiar, and that which leads us to strike out again and again into the unfamiliar and alien, the reflection of some uncanny dimension in human being.

The uneven gait of the pilgrim is a result of being pulled in opposite directions toward the finite and toward the eternal: such is human existence. Patočka writes, "A total reabsorption into reality is not even possible for us; the very fact that we always in some way transcend it, that we walk through life on legs of different length, means that we will limp." Like Kierkegaard then, Patočka sees existence as a movement between opposing poles, always in a state of tension. In the "Limping Pilgrim" essay, Patočka uses Čapek's language of the "Person" and the "soul" to describe the aspects of the self that move in constant relation to one another, each pulling its own way. In normal life, where the Person rules, playing the appropriate roles and keeping order, the soul is forced into:

> . . . the function of a mere servant with no independent say, no leading role in life, never intruding or getting in the way; the moment the soul subjugates itself in this way, it creates order and balance, biologically and socially—provided, of course, the Person is clever and successful in having its way.

However, there are moments—in Patočka these are typically moments of deep crisis and pain—in which the soul rises through the mask of the Person and changes our sense of ourselves and the world.

> In the event that the soul, that is, our unobjectified component, our connection to the infinite, does not subjugate itself, in the event that it awakens and demands its rights, then all of a sudden the way we move among things, our reactions to life become unsettled, unpredictable; things happen that never happened before—life no longer runs on automatic, but begins to be aware that it is not of a piece, that it is— limping along.

Patočka presents the possibility of a rupture with the actual, with what has been accepted as the realm of possibility. The ultimate rupture is death, and indeed for Patočka the soul is "allied with" death, insofar as it breaks away from everyday life with its certainties and calculated probabilities. A break of this kind opens up the whole in a mood of anxiety or unease. Čapek wonders, "What if the soul is nothing but unease . . .? It may not be much, but, ultimately—it is everything!" This unease is not something to be avoided, as it awakens us to something essential. Ultimately it contains an element of hope: "Things happen."

There is an advantage to our human-all-too-human infirmity. "What an odd humanism, you say, that sees humans as having an irreparable defect! Be that as it may, I believe it is this quality of Josef Čapek's humanism that sets it apart. His limping man is no successor to God, neither god nor demigod." Čapek's vision of the limping pilgrim appeals to Patočka precisely because it does not succumb to the atmosphere of titanism that dominated the end of the nineteenth century into which Čapek was born.

In this titanic form of humanism, of the kind seen in Feuerbach, Nietzsche, and elsewhere, human beings cast off the shackles of tradition and superstition and become the gods that they were always intended to be. Within this perspective,

> The moment humans break free of the clutches of illusion that obscure their full reality, the moment they rid themselves of metaphysical and mythological visions, they immediately become complete beings, heroes of the cosmos, every bit as much a product of worldly forces as the key to their meaning.

Patočka values the sense of possibility within this outlook, but he is skeptical, both of the power it promises and of the contradiction within this power: that human beings are ultimately nothing more than a force—the most powerful force perhaps—in a world of natural forces. For Patočka, as for Čapek, human life can never become fully natural in this way; there is an element of human being that the language of "worldly forces" cannot capture. The need for meaning persists, and meaning is always only achieved via a struggle, never finished.

> In Čapek's conception, the process of becoming a complete being, a sensate being with access to the universal, does not come automatically, naturally, so to speak, but only after a struggle with whatever it is that prevents us, and even then we never do so entirely and without damage, but only humanly—which is to say, partially, privately, without definitiveness. Humans may make sense of things, but only in a *finite* way.

"What prevents us," namely, our finitude, is not something that will be overcome, whatever advances humanity makes on the inherited world. Even if technology could allow for much longer life, the fact of having a limited time and a necessarily limited perspective is not eradicated. This inevitable "infirmity" implies a tragic dimension to human life, one that the death of God and the titanic dispelling of illusion do not free us from. Human being remains suspended in movement between person and soul, part and whole, finite and eternal, necessity and possibility, and the movement between these poles is something that the individual must constantly reenergize, must tend and nurture.

The Soul in the Polis

In his lecture "The Soul in Plato," Patočka shows the Platonic roots[8] of his notion of the soul and its path, again presenting the soul as a movement between opposing poles and demonstrating the need to care for the soul—both on the level of the individual and as a political necessity. Patočka portrays the ideal *polis* of Plato's *Republic* as centered on a concern for the soul's formation; the ideal social and political form would be one in which the person who has cultivated truth and justice, who has looked after the matters of the soul in themselves and in others, could "live happily and unharmed." Patočka hints at the brutality of unjust systems of governance in which the good are punished and the wicked are rewarded with power and acclaim. He describes Plato's myth of:

> ... the perfectly just and truthful man who really *is* such without appearing so (this form of life would be realized at its purest when he appears to be unjust and when he is a stumbling block for everyone else), and of his complete opposite, of the perfectly unjust hypocrite and fraudster, who cannot be distinguished from a genuinely just man by anyone who is not a philosopher.[9] The former ends up on the cross, while the latter becomes the king and ruler of this world.

As with many of Patočka's writings, the grim reality of his situation, enduring two world wars as well as living under a Soviet regime and being forbidden to teach or publish for most of his life, appears just below the surface. His description of the philosopher's task in such a society is equally telling:

> To help himself and everyone else, Plato's Socrates now undertakes the only thing the philosopher can do, and the thing that only the philosopher can do—he projects a city in which it would not be possible to do injustice to the philosopher or to anyone else, a harmonious and happy city.

Here Patočka makes explicit the link between philosophical activity—a cultivation of the soul—and a liberationist politics. While there has been much debate over how to think of Patočka's politics, with some claiming him as a figure of political resistance and others enlisting him on the side of classical democracy and civil society (both positions have merit), there is no doubt that his philosophical inquiries are bound up with the thinking of our life in common, extending to questions about the organization of the state and the education system.

Patočka's decision in the late 1970s to help draft and to lend his public support to the human rights appeal and civic movement known as Charter 77[10] was, on the surface, out of character for a man who had never been actively involved in any political movement. But it is clear that such a decision issued from Patočka's deepest philosophical commitments— commitments he had affirmed throughout his life and that were apparent to those who knew him.[11] Patočka died at the age of sixty-nine in the weeks following a lengthy interrogation by the secret police, so he was not alive to witness the eventual success of the Charter in helping to bring about the Velvet Revolution of 1989 and to usher in the writer and dissident Václav Havel as the first president of the Czech Republic.

One can see in Patočka's writings his high esteem for acts of intellectual courage, from the death of Socrates, to the founding of the independent Czechoslovak nation by the philosopher-turned-statesman Tomáš Masaryk, to the defiance of Čapek smuggling his poetry out of Bergen-Belsen. But his championing of such acts is not naive, and he is aware that many see a commitment to ideas—to non-instrumental thinking—in a less than heroic light. This comes through in a fascinating essay in this collection on "The Idea of Education." Patočka wrote this essay in 1938, in the immediate aftermath of the disastrous Munich Agreement, which gave Hitler the right to annex key areas of Czechoslovakia for Germany and opened the way to his subsequent takeover of the entire country six months later. In the essay, Patočka does not mention this event directly but instead responds to the occasion by defending—and renewing—the classical German humanistic ideal of education (*Bildung*), represented by Goethe, Herder, and others, to present a contrast to the dark reality of Germany in the 1930s. Writing in the voice of his contemporaries, and perhaps voicing reservations of his own as well, Patočka asks:

> The harmoniously comprehending individual, embracing the entirety of the world with their mind, as the humanistic ideal proposed—is this not the idealism of the dilettante who seeks only the benefits, but lacks the courage to act, or productively investigate, in even the most limited fashion?[12]

There is an echo here of Callicles' admonition to Socrates that he "let go of impractical philosophy and its paradoxical doctrines—such as that legality and truthfulness are under any circumstances better than their opposites, or that a harmonious life is happier than a wicked one" because "if he will occupy himself with or even conduct himself by his unrealistic philosophical thoughts, he will be disgraced in the city and die."[13] Yet Patočka defends the "impractical" and "unrealistic" reflective person who looks toward the whole against the charges of sterile dilettantism. The habit of distancing oneself from the conventional allows the reflective person to "go beyond their own narrowly personal standpoint as well as the perspective of whatever group they are attached to through their origin and interests." The self-discipline of an intellectually rigorous life means that "if they have the ability and capacity to act, they act not on impulse but out of understanding, and their authority is not based on putting ideas in people's heads and making an emotional impression, but rather on their ability to see into the heart of things."

Patočka recognizes that acts of intellectual courage of the kind represented by Masaryk are not available to everyone. Yet even where the reflective person is "incapable of action," where "they can understand but are not prone to act … politics in a deeper sense cannot do without their interventions; it would grow coarse and lose itself in demagoguery and utilitarianism." Such an outlook offers a framework for thinking about the political value of Patočka's philosophical activity, even though he for the most part avoids direct engagement in politics. Like Hannah Arendt, who influenced him, he sees thinking and other non-instrumental activity as the groundwork for an authentic politics. And for Patočka it is precisely when our naive faith in things is most shaken that we are in a position to think through and act toward the life in common that we want to see. He ends the 1938 essay with the admonition that education is "not simply blissful enrichment, but pain and struggle as well."[14]

The Whole and the Natural World

Jan Patočka is, at bottom, a thinker of the whole. Despite the occasional clamor about a "theory of everything," it is not characteristic of our time to raise the question of the whole, and certainly not in the way that Patočka understood this question, as grounding and orienting all of our movements in the world. The present age is characterized by a mania for distinctions and specialization, for the multiplication of particulars. And yet, what have the developments of the last century—from globalization, to world-ending weapons, to the climate crisis, to a global pandemic—shown us so clearly as the fact of being a part of a whole? Ours, declares Patočka, is the "planetary era."[15] While the economic-material whole of globalization is not the same whole that Patočka describes, we note that in insisting on the urgency of the whole, Patočka identifies a contradiction in the modern condition: on the one hand ever greater specialization and division, and on the other hand anonymous forces of unification, or perhaps more precisely, of mobilization that gather everything that is under a singular concept. A thinker who, like Patočka, offers a more thoughtful vision of the whole than the purely contingent unity of existing within the same economic forces of "monopoly supercapitalism"[16] or the same planetary ecosystem is surely a thinker for our times.

Patočka's concern for thinking the whole comes very early in his philosophical development, as he begins to think through the problem of the "natural world" in response to Edmund Husserl's writings on the subject. The natural world in question is not what we now refer to as the environment—comprising the various physical ecosystems of the planet—though it is not unrelated to this sense of "natural world" and has bearing upon it. The world Patočka describes is also not "natural" in the sense of nature as opposed to culture. It refers instead to the world of our life or the total horizon of our experience, which includes both "nature" and "culture" and which, to Patočka's mind, has yet to become the subject of philosophical treatment. Husserl goes some way toward opening up a philosophical investigation of the natural world by identifying its importance and arguing for its primacy in relation to a mathematical-scientific conception of the world.[17] But Patočka advances this investigation significantly. The centrality of the natural world to Patočka's thought is evidenced by the fact it was the subject of his first major philosophical text in the 1930s and that he is still preoccupied with it in 1967, when he writes "The Natural World and Phenomenology."

Patočka's writings on the "natural world" as the whole in which we live are occasioned by years of passionate study of and reflection on Husserl and Heidegger. Nevertheless, he is equally motivated by perennial philosophical questions about the relationship between the world of appearance and the world as it is, between mind and world, between subjectivity and objectivity. Patočka's questioning of the whole is also motivated by pressing issues of life in the present age, which has lost a connection to the natural world both in the specialized sense that Patočka uses this term and in the more general sense of our relationship to the earth and sky as the "referents" of all our activity. For Patočka, the earth is

> . . . not originally a body like other bodies; it is not comparable to anything else, because everything else that might occur and that we might encounter relates to it as the ground that is always presupposed. It is the *natural horizontal* with respect to which we assume every attitude or stance—in every rising to one's feet, every step, every movement, the earth is presupposed, at once energizing and wearying, as well as sustaining and affording peace.[18]

The natural world, as we think of it, tends to be divorced from phenomenological considerations of this kind, instead belonging to the conception of the world in the sciences. Patočka's rethinking of the natural world as the lifeworld and the earth as the ground that is always presupposed by the movements of our life offers a different starting point for our response to the environmental crisis. Additionally, Patočka raises the question of the whole against the backdrop of deep political divisions within Europe and globally. His analysis opens up a space for addressing our common human world and the crises of modern civilization.

Phenomenology, Objectivity, and Technology

The dialogue that takes place across different conceptions of phenomenology remains one of the richest sources available for thinking through our relationship to the world. Such reflection comes naturally to human beings, whether it is expressed through ritual, through artistic representation of features of the world we deem significant, through scientific enquiry, or through explicitly philosophical reflection on the self or on the nature of things. Phenomenology as a philosophical approach involves a refinement of this kind of perennial thinking, particularly in its commitment to understanding subject, object, and world in richer and more precise ways. In order to better understand Patočka's own phenomenology, it is necessary to give a general survey of the field, introducing some of the key ideas from the two phenomenological thinkers who most influenced Patočka: his teachers Edmund Husserl and Martin Heidegger. One of the rewards of reading Patočka is a sense for phenomenology as a living discipline—one that moves between and beyond the individual project of any singular figure.

Phenomenology is perhaps most immediately identified with the exploration of subjectivity or consciousness. Phenomenology's treatment of subjectivity, particularly in the figure of Edmund Husserl (1859–1938), is an important contribution to the understanding both of human and non-human being. In Patočka's reading of Husserl's project—the most extended examples in this volume are "What Is Phenomenology?" and "The Natural World and Phenomenology"—Husserl turns his attention from objects as such to the question of how things come to be available to consciousness at all. This is, in Patočka's mind, *the* philosophical question, the ground for any other kind of enquiry into the nature of things. Yet the sciences, the arbiter of truth in modernity, take the availability or givenness of the world for granted. Indeed scientific "objectivity" is meant to guarantee the full presence of the object, purged of the incompleteness, ambiguity, or biases of subjective perception. In Husserl's turn toward the phenomenal, toward the question of how things come to be manifest at all, a renewed understanding of subjectivity becomes imperative.

For Husserl, the subject plays an essential role in the manifestation of the world, as the "dative" of manifestation—that to which the world manifests itself. This is not equivalent to the strong idealist claim that the world is ultimately a *production* of subjectivity, though the subject, as in Descartes, guarantees the world in an important sense. Patočka summarizes in "The Dangers of Technicization":

Husserl seeks to base this more fundamental sense of truth, on which our worldly strivings are grounded, systematically on a specially purified transcendental consciousness which sees through all the "prejudices" of ordinary reality without sharing in them and which can see through them precisely because it does not.[19]

Husserl's notion of a transcendental subject in his late work *Cartesian Meditations* became a guarantor in this sense, providing the objectivity that the sciences could not themselves provide because they take the givenness or manifestation of the object for granted. Husserl's revised understanding of subjectivity thus entails a revised understanding of objectivity as well.

Yet Husserl's interest in subjectivity was not only the working out of a philosophical problem: he saw in the world around him—acutely toward the end of his life—the problems that could arise from a mistaken notion of truth as objectivity in the scientific sense. Patočka shared Husserl's philosophical vision of the trajectory of scientific objectivity as well as his feeling for the social and political urgency of rethinking objectivity and subjectivity in more philosophically rigorous ways. He describes Husserl's position not as a denial of the legitimacy of objectivity, but as a rejection of "its metaphysical hypostatization, for which mathematically conceived objectivity *is* reality, and the *sole* one at that."[20] One might express the problem in this way: in the present age a particular kind of reasoning has taken hold and restricted the collective imagination, skewing the understanding both of what is and of what could be.

In his *Crisis of the European Sciences* (1936),[21] originally a set of lectures in Prague which Patočka organized, Husserl sought to show how the ideal constructions of mathematics and the "mathematized sciences" stemming from Galileo and Descartes became the metaphysical underpinning for our modern conception of reality as an objective world, a world standing apart from subjective experience and open to scientific measurement and mathematical calculation. Husserl calls this conception of reality a "construction," built upon the process of abstracting from lived experience to create idealized versions of the objects that surround us and eventually seeing the world itself as nothing but a set of such objects. As inheritors of this conception, we have come to understand that the world as it presents itself in the richness and ambiguity of experience is something less than really "real." The objects of our experience lack the exactness and "objectivity" (or generality) of the objects that concern the sciences, and this unwieldy quality makes them feel less reliable. In other words, the ability to predict something becomes a measure of its reality. In Patočka's words, we "dare to decide what is and is not by the application of a dry objectivist measure."[22] As for those phenomena that scientists and data analysts have not yet learned to predict, like human action, they are available in principle to such prediction, or will be, when they are understood within the correct scientific framework.

Such an outlook strikes most of us as commonplace; after all, the situation described by Husserl and Patočka is our own. What can easily be overlooked, within the ordinariness of such claims, and with the great advances the scientific framework has afforded humanity,[23] is the threat they pose to human life. As our meaningful experience of the world and our sense of the world as meaningful become relegated to subjective perception—and, following Nietzsche, illusion—a crisis of *meaning* follows. The realm of significance, of attachments and meanings that direct our actions becomes unanchored, divorced from what (really) is, rendering our actions in the world meaningless and undermining our ability to understand the world. For Husserl and even more so for Patočka, that threat was being played out on the world stage.

Patočka's own writings on caring for the soul, on the natural world, on history, on literature reflect his sense of the urgency of the spiritual crisis diagnosed by Husserl. But his philosophical understanding of the problem is equally influenced by Heidegger's later text, "The Question Concerning Technology" (1954).[24] In Heidegger, the metaphysical hypostatization spoken of by Husserl takes on a different form, becoming an all-encompassing worldview or world "picture,"[25] one that human beings did not create but that is "a particular metaphysical fate to which we have fallen victim, a danger we must outlast."[26] In "The Natural World and Phenomenology," Patočka analyses Heidegger's account of this dangerous metaphysics with great clarity and insight. In Heidegger,

> The central philosophical formulation of this practice of metaphysics is the *principium rationis*, or principle of sufficient reason, formulated by Leibniz in the seventeenth century, after a two-thousand-year incubation: the principle that there must be a reason for everything. Heidegger interprets this principle as one of universal calculability and predictability. Nothing is, nothing exists, unless it conforms to this principle, i.e., unless it meets and is subsumed within the universal requirement that it be secured by calculation. This principle thus amounts to the rigorous, exact objectification of all that is. This objectification transforms all that exists, the *universum*, into an object placed before the subject; the subject, seeking to secure its place in the world, places the object before itself in order to master it. The world becomes a re-presentation in this sense. Thus the entire modern era is the age of the "world picture," if *picture* is understood in the sense of an "objectification," a "representation for the subject," a "counterpart to the explicit reasoning and deliberating activity of the subject," a "structure of re-presenting, of form-ing, of constructing."[27]

It is clear from this passage that a will to mastery stands behind our commonplace assumptions about the subject and the object, about what we are and what the world is. It is no surprise that part of our metaphysical fate is to face the planetary consequences of our attitude of mastery toward the earth. Following on from Heidegger's account in "The Question Concerning Technology," Patočka concludes that modernity is characterized not just by a narrow and flawed sense of reality but also by an immense technoscientific power that seeks relentlessly to uncover what is hidden, to mobilize resources. Everything that is, from human beings to the planets above, becomes a "resource." For Patočka, this project of mobilization reflects the triumph of reason of a certain kind and yet lacks any human rationale, any place in a wider field of human concern and meaning. It is epitomized by the twentieth-century development of the atomic bomb, which follows such a logic of mobilization to the end of total destruction. Patočka refers to this development as a "rationality of means" applied to an "irrationalism of goals."[28] The same dangerous combination can be seen in many of the twentieth century's horrors.

Nevertheless, Patočka shares Heidegger's sense that there is something positive in the essential core of technology, a seed that might generate new possibilities for being in the world different from the attitude of mastery and domination. Patočka writes:

> It would seem that in a technically dominated world there exists no possibility for the essential core of technology to be understood in its inmost sense and become manifest. And yet there are certain phenomena of the technically dominated world which seem to pose the question of whether a basic transformation of man's relation to truth is not being prepared in them, a transformation which might lead from truth as correctness, which is all that the rule of technology requires, to a more primordial form of truth.

It is the "essential core" of technology to uncover what is concealed. The disclosure of the present age operates only within the framework of what is manipulable and predictable, what can be mastered. However, Heidegger notes that if we grasp the essence of technology as disclosure, we will understand that truth does not lie in correct determinations, in successful models, but in this disclosive activity itself, bringing into manifestation from out of concealment.

Understanding truth as the activity of disclosure means a different role for human being in the world than that of a "force" among forces or a "resource." In "The Dangers of Technicization," Patočka offers his own account of the form this might take, namely what he calls "sacrifice." Willingness to sacrifice oneself for that which does not "count" within the framework of the real that we currently understand, a sacrifice "for nothing," demonstrates the ability of human action to realize possibilities of being that lie beyond the actual and beyond "a technical understanding of being . . . for which there exists nothing like a sacrifice, only utilization of resources."[29] This openness to being characterizes human being as such. We are creatures that are capable of truth, of letting what is show itself as it is—and this is something that we can consciously take responsibility for.

Asubjective Phenomenology

Late in his thinking, Patočka advanced the practice of an asubjective phenomenology. While questions about the nature of human being and human subjectivity remain important in this project, especially in Patočka's concern with embodiment and care for the soul, Patočka distances himself from Husserl's transcendental subjectivity: the passive witness that underpins the possibility of the appearance of the world. Patočka instead shines a light on the strands in Husserl's thought that stress the subject's active nature and intimate relationship to the lifeworld through bodily orientation and need. The natural world, the world of our life, is "not open to us like a theater, where we sit looking on and the director lets us take control, but rather a whole *in which* we are always like an embedded component that is never permitted to stand above it and never will."[30] This rejection of the spectator model of the subject who "stands above" the action is a direct shot at Husserl's transcendental subject and the Cartesian ego cogito.

However, Patočka reads elsewhere in Husserl an appreciation for our active interest in life, and he further develops this understanding in his own conception of the relationship between subject and world: "The primordial world of our pre-theoretical life is originally a world in which we *move*, in which we are active, not a world that we discover and observe."[31] Furthermore, "the world and human beings are *in mutual movement*"[32] rather than standing at odds with one another as the legacy of subject and object suggests. The language of mutuality is also intended to counter the notion that the world is ultimately a production or projection of subjectivity. We are, in a most basic sense, movement, and while we take the possibilities of our being from the world, the world also moves through our movement.

Patočka, in emphasizing this mutual movement between human being and world offers a revised, more primordial understanding of what the world is, and of our relationship to it. Rather than a "worldless" objectivity, the view from nowhere that characterizes the sciences, we are worldly beings through and through, and our connection to the earth and sky through our lived bodies makes the world always a world of our own, in which we actively participate.

All space and all that fills it, the states and transitions that we observe within it, are originally referents of our primordial movement; they have meaning only in correlation to it, and are open to us only because the movement of a being that is not worldless but has a world cannot simply *take place*, cannot be nothing but a gradual unfolding of a state, but must be *performed*, and so this movement has its own real where from/where to, its own in-the-midst-of, its own growth, its own encounters.[33]

Ultimately, as the term "asubjective phenomenology" suggests, subjectivity understood in isolation or understood solely as consciousness is not Patočka's concern. Heidegger's existential analytic had already shifted the terrain of phenomenology from subjectivity to a broader structural analysis of human being in the world—and of being itself. By the time of Heidegger's late writings, he had moved away from discussions of subjectivity altogether and turned his attention almost exclusively to being and to language as the "house of being." Though Patočka does not follow precisely the same lines of inquiry, by the 1950s the ground had already been prepared for his asubjective approach.

Building on this ground, Patočka applies himself to the task that he sees as the core of Husserl's work: developing a philosophy of phenomena or the phenomenal field—the space of emergence. He considers the explicit thematization of phenomena—as opposed to subject and object—to be a relatively recent philosophical achievement. As a result, phenomenology proper, as a science of phenomena, is still largely unworked and only beginning to come into its own. This puts Patočka's conception of phenomenology at odds with those who understand it as a moment in philosophical history, already dwindling by the 1960s and 1970s when Patočka was setting out his agenda.

Patočka contributes to the development of this new science of phenomena, building on the scaffolding of Husserl's and Heidegger's projects, through his skillful analysis of their shared concerns and their divergences. He is convinced that

> The diversity of phenomenological projects, the very differences among concrete descriptions and analyses of phenomena, depend upon the guiding idea which directs the great progression of phenomenological work, i.e., upon the progress toward concrete experience.[34]

Following Husserl's model of returning to "the things themselves,"[35] but differing procedurally with Husserl on how to achieve this, Patočka's late phenomenological texts present the ongoing drama of philosophical ideas in their relationship to one another and in their relationship to history. Indeed history is not merely an accumulation of experiences but an unfolding of the philosophical project, though not only a linear one. For Patočka, the way to the things themselves is to turn our attention toward phenomena, to the appearing of what appears as it appears.

The phenomenal field—the space of emergence or becoming— encompasses both subject and object, and so goes some way toward a new beginning of philosophy that does not take for granted the Cartesian rift between subject and world or the Kantian distinction between the phenomenal and noumenal. Unlike his predecessors, Patočka understands history as vital to the investigation of phenomena, since history is the manifestation of human movement, or the "mutual movement" of soul and world. He stresses contingent moments of rupture from the status quo that lead history in incalculable directions. History proper begins with a rupture of this kind, as human beings turn from the inherited world as a world of given meaning to a "problematic" relationship to the world. History is ultimately the story of human freedom lived out in problematicity.

Patočka's asubjective phenomenology then does not take him toward what was in recent years called an object-oriented ontology, where the question of human being was sidelined out of a worry over subjectivism or anthropocentrism. But some of the same impulses are at work in both of these approaches: a reclaiming of being as primary, defending it against the constructions of subjectivity, not least because of the disastrous environmental crisis whose roots can be located in the view that the world is ours to master. It is an insistence that *the world* reveals itself to us, but that being is not identical to thought. Part of the contemporary appeal of Patočka's phenomenology is precisely his insistence on the "equal absoluteness"[36] of the world and subjectivity, avoiding the extremes that would insist on the reality only of "things" or of mind. Patočka is interested in the human world, the world of our life, in opposition to the world as a scientific construction. However, he is deeply skeptical, especially in his late writings, of a philosophy in which we only ever see ourselves, what Heidegger calls the "delusion" that "man everywhere and always encounters only himself."[37] Being remains other and essentially "mysterious."[38]

Patočka points to Christianity as a model for acknowledging the primacy and otherness of being.

> For the Christian soul finds itself placed before something which in principle it can never master, which fundamentally surpasses it, which remains incomprehensible to it and which has to remain unconquered by it as long as it does not reveal itself to the soul of its own accord.[39]

Patočka finds in Christian theology, here that of the seventeenth-century Bohemian philosopher Comenius, an alternative to the attitude of mastery that defines the prevailing framework of modernity. Patočka's intelligent reading of religion along philosophical rather than dogmatic lines is a reminder of the reservoir of possibility held within religious thinking. The rehabilitation of Christianity in this Schellingian light is typical of contemporary speculative realism and post-secular theology. An alternative presentation of the otherness of being is offered in "What Is Phenomenology," where Patočka presents being as no-thing, that which is not in the order of beings.[40] The modern understanding of being as nothing more than a set of beings or things rests on a more primary, preconceptual sense of being as the horizon of all possibilities of manifestation.

Patočka's Aesthetic and Literary Criticism

This volume includes several of Patočka's best and most significant texts on the arts and culture, most of which are being translated into English for the first time. Patočka wrote a great deal on these topics, and his works of literary criticism in particular unfold in conversation with other philosophers and theorists working in literary studies and aesthetics, from J. G. Herder to Goethe to Roman Ingarden. His writings on the phenomenological contributions of poetry and literature, as well as on language and fantasy, were influential for later literary scholars including Paul Ricoeur and, in the Czech tradition, Milan Jankovič and Zdeněk Kožmín.[41]

Patočka's writings in this field are divided between general "theory," as in "The Writer's Concern" and "Art and Time,"[42] and philosophical expositions of a single work or author, as in his exegesis of Chekhov's *Ivanov* or Sophocles' *Antigone* and *Oedipus* plays. While Patočka does not give priority to poetry and literary writing to the same extent as Heidegger, he takes these forms seriously as a working out of phenomenological themes such as the lived experience of time, being toward death, and the horizon of a whole within which experience takes place. His forays into deep criticism demonstrate an eye for the formal and structural elements of a text as well as a keen sense of their philosophical import.

Patočka tends to emphasize the difference between philosophy and literature, since philosophy, for him, is about making "thematic" or explicit reflections on the whole, something that literature need not do. Despite this, he recognizes a distinctive philosophical contribution in literary works, and some of the philosopher's most powerful expressions of his philosophical commitments are found in his readings of literature. His reading of the Faust myth in "On Faust: The Myth of the Pact with the Devil," his commentary on temporality, history, and guilt in Karel Hynek Mácha's poetry in "Time, Eternity, and Temporality," and his exposition of Josef Čapek's humanism in "Limping Pilgrim" are all exemplary in this regard.

In "The Writer's Concern," Patočka offers an account of how the literary writer discloses a world and what role this world disclosure plays within the wider field of cultural understanding. He begins the essay by echoing Husserl's rallying cry to return to the "things themselves," and asks what might be the "thing" of the writer as opposed to the thing that concerns scientific inquiry? Where the sciences comprehend the world as a particular set of contents or things, literature orients us toward an understanding of the world as the whole horizon of our movement. It does this by offering "an *individual* capturing of *life's meaning*," as given in the author's presentation of the world.[43] This is not to say that a work of literature need be concerned explicitly with the question of life's meaning or with moral questions; Patočka instead refers to the particular way of making sense of things that is reflected in a literary work, which both awakens readers to their own frame and opens up reflection on the process of sense-making more generally. In the same essay, Patočka also considers how literature, in reflecting on the whole and on the activity of meaning-making, may offer a glimpse out of the technoscientific framework that dominates contemporary life.

His analysis here prefigures his comments in "The Dangers of Technicization" about truth as the disclosure of what is, rather than "truth as correctness." But Patočka, ever clear-eyed about the practical and societal obstacles to genuine progress of this kind, also warns of the various ways in which writing may become co-opted by the larger culture machine, being tailored to "market forces" rather than guided by its own internal demands. He decries this "traffic in writing, which makes the writer into a cog in the complex machinery of supply and demand."[44] Of course, this is a danger for both literary and intellectual writing. Yet Patočka is adamant about the social urgency of the writer's task in a world dominated by the imperatives of the technoscientific paradigm:

> The significance of literary work, therefore, in the future will grow to the extent that other intellectual fields, especially today's science and technology centers, continue to strengthen in their power to penetrate things, controlling and shaping them, which is the power of specialization and segmentation. The greater the segmentation, the greater the need for compensation and a reminder of the wholeness of life, of the undivided relationship to the universe. Literature defends this undividedness above all else. For this same reason, its place is wherever there is a confrontation of the major tendencies arising from the character of society today, in both West and East alike.

The "undividedness" of literature concerns the relationship between the world and the living, embodied subject—a relationship that has been severed in the modern conception both of the subject (as a nexus of forces) and of the world (as the objective world of the sciences). Literature rehabilitates the "natural world," the world of our life.

Myth, Guilt, and Uncertainty

Several of the texts in the "Arts and Culture" section of this volume deal with Patočka's understanding of myth as a form of cultural understanding, namely as "the original instance of human reflection on humanity's overall relationship to the world."[45] "On Faust: The Myth of the Pact with the Devil" is one of the most penetrating literary readings in this collection. In Faust, as well as in the dramas of Sophocles, the theme of myth centers on the relationship between human action and necessity, represented by the Greek notion of fate or destiny. Patočka draws from these myths an understanding of what it is to be responsible, to be "guilty" before the whole.[46] This guilt is not religious, as in the earlier Faust myths, but refers to individual human action in the face of uncertainty, the necessity of acting and being held responsible despite being unable to foresee the outcome. The possibility of failure and catastrophe looms over all of our actions, since we move always within uncertainty.

One sees in Patočka's analyses of guilt echoes of his idea of the "solidarity of the shaken" from the late *Heretical Essays*.[47] In these essays, it is clear that the soul's guilt over action in the face of uncertainty forms the basis for community—one that does not rely on national identity or any other form of identity but that responds, in anxiety, to the basic situation of human action. Patočka closes his exposition of Thomas Mann's *Doctor Faustus* with the recognition that guilt is our basic position. He reinforces and expands on this idea in his essay on the poetry of K. H. Mácha: "There can never be freedom without an act, but an act is always finite and guilty."[48] Guilt is a condition of my always limited understanding of the context of my actions, "I must be *in* a situation (not: *above* or *before* it) in order to understand it, and therefore I understand it always only in part."[49] Any action carries the burden of guilt, of being "in the wrong."

Chekhov's Ivanov kills himself over this guilt, unable to reckon with the unshelteredness of such an attitude. But guilt, as Patočka declares in "Ivanov," should be understood as the beginning of authentic action and not the end. One of Patočka's most difficult demands was adopted by Václav Havel as a motto for the type of politics he and the other dissidents were attempting: the idea of "living in truth." "Living in truth" is not in the possession of the truth, nor is it a worship of the factual ("*idolum facti*"):[50] it is a desire to risk oneself for truth. "Living in truth" then means, as Patočka writes in the Faust essay, "wanting to participate in universal justice as the only condition in which the soul can exist as such, as a being soaring out of the fall."

History and the Movement of Life

One of the features that marks Patočka's later works is a preoccupation with history, with what separates a prehistorical from a consciously historical age and with the threat posed to "historical" life by the "twentieth century as war." Understood most broadly, Patočka's philosophy of history describes the movement of human being. Just as the subject in Patočka is not an observer standing before the theater of the world, so history cannot be understood as simply a set of events or unfolding processes available to objective scrutiny. Patočka reads the movements of human life in—and as— history.

Patočka describes these movements within a tripartite framework similar to that of Arendt in *The Human Condition*.[51] Life begins with acceptance, both being accepted by and cared for by others and accepting the world as it is given to us. We put down our roots in life. The second stage is marked by a recognition of life's fragility; in response to this sense of threat to life, human being works to defend itself, striving for the maintenance of life into the future, through labor. The third movement is human action in which the inherited world and accepted meaning become problematic; in this sphere, human being takes responsibility for itself and its freedom in an attempt to live in truth or care for the soul. These movements mark both individual life and the collective life of human beings as a species, developing over time. In Patočka's account, it is only in the third movement, in the break or rupture with the past, that we enter history proper. Yet, unlike Heidegger, Patočka is not dismissive of the first two movements and sees them as an essential part of human being in the world.

"Time, Myth, Faith" and "Time, Eternity, and Temporality" both deal with the relationship of history to time. It is characteristic of the third movement of human life that it is oriented toward the openness of the future, a future for which there is no assurance that it will be like the past. Properly "historical" time contrasts with the eternal repetition of the same in what Patočka calls "prehistoric" life:

> Historical time does not flow *aequabiliter*, i.e., uniformly, like biological succession or the absolute time of Newton. There are moments of contact with what is ultimate and defining that time will never contain, yet nevertheless they may shape time and give it meaning. As a result, historical time is preparation for "the right time," "the right moment," "the fullness of time." Only in this historical time do we live with an awareness of human meaning, in the fullness of human life (whether true or illusive).[52]

The Greek notion of *kairos*, the right time or the fullness of time, suggests that historical life is not merely a series of events in a uniform spacetime. History makes "contact" with "that which time will never contain" and is shaped by this contact. In Patočka, these ruptures in time are reflective of the human capacity to go beyond the actual and thereby to change the space or course of history. "Against this backdrop [of historical life] the life of an individual human, that finite stretch of time, takes form as something capable of fulfillment or failure, of overall 'success' or catastrophe, at once shaped by these great events [of history] even as it shapes them."[53] This is what he refers to elsewhere as the "mutual movement" of human being and world.

Patočka ultimately proposes a very restricted sense of history as the project of human beings taking responsibility for themselves and their shared world in the face of uncertainty and unease. This is the "problematicity" of history, when the nature of our relationship to the inherited world becomes shaken and undone. In a sense, our reckoning with that relationship *is* history, or we could also say that history is the phenomenon of human action, human movement, which Patočka also calls the movement of the soul.

One of the main sources of contemporary interest in Patočka is as a thinker of Europe. Patočka offers to the study of history a series of what James Dodd aptly calls "provocations." One such provocation is Patočka's definition of Europe, which does not conform to any set of geopolitical boundaries but refers only to the project, carried over from Greek philosophy, of caring for the soul, of working toward the ideal community that lives in truth.

> Thus it is not Christianity, nor capitalism, nor the political and social legacy of the Roman Empire, nor imperialism and revolution, nor even the abstract ideas of freedom and democracy, but philosophy as a way of life, defined by the care for the soul, that forms the genuine heritage of Europe.[54]

The European project does not describe the *possession* of truth and enlightenment, not in any positive sense. Rather, it is commitment to care for the soul and for human life in common without the reassurances of given, traditional sources of meaning and identity. In Patočka, it is precisely this project that inaugurates history proper, when human beings renounce their sheltered existence and strike out on a fundamentally risky path.

Yet Patočka declares that the project of this ideal community called "Europe" is dead. It was, in James Dodd's summation, "overcome by the nihilism of its embrace of technological civilization and the pursuit of power and possession for their own sake."[55] While Husserl in his 1930s *Crisis* identified the threat to Europe and attempted to pull the European project back from the brink, Patočka sees more clearly that this project, by the end of the 1930s, has already come to an end. Writing in 1970 about the political turmoil of the 1930s and 1940s, Patočka describes the failure of the classical German incarnation of the European ideal, which morphed instead into the tyrannical horror of the Third Reich; the intellectuals meant to uphold and defend the formation (*Bildung*) of the soul became complicit.

> Once again, there is a "German Reich," but in a form completely different from the German classical version. Spiritual power and authority are now completely out of the question. Looking at its political structure, this "Reich" is an inheritor of the Prussian, pre-revolutionary century; after its failed attempt at world dominance, it is finally transformed, in Plato's catalogue of superseded polities, into an unprecedented tyranny, which was made into a waking reality by unleashing forces otherwise daring to appear only in the nightmares of madness. Confusion among intellectuals, who were initially still trying to build a bridge back to the age of Goethe, is expressed in stultified followership.[56]

The idea of Europe, as Patočka sees it, was only able to authorize and sustain itself on the basis that it was a movement oriented toward living in truth. The Reich becomes a "superseded polity" that can no longer claim authority from its own movements, but instead relies on subjugation and terror to enforce its "ideals."

Several decades on from the events that Patočka describes here, it can be difficult even to conjure up his idea of Europe. His announcement of a post-European age, with Europe no longer on center stage, seems far more consistent with the global developments of recent decades and will likely seem far more plausible to contemporary readers. That said, Patočka offers one final provocation, which is to ask whether it is possible to carry on the project of Europe beyond Europe's collapse? As he poses the question in "An Outline of History," "will humankind of the planetary [that is, post-European] era really be able to live historically?" Patočka suggests that reckoning with Europe's failings must be part of any "post-European" project of moving forward with the open soul as a political ideal. His writings on this subject do not offer an answer to the question, and he moves between despair and hope about the possibility of such a post-European project. On the side of pessimism, it must be noted that the "biologism" which dominates contemporary life is a major obstacle to living in truth, since such a framework does not recognize any good beyond bare life, so does not recognize the third movement of human existence at all.[57] On the side of hope, we note that it is characteristic of "historical," problematic human life that: "The main thing, what is most important, always lies ahead of us, however far we go. And yet its very absence may shape what comes next for us, our concrete future."[58]

Notes

1   Patočka held courses on the Pre-Socratics, Socrates, Plato, and Aristotle between 1945 and 1949, and in 1946 he published an important monograph on Aristotle, which has recently been translated into French: Jan Patočka, *Aristote, ses devanciers, ses successeurs*, trans. Erika Abrams (Paris: J. Vrin, 2011).

2   Jan Patočka, "Sixth Essay: Wars of the Twentieth Century and the Twentieth Century as War," in *Heretical Essays in the Philosophy of History*, trans. Erazim Kohák, ed. James Dodd (Chicago: Open Court, 1999), 119–37.

3   See *Thinking After Europe: Jan Patočka and Politics*, ed. Francesco Tava and Darian Meacham (London: Rowman and Littlefield, 2016).

4   "An Outline of History."

5   Simona Forti, "Parrhesia Between East and West: Foucault and Dissidence," in *The Government of Life: Foucault, Biopolitics, and Neoliberalism*, ed. Vanessa Lemm and Miguel Vatter (New York: Fordham University Press: 2016), 187–207; Darian Meacham, "Biologism and Supercivilisation," in *Thinking*

after Europe: Jan Patočka and Politics, ed. Francesco Tava and Darian Meacham (London: Rowman and Littlefield, 2016).

6   Josef Čapek, *Kulhavý poutník: Co jsem na světě uviděl* (The limping pilgrim: What I saw in the world), in *Spisy bratří Čapků* (The works of the Čapek brothers), vol. 37 (Prague: František Borový, 1936), 181–217.

7   "Limping Pilgrim Josef Čapek."

8   The Aristotelean roots are equally important, and Patočka's readings of Aristotelian motion influence his reading of Plato in this text. See Patočka, *Aristote*, 2011; *Body, Community, Language and World*, trans. Erazim Kohák, ed. James Dodd (Chicago: Open Court, 1998).

9   Plato, *Republic* 360d–e.

10 The authors of the main Charter text were never declared, but Patočka wrote several short statements that gave Charter 77 a deep moral appeal. He was one of the first three spokespersons of the Charter, along with Václav Havel and Jiří Hájek (Minister of Foreign Affairs in spring 1968).

11 See the account of Patočka's death in Costica Bradatan, *Dying for Ideas: The Dangerous Lives of Philosophers* (London: Bloomsbury, 2015).

12 "The Idea of Education and its Relevance Today."

13 See Patočka's essay "On the Soul in Plato."

14 "The Idea of Education and its Relevance Today."

15 "An Outline of History."

16 "An Outline of History."

17 Edmund Husserl, *Crisis of the European Sciences*, trans. David Carr (Evanston, IL: Northwestern University Press, 1970).

18 "The Natural World and Phenomenology."

19 "The Dangers of Technicization in Science According to E. Husserl and the Essence of Technology as Danger According to M. Heidegger."

20 "The Natural World and Phenomenology."

21 The Prague lectures were given in November 1935. One of the lectures formed the basis for the first two parts of the *Crisis* book, published in 1936, while an expanded version was published posthumously. Edmund Husserl, *Die Krisis der Europäischen Wissenschaften und die transzendentale Phänomenologie*, in *Philosophia: Philosophorum nostri temporis vox universa*, ed. Arthur Liebert, vol. 1, no. 1 (Belgrade: n.p. 1936).

22 "The Truth of Myth in Sophocles' Theban Plays."

23 Patočka's position should not be confused with either Luddism or a rejection of science. On the contrary, like Husserl, he has great admiration for the sciences as such and for the possibilities they have unlocked for human being. Further, in "On the Principle of a Scientific Conscience" he demonstrates his respect for scientific inquiry in a passionate plea for the freedom of the sciences from dogmatic political demands or from bureaucratization.

24 "The Question Concerning Technology," in *The Question Concerning Technology and Other Essays*, ed. William Lovitt (New York: HarperPerennial, 1977), 3–35.

25 See Martin Heidegger, "The Age of the World Picture," in *The Question Concerning Technology and Other Essays*, ed. William Lovitt (New York: HarperPerennial, 1977), 115–54.

26 "The Natural World and Phenomenology."

27 "The Natural World and Phenomenology."

28 "Two Senses of Reason and Nature in the German Enlightenment: A Herderian Study," in *Jan Patočka: Philosophy and Selected Writings*, ed. Erazim Kohák (Chicago: University of Chicago Press, 1989), 157–74.

29 "The Dangers of Technicization."

30 "The Natural World and Phenomenology."

31 "The Natural World and Phenomenology."

32 "The Natural World and Phenomenology."

33 "The Natural World and Phenomenology."

34 "What Is Phenomenology?"

35 Edmund Husserl, *Logical Investigations*, 2nd edn, vol. 2, trans. John Niemeyer Findlay, ed. Dermot Moran (London: Routledge, 2001), 168.

36 "The Natural World and Phenomenology."

37 Heidegger, "The Question Concerning Technology."

38 See, e.g., "The Writer's Concern," "The Natural World," and "What Is Phenomenology?" in this volume. See also Patočka's remarks in the third heretical essay (Patočka, *Heretical Essays*, 75).

39 "Comenius and the Open Soul."

40 The basis for this discussion is Heidegger's analysis of the nothing of being in *What Is Metaphysics?*.

41 See Jan Tlustý, "Contemplating literature with Jan Patočka: phenomenology as an inspiration for literary studies," *Bohemica litteraria* 23, no. 2 (2020): 81–98.

42 For secondary sources on these texts, see, e.g., Erin Plunkett, "'New Human Possibilities' in Patočka's Philosophy of Literature," *Bohemica litteraria* 23, no. 2 (2020): 69–80; Jan Josl, "The End of Art and Patočka's Philosophy of Art," *Horizon Studies in Phenomenology* 5, no. 1 (2016): 232–46; Miloš Ševčík, "Dominant science and influential art: Jan Patočka on relations between art and science," *AUC Philosophica et Historica* 1, Myth, Philosophy, Art and Science in Jan Patočka's Thought (2014): 73–84.

43 "The Writer's Concern."

44 "The Writer's Concern."

45 "The Truth of Myth in Sophocles' Theban Plays."

46 This is also a theme in "*Ivanov*" and "Time, Eternity, and Temporality."

47 Patočka, *Heretical Essays*, 135.

48 "Time, Eternity, and Temporality in the Work of Karel Hynek Mácha."

49 "The Natural World and Phenomenology."

50 "A Few Remarks on the Concept of World History."

51 Hannah Arendt, *The Human Condition*, 2nd edn (Chicago: University of Chicago Press, 2018).

52 "Time, Myth, Faith."

53 "A Few Remarks on the Concept of 'World History'."

54 James Dodd, "Jan Patočka's Philosophical Legacy," in *The Oxford Handbook of the History of Phenomenology*, ed. Dan Zahavi (Oxford: Oxford University Press, 2018).

55 Dodd, "Jan Patočka's Philosophical Legacy."

56 "The Spiritual Foundations of Life in Our Time."

57 See "An Outline of History."

58 "Time, Myth, Faith."

PART ONE

Early Texts

These two early texts introduce some of the main themes of Patočka's work: a critique of the prevailing notion of objectivity, a concern for the role of history in our understanding of human being and world, and a commitment to cultivating the spiritual dimension of human being in the face of grave historical and political obstacles. Here, spiritual does not denote anything religious but instead marks out that element of human being which is capable of more than mere survival, which would be the subject and the agent of both "history" and "education" as Patočka presents them.

"The Idea of Education" was written in 1938, just after the signing of the Munich Agreement, which authorized Hitler to seize key border areas of Czechoslovakia and spelled the beginning of the end of the nation's sovereignty. In response to this political disaster, Patočka launches a challenge to his fellow citizens, especially to intellectuals, asking what they stand for, whether they still possess the power to ask what kind of country and society they want to be. He centers this challenge on the idea of education and what a meaningful education entails. Education, he argues, cannot mean simply cramming the head with facts, nor should it be an intellectual exercise; it must train learners to develop a new relationship to themselves and to relate to the world differently, responsibly. Sympathetic to but also critical of the classical German ideal of education—*Bildung*—Patočka presents a portrait of education that emphasizes the struggle it involves, the break with previously accepted forms of meaning and value. "There is no harmonious, blissful development here, as in the growth of a tree from a seed, but a piece of concentrated life, an indispensable moment in the life struggle, that moment in which one fights for standards and models not only for oneself but for everyone."

CHAPTER ONE

A Few Remarks on the Concept of "World History"(1935)

Translated from the Czech by Alex Zucker

1. On another occasion, the author of these lines sought to show that pure intellectualism in the theory of history is impracticable, or better put, that it leads to a false, decadent understanding of history. We can best realize this if we seek to carry through to its consequences the fiction of pure intellect regarding history. The ideal of pure intellect is "objectivity." This "objectivity" has an important prerequisite: a sharp dividing line between "subject" and "object." Only under this assumption can an "object" be perfectly captured, described, analyzed. If not for this strict distinction, the "subject" coming to know the "object" would at the same time have to come to know itself, which is "impossible for the same reason that I cannot walk down the street and look at myself out the window at the same time"; this would steer the process of cognition down the path of infinite self-perception, which lacks the requisite perfect perceptibility.[1] In other words: pure intelligence gains knowledge by way of pure self-forgetting, in fact explicitly severing any ties that might bind it to the object, so that the object appears completely separate and independent. Only then does the process of apprehending the essential aspects and structures of the field toward which it is turning, and the attempt to exhaust the entire field by way of deduction, or at least systematic description, commence.

The result of that in looking at history would be a reduction of it to what can be objectified, to what insight can be gained from history through recollection. Though an "object" may be inexhaustible, which is to say infinite, still it must be *complete* in its being. Every physical object, for example, is de facto inexhaustible in its possibilities; but all of its aspects are equally real at the same time. The possibilities of an object such as this exist in the form of *forces*. What happens to it is a regular *process*, codetermined by these forces. Applied to history, this perspective gives a particular picture of it: history is the human past conceived as a series of processes played out with human objects. History then is a simple description of these processes, and philosophy of history is the interpretation within this description of processes perceived on the basis of the lawful operation of the great forces that determine what happens to objects. In short, we would arrive at the familiar view of history as practiced by naive historical positivism; all "processes" in principle unfold on the same level, history constitutes a set of interrelated causal series, which need only be mentally reconstructed for the goal of historical knowledge to be achieved.

It has been observed (by Rickert) that this widespread view of history is not employed by historical science nor would it be feasible for it to do so. To begin with, the principle of choosing which parts of the human past are suitable as historical material is absent. And yet when we contemplate history today, it is a view that readily comes to hand, a view we quickly relapse into whenever we start to reflect on history, a view we find it difficult to disengage ourselves from. One of the main reasons it comes to us so naturally is the ahistorical understanding of humanity that has been at home in all of Western philosophy, with several exceptions, up until the modern day. In antiquity and later, in analogous fashion, in the medieval view, human beings were conceived of as a level of the cosmos, a segment in the eternal order of ideas. In modern times the situation is reversed; if, before, the concept of *physis*, "nature," was subordinate to the concept of *cosmos*, "the order of the whole," now all order is dependent on nature, its rules and forces. But the static, ahistorical view of humanity has not changed; what was cosmic has merely become naturalistic. Modern anthropology, plotted out by the names Descartes, Hobbes, Spinoza, Locke, is characterized by the process of naturalization of the traditional conception of humanity. The outcome of this process is modern psychology, the doctrine of the objectively natural foundation of human experience, which ultimately understands experience itself as a factual, objective process. The popular, most readily accessible thinking of today sees humans as a part of nature. History as a process that plays out on the stage of humanity therefore becomes a process of nature.

Naturalistic anthropology found itself in crisis when the consequences it had in human life became apparent. The decadent phenomena of our modern life are in large part related to it. Examples of these phenomena are skeptical relativism, the indifferentism of pure intellectualism, and noncommittal aestheticism. The phenomenon of self-alienation emerges and spreads, the subjugation of spontaneous humanity to an alien norm. One partial phenomenon here is the feeling of "cultural discontent," which can be seen in European civilization from the sentimentalism of the eighteenth century to this day. The introduction of notions of the whole, of form, of structure, of "teleological" factors into at least some areas of the concept of nature is of no help to the more recent era in seeking to replace the purely mechanistic concept of nature that dates to the beginnings of modernity. All because, in spite of all the reforms in the *form* of being, it remains stuck in the same fundamental type of being, the same ontological sphere. One of the consequences of this is, as noted, a misunderstanding of history, which can also be counted among the reasons for the nonsensicality of naturalistic anthropology.

What we would like to attempt here is to reverse the position: seeking to penetrate in original form to what makes history history, we will seek to deduce from that the consequences for philosophical anthropology and for an epistemic ideal that can stand in opposition to the ideal of pure intellectualism sketched above.

2. Assuming we accept the fiction of pure intellect, we may note first and foremost that it engages its material too broadly, mixing the non-essential with the essential, reducing both to the same level (a variation on Rickert's objection). Even more important, however, is how much this view is missing. It lacks not merely a connecting link and a guide, but the creative energy of history itself.

What do we mean by this creative energy? The best way to arrive at this is to start from the approximation that it is that which causes individual efforts to follow on one another within the historical process. The codetermination of human activity by the past is a basic feature of historicity, assuming of course that codetermination is conscious. There is no historicity where something utterly new is being created, yet it is everywhere connection occurs, a spilling of one will into another so to speak, however obscure and complex the paths of that connection may be. Historicity can be anonymous, but it cannot be unconscious. Thus there is historicity when, feeling a communion of interest with something in the past, we co-create a work whose meaning lies deeper than on the individual level. Even when acting on the basis of individual motives, historical figures see themselves as supporting a deeper cause.[2] The process of history is the transmission of the creative impulse. This transmission is a conscious, voluntary effort: that is the reason why humans instinctively understand history. The world of history is our practical world, the world of our (conscious) interests.[3] To comprehend history historically, then, does not mean to interpret (e.g., psychologically, economically, etc.) these interests, but to conceive of them as supporting the typical forces governing humanity, human life and the world. If we ask why something happened in history, the question does not mean the same as it does in natural science. Because in this case we are not simply asking after the natural constellations that lead to certain processes, but rather we wish to understand them on the basis of those original forces that govern our existence and which we too may "experience," "feel," "consider," "overcome."

The forces that govern our lives cannot be simply calculated or deduced from principles. Later we will say why. But they are all fundamental determinatives of individual and social life, which we feel as impulses within ourselves and thanks to which we are able to see life not merely filled, but in fact fulfilled. In history, people seek to give their lives objective meaning through active creation. This meaning is not some mystical notion, but the creation and realization of one's own will. The "search for the meaning of life" is nothing other than the effort to discover and clarify one's will. On the other hand, one must bear in mind that the lack of impulse, energy, will is equally a life-governing force, even a very important one. Nonsense, however, gets its definition from sense, lack of force from force.

As an example of these original forces, let us consider the ambition of a government with great variation in capacity to govern, leading to imperialist expansion as well as to a lawful consolidation of civil society within the state. Another such force is what is often referred to as "spirit," that is, the conscious connection of a person to the world through the forms of philosophy (and science), the arts, life wisdom, and religion. Every such force occupies a position within the polarity of individual vs. social tension, being both an individual and a community matter, but in varying degrees and proportions. And none of these forces is given prior to history, which would make them, so to speak, extrahistorical explicans of history, but they themselves are also still subject to the historical process. The process of history is essentially the process of creating these forces, which govern and effectuate life. We may also express this paradoxical phenomenon by saying that there are goals created in the course of history, and it is only in proceeding from them that we are able to comprehend life (in its historical form).

When we talk about the "forces" that govern life, we are actually speaking in the abstract, which could lead us to make the error of compromising the historicity of these concepts. In fact these forces are real only in concrete historical periods, in concrete philosophies, in concrete impulses of political power and state formations. Yet there is something in common that holds throughout this diversity of historical formations that allows us to speak of a unitary historical force; this is not a general concept in the natural sense, but in the specific historical sense that presupposes a continuity of the fundamental impulse, of the fundamental "creative energy," as we explained it above.

This "creative energy," introduced to history by certain personalities within the historical process, is neither a spatially nor, in the last instance, a temporally individuated fact. Let us take for example "Plato's philosophy." This philosophy is not simply what Plato thought in a particular place at a particular period in time, but all that Plato introduced to intellectual history: it lives on within that history independent of his individual existence. Nor is it rigid in its ideal content, like the content of a theorem in geometry, but in fact it *lives on* in history. In the same way, as long as they affect us, the impulses of power and politics live independent of their creators; in the same way, ideas, styles, artistic devices live in history. Whoever introduced them to historical life has the right, so to speak, of discovery, not of exclusive possession.

The "creative energy" of history that is passed on from our life to our will, and because it is never perfectly individuated, cannot be captured in a view taking heed only of "facts" and "processes." Yet there is another, deeper reason for it, related to that insufficiency of individuation. Creative energy is a reservoir of possibilities, a set of potentialities that beckon to those working toward them as a reward for their efforts. These possibilities are, again, not mere logical possibilities; their innermost essence cannot be thought of as given ideal facts, but rather something that is created through the process of the self-objectification of life: consequently, even here we remain on the ground of history. This reasoning is a matter of abstract metaphysics, however; let us return to the consequences that follow from what has been said for history.

3. We can now make a distinction that is in fact widely used in thinking about history, despite its not having been philosophically substantiated: the distinction between deep, internal history and superficial, external history.

Superficial history is constituted by the human past conceived as a *process* in the above-mentioned sense (see section 1), regardless of the energy that sustains it and the conflicts that occur in this sphere of energy itself. Internal or deep history is shaped by the development and conflicts of those creative energies, the powers one consciously places one's life at the service of. Corresponding to this distinction then is the distinction between two types of historiography or, better, two trends within historiography: superficial and deep. A history is superficial when processes and the people who carry them forth are described with no consideration for capturing their vital *significance*, i.e., with no consideration of the energy that sustains them and of the conflicts in the sphere of energy; deep history, on the other hand, means following development and conflicts in the sphere of energy. For example, where Thucydides describes the outset and course of the Peloponnesian War, he is writing superficial history; where he explains its origin and continuation based on Athenian power and lust for glory, encouraged by the Hellenism that exploded amid the success of the Greek wars, as well as on the Athenian and Spartan forms of life, he is practicing deep history. Each concrete historiography involves working in these two layers in parallel. A superficial history includes everything in history that can be *ascertained*, established as a simply localized fact. It is not simply history from a behavioristic aspect: it includes also facts from character studies of unifying figures, which is important to it from a purely biographical standpoint as well, facts from the character of the communities involved, incidental mental dispositions and indispositions, in general everything in history that falls under the heading of chance; furthermore, everything in history that can be conceived of as a *natural vis a tergo*,[4] as the natural cycle of our organic life in operation, the unpredictable play of natural forces, causing crop failures, disease, pushing humanity off the historical stage, etc.

In contrast to this, a deep history cannot be directly ascertained by way of facts. The "form of life" or "life ideal" of nations or individuals may be reflected in their deeds, but nowhere in them is it wholly and directly contained. "Form of life" is an idealized representation of the normal functioning of individual and social life within a specific historical group; it includes the group's relationship to nature (within the limits of normality), type of occupations and their regulation, norms of social coexistence, relationship to spiritual forces, etc. Hence form of life is a synthesis of the original forces mentioned above; it is the product of their constant flowing and counterbalancing. Yet, on the other hand, considered in themselves these powers are nothing but abstractions that we draw from that group erected within the stream of life, which we refer to as the "form of life" or *world* of a specific historical community or specific historical individual. Deep history, therefore, in the eminent sense of the word, is world history, which is to say the history of the human world, of that constantly present yet endlessly changing concrete form in which all of our individual life, all our dwelling over individual details, takes place.

Now, further, we must demonstrate that even superficial history is indicative of deep history, that it is contingent on it, and hence superficial historiography is dependent on deep historiography. Even those authors who record "pure events" as chroniclers, i.e., as authors approaching the ideal limit of superficial historiography, do not work without guidelines. These guidelines are given on the one hand by the historians' field of view,[5] and on the other by their own (historically formed) interests and the form of life and life ideal of the community to which they belong. These interests guide them in their selection of facts. Therefore, if we are compelled to change our view on the course of superficial history on the basis of our own better knowledge of the sources, the chronicler's view remains nonetheless an important source for understanding the historicity of a specific period, that is, the way in which the period itself understands its events. Yet even historians who lack thorough knowledge of the rules of historiographical criticism may have a greater understanding of deep history than historical positivists who are as industrious as ants: it depends on the depth of their own interest, hence on an understanding of those same creative energies as they manifest themselves in history; when criticality and a sharp mind, capable of penetrating the surface of situations, interests, and intentions, are joined to these, it results in a great work of history.

4. Given that historical energy is not an abstraction in history—in the dual sense already mentioned: it always takes the form of a *specific* impulse and is always in the context of a specific *overall* structure, which we have designated "the world"—in deep history, strictly speaking, no aspect can be separated from the others; this is also why, if we study, for example, "the history of philosophy," "the history of national economy," or "the history of literature" in isolation it gives us so little satisfaction; this is why, again, we

see the need to understand other aspects and branches of life, in order for us to broaden our angle of view. Essentially only one history exists: the history of a particular life in the fullness of its givenness.

Yet the individual and the collective world alike are both subject to change. Not only does the *content* of the world change, but the world, the "form of life" (as we have designated it using another term) itself. The world in this sense is the set of possibilities open to a person at a given moment, possibilities in which they live and to which they are constantly related through their actions. Conceived in this way, the world is submitted on the one hand to a specification and expansion of its structures, on the other to more radical modifications; an altogether new possibility may be discovered. Thus, for example, with the appearance of philosophy a wholly new possibility was created for humanity, the possibility not only to live in the particulars and understand the particulars out of the whole, but to live in the essential things, to live *in the whole*, in the whole of the world. This possibility does not exist for the naive person, in the sense that the naive person does not know about it, for substantial reasons being unable to grasp it. With the creation of philosophy, however, the human world changed in the same way as it does on the basis of every other "spiritual" activity. Likewise, our world also changes passively, through the mere continuation of time; even if nothing original, or notable, is happening, the world is changing, despite things still appearing to be the same. Even when it seems that nothing is happening or being created, that there are no attempts at a new common will and a new understanding of life, which would naturally have an active impact on our perception of the whole, this too is a *process*, not a state of *static* rest.

The world, then, is what governs our understanding of individual details. Consequently, we must realize that any historical documents that come to us in the context of a world other than the one in which they were created mean something different to us than they did to the people for whom they were meant at the time of their creation. There is a twofold anachronism: an anachronism in the data and an anachronism in our understanding of the data.[6] This is also one of the main reasons why, in writing history, it is not enough simply to ascertain what the sources say, and why interpretation is necessary (in a particular, specific sense, which will be elaborated below): historical facts, situated always in the context of a changing world, are themselves subject to change. Any work of history that is purely superficial thus proves, once more, in a different way, to be contingent on transformations of historical energy: the ascertainment of processes is itself possible only on the ground of a specific overall understanding, i.e., always only in a specific cross section of history, and other periods will not only see the same processes differently, but often take note of other processes as well, lifting them out of their previous anonymity (for example, from the Hellenistic standpoint, the fact that the origin of Christianity is nowhere documented in its historiography is quite normal; this same fact takes on a central importance in the medieval outlook).

Assuming, then, that written history should offer us a reconstruction of the past, it must not be led down the wrong path by the suggestiveness of facts, *idolum facti*. We saw the source of this *idolum facti* already in naive intellectualism and its objectivism: from this perspective, all processes unfold, we said, in principle on the same level. This view must be replaced by an awareness of the variability of the all-encompassing horizon within which human life takes place, and hence an awareness of the fundamental non-transferability, the incommensurability of processes within different historical horizons. The task of history then can no longer be the simple reconstruction of historical "facts"—understood in the sense of strictly localized processes. Historiography must primarily obtain *access* to the historical facts, being conscious that we must begin from ascertainment *in our world* and follow the path from there to ascertainment in the world of the past. Historical sensitivity and tact are not merely synonymous with the clear-sightedness of the politician or the profundity of the philosopher, but at the same time encompass something entirely original, that awareness of the variability of the human world, combined with a sense of historical style, of what is possible and impossible at a specific moment in time based on the categorical composition of that period. There are, so to speak, various degrees of historiography; it may be a recitation of events within the author's own world or it may be an attempt to reconstruct another. Thucydides set for himself the first task—in general it is typical of ancient historiography that it understands history only in this first sense (not so much because it is lacking in any historical sensitivity or tact as because it is darkly aware of the fundamental paradoxes posed by "world" history). The second task is reserved for us with our modern-day, universalist orientation; it is a purely modern task. A true "world" historiography cannot arise where an awareness of the fundamental variability of the human form of life has not penetrated— and indeed we see that in periods of history marked by static self-containment, the absolutism of ideals, and supra-individual norms that are totally binding, world history is nowhere possible, and hence does not arise in the sense that we are using it: examples of such static interpretations can be found in antiquity, the Christian Middle Ages, and ancient China.

Historians handle this task intuitively, without explicit clarity about its fundamental meaning and philosophical reach. Only the philosophy of history can lead to fundamental clarity, which is at the same time a metaphysical clarity. In fact the task of universal history is, in its ultimate essence, a philosophical task, not a historical-empirical one, since the methodology for reflecting on the world as a whole and its variability is philosophical reflection. Philosophy and historiography here must work, so to speak, hand in hand. It is philosophy, taking as its starting point the original givenness of the world, that reveals to us the structures within the world that are capable of variability, and thus the possibility of different historical worlds; history is here with the fullness of its facts as a constant empirical treasury and control.

5. What has been stated above in sections 2–4 suggests that the task of philosophical anthropology is to ask: What is the essence of a historical creature? and What is "world history?" Static, objectivist anthropology may ultimately be replaced only by an anthropology that fundamentally reckons with questions of the philosophy of history.

Let us now radicalize our thesis to say: only historical philosophy can lead to a true philosophy of history. Historical philosophy is that philosophy which is able to capture the essence of historicity without distorting it. We have described the essence of historicity as the stream of life and its possibilities, which, gathered into the present unity, constitute the world. There are two histories of the world, one which is the task of philosophy in general (metaphysics), the other which is the task of the philosophy of history. The first, the philosophical history of the world in general, is not an analysis or description of the development of the temporal world: it is an analysis and creation (constitution) of the world and time, of the world in time and of time itself from the perspective of philosophical reflection; by contrast, the philosophy of history is world history in the proper sense, as indicated in section 4.

Philosophy seeks not merely an image of the world, nor simply the form of the world, but the *origin* of the world in a radical sense. It is historical therefore not only because it is concerned with changes in the world, but also and notably because it examines the essence and origin of the world. It can examine the origin thanks to its method of continuous reflection and the escalation of philosophical abstraction, which give it access to the site of its origin, and this site is the stream of life, which creates every valid form on the basis of itself.

The fact that it has access to the origin of the world means philosophy has access to the form of the world, and the fact that it has access to the form means it has access to the contents, which under the law of form stand as historically valid, relatively constant variations on the same form of the world. Those philosophers who study the origin and development of the world are, of course, limited in that they must proceed from their own specific, limited historical situation, even if they mean to transgress the relativity of this situation with their philosophical knowledge. The possibility of transgressing this situation of course presumes a reflective attitude and abstraction on their part; but neither purely theoretical reflection nor abstraction alone enable this transgression; reflection and abstraction are in and of themselves sterile acts. The only thing that makes this transgression possible is the capacity for variation of our experiential structures; that capacity for variation, which makes possible historical consciousness in the proper sense, that "gift of historical empathy," the "historical tact" so often spoken of in history, lies within our possibilities. But the breadth of that capacity is given differently to different people, and in particular it is difficult to implement those possibilities as radically as philosophy and history require. Only the creative person who seeks to seize hold as personally and as broadly as possible of the possibilities of genuine humanity that are given them has the prerequisites for the capacity for variation that we demand. Only those who see philosophy, art, the rational regulation of life as their own internal project in which they are engaged can understand also the *history* of these mental activities. For only they bring the deep store of possibilities needed to allow them to grasp the historically given as various aspects of existence. The primordial impulse for transgression resides in the creative impetus that is not content with what is brought to us by superficial tradition, but seeks to penetrate through this deadening layer to the sources of life, "to the mothers."

Those thinkers who approach philosophizing from the standpoint of original transgression must, to a certain extent, abandon the ideal of timelessness inherent to all ahistorical philosophy and science. Proceeding from their own historically given possibilities, they may work their way through to multi-temporality, to an understanding of *specific* historical periods and the like; but what if understanding certain structures of life is inevitably related to not understanding others? What if all history is just one big dispute? Is there any hope that the philosopher can work out a way at least in part to escape these problems, which demonstrably threaten the traditional notion of truth and knowledge itself?

At another time we will attempt to explain our stance on the problems of historicism.[7] For now it will suffice to point out that, in historical knowledge, the subject is not something foreign to the object, there is no strict boundary between one and the other. Humanity is not in a position of *actus purus* against the world, but historical knowledge goes deeper, to the very awareness of the variability of the world; in a philosophically guided history, the relativity of this division, absolutized by objectivism, stands out clearly. Thus the understanding of the historian, once mingled with the philosophical spirit, is a contribution to self-understanding; not the individual self-understanding of the historian, but the self-understanding of that original "energy" which courses through historical formations as well as through the historian themselves, a stream of energy that the historian cannot escape.

Notes

1   Cf. the contributions to the problem of self-perception by Fichte and Herbart.
2   The Hegelian "List der Vernunft" ("cunning of reason"), then, is an unnecessary concept. The reality is the opposite: an awareness of historical meaning where in fact there is none.
3   That is, a naive world, the opposite of the world of modern science.
4   A force operating from behind, a propulsive or driving force (Ed.).
5   A historian's field of view is their knowledge of the social context within which the society whose history they are writing is located.

6   I have attempted elsewhere to show how St. Thomas, the brilliant interpreter of
    Aristotle, interprets the Greek philosopher in a different world than his own,
    and the consequences of this interpretation for the reception of Aristotle in
    Aquinas's theology. (Citing Jan Patočka, "Několik poznámek k důkazům boží
    jsoucnosti u Tomáše Akvinského" (A few remarks on the proofs of God's
    existence in Thomas Aquinas), *Česká mysl* 29, no. 3–4 (1933): 138–48.)

7   "Dějepis filosofie a její jednota" (The history of philosophy and its unity),
    Česká mysl 36, nos. 2–3 (1942): 58–72, 97–114.

CHAPTER TWO

The Idea of Education and its Relevance Today (1938)

Translated from the Czech by Alex Zucker

People of the last century had in the word "education"[1] the bond of an ideal that was truly alive in them. The best of them did not shy from shielding their efforts behind this name. Goethe's life was one long impulse for education, for inner enrichment and coming to grips with all the worlds of the mind. The Humboldt brothers, who supplied the ideological formulation for the organization of German higher education, were sustained by this humanistic-educational ideal, formed in the eighteenth century and elaborated chiefly by Herder; education in this scheme was no mere means, but an end in itself, upheld by the idea of the importance of humanity in the universe as a whole, by the idea of humans as "liberated from nature," simultaneously concentrating it within them and transcending it, working on themselves as one would work on a masterpiece of art. This ideal was in short a partial but integral aspect of the idea of humanism, which formed the cornerstone of the life outlook for the leading strata of the day, especially the increasingly important bourgeoisie. It is by nature an individualistic ideal, just as all education is essentially individualistic, grounded as it is in the individual and having its main effect at that level, rather than at the external, utilitarian-social level. We can still see this individualism, exaggerated to the point of aristocratism, for example, in the young Nietzsche, who speaks from this perspective in his lectures on the future of educational institutions. From Germany, which represented the most energetic as well as the most turbulent example of this educational impulse, it came to the Czech lands along with its ideological underpinning, the idea of humanism, whose three main variations—scientific (Dobrovský), national (Kollár, Šafařík, Palacký), and sociopolitical (Masaryk)—pervade our nineteenth century. In all three variations, the idea of humanism went hand in hand with a powerful thrust to intensify the expansion of education, although differently in each case.

The critique of humanistic individualism has grown increasingly strong with time. New ideas of ethics have emerged, which evaluate the individual by collective standards, and viewed in their light the idea of humanism has begun to appear incomplete and in itself shaky. The educational impulse of humanism has shown itself to be a trivial game, removed from life, if not selfishly exclusive. Today, for example, we constantly see Herder as humanist criticized for his educational aims, while his teaching on national organisms are emphasized, perhaps to an excessive degree (see, for example, Friedrich Meinecke's *Die Entstehung des Historismus*[2]) we see Humboldt faulted for a lack of vitality (Kähler),[3] which then troubles the whole humanistic ideal. In addition to that, the "intellectualism" of education has been counterposed to life; to be "educated" and "educating oneself" as a goal and ideal is virtually synonymous with being vague, pointless, inauthentic, bloodless, and corrupt. Then again, on the other hand, the methods of modern intellectual work seem to vindicate the view that the ideal of the educated person was a delusion. The harmoniously comprehending individual, embracing the entirety of the world with their mind, as the humanistic ideal proposed—is this not the idealism of the dilettante who seeks only the benefits, but lacks the courage to act, or productively investigate, in even the most limited fashion?

Amid the immense historical upheaval caused by the new collectivisms and their powerful antagonisms, humanistic and educational ideals have either been lost or transformed, so that thinking about them now seems at first a purely theoretical matter. In Marxist socialism, humanism is ascribed at least a conditional validity—once the main historical tasks have been completed, in the final stage of human history; for Marx in fact humans become their own goal, once they overcome their "self-alienation," once they overcome their individualistic prejudices and comprehend themselves as beings both sensory and social; in short, once historical conditions permit them to attend to themselves. New types of people will then emerge, which Marxists—as is characteristic for them—often see in terms of ideal humanistic models. "There will be talents standing on every corner, throngs of Platos, Brunos, and Galileos" (Labriola). "The human average will rise to the level of an Aristotle, a Goethe, a Marx. Above these other heights new peaks will arise" (Trotsky).[4] By contrast, the more vigorous collectivism of German National Socialism, for example, "legitimates" culture only as *the expression of* a naturally national collective essence, putting it always and forever at the service of political circumstances and goals. Humanity, says Alfred Bäumler, is originally subject to an innate and natural order of forces. "Our humanity resides not in the fact that we rebel against the laws of nature, that we seek to destroy and replace it (= civilization, 'humanization' [JP]), but primarily in obedience to the order that created us (= the order of racially and nationally dependent creative forces [JP]). Only once we have shown obedience to this order in its essential, not easily discerned features, can we build a human world of our own in accordance with the eternal harmony of things, and consequently, with the expectation of permanence."[5] However, this order is political and never envisions the liberation of human beings, whereas Marxist socialism at least promises liberation at the end of history. Bäumler's most powerful contempt is reserved for bourgeois liberalism and its "intellectualism," a "degraded idealism" that assumes humans are naturally free and naturally pursue spiritual goals—a prerequisite of *every* humanism. The "intellectual" is a creature parched in body and soul: one having sacrificed body and soul alike to a falsely understood "spirit."

It strikes me that there should be more reflection on these circumstances, in our country especially, than there currently is. Here at home, Masaryk's humanistic thinking produced the strongest agitation, and it has long been the main profession of faith among our intelligentsia; since the time of the national awakening, there has been nothing on a par with Masaryk's intellectual achievements, his critique of the revival, of Marxism, world events, revolutionary ideologies, and realities here at home, the result being that Masaryk has become such a powerful force that he has influenced even his opponents and served to unite even opposing camps. Yet today we see—it must be said openly—the absolute collapse of the Masarykian tradition. After Emanuel Rádl, who has fallen silent, there is no one in this country actively deliberating on the major issues using the categories introduced by Masaryk. Does this mean humanism and the idea of education are outdated ideologies of the past, or is it just a momentary crisis of weakness for today's "intellectuals," disoriented by the wave of ideological antagonism? Is it true what we often hear today, albeit rarely in public, that there is no important message we can take away from Masaryk as a thinker?

It is one of the saddest phenomena in our public life that we could even arrive at such an understanding, that such voices could even be heard, and the guilt lies not least of all with those who copied Masaryk without so much as a fraction of his intellect, who gave us all those popular summaries of his ideas, which came nowhere near doing justice to Masaryk's significance, making certain of his views into a dogma while failing to penetrate to the foundations of his thinking. Masaryk himself did not subscribe to any dogmatism; he could see there were limits to the power of the mind, but he refused to believe in any external limits to history that lay beyond the reach of intellectual effort itself and the freedom of the mind. This is why he accepted religious faith, which allows the powers of the mind to take flight, but for example rejected Marxism (along with other doctrines of historical, collective determination), disagreeing with its reduction of the human being to a set of "relations" and "forces." He was opposed to dogmatism in the classical sense, i.e., to that lack of faith in inner life which relies on "things themselves," on their ostensibly readymade inner truth. All that too was faith, but an active one, thinking and intervening at every moment. And out of this activist faith, free of dogmatism, Masaryk managed to act. Therein lies his significance. This is why, for us today, Masaryk's experience means that "intellectuals" can act precisely on the basis of their intellectualism, on the basis of their "education," provided they actually set themselves the goal of taking action.

This is why Masaryk should be not a problem for us, but proof. By the word *proof* I do not mean just an empty phrase encouraging hollow enthusiasm for Masaryk, but an enthusiasm which, in concrete terms, must be submitted to the most serious critique in judging his intellectual and critical output; a critique that is truly educated, i.e., ultimately upheld by the same ideal Masaryk paid tribute to as one aspect of the humanistic, i.e., inner human ideal. This is why Masarykism, assuming it can still exist here in our country today, having been compromised by so many mindless interpreters, ground to a fine meal for the toothless, and put at the service of party and often personal politics—and it will *have to* exist, lest we entirely resign ourselves, giving up on all we have wanted and longed for, dating back to the time of the national revival—this is why Masarykism will have to fall back on the true foundation of Masaryk's thinking, namely, the idea of European education. This is not a timeless task, lying entirely outside the frame of our historical situation. We cannot come to a stop where we are, but must continue forward. However distracting and difficult our national and political situation,[6] we must be mindful to keep our focus. Did Dobrovský, Palacký, Šafařík not work creatively under pressure?

Of course our "work under pressure" today has to be different, in accordance with the changed situation. It is not a matter of awakening the nation to the first rudiments of cultural self-rule, but rather of identifying them more precisely, improving their quality, establishing genuine contact and entering into active collaboration with the culture of the rest of the world. This is far more difficult than it seems at first glance, however. The difficulties are on the one hand societal and on the other intellectual. The societal difficulties have to do, first, with the fact that our middle class is still relatively weak in comparison to that of other societies, and has to fight quite hard for its position; as statistics and unprejudiced sociological observation show, it is this class alone, through a natural, near-biological process, that gives rise to members of the intellectually active strata. The middle class is where they find their natural milieu, their echo, the basis of their influence and the indispensable backbone of all their activity. Further societal difficulties stem from the fact that the middle class is at risk of being riven, assuming it has not been already, especially among its wealthier elements, by intellectual and moral anarchy and unruliness, by the fact that it is intellectually out of touch with reality and therefore prone to an inability to distinguish between ideas and mere slogans, taking sympathy and hatred to be valid criteria; above all, its poverty shows in its false education and lack of honesty, which we encounter at every turn.

Here we have already entered into the realm of intellectual difficulties. At root is the fact that a part of the bourgeoisie lacks definite ideals, feeling only resentment toward those ideals that do not suit them, and often toward their representatives, whom they find personally unpleasant. The word "nationalism" is no longer enough today. Its weight lies all in its social and cultural content, in the adjectives "humanistic" or "racial," "democratic" or "totalitarian," etc. The "programs" of today, with their chaotic ambiguities, often swing from one to the other not only with no ideological clarity, but not even an attempt at it. Another aspect of this intellectual poverty lies in the fact that true education is always the product of long-standing tradition and great thinking as well as other intellectually creative work. This type of work alone is capable of supporting the life system of a national society as a whole, and developing it institutionally, that is, incorporating it into a distinctive, truly vital program of national education that meets all the essential needs of society and provides its members with the necessary clarity about the circumstances of the existence and advancement of that society, protecting them from a mistaken under- and overestimation of self, while at the same time culling from human history what is vitally necessary, great, and noble, so they can rely on it for real support in difficult periods of the nation's life as well as of their own.

Obviously, these are not problems that can be solved by a few magazine articles, but we must look the facts in the eye and recite them for those who do not yet see them; we must be hard on ourselves in the same ruthlessly critical spirit that Masaryk was distinguished for; criticism born of love must be harsh. All of this is needed today especially, when the outlines of a tragic situation are taking shape, a situation our generation will have to take on and be responsible for. Yet everyone has to think for themselves, and the seriousness of this thinking will be proven by the depth of the work in which it is embodied, made concrete. We can benefit our society, our surroundings, our people above all by showing how unconditionally we are able to believe in something, how seriously and unselfishly we intend to work, how large are the goals we intend to set—all of this, together with the pursuit of national and social justice, must be convincing and inspire respect. It must be the type of societal force that we so need in our country today. Not that we should count on success and the respect that comes with it, or attempt to gain that success and respect by duplicitous means; but first and foremost we ourselves must feel it as a commitment we have taken on, a part of our living faith that we cannot betray, a faith that believes even when everything around us is toppling. For it is a faith that has stood European humanity in good stead now for thousands of years, a faith that has always lifted its head again after every world transformation, that lives quietly the world over, undrowned by the torrents of politics, unnoticed or muzzled, but inextinguishable. If we ourselves want to exist, we must believe that Europe will exist again—a Europe no longer formulated by the same humanistic ideals that it believed in before, and yet in essence the same only deepened and consecrated by the pains and struggles of today. Let us not rely on pure politics, but rather let us regroup our thoughts, let us once again—*let us not be afraid to*—set ourselves great intellectual goals. They will not disappoint us, they cannot, for they will remain a part of Europe, just as Komenský, Dobrovský, Palacký, and Masaryk did.

I do not intend to deal with the objection that the spirit blows where it will,[7] and that to concentrate on higher culture means to require genius. Genius is of course a matter of grace and chance, but to develop it requires—as everyone has known always, up until this day, even if now we forget—education. This is why it is so important for us to reflect on the concept of education, this is why it is in fact a *necessity*. This is why we ask *what education is*.

*　*　*

The educated person stands in contrast to the unstudied, naive person, as well as to the superficial, poorly educated one. The naive person accepts the world as it is, and does not believe there are uncertainties and problems that can be solved by force of one's own reason and will. Similarly, those whose education is incomplete also see everything as obvious; like those who are naive, they have never felt the thorn of a true dilemma, but have found their eternal truth lying in the street, so to speak, and brandish it like a weapon at whatever circumstances bring within reach. They do not devote themselves to any question or activity for its own sake, seeing these solely as an opportunity to assert their "convictions" and, in the process, ultimately themselves. They have a "world view" that answers all their questions for them, and in the event something should slightly unsettle their view, there is a central authority to provide them with a suitable response. Should they choose not to inquire of said authority, being "liberal," it is only because their "principles" and "views" on the matter more than suffice. In both senses, it is hard to say exactly how the educated person differs from the uneducated one; for our purposes here, this approximation will do: the uneducated person moves on the ground of the definitive, the ground of the (ostensibly) self-evident, whereas the educated person (which in essence means self-educating, it being merely a defect of language that presents us with factum instead of fiens)[8] moves on the base of the unfinished, the indefinitive, the uncertain or not fully secured. Not out of any preference for the skeptical mood; nothing could be more alien to the educated person than a capricious flirtation with arguments that might have an adverse effect on unstable dispositions and personalities and propagate an atmosphere of arrogant self-satisfaction. Banal skepticism to the educated person is every bit as contemptible, perhaps even more so, than naive dogmatism.

Education is where the free, autonomous ideal lives and breathes, so it cannot be replaced by any exclusive, definitive *forming* of the human mind. One shortcoming of many modern theories of education is that they ignore the difference between education and formation; this of course greatly simplifies the problem for them, turning it into a mere subsidiary of political questions without causing any difficulties on the level of fundamental "world view." (See German critics of the theory of classical education, e.g., Bäumler.) Education presupposes formation, discipline, strict demands on oneself, but in such a way that spontaneity remains the guiding force, that it remains clear who is the master. At the same time, the educated person shows full humility toward their ideal; they may be harsh toward other people, yet they know there is something more important than themselves, their own role and their intellectual forays, and that important thing is all that matters to them.

Education is the fruit of long fumbling, its ideal materializes and takes root only in those highly refined individuals who have managed to preserve their moral health intact, or at least successfully overcome the childhood illnesses of their moral condition. Education is in no way synonymous with a turning away from the world, with vocational training, with service to impractical ideals; on the contrary, it is the only way to make eternal ideals *truly* practical, as opposed to implementing ideals by depriving people of their freedom.

The essence of the matter is that the educated person adopts a different *attitude* toward things and ideas than others do. They do not let themselves be carried away, and still less controlled; they always maintain a certain reserve that enables them to stand above it all, so to speak, to deliberate on and assess things objectively, in fact from the standpoint of higher relations of deeper meaning. While they may be excited or saddened along with others, in them these emotions have a different origin and a different object. Not that they indulge in the common "*odi profanum vulgus*."[9] It simply brings them to search for reasons and to seek to have a transparent world.

Education then involves a certain relationship to oneself, to one's own human powers and their use; it is not stuffing the head with material. There were educated ancient Greeks with less positive knowledge than our fourth-graders, and they were intellectuals in the fullest sense of the word. What they were not lacking, however, was a genuine relationship to all the great powers of education, to everything that deepens one's humanity: to the poetic, which captivates, cleanses, and constructs paradigms; to rigorous awareness, which clarifies and specifies; to the heroism of one's own history, which teaches one to see clearly one's own situation; to philosophy, which reveals the whole. The Greeks, of course, were a nation of brilliant individuals, and succeeded in creating a culture based on their own intrinsic strengths; the ideal of the educated person and the concept of being educated, as well as the word for education, *paideia*, are all of Greek origin. What the Greeks achieved, no one alone can do in the midst of a world where life has become extremely complicated from a material point of view. The Greeks could draw on their own resources, since history in fact began with them; true history—in the sense of a tradition of education as conscious individual effort, rather than merely a mysterious power, controlling, stylizing, shaping life—is a Greek creation. Everything that can act on *us* as an educational agent is either a creation or a part of this history, which makes this history an educational subject par excellence.

Of course there are historical creations that can be easily removed from the ground that gave rise to them, becoming autonomous. All purely exact knowledge falls into this category; in this way it is superhistorical albeit truly educative. One could claim that it was only mathematics which gave humanity the norm of truth, that only mathematics taught us to distinguish rigorously between what is and is not. But there can be no covering up the fact that any education consisting solely of such abstract, timeless elements is too rudimentary. This is nearly the lowest mode of education; colorless, inhuman, anational, ahistorical, an education perhaps for people whose thinking is too straightforward and simplistic for them to be able to concentrate otherwise, an education that undervalues the vital ground from which it sprang, which it must return to periodically to draw from again. This mode of education inevitably predominates where it helps to penetrate beyond the walls of narrow national autarky and contented provinciality. Yet there is no such thing as a culture oriented exclusively or even predominantly on mathematical–natural scientific thinking, nor can there be any such thing. It cannot exist, because the key to the question of human life and destiny cannot be found by this route.

In this respect, the artistic (I am not saying aesthetic!) mode of education is far higher. I do not include here all artistic activity, insofar as it has an impact on social life, but primarily *great* art, dealing in some way with *all* the essential human questions. Literary works in particular possess this relevance, but other arts as well strive toward it. It is only within the framework of these great creations, laying out the goals, boundaries, and divinities of life, that smaller, more subtle efforts can be understood, which in themselves may not appear to be of any significant interest tied to art but which are nonetheless gripping and full of radiant life. Anyone who does not have the courage and patience to see the creative struggle in art over the ultimate questions of humanity, over its self-assigned vital content, and who sees in it only an echo and reflection of the situation in society, essentially political, must be either deaf or sterile. They degrade art to the level of mythology. Though art may spring from a collective foundation, it wields this foundation masterfully as the raw material on which it makes its mark. Art gives life to our gods, inserting them into it, making them concrete. We see this in Homer, in the Gothic cathedral; but our modern god, too—harsh reality, free of illusions—is solidly probed to its depths in the works of writers such as Cervantes and Shakespeare. Hence the importance of literary education, rigorous, analytical, going to a depth rarely seen in our country; let us ask only what our students learn to truly *comprehend* of the world's great literary creations—and we see how we are missing what is most important, what could create standards, models, great horizons. It is this that is most important in the historically grounded structures of education:

we have no standards other than the works that have been created throughout history, attested to by us and ceaselessly disputed. We have no values other than those hard-won and -established.

Still another mode of education is one that consists in reflecting on the historical facts themselves, the historical-political model. It is represented not by the political fanatic but the reflective type, who seeks to find a meaning in real-life events that eludes the superficial observer or actor. For those who are reflective, the train of history stretches far into the past, including things, people, and events that would seem to be uninvolved. These reflective types are able to go beyond their own narrowly personal standpoint as well as the perspective of whatever group they are attached to through their origin and interests. If they have the ability and capacity to act, they act not on impulse but out of understanding, and their authority is not based on putting ideas in people's heads and making an emotional impression, but rather on their ability to see into the heart of things. It may be also that they are incapable of action, that they can understand but are not prone to act; yet politics in a deeper sense cannot do without their interventions; it would grow coarse and lose itself in demagoguery and utilitarianism. It is important for practical reasons that reflective people like this be active in political society and that they be granted the broadest possible influence; in our situation it is critical that analytical, discerning, informative journalism, in short journalism that educates, gain the upper hand over journalism that is narrowly partisan, operating with no methodology or independence.

The philosophical mode of education aims to bring reflection to bear on all of human life, on the relation between its purpose and destiny, as well as on its framework as a whole, which is the world. To be philosophically educated is not the same as to be philosophically gifted or possessed with philosophical passion; nor does it mean a person went to any particular school; on the contrary, school may have deprived them of access to any serious philosophical education. A person who is philosophically educated is familiar from their own experience and own original thinking with the major interests of philosophical thought and the major historical attempts that have been undertaken to address them. These then, again, provide the necessary standard. It is quite possible for a brilliant philosopher to have a relatively poor philosophical education; however, without people who do have a philosophical education, it is impossible for that person to gain authority and influence, to find a suitable environment in which to work without losing hope. So a thorough philosophical education is every bit as important as original thinking, and all the more so because it can always be worked on, whereas to be a real thinker is a matter of grace. The educated tend to be modest and unpretentious, whereas those who insist on styling themselves "thinkers" are more likely to come across as lumbering in thought.

All these higher modes of education, evidently, must draw their material *from history*. All education has a *historical* horizon. For every modern nation, this horizon is segmented into a horizon of its own national history and a horizon that is universal. The horizon of education is not continuous in structure, but has its peaks and valleys, its moments of fullness and gaps; in short it is punctuated by emergent zones that constitute the milestones of historical development. It may happen—in fact it tends to be the rule—that the significance of the milestones shifts over time to other places; however, there are certain, so to speak, historical constants, whose valuation may vary but whose overall significance cannot be underestimated. Part of the essence of being an educated person, then, is living in the universal horizon of historical events. It follows from this that to be educated means to outgrow any sort of narrow-mindedness, bias, or limitations.

What we lack today is the assurance of that universal horizon which could provide standards and landmarks. We do not mean to claim that there is a lack of educated people in our country; but those here typically have their own individual interests attached to some particular corner of world life without any lasting positive values being created for our domestic educational life, without their work putting down solid roots at home. Universities are the institutions that should keep such a set of intellectual values alive in the mind of our society; however, they have many other tasks to attend to as well, and cannot be in charge of cultural life. But if our education is ever to stand on solid ground, we must keep the relationship to this universal goal constantly in sight, and the major points of orientation offered by history in such abundance must be more than simply a register for us, to be clearly and humbly aware of the full extent of what remains to be done. Let us cite here a few such requirements; of course these are only examples, and as such of course are drawn from the areas closest to the writer.

We are one of the few nations that lacks a lively relationship to antiquity. This is evident not only from the continuing decline in the study of antiquity in our life and the disappearance of classical education, but also in the helpless attitude of many of those professionally engaged with it. Characteristic of this is the fact that we have our first complete and high-quality translation of Plato (by František Novotný) only now. Also characteristic is the overall lack of public interest in it. We should be studying primary rather than secondary phenomena, and in doing so, we should set ourselves the task of collaborating with others to address current issues, not just "informing" people at home about goings-on elsewhere. Far from being behind us, antiquity still awaits us. In particular, it is awaiting study *by our philosophers*. We are still talking about how we mustn't fall under the thrall of German thinking; but surely the best way to ensure that would be the study of the origin of all philosophy itself, which remains unsurpassed and is found in antiquity. In all philosophy, we still have nothing more powerful than Socrates, Plato, and Aristotle. What do these names mean to us? Our own philosophy developed at a time when there was an attempt to make a break with the whole tradition of Western European philosophy and start anew with no regard for history, on a purely modern foundation. This attempt, positivism, failed. Today we have a heightened obligation to find our bearings within a tradition that has as yet never been organically alive for us, that we have as yet never been able to build on for our intellectual and spiritual life and creation.

And what do the great modern national cultures mean to us in real terms? Where are those among us who can identify with them, live their spiritual rhythm and bring it into our lives? For example, we have a surprising lack of work on the French classics addressing the problems they raise or at least indicating their scope. The first thorough work on Descartes in Czech appeared only two years ago.[10] The Pascal we have is still the version that Masaryk presented in such a subjective and inadequate way.[11] The French Enlightenment is just a cliché for us; its actual life, its interests and ideals, which we so readily invoke—who among us knows the genesis of them, who knows them in all their richness and depth? The same holds for our relationship to German culture. While "*in ea vivimus, movemur et sumus*"[12] still holds true, we ourselves are not conscious of it and lack the knowledge either to comprehend or criticize it. It is precisely the major and most important phenomena that are either neglected or viewed in too isolated a manner, with no consideration of the greater goals and ideals. To remain just with philosophy: for example, there has been plenty written in Czech about Kant, but the level of the writing, the level of its *expertise*, is worse than poor; all that has been done about Fichte and Hegel is mere clichés.

One indication of an immature culture is that it demands others take an interest in it, without asking what might more deeply justify this interest. Any greater interest in us must come from us ourselves, from a deeper, more universal effort to explain and ignite passion for our own culture. That, however, first requires a humble and devoted interest in the world, in its universal interrelatedness, in its truly enormous problems. Perhaps today we are sufficiently mature for that; provided we can do so more diligently and conscientiously than we have up to now, the outcome will be not contempt for the domestic, a negligence that carries with it an air of insincerity, but rather increased respect for our own culture, forged in the fire of the most stringent criticism, a respect no longer stigmatized by any pang of inferiority that we would rather avoid.

Does this all add up to a return to the older, harmonious conception of humanity as Herder for example envisioned it? Does this mean a renewal of the experiment that failed to stand the historical test? Do we too believe that the spirit naturally achieves harmonious form, the spiritual joy of genuine culture? Despite our accepting its core principles, namely freedom and spontaneity in all cultural endeavors, we partially blame this cheap optimism for the failures of the earlier humanism. Education is something other than intellectualism, than curiosity, polymathy,[13] dialectical and intellectual artfulness; it is a purely spiritual effort at discipline that sees in the ideas of greatness, universality, wholeness an effective antidote to the comfort and decadence that threaten every one of us internally. So why do greatness, universality, and wholeness of all things play this role? Because in them is exhibited the power of the spirit to summarize and examine the things that initially marked its boundaries, to overcome its limits, to overcome itself in every naive, naturally given form of itself. In the process of this overcoming, in the process of this deepening of self to the ultimate possibility, the fullness of one's essence must ultimately be revealed, its inner tension, its intense moods, its conflicts and pains, as well as its redemption. There is no harmonious, blissful development here, as in the growth of a tree from a seed, but a piece of concentrated life, an indispensable moment in the life struggle, that moment in which one fights for standards and models not only for oneself but for everyone. It is a struggle that presupposes absolute freedom, yet this freedom must of itself be directed toward authority, discipline, toward submitting to clear overall positions, in short to legislation, which everyone may freely contribute to, albeit under the strict watch of the guardians of the existing standards (who may not be just people, but certain intellectual acts). Education is not simply blissful enrichment, but pain and struggle as well. Greek philosophy, the pinnacle of human cultural endeavors, would be nothing without Socrates and his firmly controlled inner tension. Passion grows from this tension alone—and every true cultural endeavor must be passionate. For all *meaning*, the true meaning of life and the world, appears to us first in the passion that attracts us, not in the calm, harmonious development of our natural abilities and strengths. Therefore we can ultimately formulate our humanism as the struggle against cliché, against comfort, against spiritual hedonism in favor of greatness, of the courage to withstand stress, the courage to feel passion and pain. Education is work, it is discipline. Perhaps many generations of painful searching will pass before we arrive at a new happiness. But the search itself is its own reward, because the search has meaning.

Notes

1   The Czech *vzdělanost*, translated here as education, approximates the German *Bildung*, which means formation, education, culture, or cultivation (Ed.).

2   Friedrich Meinecke, *Die Entstehung des Historismus*, vols. 1–2 (Munich and Berlin: R. Oldenbourg, 1936) (Ed.).

3   S. A. Kähler, *Wilhelm von Humboldt und der Staat* (Munich and Berlin: R. Oldenbourg, 1927) (Ed.).

4   Both Labriola and Trotsky cited according to Werner Sombart, *Deutscher Sozialismus* (Berlin-Charlottenburg: Buchholz and Weisswange, 1934), 104, 105 (Trans.).

5   Citation unidentified. Bäumler makes a statement along similar lines in *Bildung und Gemeinschaft* (Berlin: Junker and Dünnhaupt, 1942) (Ed.).

6 Patočka wrote this text in response to the Munich Agreement of 1938. The agreement, an effort by the world powers to appease Hitler, forced Czechoslovakia to cede significant territory to Nazi Germany. In the year following this concession, Hitler annexed the whole of Czechoslovakia, and it remained in Nazi German hands until 1945 (Ed.).

7 John 3.8.

8 "that presents us with a fact instead of a deed" (Ed.).

9 "I detest the vulgar crowd [or "uneducated rabble"]—Horace, *Odes* III, 1, 1 (Ed.).

10 Josef Beneš, *Descartesova metoda ve vědách a ve filosofii* (Descartes's method in the sciences and philosophy) (Prague: Československá akademie věd, 1936) (Ed.).

11 Tomáš Garrigue Masaryk, *Blaise Pascal, jeho život a filosofie* (Blaise Pascal, his life and philosophy) (Prague: Jan Otto, 1883) (Ed.).

12 "in it we live, move, and have our being"—New Testament, Acts 17.28 (Ed.).

13 "acquaintance with many branches of knowledge"—Cf. Hermann Alexander Diels and Walther Kranz, *Die Fragmente der Vorsokratiker*, vol. I (Berlin: Weidmann, 1951), Heraclitus, B40: "The learning of many things does not teach understanding" (Ed.).

PART TWO

Care for the Soul

The term "care from the soul" has its origins in ancient Greek philosophy, and specifically in a Socratic conception of a radical self-questioning. Soul here is not a theological term but instead describes the activity or movement of human being toward a life in truth. In Patočka, truth is an activity with a certain orientation, rather than something one "has" or "knows." He acknowledges that the need to care for the soul is not obvious within the framework of instrumental reason or "biologism"—the organization of society around physical life and health. It is instead affirmed in acts like Socrates' willingness to die for a truth beyond the status quo, or the painter and writer Josef Čapek's decision to write poetry from a Nazi concentration camp. Care for the soul is a commitment to and orientation toward a deeper source of value than those on offer in any given social framework. In Patočka, care for the soul is always, at the same time, care for the *polis* or the city—the space of life in common. In this sense, it is always "political."

CHAPTER THREE

Limping Pilgrim Josef Čapek (1950–3)

Translated from the Czech by Alex Zucker

Josef Čapek is less brilliant, less a virtuoso, less turned toward outer life than the other Čapek Dioscurus.[1] Paradoxical though it may sound, Josef Čapek, painter, a man of the world of shapes and colors, of space and outward appearances, is inward-facing when it comes to his main interest. As is his art! And this inwardness is what made him a thinker. A thinker, albeit not in the sense of professional expertise. Having read all the books and essays in which he most deeply ponders the questions crucial to him, we do not hesitate to deny him the title of philosopher. Čapek himself laid no such claim; the truthfulness of thought that he pursued was of a different variety than the truth of a systematic structure. It never occurred to him that the ultimate secret of being could be teased out through the roundabout route of a conceptual lacework delicate as breath. Although his thinking too was delicate, in its immediate urgency and drama it was quite different. Josef Čapek was a seeker of life wisdom; that is, thinking concerning life and death. Life wisdom, in the sense that Čapek understands it, is the ultimate source of stability in life when a person is faced with the important crossroads and experiences that always come up for a person (or can, assuming they are not avoided out of cowardice or inanity). In short, as a seeker of wisdom, Čapek lives in thought and thinks through life. This gives him a kinship with many ancient thinkers and poets, from cultures as far-flung as the ancient Greeks, the ancient Chinese, and the late-medieval seekers of God and truth, whose quotations fill the pages of his book about the limping pilgrim.[2] What Čapek has in common with all of them is an absolute earnestness and righteousness that prevent him from straying even a step from his inner center of gravity, from experimenting, from tinkering with thoughts and ideas. It is that melancholy that does not give ground on matters of principle, that melancholy that causes the pilgrim in search of the absolute to tread so heavily, to limp the way he does. But if Čapek has a kinship with those who think but a single thought, the internal monoideists, it does not mean that he was detached from his times, or that he sought an artificial and unnatural timelessness. On the contrary, as the author of a study on the creative nature of his own day and age,[3] he was acutely aware of his connection with the times. And the facts underlying his lifelong concern are clearly stated there.

> [T]he whole nineteenth century was a period of complex and passionately lived life, for individuals and collectives. In the midst of this exhilaration, religion ceased to have any general validity, and every new challenge humanity found itself confronting was addressed with the broadest possible scope of intellectual energy; new sectors of social and ethical life sprang up, new conditions in the lives of states, in politics and in mass social movements, new organizing concepts, new opinions, new scientific hypotheses, which in many cases were able to replace the loss of religious faith.
>
> The need and necessity for new creations applies in every field of human endeavor. . . . Natural faith and unrestrained devotion to this dynamic exhilaration contain within themselves the capacity for a spiritual and ethical synthesis of a new humanity as powerful as the religious conceptions of yesteryear. The need for faith, as deep-seated in modern humans as it was in our faithful ancestors, certainly does not appear to be founded on the divine principles of the religions of the past . . .
>
> The modern atheistic spirit also flares upward in the direction of the unknown with a near-religious intensity; yet it is a bold thrust, expecting no succor or final absolution from above. It is action itself, a sharp ray of light cast on everything: it seeks to permeate and overpower the materiality that it acknowledges; to expand the narrow confines of the concepts of three-dimensional space and mechanical time, to overcome the laws of gravity, velocity, those that govern physics and chemistry, by way of the most remarkable feats.[4]

The particular content with which Čapek's wisdom seeks to engage is the spirit of this "atheistic" age. The spirituality of an age in which God's place in the scheme of things has remained unoccupied. The spirituality of a technological age, which seeks to reshape and transform all that is given, which aims to use that which already is as a springboard to a higher end, not yet accomplished. An age for which the world, the external, nature, matter all exist. Čapek even opens his study by citing the "materialist poet" Walt Whitman. And yet it is spirituality—not mere technical and external control, for which manageability, government, mastery are the alpha and omega. In short, Josef Čapek here, in his period of youthful rebelliousness, is getting at the question of humanity's autonomy in nature and the world, the question of the importance of spirit in an age of humanism, when humans are the highest form of life in the cosmos and our task as humans is to make sense of the universe.

As formulated by Čapek, this task may seem somewhat reminiscent of titanism—but we will see how he managed to avoid this pitfall. Nevertheless there is a romantic core to it, and just as the nineteenth century's whole second half and the early part of the twentieth were a peculiar amalgamation of romanticism and positivism, these alleged opposites came together in their most typical representatives, including Balzac, Comte, Wagner, and Häckel, as well as in poets and artists of the twentieth century, so that the young Josef Čapek held both within him at once. This whole trend was part of the central problem he inherited, which we might call the great dialectical problem of the humanistic period: humanity at once both as a part of nature and overcoming it, humanity understood on the basis of the world, yet at the same time making sense of and interpreting it. In this sense, one could say that the entire nineteenth century was in some way Hegelian, both humanistic and titanic at once.

This human autonomy within and on the basis of nature appeared to Čapek to be embodied above all in art. Perhaps it would not be mistaken for us to assume that this was the root of his enthusiasm for modern art with its attempt to start from reality as the basis for going beyond it. We know too how heartfelt was his conviction that art, as he understood it, is not an intellectual game for a circle of the select few, but that, in its endeavor to create a new reality, art is an elementary human necessity, thrusting to the surface with the same intensity in the magical drawings of the Magdalenian period or the primitive Bushman as in the "humblest art" of shop signs, the ceramics and folk art of village fairs, souvenirs, and photographs, old and new alike; in all of this, even the exhilaration with which the village room-painter captures the stark, hard reality of death in the face of a woman in a coffin, Čapek sensed the same movement that guided his art as well, a movement from interior to exterior, not slavishly copying that which is already there, but genuinely transcending it while avoiding untruthfulness; because human beings, the human heart and soul, human imagination, these too are reality, and more resolute and responsible than a passively presented one.

But I do not wish to repeat in shadow fashion what those more informed have said, so I will turn to the document that shows how Čapek not only felt the necessity to express through unmediated creation that human essence which is more than just what is ready-made, but also how he struggled with it conceptually, endeavoring to capture it with his mind alone, by way of reflection. Not merely to achieve or to grasp this transcendence artistically, but to experience and crystallize this "more" in its entirety, in all its significance for life. What I wish to speak of is *The Limping Pilgrim*.

The Limping Pilgrim is evidence of Čapek's humanism—while at the same time evidence of his renunciation of any sort of "humanistic overreach."

The limping pilgrim hobbles along the path of life—what vast, far-off perspectives these words evoke. The oldest, most ancient philosophemes are linked to the image of the path.

Parmenides encountered the Truth on "the path that leads the man who knows through the universe."[5] The Tao is a path that itself leads us along it, rather than being walked. Heraclitus knew that the road up and down, of origin and extinction, was one and the same. In the sophistic parable, Hercules encountered Vice and Virtue at the crossroads of life. Wandering, paying no mind where from or where to, yet hoping we will not be abandoned by the beneficent deities, who know our final destination—this is how life appears to Socrates in his old age.[6] Čapek is drawn to this image, and he is drawn to those in whose minds this image has been etched: Comenius, for one. But the pilgrimage for him truly is a path from the unknown to the unknown, from darkness to darkness. "I was not—*I am*—I will not be."[7] This is how Čapek describes the line of our path, our finite time. This trinity, with its clear reference to time, this dual frontier of our own dynamic, at once moving and standing still—interval and movement, a restlessness frozen in place: this is the path, this is our time. The oldest philosophemes use the imagery of the path and the pilgrim to allude to the connectedness of the questions of being, time, humankind; the limping pilgrim walks the same path, but with a heavy, unfanciful, non-speculative gait. He travels slowly, his feet struggling to lift from the ground; one foot forever resting on the earth, he cannot break away from it; the world, nature, matter exist for him. The world for him is an eminent reality, which no metaphysical trick can make disappear. And he cannot be talked out of believing in it. The world is full, crowded with being; it does not lie at the bottom of a void. In fact nothingness, as Čapek reflects later in *Written in the Clouds*,[8] is not possible; the material world, with its attributes of space and time, is as old as the ages. And its dynamics, the immensity of actual and possible movements and events within it, are age-old as well.

But having a limp does not mean simply this realistic acceptance of facts, an attachment to that which we know exists based on our own life experience and common sense. A total resorption into reality is not even possible for us; the very fact that we always in some way transcend it, that we walk through life on legs of different length, means that we will limp. The Hegel of old once used to maintain that humanity was like a sick animal; in the sense that we are biologically incomplete, imperfect creatures. Among other things, the image of the limping man refers back to that. This infirmity as such, however, would not interest us were it not balanced by something on the other side of the scales. The lack of adaptation to that which is near, familiar, and certain may mean, to an extent, adaptation to something else: to that which is great, unfamiliar, distant, problematic.

And indeed the Limping Pilgrim praises his infirmity: "There was also something he gained thanks to his shorter, less mobile leg, which impaired him in his pilgrimage through life: like his awareness of his shorter leg, his experience of some things in life and the world was more evocative, more acute. Growing in strength and gratefully devoted to serenity, he perceives large phenomena, as grand as the heavens and the expanses of the earth, at the same time as those very small, such as a bird or a butterfly." In short, he has discovered the virtue of limping. And he speaks to us in order to persuade us of it.

What an odd humanism, you say, that sees humans as having an irreparable defect! Be that as it may, I believe that this is precisely what is specific to the humanism of Josef Čapek. His limping man is no successor to God, neither god nor demigod. On the contrary, his outward appearance inspires no great enthusiasm: less the embodiment of harmony and strength than constitutionally weak and defective. We might add that it is a defect which is insurmountable. The classical humanists of the nineteenth century saw things differently: for them, defects belonged exclusively to the past and the present, not to the ultimate stage of human development. This is why they so often saw humans as infinite, total, universal titans making sense of the universe, plowmen hitched to the plow of creation, the word liberating heaven and earth. The moment humans break free of the clutches of illusion that obscure their full reality, the moment they rid themselves of metaphysical and mythological visions, they immediately become complete beings, heroes of the cosmos, every bit as much a product of worldly forces as the key to their meaning. In Čapek's conception, the process of becoming a complete being, a sensate being with access to the universal, does not come automatically, naturally, so to speak, but only after a struggle with whatever it is that prevents us, and even then we never do so entirely and without damage, but only humanly—which is to say, partially, privately, without definitiveness. Humans may make sense of things, but only in a *finite* way. This finiteness manifests itself above all as mortality. Mortality is the most conspicuous expression of finiteness, but is not itself its basis, its essence. Hegel and the young Feuerbach saw mortality as just a tax that humans must pay for their own internal infinity, the infinity of their spiritual essence, as it manifests itself in society and history. For them, death was merely the certainty that individuality is not the true essence of humanity, but that humanity's essence is universal and spiritual in nature; the meaning of an individual's death lies precisely in the transcending of finiteness. Death, as they saw it, serves to oppose individuality. Whereas, in Čapek's conception, death individualizes. The idea of death—not sentimentally mourned or disguised in any way—serves to make the finite life lived that much more intensely, enjoyed more authentically:

Here, however, contrary to custom, the end of all our stories is placed right at the beginning, thus becoming something of a starting point, a key to all the rest. Or, to put it this way, being aware of the certainty of the end, we can start by drawing an imaginary line under everything that we will have to leave behind, and fill in this final column to end all columns with an approximate total, arriving at a balance of what is most important.[9]

Thus death becomes a dividing line between what is genuine and what ultimately matters, what I live by when everything external and ephemeral that death stops, pulls up short, and discards, ceases to be effective and valid. So the idea of death is at root distinct from any notion of *vanitas vanitatum*. Death is neither confirmation of a universal *nihil*, nor, on the other hand, proof that human beings are, at their spiritual core, masters and sensemakers of all reality: death is an opportunity to confront what remains safely hidden from us in life, because we face, or so we think, more urgent matters, though in fact they are distractions; death serves to concentrate; only under the strict gaze of death are we made whole—we are not only who we are engaged in this or that activity, whether important or not, but ephemeral humans living in the face of the universe, in relation to its eternity, and therefore *sub specie aeterni* alone.

Death does still one other thing apart from individualizing life, making it fully ours: it dramatizes it. Life is not a simple fact like the structure of an atom, a crystal, or a sunset. Life is a story, a dramatic event where there is something happening, even in the case of a short, impoverished life, lacking in any superficially rich content. Even a life not poised at the helm of the world, even a life that does not feature on the stage of great world events has its own inner drama, its own unique plots, whether full of depth or not. Čapek sings the praises of life, of vegetative life, a simple life whose roots are grounded in what is closest to it, like plants and trees, a life that, rather than looking to animal models, tends to parallel that of molds and mosses, dryland herbs, stalks of grain, forest-dwelling shadow lilies. It goes without saying a life like this is of no general significance but only private; it is not important so much to others as it is to itself; but private significance, private meaning, is, in the end, all the meaning we have as humans, and our belonging to the whole is indirectly also the meaning of the whole.

The path of the Limping Pilgrim is human time. Human time, that line between birth and death, is possible only where the end is already present in advance at every stage. There are encounters along the way, and this is the sum of the pilgrim's adventure. The Limping Pilgrim is passive, perhaps too much so.

Yet he will have to do battle and free someone along the way. The path leads through being. Where from and where to? "From one indefinite place to another still less defined. In truth I am going from nowhere to nowhere, just wandering *within something*; rather than leading me through places the path is more a certain duration, a moment of tension in time, more just a state or condition."[10] "Where from–where to" is a question that serves a dual awareness. On the one hand, awareness of the immense whole in which we are embedded and from which we emerge in such an odd way—nature and the material universe clearly behave as if we, our individuality, our inner selves and lives, did not matter, and yet our inner selves, lives, and individuality are here. There are filiations everywhere, immense and extending indefinitely. The filiation of our living from the universal reservoir of biology is undeniable. Yet the biological layer itself rises to the surface from somewhere in the inorganic substrate; is that all there is? To be able to say definitively where from and where to would require us to survey the whole definitively, down to the deepest depth; and to decline to answer the question "where from–where to" requires us to acknowledge the unrevealed nature of our being within the whole, at least in the positive and substantive form that our minds typically call knowledge. Our awareness of the whole, then, is at the same time accompanied by a second awareness: ignorance. We do not know where from or where to. This also means we do not know *what* we are traveling toward. Neither nature, nor any other source and origin, but also neither the conclusion which we are drawing toward, can dictate its demands to us in full and without question. Even if it were true a hundred times over that all that matters to nature is the species, the whole, the group, and that the individual is merely an instrument—our life after all is still only our own. So the awareness that comes from the question "where from–where to" is both total and negative; it is an all-encompassing question, a sort of knowing ignorance, *docta ignorantia*.[11] It is both poor and boundless. This boundlessness is manifested in the new relationship it allows us to form with ourselves—immense and eternal.

> It [this boundlessness] does not begin out there somewhere, on the other side of a border, beyond the end of something; we are right here in it now . . . It passes through us, permeates us, encompasses us within itself here, in the same way as it does there, on the other side, in the hereafter; it is already here among us and within us. Life is but one of its manifestations, accessible to us in fragmentary form at least, in part if not more, by way of our senses . . . more than once I have read that the Gateway to Eternity stands before us everywhere, no matter where we are, open wide . . . You asked where I am coming from and where I am going. We are on the same journey: I am hobbling through the Gateway to Eternity.[12]

What might we encounter on this journey in the company of the Limping Pilgrim? Will the path take shape differently than the way we create it every day as we hurry along in pursuit of other things, with no aching leg forcing us to think about the path itself?

The answer is already clear: Have we not already discovered things so magnificent that they take our breath away? Have we not already encountered the immensity of being, urging us on even as it hides itself from open view? First we confronted the mystery (more than the question) of being. But what comes next is inseparable from it: anyone for whom the whole is of pressing importance, for whom being poses a question, who has a sense of the eternity in which we unceasingly are, and from which—whether we know it or not—we are not able to take even one step back, discovers that they have—a soul. Our Limping Man has something in common with the ancient Socrates, in that his knowing ignorance, inflamed by the urgency and unanswerability of the ultimate "where from–where to," is at the same time a care for the soul, *tēs psychēs epimeleisthai.*[13]

Against the solid backdrop of what is given and certain, against the backdrop of the definitiveness of existence, which manifests itself through age-old laws and forces, through the preponderance of material and forces, trembles something not fully defined, the human question of what is the ultimate "where to." Not everything *in the world* is given forever in advance. We can see that in the fact that we ask without finding an answer. There is no answer here—we cannot deduce it from anything external in heaven or on earth, we cannot depend or rely on anything outside ourselves when it comes to the ultimate questions, no such thing can serve as our ultimate authority and answer.

> Matter may rule to the uttermost limits—the soul is still the farthest and highest that the evolution of life has been able to attain. Yet no Superman or Übermensch; I do not like any such Nietzschean arrogance.
>
> A human is quite enough for me. A human being with a soul. A creature of unease. Yes, unease about both change and persistence. About temporality and eternity, life as well as death. Unease about the meaning of it all. And what if the soul is nothing more than unease, nothing but distress and weakness, nothing but a noiseless cry of despair into the dizzying void? It may not be much, but, ultimately—it is everything! The soul is the ultimate and supreme question that life can pose within an individual. But a question is not an answer. No, it is not. With perhaps but one exception, and that is: when the question is at the same time already the answer.[14]

Thus, in dialectical fashion, the pilgrim seeks to move out of the question itself, away from a lack of knowledge, away from a negative, toward the answer, toward the positive and the substantive. If life, conscious life, cannot find what it requires in the universe—meaning, purpose—that is not to say that it is without meaning or purpose. At least not so long as there is a soul, the guardian and shepherd of this question, of this relation to the existing whole. What was in the past considered obvious and given, a gift from the hand of God, is now again a question for humanity today—yet this means greater, not lesser, responsibility, it means living within the whole, it means breaking out of human smallness and the defensiveness that continuously, automatically, dogs humanity's heels. The whole world is a sort of striving toward self-overcoming; the purposelessness of matter is overcome in life, a life in consciousness, a consciousness that in humans is purified into pure mentality, into a steady relation to things that are ultimate, permanent, and therefore eternal. Perhaps these pilgrim's formulas are insufficiently clear, perhaps they are lacking in sophistication. But they demonstrate the point: that even with the greatest affinity for nature, humanity is a turning point, and if we do not get our answers from God, from what is higher, neither can they be dictated to us by nature, i.e., what is lower. Even an ordinary life, as Čapek later said, cannot escape being impinged upon by metaphysics. Not the metaphysics of speculation, but the metaphysics that we are.

This impingement of the whole of being on life is the essence of the soul. Anyone capable of relating to the whole in this way, anyone with a sense of the *honor generis humani*,[15] has a soul. On the other hand, there is an aspect of humanity that shortens our perspective and our breath, an aspect that is no less ours than our soul: that aspect of our personal success in life, which we constantly measure against that of others, which drives us forward, up the social ladder, seeing only functions and actions, that aspect which changes our life path into a career, that aspect which thinks, feels, and lives only for itself. Profit, advantage, loss, struggle, these are the finite perspectives of our overly human arithmetic—this is the domain of the *Person*, which competes with the soul for dominion over humankind. The soul cannot count, at least not in the usual way; its field is the infinite, and within that field the part is not less than the whole, within it there is no possible or clear progression, nor gain nor loss—the soul seeks to live, and lives in full, because it is in relation to the whole. And being in relation to the whole, to everything, the landscape of the soul is solitude. Not the kind that closes itself off to other people, but the kind that creates along with its own humanity yet another.

The Person, then, is the second encounter on the path of life, simultaneous with meeting the soul. The Person is the soul's double, standing in so perfectly for the soul that for many, preoccupied with their own Person, it will never cross their mind that behind its broad shoulders is yet another being, slender and timid, quiet, solitary and taciturn, yet without whose blood the Person would not survive even a moment. The Person is sustained through transfusions: for all our relationships in life are, ultimately, relationships to the great Whole, whereas the Person seeks to live on the basis of its own self alone: it is self-sufficient in the sense that Comenius uses the word.

Earlier we said that for Čapek humans are not solely creatures of meaning, of the whole, of infinity, of eternity, and that we are also not such beings automatically. We do not have a soul in the same way we have arms and legs. Humans have a soul only so long as we are willing to fight and greatly sacrifice for it. And even if we do fight and sacrifice, it may still not secure for us the role of undisputed master and sensemaker of things, but only our own private meaning in life, our own human dignity and majesty.

We must fight with the Person over the soul. The reason for this lies in our finitude, of which the Person is the foremost exponent. The Person stands between the soul and the whole like an opaque shield, ever present, only occasionally offering a glance around its edge into the limitless firmament of the heavens.

The pilgrim speaks of the Person with utmost bitterness, regarding it as practically evil incarnate. The Person is demonic, a demon of complacency, he says. The soul is not in a battle against the body, assuming we understand the body to be materiality and sensuality, but rather against the Person. The "bodily" aspect is part of the Person only to the extent that those selfish instincts that seem to make us the center of all our actions and that the Person seizes upon, so to speak, as its own found property the moment it turns to building its own empire, an empire "of this world," are part of our natural, animal side. The way the Limping Pilgrim speaks of the Person may initially give the impression that the Person is a sheer parasite in the overall plan of life, something thoroughly superfluous, which we can do without.

> The encounter with the Person, then, is one of the great adventures of this journey, an adventure notable because the Person is a very dangerous creature for a human. It has no respect or regard for the human being at all, and how could it, given that, unlike the human race, it did not come directly from the workshop of creation? Its origin lies someplace else entirely, and I daresay, it is more than a little proud of that.
>
> So who did create the Person, if it wasn't born of a mother? Like so many other detrimental things, each of us creates the Person for ourselves, and having elevated it above ourselves, we bow down in obedience to its authority. And yet the Person is not built of better material, nor is it in any way more beautiful: in none of these respects does it have any reason to pride itself as superior ... And yet always, through and through—however indistinguishable it may be from us—it is a derivative product, in fact artificial, and to a large extent a parasite, living off of our bodily and mental juices. It is said of unhappy people that they are victims of their darker instincts, their passions; yet how many of them are victims of their Person! That insidious monster that clings to their bodies with thousands of little hooks; that puts them on like a costume and, pretending to be them, speaks their words, imitating their gestures and actions.[16]

The Person—we hear again other times—is social in origin: we must cut the cloth of our nature to fit the pattern of society, whatever look is now in vogue that can be imitated and adopted for use ready-made, making our lives easier. This making easier, making simpler, encourages our inner weakness and cowardice: it accommodates our tendency to hide from duties, obligations, difficulties. Ultimately, our complacency breeds a tendency toward the Person: we seek superiority, competition with others, and the

Person, which is an entirely external pose, a role, something objective, real, and imposing, helps us do so in a tangible way. In short, the Person is false, objectified spirit, transformed and reduced to a thing.

We must make sure that the Person, in Čapek's sense, is not a mere construct, that it is a phenomenon which everyone can observe in themselves and others alike. Life carries this inner falsehood with it constantly. Humans are incapable of being fully and entirely truthful, or, some say, sincere. Sincerity is precluded by our very essence, some moralists have tried to claim. Čapek, understandably, does not go to such outlandish extremes. Yet there is still a question as to whether he has succeeded in fully conveying the vital importance of the Person. Surely there is something demonic in this fascination with the Person, which at any given moment makes us into something other than what we truly feel ourselves to be, which causes us to tell a lie instead of speaking the truth; instead of people we see masks, instead of reality a masquerade—in short, a world of semblances instead of a world of true being, or *ontōs on*, as the ancient philosophers called it. Yet on the other hand, it is likely that humans could not even exist, could not live, without this principle of finiteness. The principle of decline is inseparable from being human. We need only look a bit further into the other effects of the Person to convince ourselves of this. It is understood that the Person is largely a social creation, but—*cum fundamento* in re, i.e., in natura.[17] This is why humans must create a Person and then submit to it in servitude, since, unlike other creatures of nature, we are not mere organs of the universe, like a crystal, an ear of wheat, or a bird in the air—but rather, being in the midst of the existent and incorporated within it, we are also independent. After all, Čapek himself says at one point, "We share with nature a noble origin, being parts of the universe and of the same materials as it. Many a bad thing, then, is rooted in the fact that this human particle has such a fateful passion for doing for itself, establishing itself under the rubric of a Person."[18] In this view, our individuality, our independence with respect to nature, is related to the Person—as is then, also, the individualization of our soul. This independence, this simultaneous inclusion and exclusion, means there must at all times be *two* opposing tendencies at work within us, a dual direction and flow of life: one which consists in appropriation, the assimilation of being—essentially not finite—by our limited self, the other which presents our excluded and finite self again in connection with and dependence on the immense and eternally untamed. These two tendencies, as closely connected with human life as systole and diastole are with the movement of the heart muscle, are in essence what we call Person and soul. Both are involved in every impression we have, no matter how slight; the merest glance, the simplest visual quality, contains in some way the infinity of the existent—yet this perception cannot merely be; it must also serve us. It must mean something in the context of our practical objectives, therefore it must be conventionalized, categorized, labeled with words, and stripped of its originality. It is through the joint efforts of both, soul and Person, that we ultimately arrive at that aspect of human life which Čapek so aptly describes: a complex scene, played out within a single person.

> You know . . . there are lots of things one can find to be fulfilled. But then again, there's so much emptiness to fill. The way you see me here, you, all of you, I'm kind of like that shell in the hands of the child old Saint Augustine was looking at. Yes, that shell is me [a human being]; and that little boy, scooping water from the ocean with the shell, that's me too [is it not ultimately me–the Person trying to find an end to the immeasurable?]; Saint Augustine, taking a lesson from this, is, with all due respect, at least a tad me as well [the soul, which knows both about true infinity and the Person's actions in vain]. And in fact, if I stop to think about it, the ocean is also partly me [ocean of being]—at least as much of it as the child managed to slosh up on shore with his shell . . . I don't much like metaphors; but the one truly unique advantage of a parable is there are some situations where it fits so well it hurts.[19]

Of course, even though both antagonists are inseparably present in our lives, that does not make them any less antagonistic, and each tries to win control of the field as exclusively as possible—a victory which, of course, would result in the suppression of the winning party itself. After all, the Person furtively and shamelessly provisions itself from the soul; the soul cannot take its content from the Person, however, as the Person has nothing to give (being sheer taking), but without the Person it could not survive, or it would merge with the universe. In reality, the result of this antagonism in normal life is to force the soul into the function of a mere servant with no independent say, no leading role in life, never intruding or getting in the way; the moment the soul subjugates itself in this way, it creates order and balance, biologically and socially—provided, of course, the Person is clever and successful in having its way. In the event that the soul, that is, our unobjectified component, our connection to the infinite, does not subjugate itself, in the event that it awakens and demands its rights, then all of a sudden the way we move among things, our reactions to life become unsettled, unpredictable; things happen that never happened before—life no longer runs on automatic, but begins to be aware that it is not of a piece, that it is—limping along. For ultimately the Limping Man is nothing other than a human being with its two essential organs, the organs of semblance and truth, of realities and reality, parts and the whole. A human being with an organ of finiteness, allowing them to adjust boundless reality so as to be able to live in it, cope with it, take control of and subjugate it, and with a connection to the infinite, which tells them every time they try to dictate to the ultimate truth that the truth is not in their power, that they do not rule over it, but on the contrary, it rules over them. So, as it turns out, the soul, for all its passivity, is at the root of its own ethos: the soul is its own truth and, as a result, as we shall soon see, its own good.

The soul, then, is truth, but it has many disadvantages in life compared to the Person. One such disadvantage is the soul's eternal uncertainty. The soul is not anchored in unproblematic, objective knowledge, but in knowing ignorance, a puzzle par excellence! So it never has the reliable, albeit relative, certainty that applies to objective truths. Ergo the Limping Pilgrim's oft-repeated reflections on the essence and fate of the soul. Does it come from nature? Or from something even more far-reaching? Is there something like a soul of nature that speaks to us in the landscape and is composed of the things and beings forming a wrinkle of nature's gown? Do our souls dissipate once our material structure decomposes, returning again to merge in the universal soul of nature? All questions that are merely a game; there are no answers, nor can there be.

This uncertainty, rooted in immateriality, is another disadvantage that the soul faces in comparison to the Person; yet the soul has a powerful ally. Only now can we say more fully what at first was merely hinted at: why the soul is connected with death. That ally is none other than death itself. This is where the Person's self-interest comes to an end, having run out of plans and projections;[20] no dodges and rationalizations are of help here; reason and spirit desert to the other side. But the stages of life also stand out in sharp relief from the standpoint of the soul: the three islands of life, childhood, adulthood, and old age, appear against the backdrop of the sea of the universe; the first, the island of children, a garden of magic and fantasy, is also a place of bravery and yearnings for joy and tenderness; on the large middle island, the Person resides, with its manufacturing and entertainment businesses, but also districts of the poor; the island of the old, gray and desolate, has spots glowing with radiance. The biological age, the age of existential struggle, the age of accommodation. "We are given plenty of opportunities to reckon with the facts of life. We may do so by suffering, existential maneuvers, or accommodation. Of all these options, accommodation, which is present in all of nature, hardly seems the worst to me."[21] It would be a mistake to interpret the human struggle for the soul and against the Person as the struggle of the individual against the social, against integration into human society with its objectives and needs. The world and life of humans is collective, communal. The soul in society: that is moral life. The world of the Person is narrowly utilitarian, a world of personal, egoistic expediency. "Morality until it is recalled, sacrificed at any time for the sake of individual profit, for the benefit of the parts, for the majority way of thinking. Ethics exploited to the point of being nothing but a polemical flyswatter."[22] The desire for good appertains not to the Person, but to the soul; the will to have a conscience: "feelings, even more, an awareness of solidarity with the human community—and of course—a degree of complicity along with that. Complicity in the miseries of the world, which come about because the human community allows it."[23]

Responsibility for everyone and everything—that is what the soul, whole and integral, feels and demands, in this relation no less than in all its others.

Any particular individual is human society, provided the Person does not expand to fill society with its arranging, technicizing, and mobilizing of everything, but instead has, and wants to have, a conscience. And, needless to say, on our journey with the Limping Man we will also discover the art, books, and pictures that are the true voice of his soul:

> I don't want just stories, I want the word! I don't want information, I want knowledge! I don't want half the truth, but I'll settle for being totally captivated. I want books I can read over and over again, and every time they'll have something to say to me, something to make me stronger, something to spur me on . . . Eternal youth . . .[24]

There is just one great thing the Pilgrim does not meet with on his way, and that is God. Čapek once later said of God that he would surely love him more than life and that the idea of God may have cost humanity a great deal, but it had also given it a great deal in return. Čapek's atheism is not blasphemous. Nor is it the "postulatory atheism" of so many modern titans who see or have seen in God a usurper of humanity. For Čapek, God is an unoccupied place in the geometry of life's vanishing points. Still, there is something great that lies beyond the axis of our lives, to which Čapek cannot relate through either deed or affect. And since, if he is to be quite candid, he does not know God, he is alone in his final human task, alone with his soul.

There is something melancholy in this conclusion, no gushing here of exuberant pride. Čapek's wisdom is heavyhearted in a manly way, though free of self-pity and artificially heroic posturing.

But Čapek's melancholy, laden with the heavy burdens of life, while neither despondent nor frantic, is also a happiness. He had already said in *The Limping Pilgrim* that he was a happy man,[25] and he said so again in his tragic book *Written in the Clouds*: "In fact I am a happy person. But I have no occasion to show it. Why, how is it that a person should be unhappy when he has within him so many loves which might make one happy?"[26] The source of melancholy for Čapek is not that, lacking God, he is bereft of substance and meaning. Substance and meaning for him come from the struggle of the soul and the struggle for the soul. His melancholy springs from the fact that even a being so significant as a human is not up to the task of serving as the meaning of the universe: "The starry cloak of the universe is surely not made to human measure. What giants we would have to be not to be tempted to invent the gods!"[27] And: "If there is no God, perhaps it is because nature the creator took it too far with humans, launching us on a trajectory that, lacking any higher goal or further destination, could only have a meaning and purpose within itself. Any adventure or task must be borne bravely."[28] These statements are typical of Čapek's hard realism, his attitude free of illusion, yet full of faith and hope. It is as human as one can be; so natural, so vital, so fragile.

I will not and cannot go into here the evolution of Čapek's views that we see in his second book of essays. In this book he has chosen a different form: it is no longer that of a dialogue with his true self, but aphorisms, a form that is rare in our literature. To read a book of aphorisms without feeling bored is a sign of the author's wit, but Čapek wants more than just that. His aphorisms are the interior diary of a man who has fallen from basking in onerous glory, from a state of gloomy happiness, into the horrors of a terrible disaster, first collective and then personal as well. There came moments for this melancholiac of human weakness when the wisdom he had gained in life, the wisdom of a soul hushed in its solitude, had to endure alone, without the aid of a higher reality, the onslaught of the most terrible, most scandalous events, bit by bit losing the supports of his life in society as he lived through the collapse of Munich and its aftermath, followed by the loss of his brother, when the bread turned bitter in his mouth and all his thoughts kept rushing back to that one painful blow, as the danger to him personally began to take shape, threatening to tear him away from his family, from the ones to whom he clung with the greatest, most devoted love. The world turned from something sweet and deep, attractive and hopeful in spite of it all, into an insulting, humiliating shambles, and finally was reduced to total ash, negative to its core and capable only of hurt. *Written in the Clouds* is a book that shows what the wisdom of the soul is for a person at a time when darkness is falling.

What was the book to him? In short: he remained faithful to it and it remained faithful to him. "Wistful, bitter—but faithful," he writes in late 1938. "Though I suffer, I still believe, I still hope: I am alive! What will become of me if woe betides me? *But what will become of everyone?!!*"[29] This is almost the only personal reference to have made it into the book, which is otherwise entirely given over to the life of the soul, its ideas, thoughts, hopes, its self-encouragement. We will not delve any further into its philosophical themes, which continue consistently along the pilgrim's path. Its political themes suffice to show how firmly he holds his ground.

Humanity, freedom, justice, law dragged in the mud? Fine, they'll pick themselves up from there one day, from down there on the bottom. Maybe people will have a better understanding, maybe they will better learn, if the great cry of humanity, freedom, law, and justice rises from the deepest depths, from the dust of the earth, from the very bottom itself![30]

It is bad, woefully bad, people have lost their way, indulging in foolish dreams, and only facts, facts, they say, will set them on the right path and cure them. All else is but a delusion, only facts are true and sound.—As if there were no need to add faith to facts (especially when it comes to the overwhelmingly evil ones); facts, after all, have no lasting and permanent value; that comes and only ever will come from the capacity for faith: the faith that today's facts may at some point be rectified and overcome—rendered null by better facts; that what is a fact ten times over today may be a monstrosity of the past come tomorrow.[31]

Here too, Čapek remains faithful to his idea of not reducing humans, not assessing them on the basis of what is given, not relieving them of their responsibility or depriving them of the possibility of an authentic life: "For many of us, nearly the whole world collapsed that fall of 1938. We live in the ruins, our ideas about the justice of history, about the value of morality and the solidity of the truth badly shaken—what misery, and yet—what a life challenge!"[32] And, one of his most personal and perhaps deepest thoughts: "A tragic impression of life is not at all the same as a negative sense of life."[33]

That, I think, best expresses the message of *Written in the Clouds*: Čapek's melancholy here grows into the tragic. His sense of the human situation in the world is essentially tragic: it is an enormous challenge, in fact beyond our strength, but there is no escaping it; every way out is closed—the brave path through the objective forces of nature and history, the cowardly path, the barren path of personal privacy—this true human, this true soul, closes them off to himself. And so he strides with his head held high, stepping onto the open plain where thunder booms and the outcome is certain, only the when and where of it are uncertain for him. And the Limping Pilgrim was walking in the same way when assailed by the blow that ruined his personal privacy for good.

And after that, we have no other aphoristic entries from him. What we have is verse. Sincere, often breathtaking verse, the kind the Limping Pilgrim loved, verse that, making no attempt at descriptiveness or documentation, captures for eternity those moments of utter darkness in life, of the bare existence at life's freezing point that has now become his. Here too he is faithful to himself. He protests, he fights, he believes, he nourishes hope: he does not give in to ready-made conclusions.

You who in prison
weave your longingly embellished dream of life,
what—if your faith in life is nothing more
than a sign of despair? . . .
that life you so believe in is your murderer!
what else is that faith of yours but despair?
. . .
it is not by life I feel wounded, but by human cruelty
—and yet life enfolds all that is human within it:
what is a human if not life? am I not life myself?
if I do not believe in life—where am I to find trust in myself?
as long as I live, however unhappy, however consumed by despair,
I want to believe in life—and despairing—still I do not despair![34]

Then there are tiny fragments of nature that surface like memories from a different sphere of life into these dark or gray lines of verse, autumn grass that refuses to be plowed under, shepherd's purse blossoming behind the barbed wire, symbols of a resurgent, if trampled will to live. "The gods, I take it for certain, knowing everything in advance, are unacquainted with hope; humans created hope for themselves out of their own mortal strength."[35] They rise up, time and again, in a final painful struggle, where the choice is either to let go or hold tight still one more time. And how wondrously this strong soul, which once knew such gilded and bitter happiness, holds tight each time yet again! What domestic tenderness and beauty waft from his verses about woman, the soul, the home, some of the most moving verses ever written in Czech. The soul rings out as roundly in them as in days of ease, as if with an accompaniment from another world, a tragic accompaniment all its own. And then, for the last time, the last appeal of that strong soul as it makes its return to life, willing to trust it, and yet in full awareness of its tragedy.

> Back to life or into the jaws of death,
> —what lies at the end of the road?
> Thousands are going, you aren't alone . . .
> Will you be lucky, or won't you?

> The day of the great journey has come,
> long have you been prepared for it:
> a harvesting of life or death—
> either way you're going home—you're going home![36]

Notes

1   Patočka likens Josef and his brother Karel to the "heavenly twins," Castor and Pollux (Ed.).

2   Josef Čapek, *Kulhavý poutník: Co jsem na světě uviděl* (Limping pilgrim: What I saw in the world), in *Spisy bratří Čapků* (The works of the Čapek brothers), vol. 37 (Prague: František Borový, 1936) (hereafter cited as *KP*) (Ed.).

3   Josef Čapek, "Tvořivá povaha moderní doby" (The creative nature of the modern era), in *Volné směry* 17, no. 4–5 (1913): 112–30. Published in book form as J. Čapek, *Co má člověk z umění a jiné úvahy: Výbor z článků z let 1911–1937* (What a person gets from art and other essays: A selection of articles from the years 1911–1937) (Prague: Výtvarný odbor Umělecké besedy, 1946), 34–44; also in J. Čapek, *Moderní výtvarný výraz* (Modern artistic expression) (Prague: Miroslav Halík, 1958), 83–94 (Ed.).

4   Josef Čapek, "Tvořivá povaha moderní doby" (The creative nature of modern times), *Volné směry* 17, no. 4–5 (1913): 113–15 (Ed.).

5   Parmenides, B 1,19, in Hermann Diels and Walther Kranz, *Fragmente der Vorsokratiker*, vol. I (Berlin: Weidmann, 1951), 228 (Ed.).

6   Plato, *Phaedo*, 107d–108c (Ed.).

7   Josef Čapek, *Psáno do mraků* (Written in the clouds) (1936–39), in *Spisy bratří Čapků*, vol. 50 (Prague: Miroslav Halík, 1947) (hereafter cited as *PM*), 35. Cf. also the chapter titled "Kráčí člověk" (As we walk along), describing youth, adulthood, and old age, in *KP*, 113 ff. (Ed.).

8   J. Čapek, *PM*, 132, 232–4 (Ed.).

9   J. Čapek, *KP*, 24–5 (Ed.).

10   J. Čapek, *KP*, 36 (Ed.).

11   "learned ignorance." See Nicolai de Cusa, *De docta ignorantia*, in *Nicolai de Cusa Opera omnia* (Leipzig: Felix Meiner, 1932) (Ed.).

12   J. Čapek, *KP*, 43ff.

13   τῆς ψυχῆς ἐπιμελεῖσθαι—see Plato, *Apology of Socrates*, 29e (Ed.).

14   J. Čapek, *KP*, 75–6 (Ed.).

15   "the honor of the human race" (Ed.)

16   J. Čapek, *KP*, 67–8 (Ed.).

17   "with a basis in matter, that is, in nature" (Ed.)

18   J. Čapek, *KP*, 144 (Ed.).

19   J. Čapek, *KP*, 46–7. The text inserted in brackets is Patočka's (Ed.).

20   The text added to JČ2–4 ends here (Ed.).

21   J. Čapek, *KP*, 138 (Ed.).

22   J. Čapek, *KP*, 155 (Ed.).

23   J. Čapek, *KP*, 157 (Ed.).

24   J. Čapek, *KP*, 176–7 (Ed.).

25   See J. Čapek, *KP*, 156 ("Well! And yet you stubbornly insist that you're happy.—True. And I am. It turns out dissatisfaction with oneself is no misfortune at all.")

26   J. Čapek, *KP*, 123 (Ed.).

27   J. Čapek, *KP*, 156 (Ed.).

28   J. Čapek, *KP*, 323 (Ed.).

29   J. Čapek, *KP*, 253ff. (Ed.).

30   J. Čapek, *KP*, 253ff. (Ed.).

31   J. Čapek, *PM*, 258 (Ed.).

32   J. Čapek, *PM*, 262 (Ed.).

33   J. Čapek, *PM*, 272 (Ed.).

34   J. Čapek, "Ty, který . . ." ("You who . . ."), in *Spisy bratří Čapků* (The works of the Čapek brothers), vol. 48: *Básně z koncentračního tábora* (Poems from a concentration camp) (Prague: František Borový, 1946), 125. The collection was assembled by Vladimír Holan, though he is not credited as editor in the book (Ed.).

35　J. Čapek, "O naději" ("On hope"), in *Spisy bratří Čapků* (The works of the Čapek brothers), vol. 48: *Básně z koncentračního tábora* (Poems from a concentration camp) (Prague: František Borový, 1946), 127 (Ed.).

36　J. Čapek, "Před velikou cestou" (Before the great journey), in *Spisy bratří Čapků* (The works of the Čapek brothers), vol. 48: *Básně z koncentračního tábora* (Poems from a concentration camp) (Prague: František Borový, 1946), 228 (Ed.).

CHAPTER FOUR

On the Soul in Plato (1972)

Translated from the Czech
by Jozef Majerník

My subject is the problem of ψυχή (soul) in Plato. In a short lecture, I do not believe it is possible to do more than present an outline of this problem, which has been of enormous interest to me and still somehow keeps me in suspense. I am not sure if I will manage to share with you some of the intensity I feel in this subject, but enough with the long introductions, let us proceed to the matter at hand.

A frequent solution of the early aporetic dialogues, which leave the reader at a loss about the nature of the ἀρετή (excellence) being defined, is (as is well known) that the given excellence, or better said *genuineness*—be it courage, moderation, piety, or being dear to the gods[1]—cannot be apprehended for itself, but is factually and intellectually inseparable from excellence, genuineness, truthfulness, as a whole. Thus the topic is, e.g., courage, or moderation, σωφροσύνη, or being dear to the gods, and in the course of the examination it will become apparent that these questions have to fall by the wayside, and the reader will not get a ready-made solution. That solution lies between the lines and consists in the realization that the given ἀρετή (excellence) cannot be defined without the other components of the *one* ἀρετή (excellence). Ἀρετή, genuineness, thus shows itself as *one*, as opposed to the *multitude of weaknesses and falsities*. There is no motive more Platonic than this starting point. The dualism that always comes to mind with Plato's name is, in the first place, this dualism of the basic possibilities in which the human being always exists—either truly, in the full sense being what a human is in its essence, or in a fallen form, realizing its essence only weakly and formally. An analogous opposition also exists in the case of animals, organs, and tools. The animal too has its ἀρετή (excellence), as does an organ like the eye, which functions either fully and correctly, or defectively, and the same holds true of a tool. However, the human being exists in this duality in a peculiar way, namely by always explicitly relating to it, by somehow knowing about it and being "responsible" for it. But what is human being in its essence? What does its being consist in? This question is not explicitly posed in Plato, but it is nevertheless omnipresent in his thinking. Our most important matter, πῶς βιωτέον (how to live), is only meaningful if what is essential in us, our being, is bound to it; and this essential core within us is the ψυχή (soul). That is why philosophy, whose task it is to explicitly pose, clarify, and treat the question of how we should live, can be defined as ἐπιμέλεια τῆς ψυχῆς, care for the soul, as is said in the *Apology*.[2] Philosophy is relevant for the ψυχή (soul) and its question of πῶς βιώτεον (how to live) because knowledge as clarity, as a confrontation with the determinate, the precise, the pure, also determines in a corresponding way human life and the human way of being.

We encounter the opposition of pure and impure shapes in geometry, and even more so in its practical use, in measuring. In geometry we use visible, drawn, material bodies, and speak about them as if about the geometrical bodies themselves; in reality, however, what we have in mind is not the visible bodies, but the precise and pure bodies of which the former are mere likenesses.[3] In the visible world there are no precise lines without width, there are no precise circles; the nature of the visible realm does not allow us to find anything other than a greater or lesser *likeness* of the line or of the circle. We could say that the possibility of attaining an ever-greater precision *ad infinitum* is the best sign of the essential imprecision of the visible. From this further follows that in the realm of the imprecise we can never return to the same thing, namely to *precisely* the same thing; that is beyond the limits of its possibilities. There is no precisely determinable *identity* here. As a consequence, nothing can be precisely known and proved here. What geometry teaches us is not true of visible figures, but rather of their (as we say) idealized counterparts in the realm of *the pure*.

In the realm of the *impure* we always have a certain scale of some *more and less* that is capable of increasing and decreasing *into the indeterminate*. Therefore it is also the realm of the *uncontrolled multitude*. The realm of the pure is dominated by *unity*, and *multitude is controlled by the unity in it*. The impure is at the same time the *limitless*. Measure does not come from it; it is originally foreign to it. A characteristic feature of the pure is *the limit*, transparency, apprehensibility. Its center is *the measure*.

If there is no rigorous identity in the realm of the impure, the indeterminate, and the limitless (i.e., if it is impossible to fix the object of our utterances), then neither can we apply the word "is" in the proper sense here—that is, the word which forms the basis of any utterance or speech that pretends to be true or false. Therefore it is fully consequent and comprehensible that even when the object of Plato's speech is not a process, but rather a time-independent predication in the realm of the impure, he does not use the words εἶναι, τὸ ὄν, or ἡ οὐσία (to be, being), but rather γενέσθαι and γένεσις (to become, becoming).

How is it possible that in geometry we use visible sketches while what we "actually" have in mind is something different from them? In geometrical proofs we have an imprecisely sketched triangle, but we do not mind its impreciseness at all; we use this sketched triangle in further constructions, and we use those constructions to make proofs—but what we have in mind in those constructions and proofs are not the things drawn here, but rather the precise, ideal triangle which is not in front of us. In the common practice of measuring, weighing, and evaluating we are not conscious of this difference between the impure and the pure. We are in a kind of twilight, we do not see the ambiguity of our words, which aim both at the impure and at that of which the impure is a "likeness." Geometrical measuring and proofs are mental acts, and all activities of our mind are dependent on the center of our being, on our ψυχή (soul). The fact that geometry is an activity performed *with the help of* the impure, but "actually" takes place in the pure, shows that here—just as when the subject is courage, wisdom, and ἀρετή (excellence) in general—our ψυχή (soul) stands on the borderline between the genuine and the non-genuine. In geometry the difference is between knowledge and ignorance, in practical activity between ἀρετή (excellence) and κακία.[4] Both knowing and practical activity define us further and more precisely; they make us knowledgeable and capable of learning further pure truths, or capable of further, more solid and more conscious ἀρετή (excellence)—and, on the contrary, the negative decisions make us into a being incapable of understanding anything genuine, pure, and true, and incapable of *being* in that genuine way which is characterized by the word ἀρετή (excellence).

This means nothing less than that the ψυχή (soul) itself depends on its accomplishments, on its activity. How does the ψυχή (soul) depend on itself? It is solely *its own* possible accomplishment that the sphere of the pure reveals itself to it, because the pure is the object of knowing, and knowing is impossible without the ψυχή (soul). But this means that the opposite thereof, the *loss* or covering-up of this sphere and the fall into the realm of confusion and of the limitless, is an act of the ψυχή (soul) as well. This change, this emerging or submerging, is thus at the same time an *alternation* between purity and confusion, unity and multitude, identity and difference. This alternation in the overall character of that which appears is thus the work of the ψυχή (soul). From the appearance and disappearance of the sphere of the pure arises for the ψυχή (soul) the possibility of really becoming *one*, of unifying itself, of eliminating confusion, disharmony, and contradiction—or of falling into them. Socrates speaks in the dialogue *Gorgias* about all the things he, *being one* (ἕνα ὄντα), would rather suffer than to be in disharmony with himself and to contradict himself.[5] Self-unification and creation of harmony in its opinions is the self-formation of the ψυχή (soul) by philosophy, and it is the aim of the Socratic ἔλεγχος (elenchus). If such unifying does not take place, the ψυχή (soul) falls into the opposite state and sinks into the opposite sphere.—From the polemics about the concept of κίνησις in the third book of Aristotle's *Physics* we know that in the Academy—apparently at Plato's behest, but certainly not in opposition to him—motion, κίνησις, was defined with the help of the categories ἑτερότης (difference), ἀνισότης (inequality), and τὸ μὴ ὄν (non-being), and the text can be understood as saying that this is the case *because motion is no more a movement from identity to difference, from equality to inequality, and from being to non-being, than the other way round.* We can in turn apply this to our question: it shows that the ψυχή (soul) is, according to its Academic definition, in motion, namely in such a motion that depends on the ψυχή (soul) itself, in a motion that the ψυχή (soul) itself determines: ψυχή is τὸ αὐτὸ ἑαυτὸ κινοῦν = τὸ αὐτοκίνητον, that which moves itself.[6] This is the definition of the soul that we find in Plato himself (although only in late works such as the *Phaedrus*, and in contexts that are also ontological and cosmological), and that is reported as Platonic and polemicized against in Aristotle's Περὶ ψυχῆς.[7] Now we have to understand what this strange definition, that the soul is that which moves itself, actually means. What to make of this? I am attempting to understand it from that basic opposition in which the human being always exists, that one is always either in the state of fallenness, in the state of non-genuine being, so to speak, or in a surging- and rising-up to what could be called genuine being or a genuine way of existing—and that this twofold way, this twofold fundamental possibility in which the human being exists depends on the human being itself—one determines oneself to being one way or the other.

In my opening remarks, I tried to characterize this twofold possibility more precisely with the help of the concepts of the im-pure, the in-determinate, the non-existing, with negative determinations on the side of the fallen or non-genuine being—and with unity, determinacy, measure, and limit on the side of the possibility of truth.

Now it is necessary to characterize the limitless realm, the realm of the im-pure and indeterminate, the realm of "indeterminate fluid generality" (in the words of a modern thinker),[8] from yet another side. Plato characterizes it as *the realm of the visible.* Here we have to remind ourselves that Plato's theses about the visible and the invisible cannot be understood in the sense of modern, objective science, e.g., in the sense of the physiology of the nervous system, but rather in the sense of phenomenal *experientiality.* When we see something, in a certain way we experience not just the seen thing, but also the bodily act of seeing, etc. We know that our body participates in it. The way in which we are conscious of this, in which we have an experience of this, is complicated and we will not go into it here. What is certain is that we have certain phenomenal data about it. But there is a phenomenal difference in the case of thinking: we do not simultaneously experience both the thing thought and the organ with which we think. We simply are not aware of it while we think. Our thoughts unfold in front of us without our knowing or being conscious at all that there is something like brain processes etc. In relation to this we can now say that the realm of the visible (that is, the limitless, indeterminate realm bereft of purity) is also the bodily realm, the realm where the ψυχή (soul) works in relation to the body and through its mediation. I say that it is limitless, indeterminate, and bereft of purity, but we have to understand this as follows. A seen thing with its shape and color, with all its properties, is a thing whose shape can be characterized, for example, like this: this tabletop is a rectangle, or rather it is rectangle-like, since it of course is not a precise rectangle, a rectangle in the geometrical sense. But if I want to define a perceived shape, I have to speak in this way, I have to say that it is rectangular. Or that this is a straight line, a straight edge, but naturally it is not an actual straight line. Any such shape naturally has certain further determinations. For example, we can measure this desk and calculate its surface; our measuring will naturally be imprecise, but it can be made more precise *in indefinitum,* and by analogy the same holds for all similar particular determinations. This is related to the fact that the object here in front of me, in the field of my perception, is not a geometrical, but a practical object, and its objecthood and the truth of statements about it is practical truth rather than geometrical truth. This is the sense in which I mean that the visible is the realm of the impure, the limitless, and the indeterminate. It is also the realm in which the ψυχή (soul) works in relation to the body and through its mediation. Thus all actions that aim at the satisfaction of bodily needs—eating, drinking, labor and other tasks, the sexual act—are activities of the ψυχή (soul) in cooperation with the body and through it. From the perspective of the human person, this realm is thus—expressed in a modern way—the realm of our instincts, needs, habits, and skills, of our physical satisfaction, of our skillful interventions and personal accomplishments.

The opposition of these two spheres between which the motion of the soul takes place thus can be formulated as the opposition of the bodily and the non-bodily. The soul which moves in the bodily realm tethers itself to it, succumbs to it; everything in it becomes bodily in the sense that corporeality is participating and dominating in these acts; even thinking becomes mere opining that is incapable of understanding that which is pure, unmixed, and one, as opposed to the multiplicity that surrounds us. From this perspective we can comprehend the opposition made in the *Phaedo* between the two ways or possibilities of the existence of the ψυχή (soul) as the opposition between bodily and non-bodily existence, that is, the opposition between the genuine and the non-genuine, further characterized as the opposition between the pure and the impure, the precise and the confused, is at the same time also the opposition between the non-bodily and the bodily. And if we conceive of death as the separation of the soul from the above-mentioned cooperation with the body (the dead person does not see, does not feel, does not make any bodily movements), it also becomes comprehensible that philosophy is defined here as an orientation toward death and even as a will to die; τῆς ψυχῆς ἐπιμελεῖσθαι can in this respect be understood as ἐπιτήδεια τοῦ ἀποθνήσκειν καὶ τεθνάναι, the intention to die and to be dead.[9]

The ambiguity of the terms "body" and "bodily" or "corporeal," which mean now the phenomenal body (as indicated above) and then the objectively real body, surely deprives Plato's argument in the *Phaedo* about the separation of the body and the soul and about the immortality of the ψυχή (soul) of any philosophic relevance for us; nevertheless, we understand independently from it the *phenomenal* significance of the Phaedo's emphasis on the non-bodily in relation to *purity*. Plato speaks there of pure seeing and knowing, of pure knowledge, of cleansing oneself from bodily nature, of how an impure person should be barred from contact with the pure, etc.[10] Plato's doctrine of the ψυχή (soul) can be understood as an investigation of the phenomena that are related to the essential core of human being, to the experienced and intelligible principle of human life; and we even venture to say that it is from this center alone that Plato's most important doctrines can be understood. The soul as that which moves itself—and as a human soul it moves especially between the realm of pure, determinate limitation and the realm of indeterminate limitlessness—can give us an understanding of the doctrine of the Ideas and of that which grounds this doctrine. It also enables us to understand Plato's theory of education, his ethical doctrine of the formation of the harmonious human being as the subordination of the limitless to limit and measure, his doctrine of the πόλις (*polis*) and of spiritual authority as the basis of a happy city, his cosmology, and his most important myths. In particular we hold that only from this perspective can we understand the systematics which Plato was the first to bring, on a grand scale, into the questions of the psychic: of psychic functions, of psychic acts, of levels of the psyche, of questions of character, and of questions which today are described as belonging to depth psychology. Beholding this great systematic accomplishment then is not just an act of historical reflection and remembrance; it also takes part in the system of the psychic, which has never ceased to be living and urgent.

But we have to explain yet another side of psychic motion before we come to these expositions. Psychic motion is in the most original sense uncovering and concealing; but concealing is also a kind of uncovering—even where the realm of the pure and the genuinely existing is hidden, something shows itself to us. A confused uncovering is still an uncovering. The uncovering of things like this table, or this room, or our neighbors naturally belongs to the realm of indeterminacy and confusion, even though we usually consider it to be uncovering in the most proper sense. However, it is an uncovering that is missing the very core of that which is being uncovered; it is an uncovering that lacks the capacity to distinguish between appearance and reality, which according to Plato is the essence of the *dream*.[11] In the realm of confusion we live in a peculiar relationship to that which uncovers itself, because it is missing the very core of what makes uncovering into uncovering, namely, the possibility to say that that which uncovers itself also *is*. We have given the reason why we cannot say *it is* in this realm right at the outset: because it is the realm of the indeterminate.

Wherever we can say *it is*, we can always return to this *it is* and we can assert that this *it is* is true now, was true before, and will be true in the future; whereas wherever I cannot identify the thing with precision, wherever there remains the possibility of an escape, wherever there remains such an unidentifiable scale of more or less—the verb *to be* in its proper sense does not apply. Nevertheless, in this realm we satisfy our needs, we give ourselves up to our instincts, we work and perform other tasks, and our ψυχή (soul) is responsible for all this. Thus the ψυχή (soul) moves not just from one realm to the other, not just from the pure to the impure and back again, but also within them: also by satisfying our needs, etc., a change occurs in it—namely the ψυχή (soul) makes the body persist in its ceaseless activity and exchange with the outside world, in those periodic lacks which we feel as hunger, thirst, and other needs. By all this the ψυχή (soul) also modifies itself, it attaches itself to the bodily realm no less than it adopts and assimilates this realm; it attaches itself simply by being yoked to this eternal cycle of needs and by, so to speak reveling in them. The whole of comportment in the *bodily realm* and in relation to the particulars within it is not just movement of the body mediated by the ψυχή (soul), but also a movement of the ψυχή (soul) itself. It is similar on the other side, in the realm of the pure: here too the ψυχή (soul) influences itself by its contact with the pure. Thus the ψυχή (soul) is not motionless even when it does not rise or fall, not even here does its αὐτοκίνησις (self-movement) cease. We could figuratively say that the human ψυχή (soul) carries out a kind of spiraling movement—if a movement within a certain area can be depicted as a circle—out from itself to the things which the body or the ψυχή (soul) itself lacks and needs, and from them back to itself; and the movement of ascending or falling, the movement between the two realms. What the ψυχή (soul) moving in the realm of the pure lacks is nothing but the possibility to embrace this entire realm at once—the ψυχή (soul) can attain the totality and unity of this realm only gradually, through movement. No one can think at once the entire wealth of a certain, say, mathematical discipline, no one can think through all the categories and their relations at once—we rather have to exhaust them step by step, posing the problems one after the other. That is why not just the human ψυχή is in motion, but the myth of the *Phaedrus* shows also divine souls in motion, and the cosmology of the *Timaeus* shows specifically the world-soul in motion.

These are our basic presuppositions, an account of what I understand by the term "self-motion of the soul." Now I will move on to the individual chapters of Plato's philosophy that assume a special importance from this perspective. To wit, I believe that Plato's entire philosophy is in its nature, in its substance a doctrine of the ψυχή (soul), even though Plato does not explicitly interpret it as a doctrine of the ψυχή (soul).

How does the doctrine of the Ideas relate to the thought of movement between the realm of the pure and its opposite? How does it relate to the thought of the twofold possibility of our being, of being in fallenness and in genuineness? Is it not the other way around, that this thought itself is conditioned by the dualism of the world of the Ideas and the world of appearances? Is this thought not contained precisely in the dualism between the pure and the limitless and indeterminate?

Certainly, the movement between those two possibilities is inseparable precisely from what shows itself in this movement, and that is (among other things) the world of the Ideas. If the realm of the pure shows itself to us, that means that the Ideas show themselves to us. But[12] do the Ideas teach us about ourselves, or does our essential motion teach us about *the meaning of the Ideas*? How could we ever detach ourselves from appearances and conceive of the Ideas were it not for the fact that the ψυχή (soul) can internally feel the need for unity, and is thus capable of carrying out that vertical movement (which is presupposed by this need) even when it is almost completely bound to the realm of the limitless and of impurity? We arrive at the Ideas, at these pure units, through the unbearable nature of our internal contradiction, and this unbearableness is an indication of the essential (albeit unrealized) unity of the soul even in its dispersedness and fallenness. Fallenness is a movement, a fall, that points in the opposite direction. The seventh book of the *Politeia*[13] gives an account of how we arrive at the difference between the world of the Ideas, which is intelligible and accessible only to thought, and the visible world. The problem is to find something *in our ordinary experience* that can first bring us to doubt that the visible is genuine being, and can then lead us to make explicit the distinction between the genuine and non-genuine. The fifth book of the *Politeia* has already showed[14] that between knowledge and ignorance, the former of which relates to what is and the latter to what is not, we also have to presuppose a middle element that neither fully is nor is not, and this middle element is the object of *opinion*, of *seeming*, of δόξα; δόξα is thus at the center of a contradiction that is unaware of itself. It is further concluded that the entire realm of the visible belongs to δόξα (opinion). Plato subsequently shows[15] that this realm, in which only a multitude of beautiful things is acknowledged, but no beauty in itself, a multitude of holy things, but no holiness, is also a realm in which each of the multitude of things has contradictory aspects and properties: the beautiful is always also ugly in some respect, the great is also small, a half is the whole and the whole is a half, etc. Now, the seventh book of the *Politeia*[16] distinguishes between visible things, which we can experience through the senses (ἐν ταῖς αἰσθήσεσι) and which do not call upon our νόησις, our insight, to participate in the examination, and things that provoke this capacity of ours. The former kind of thing is such that a sensual impression itself is sufficient to evaluate them: a finger is a finger, the color red is red. In contrast, impressions that go beyond the domain of a single αἴσθησις (perception) and enter into the domain of another (ἐκβαίνει εἰς ἐναντίαν αἴσθησιν) directly provoke our reflection in that they make us conscious of a contradiction. Here belong the impressions that show, as we say, the relativity of the respective properties:

the ring finger is simultaneously longer than (the little finger) and shorter than (the middle finger), the same brick is hard compared to clay and soft compared to steel, etc. The ψυχή (soul) is at a loss in such cases[17] and it calls upon λογισμὸν καὶ νόησιν, calculation and insight, for help, to see whether one or two things are at stake here; it is then capable of distinguishing between them. It happens in the same way in the case of that general contradiction which consists in our giving universal determinations to things without seeing that these determinations are units that have to be thematized for themselves if we are to avoid a basic confusion and contradiction.

The insight that εἶδος, the general unit, truly, in the full sense, *is*, is then possible only because when it comes to opining, the ψυχή (soul) is so to speak *between* the two spheres, because it embraces them both—that is the sole reason why it can notice the contradiction between them, even when the ψυχή (soul) has been desensitized to it by exclusive contact with visible things. It embraces both of these spheres because its place is in this movement between them. We are reminded of this movement across the entire spectrum of entities by the famous analogy of the divided line, the two parts of which are again divided in the same ratio: here we have the two parts of the visible—images, shadows, and reflections on the one hand, and the realities of our surroundings on the other. The interpretation or understanding of an image is possible only by a twofold intention, a twofold act; we have to *know* realities in order to understand images, even if our attention is turned to the latter; and likewise, in a certain sense we have to *know* the invisible in order to be able to speak and make utterances about the visible, in order to determine, measure, and count it. All this shows that even when the ψυχή (soul) dwells among visible things, it is still capable of movement between the two spheres, and that also in the visible realm there is something like a possibility of ever-greater distancing from the invisible with its unity and preciseness, and thereby a "vertical" movement. And the most famous analogy of the *Politeia*, the parable of the cave,[18] can likewise be understood only from the perspective of upward and downward psychic movement.[19] At the beginning of the analogy, two extreme states of the human being are discussed, states which the analogy is supposed to present to us—a human being in a fallen, unfree state, left wholly at the mercy of the moving shadows conjured by the flickering light from a derivative source—that is the state of ἀπαιδευσία, the state of human unfreedom and formlessness whereas the *turning*, the rising up, first within the cave and then to the light of day, is παιδεία (education), the peak of which is the pure intellection (*noesis*) of the source of all entities and the origin of all light. The turning point itself is nothing but that ἀπορία (aporia) which we mentioned above, and to which the Socratic ἔλεγχος (elenchus) and Socrates' maieutic activity lead. Socratic ἔλεγχος (elenchus) of others is rooted in the fact that they themselves have become conscious of the contradiction; their ψυχή (soul) has thereby embarked upon an upward movement, it has given itself an impulse toward unity, toward entities, toward being, knowledge, and truth.

The characterization of the two basic possibilities as ἀπαιδευσία (ignorance, lack of education) and παιδεία (education) also shows that the movements of the soul are at the root of Plato's theory of education. Education is possible only because the ψυχή (soul) is responsible for itself, because it influences itself through its own impulses and acts. Already in the *Phaedo* we hear that pleasures and delights affix the ψυχή (soul) as if by nails to the bodily and limitless realm; thus it is the soul's own movement that places it there. But the task the ψυχή (soul) is faced with is παιδεία (education), and παιδεία (education) consists, on the one hand, in the preparation for turning upward already in the lower realm, and, on the other, in the strategy and tactics of this turning itself and in the tethering of the ψυχή (soul) to the upper realm. The preparation consists in making this irrational realm become what it is capable of being without knowing it, namely *a realm of unconscious rationality*: and we do this by not permitting any of the activities of life in the realm of bodily seeming that would be contrary to the future life turned toward being, to explicit genuineness and truthfulness. Education thus has two stages: first the preparatory, more or less negative stage in which we simply do not permit anything that could at some point conflict with the higher life, then the actual positive stage, which means the strategy of turning. In order to carry out the latter, various mathematical disciplines are examined according to the degree to which they are capable of bringing about the beneficial *aporia* in the ψυχή (soul), the consciousness of the contradictoriness in the generality of seeming, in δόξα (opinion); cultivating this problematicity and aiming at resolving it by dwelling in the realm of the pure is the central moment of this positive education. Thus it consists first of mathematical disciplines, and then of the actual philosophical investigation of the Ideas, in dialectics. That this does not mean some pale intellectualism follows from the fact that what is at stake here is not mere knowledge, but rather the being of the ψυχή (soul) itself. The turning which is effected by παιδεία (education) lifts the human ψυχή (soul) beyond time itself and armors it against petty fears and appetites; in this sense it protects the ψυχή (soul) from the dangers of being an intellectual, whose provocative criticism of all tabooed traditions easily ends in skepticism unless this criticism is moderated by the orientation of the entire ψυχή (soul) to the enormous responsibility of the task of actually becoming what it *in potentia* and in its essence is—namely something that belongs to the realm of the eternal and is itself capable of eternalization. Here is another, deeper sense of the eternity of the ψυχή (soul) than the one discussed in the *Phaedo*, which occurs by separation from the body.

Let us now briefly remember another substantial Platonic teaching, his moral doctrine, which is related to the clarity of the ψυχή (soul) about itself, to self-knowledge. The way in which the ψυχή (soul) comes to dwell in one of the two realms follows an overall way of life, βίος, as the order of values and imperatives of life; thus also a certain overall view of life, of its goal, of its success and failure, of unhappiness and happiness. Those who fully and consciously abandon themselves to appetites (and appetite is essentially limitless, since in essence it can always demand more) belong to the limitless realm of that bad infinity characterized by the possibility of a constant "more or less" with no precise measure. They are led to consider their unleashing as the actual meaning of life, to consider the intensity of experience as the growth of one's ψυχή (soul), of one's being, or as the true freedom in which the individual is not bothered and hampered by anyone. All their effort, not only their will but thought as well, is then yoked to the service of the appetites. This is essentially related to the view that moderation, legality, and justice are mere conventions whose preservation is socially advantageous to the multitude of weaklings who thereby enslave the strong individual; and to the related view that although law and justice are valuable, they are not valuable in themselves, but only as a means to prevent the worst possible outcome, which is the possibility of suffering a wrong at any time from anyone. In the background of these views is the thought that pleasure is the sole good, and that the more intense the pleasure, the greater the good. But bodily pleasure too belongs to the realm of things that can be intensified into the indeterminate; pleasure has no measure in itself. Those who hold this view do not realize that it seems self-evident to them only because they have bound themselves to the realm of the limitless and the impure, where only mixed pleasures and joys exist (why mixed? because something like a bodily pleasure is always possible only as a satisfaction of a need; a need is something negative, it is the very opposite of satisfaction—thus we have here something negative mixed with something positive, resulting in an impurity) and these demand always further, limitless satisfaction, thus leaving us to circle in the bodily realm with no way out. It is not just that pleasures and pains are a bad infinity here, but that they are impure in the sense that none of them is possible except through and in the presence of its opposite. Mixed pleasures and pains are the ownmost movements of the soul in this sphere; the ψυχή (soul) tethers itself through them, and the human being falls prey to dissolution, or, to put it in a modern way, to one's instinctive-biological basis, obscure and tending toward extreme excesses. What thus appears in the man of the limitless, of pleasure, and of appetite is the secretly present tyrannical man, the man of extreme fallenness who instead of the desired freedom actually lives in worry, endless dependence, fear, and anxiety; everything limiting, all measure, and with measure also being, truth, and knowledge, have disappeared from his horizon; his life has drowned in the whirlpool of limitlessness, in ἀπειρία. The opposite of this life, a completely different *overall* form of life, now is not (as we could perhaps expect in line with the *Phaedo*) the complete separation from the sphere of the limitless—that is the life of the gods and perhaps of the blessed heroes—but rather *formation*, the union of πέρας (limit) and ἄπειρον (limitlessness), their harmony, a combination of the psychic movement upward—of the insightful life—with *pure* joys and bodily necessities. The form of life that arises in this way is one of those entities that is a combination of the limit and the limitless, discussed in the *Philebus*, whereas the immoderate and dissolute life is limitlessness bordering on non-being.

The representative of the views typical of this dissolution and secretly tyrannical thinking, widespread in the seemingly lawful, free, and liberal-minded Athenian city, is of course Callicles from the *Gorgias*. It is in line with his overall views when he advises Socrates to let go of impractical philosophy and its paradoxical doctrines—such as that legality and truthfulness are under any circumstances better than their opposites, or that a harmonious life is happier than a dissolute one—whereas if he will occupy himself with or even conduct himself by his unrealistic philosophical thoughts, he will be disgraced in the city and die. This friendly if uncomprehending admonition is then followed up in the *Politeia* by Plato's great myth of the perfectly just and truthful man who really *is* such without appearing so (this form of life would be realized at its purest when he appears to be unjust and when he is a stumbling block for everyone else), and of his complete opposite, the perfectly unjust hypocrite and fraudster, who cannot be distinguished from a genuinely just man by anyone who is not a philosopher.[20] The former ends up on the cross, while the latter becomes the king and ruler of this world. To help himself and everyone else, Plato's Socrates now undertakes the only thing the philosopher can do, and the thing that only the philosopher can do—he projects a city in which it would not be possible to do injustice to the philosopher or to anyone else, a harmonious and happy city. The construction of this city will fulfill the demand of Plato's brothers that right and justice be treated and observed not just in their external outcomes and consequences, but also in how they work within the ψυχή (soul) itself. The task here is thus to think through the problem of founding a city in which the perfectly truthful and just man can live happily and unharmed. Perfectly truthful and just: i.e., one for whom it would be impossible—because of internal reasons, because of the way in which his ψυχή (soul) is formed and because of the place in which it dwells—to think and act otherwise than he does in front of others, even if he had Gyges' ring of invisibility; a man perfectly transparent to himself and mastered by himself, perfectly responsible, always able to account for his actions, never overstepping his clarity about himself. It is thus apparent that the problem of the city too is being treated with regard to the ψυχή (soul) and its fundamental possible positions, and to the forms of life which follow from them. First we get an ideal genesis of a healthy city in which humans can simply live, because they unwittingly help each other by division of labor. When additional demands and artificial needs arise—that is, when the limitless penetrates into the heart of the city—the fallen, bloated city comes about, but this city has in itself the condition for its own cure. The bloated city can exist only if it is expansionist, and for that it needs an army. But the army, the defenders, is the potential *vehiculum* of universal moderation. The bloated city can be cured—it can be transformed not into the primitively healthy city, but rather into the city of justice and happiness—provided that the principle on which the healthy city unwittingly rests is applied consciously in it: that everyone has to fulfill their own function, to which they are most suited, both by nature and by education; each person thereby perfects themselves and is able to help both themselves and others. The most important matter in the city will be this sharp delimitation of functions, so that the guardians are exclusively guardians, the producers nothing but producers. However, everyone has to agree that this way is best for the whole: for the producers, privacy, family, and prosperity within the appropriate limits; for the guardians, a public life, no property, group marriages and families, and sustenance as their only wages, but also a perfect education in the sense discussed above. A further selection from the guardians then takes on the highest function, watching over the preservation of the whole, and above all ensuring the harmony of the basic components of education, of music and gymnastics ... The city thus composed and attuned is ruled by harmony, it is a city that is wise because of its highest class that preserves its spirit through education and versatile foreign policy, courageous and safe because of its guardians, moderate because of the conviction of all about the excellence and unselfishness of the rulers and about the impartiality of their selection. The city will then evidently be harmonious (healthy, without extremes, it will be the correct combination of the limitlessness of needs and of the limit that is given by insight into the higher imperatives of unity and wholeness) and happy as a whole, but also in its components and functions it will show that feature of ἀρετή (excellence) which makes each thing fully what it is. A city thus founded will have all components of ἀρετή (excellence), wisdom in the *nomothetes*, courage in the guardians, moderation in the mutual relations of everyone—but especially in the producers—and justice in everyone, since everyone, in doing their work, will fulfill themselves in the highest sense, help all others, and will not encroach on anyone else's domain and rights.

What does all this have to do with the ψυχή (soul) and its capacity of self-motion? Each of these components of ἀρετή (excellence) comes to the city from individuals. The city shows more readily than the individual—who usually cannot decide for themselves (unless they are a philosopher) which way of life to choose—how happiness, being, truth, justice, and the other ἀρεταί (forms of excellence) go hand in hand. The ideal genesis of the city is a guiding thread to the understanding of the life of the individual, of the right choice of the way of life, and of the related structure of our ψυχή (soul). The ideal genesis of the city thus is a contribution to self-knowledge, it is a doctrine of harmony also in the individual, in his ψυχή (soul).

Yet harmony cannot be realized unless the ψυχή (soul) itself has *various* functions, just like the city. That means that the ψυχή (soul) has to carry out various movements in different realms simultaneously—various, but nevertheless harmonious movements that do not impede one another. The city and its composition out of autonomous functions, the ἀρετή (excellence) of a well-ordered city, is the guiding thread to understanding the structure of the functions of the individual soul. It is not that it would be sufficient to look into ourselves by some mysterious act of internal apprehension in order to grasp the ψυχή (soul). We do not become conscious of ourselves in this way, we do not understand ourselves in this way. Plato knows nothing about reflection in the modern sense, which, by the way, is a modern myth. We need a certain guiding thread for self-understanding, a factual guiding thread, and this factual guiding thread is the city, its composition, its functions, and its ἀρεταί (forms of excellence). Consequently, the ψυχή (soul) itself is understood as a kind of city. The result corresponds to what was ascertained in the ethical examination, but is now more detailed and clearer: the ψυχή (soul) itself is a kind of city, it is not a single movement, but a plurality of movements with tension between them; the appetites strive to drag it *whole* down into the limitless, and in this they are sometimes aided, yet at other times and more often hindered, by an irascible self-regard, burning with anger and energy against anything that disturbs its circles.[21] But above both of these, insight rules with its power of distance, enabling mere internal forces to subordinate themselves to self-rule, to be clearly seen and put in order. The harmonious individual will thus be one with transformed and clarified instinctual impulses. The instinctual basis within us is originally not just untamable and licentious, but outright criminal, mocking all regulations, everything that forms the basis of *human* coexistence: it is bloodthirsty, incestuous, libidinal without any limitations, and this manifests itself not just in dreams (which often are a fulfillment of such untamable wishes), but also in reality—when the tyrannical person yields to their appetites for good. The harmonious form of life will result in the same ἀρεταί (forms of excellence) in the individual as in the city: in σοφία (wisdom), ἀνδρεία (courage), σωφροσύνη (moderation), and δικαιοσύνη (justice), the last of which is actually harmony *par excellence*.

However, the genuine and just city, the city with all the ἀρεταί (forms of excellence), is not *possible* or realizable unless the legislators of this city, those who regulate its fundamental law, which is παιδεία, education, are *philosophers*. That means: the entire city must be dominated by the movement of the ψυχή (soul) upward, by the movement toward being, knowledge, truth, and the other ἀρεταί (forms of excellence). The city in which the truthful person can live unharmed is the city governed by truthful people. The problem of the city thus actually is the problem of spiritual power and authority. This problem is thus bound up with that upward movement, with the ascent of the ψυχή (soul) to its actual spiritual, pure, eternal essence that is its genuine, authentic being.

We can now look back and present the following schema of the nature and structure of that peculiar self-moving entity which is unlike any other, which is responsible for our life, which is called ψυχή (soul) by Plato.

Its basic feature is the movement between its two fundamental possibilities—the fallen, limitless possibility that is devoid of measure, on the limit of non-being, knowing nothing but corporeality and the visible, and the opposite possibility, whose ultimate limit is a complete spiritualization that is not possible within the bounds of the human; therefore it is replaced by a harmony under the dominance of mind, measure, being, and truth over the limitless nature of appetites, affects, and passions.

Here we could mention that this essential position between two fundamental possibilities is what Kierkegaard called existence. Kierkegaard talks about existence as the synthesis of time and eternity—those are Plato's two fundamental possibilities—that relates to itself, i.e., which determines itself, or said with Plato, which brings itself into motion: τὸ αὐτοκίνητον.

Within the framework of these fundamental possibilities—in essential cooperation with phenomenal corporeality on the one hand, without it, on the other hand, in the domain of opining, expressing, insight, thinking, and knowing—the secondary movements of our soul play out, movements within the chosen realm, on the one hand movements toward the visible, in order to deal with the ceaseless demands of our bodily needs, and on the other toward the intelligible, in order to satisfy the most fundamental need of the human being—the need for being, clarity, and truth, so that our own being may *become* being in truth, a truthful being. Here we must forego the study of *these* movements, that is, the psychology of the functions and acts of physio-psychological behavior as well as of the movement of thought, of mixed as well as pure affectivity—we do not have the time for that. These acts are themselves carried out within the framework of certain *functions* (such as the appetites on the one hand, the sphere of one's own personality on the other, and finally the purely spiritual sphere) that can be characterized as more or less invariant within the framework of each of the two possibilities. *Characterological* studies have a special place within the framework of fallenness—they build upon the guiding thread provided by the parallelism between the functions of the city and the functions of the ψυχή (soul).

The relation between the instinctual basis of our entire existence, between instinctual limitlessness and responsible existence, is not a relation of mere antagonism and exclusion, but rather a relation of transformation, harmonization, and ordering into a unanimously working whole, into a single complex movement controlled from the top. These are the problems described in the modern era as depth psychology.

Thus we see that unlike all its predecessors, Plato's thinking about the ψυχή (soul) forms a genuine systematic account that consistently arises out of the conception of a self-determining movement, which we venture to call the movement of existence.

I have to briefly mention two points which I cannot develop here. The ψυχή (soul) as αὐτοκίνητον (self-movement) seemed to Plato a concept suitable also for the foundation of *cosmology*. That which brings itself into motion is also the first source of movement for everything else. Therefore the original place of the ψυχή (soul) in the visible universe is not here on earth, but rather at the source of all motion, of generation and corruption, of the circulation of the elements, of the orbits of the heavenly bodies, of the periodicity of natural processes: up in the heavens. Hence the problematic of the world-soul and of its relation to our human souls. But we must forego this problematic and its relation to the preceding. Let us just point out that another "proof" of the immortality of the soul (of course just a pseudo-proof), given in the *Phaedrus*, depends on this cosmological-physical understanding of the concept αὐτοκίνητον (self-movement)—but this proof carries no more weight than the proofs in the *Phaedo*, as it is based on the μετάβασις εἰς ἄλλο γένος, on the passage from the realm of the movement or process of existence to the realm of physical processes.

The immortal soul is nevertheless at the center of Plato's myths. If the soul is immortal, it has a prenatal and posthumous fate, which is treated by Plato in accordance with his overall orientation toward universal justice and judgment, reward and punishment.

But there is yet another Platonic myth of judgment, one which is not posthumous and transcendent but rather worldly, or better said: global. This myth is related to the above-mentioned motive of the perfectly truthful man who time and again must suffer the fate of being killed until the city of justice is built, a state which protects the completely truthful man with its spiritual authority; he will time and again be condemned, while the Enemy, perfectly imitating the appearance of justice, will sit in judgment over him. But the judged one will turn this verdict into a trial of his judges, as Socrates did in the *Apology*, by the force of the truth which is contained in his thought of helping both himself and everyone else. Because if the state of justice belongs to the essential content of human history, then this history is a trial of the judges of Plato's Socrates.[22]

Notes

1   τὸ θεοφιλὲς. See Plato, *Euthyphro* 11a.

2   *Apology* 29e.

3   *Republic* 510d.

4   incapacity, incapability, incompetence, wickedness (Ed.)

5   Plato, *Gorgias* 482c.

6   Plato, *Phaedrus* 245c–e; *Laws* 896a; *Timaeus* 37b.

7   Aristotle, *De Anima* 406a.

8   Edmund Husserl, *Cartesianische Meditationen*, in *Husserliana*, vol. 1, 149. English: *Cartesian Meditations*, trans. Dorion Cairns (The Hague: Martinus Nijhoff, 1960), 8.

9   *Phaedo* 64a.

10 *Phaedo* 66d ff.

11 *Republic* 476c.

12 When delivering the lecture, the text from this point up to footnote 19 was modified (Ed.).

13 *Republic* 523a–524d.

14 *Republic* 477a–b, 478b.

15 *Republic* 479a ff.

16 *Republic* 523a.

17 *Republic* 524a.

18 *Republic* 514a–517b.

19 When delivering the lecture, the text from footnote 12 up to this point was modified as follows: "But do the Ideas teach us about what our life is and how we live, or do we rather have to start from this internal movement of ours, from this motility of our existence, in order to understand what the Ideas actually mean and what can they mean for us? I think that we can precisely understand what the Ideas *in concreto* are when we realize what they mean for our life—namely that when we relate ourselves to the realm of the pure, we ourselves become the kind of thing that belongs to this realm, that our own being transforms itself, that it assimilates itself to this kind of being, that it ascends beyond dispersedness and indeterminacy, beyond the entirety of time, and that it arrives into the realm of that which truly *is* and of which we can use this word in its full sense and with its entire force, where identification, unity, and precise shapes are possible—in a word, that by relating ourselves to the Ideas we are becoming something that *is*; our own being becomes true being.

This access to the world of the Ideas is opened up to us simply by (said in a modern way) our becoming aware of the enormous, general contradiction that characterizes the entire visible world of im-purity, the contradiction which consists in the fact that we see *one* as many in a manifold sense, in the fact that we see the particular things we encounter (such as tables, our neighbors, or various other entities) from the perspective of universality. When we ask: 'What is this?', we answer with a universal; we say: a table, a dog, etc. We answer with something which, if we are to characterize it more precisely, we have to conceive as a unit, but in this reality of ours this unit is necessarily separated from itself and divided into the greatest—actually infinite—diversity of exemplars, and again those exemplars are characterized by that indeterminacy and limitlessness which we discussed at the beginning of our argument. Therefore the actual impulse, the moment in which the ψυχή (soul) conceives something like the passage to the realm of the pure, the *in concreto* passage to the Ideas, is becoming conscious of this contradiction. And this means that the ψυχή (soul) is in its core in need of unity, in need of pure being. Thus the insight that εἶδος, that universal unit, *is* in the full sense, is possible only because even when the ψυχή (soul) lives in the realm of mere opinion, in the realm of indeterminacy, it is still in need of the opposite thereof; this insight is possible because, as a consequence of the soul's motility, it is constantly in motion between the two spheres and embraces both. Only because of that is it capable of noticing their contradiction, even when it has been desensitized to it by that long, original, and maybe even exclusive contact with the visible things. This is to emphasize the relation between the soul as motion and that basic feature of Plato's philosophizing which is the doctrine of the Ideas. You all know that

Plato characterizes the relation of the realm of the Ideas and the things around us, of those two realms that somehow essentially belong to the fundamental possibilities in which we always exist, by the great analogy at the beginning of Book VII of the *Politeia*, by the parable of the cave. Also this analogy is so conceived that it speaks directly about movement upward and downward" (Ed.).

20 *Republic* 360d–e.

21 A reference to the Greek mathematician Archimedes. When Roman soldiers came to seize him, he is said to have implored them not to disturb the circles he was drawing in the sand. One of the soldiers then killed him. It is an example of the kind of brutality against the good that would be impossible in the ideal city (Ed.).

22 Several notes by Jan Patočka have been appended to the manuscript:

> "But one of the greatest teachings of Plato's doctrine of the ψυχή (soul): the soul *originally does not know itself, precisely because it is* in motion, because it does not observe itself like an audience observes a stage; it has rather always already decided about itself, and consequently about what it can see, know, understand *of things as well as of itself*; the ψυχή (soul) sees itself according to how it *is*, and not the other way round, that it would *be* the way it sees itself. What we see and know depends on our being, and being does not depend on our knowledge—that is the doctrine of the ψυχή (soul) of this 'idealist'. But, unlike the parallel modern ideas that first conceive a certain biased idea of being, to which they then—in a vicious circle!—subordinate the being of human beings, Plato starts from *the being of the human being* in its basic κρίσις (crisis) and problematicity, which is essentially *moral*, i.e., such that it concerns our being and non-being in *partial* dependence on us, on our decision, on our ἑαυτὸ-κίνησις (ownmost movement).* Plato does not start from *cogito sum*, from *certainty*, but rather from the original confusion and uncertainty of existence, from its *movement*, whose meaning is clarified only in its being carried out and by itself, that is, never independently and definitively . . .
>
>   One could say with a modern thinker that the ψυχή (soul) shows itself to itself, that it comes to know itself according to whether and how *being* uncovers itself to it; but we also have to emphasize that αὐτὸ-κίνησις (self-movement),* we have to emphasize that being does not uncover itself independently and arbitrarily, with that metaphysical gamble which the late Heidegger propounds, but rather in accordance with how the ψυχή (soul) *is—responsible* or *irresponsible*—i.e., in accordance with a decision that is *not* arbitrary. The moral aspect, responsibility, does not uncover the *other* world, as in Kant, but rather *this* world."

> * The emphases on ἑαυτὸ and αὐτὸ have been restored on the basis of the manuscript (Ed.).

CHAPTER FIVE

Comenius and the Open Soul (1970)

Translated from the German by Andrea Rehberg

The human soul has often been put at the center of philosophical inquiries by ancient and modern philosophers. In the modern period, the basic division in all philosophical attempts to develop a theory of the soul can be summed up as the contrast between the open and the closed soul. The closed soul is that which identifies in one way or another with the absolute or which defines itself in relation to the absolute. Thus there is nothing that would be fundamentally external to it, that could present a limit to its infinity and a constraint to its freedom. And yet—paradoxically—we call this infinite soul closed. It is enclosed within itself, precisely because as infinite it cannot encounter anything other than itself. For it, there is no outside. Thus there is also no problem with which it should or could not be able to deal through its own faculties and means. That is why it sees its essential tasks as mastering, acquiring power, and assimilating.

The closed soul exists both in idealist and in materialist versions. Naturally, the term "closed soul" evokes first of all the views of speculative idealism and formulations like that concerning the closed nature of the universe that has no power to withstand the cognizing spirit; it evokes views that interpret the world as the matter of duties, etc. But the closed soul also prevails where it is regarded as the greatest exponent of a fully comprehended and dominated world, where it is viewed as the most powerful and—since it is familiar with all the snares and obfuscations, the interests and wiles of power—as the only free and dominant entity. The closed soul is the apex of the world; there is nothing that would in principle surpass it in value or sense; there is nothing before which it would have to halt as before a barrier that fundamentally exceeds its capacities.

The conception of a closed soul has become familiar, even obvious to our contemporary period, and for the most part it does not even occur to us that there could be another possibility of thinking about the soul. And yet the understanding of the closed soul is not all that old; there was a time when it was new and previously unheard of. In the Europe of the late Middle Ages and the beginning of the modern period it confronted the prevalent Christian conception of the soul, which, although it was not the only example of the "open" soul, was yet one of its most important historical forms. For the Christian soul finds itself placed before something which in principle it can never master, which fundamentally surpasses it, which remains incomprehensible to it and which has to remain unconquered by it as long as it does not reveal itself to the soul of its own accord and empowers it to do that to which the soul's freedom in principle enables it, but which is factually not available to it—that is, the soul is placed before God the creator and redeemer on whose revelation and grace it depends.

The emergence of the conception of a closed soul is closely connected, but not identical with, the emergence of the modern view of life and the modern world picture, to which modern natural science and technology, and modern scientific philosophy, belong as its cornerstones. Modern science is one of the heroic acts of the human spirit, by means of which it begins to hold sway over physical nature, although it finally also hopes to be able to hold sway over its own nature. To the great minds of the seventeenth and eighteenth century we owe the beginnings and, at the same time, the first successful implementation of those endeavors we call the mechanistic worldview. If these great minds could rise again and assimilate the advances of contemporary natural science (despite all divergences of research areas and the incomparable, unforeseeable results of the new scientific method), they would recognize in those advances the fruits of the same spirit that had already inspired them. It is therefore conceivable that they, if transported into the situation of contemporary science, would drop the husks of alien thought formations—e.g., Galileo's and Kepler's concepts of the cosmos, or Descartes' theological residues—if only the successes of the objective, mathematical method were brought home to them in a sufficiently comprehensive manner.

But at that time there also existed figures who, although usually equally praised as forerunners of modernity, would strongly reject their role as forerunners of modern endeavors in their chosen field. Among these figures the venerable founder of systematic didactics and educational theory, John Amos Comenius, seems to me to belong. One can find the reasons for this estimation set forth in Klaus Schaller's works on Comenius. The work of the "forerunners" or "founders" of modern natural science is the fruit of *ratio*, which, according to Cartesian formulas, is conceived as the *possession* of human being, as its asset and property, by means of which it develops into a subject. In our terminology, this *ratio* can be adduced by the closed soul as a fundamental argument for its worldview. This *ratio* is superordinate to its matter; in the encounter with its matter it does not meet anything foreign to it, but only pure self-realization. The Comenian didactic, by contrast, is not at all the fruit of such a *ratio*. Comenian reason is no natural light that finds its principles, i.e., itself, in the things it investigates. In order to apprehend things as they are, it must first of all learn to comprehend that its tendency to measure things according to itself can only yield true results if it opens and subordinates itself, including its entire soul, to a wholly other, a higher authority. Thus it is not an a priori sovereign reason that is the apprehending organ, but reason as one faculty among the other faculties of a whole soul that is harnessed and woven into the whole of the universe—including God—and that must first of all ascertain and maintain its rightful position in this whole—this is the point of departure for Comenius. Only after the soul has experienced itself in its essence as dependent on a wholly other and knows itself to be bound to this other can it also hope that its apprehending reason comes to feel and taste (*sapientia*) the things themselves in their own being and sense.

In this "going beyond the natural self," going beyond one's own domain must be carefully distinguished from the positive attachment to divine guidance and to the true light of revelation that emanates from God. It is at this point that Comenius's theologico-metaphysical speculation begins, his leap into the *revealed* absolute. On this leap there rest the *contents* of his didactic and his universal reform (*panorthosia*), which are most intimately connected. But the open soul and its basic movement—which is not to lose itself to worldly beings, to beings in the world, but to dedicate itself to and to expend itself in things, in human beings, even in God—is largely independent of this leap.

The originality of Comenius's speculation can best be demonstrated in his Czech writings. This too Klaus Schaller was the first to see. The point of departure in this is his encyclopedia, the presentation of the universe in its significance for human being and for the whole of beings. This significance is then explicated by a consideration of the position and fate of the human soul, especially through the myth of the errant path and of the pilgrim's finding their way back home in the *Labyrinth*; a myth whose essential trait can be interpreted as a self-portrayal of the open soul. In the depiction of the *Labyrinth*, and even more in the *Centrum securitatis*, and especially in Comenius's later, Latin writings, one finds a *metaphysico-theological interpretation* of this fundamental experience, since reason, guided by Jesus and centered in God, sees itself capable of experiencing the complete sense of the world. The most important thing that thereby emerges (and that is not yet contained in the consolatory writings) is the insight that this complete sense is no mere depiction and copy of what exists, but that it poses a tremendous task that is conferred upon human being to accomplish (*res humana*):

— human being placed in and integrating itself into the whole order determined by the divine being;
— education, in which the art and science of education, didactic, instructs us;
— the reform of all things that make human being human, a reform that is instigated by education and that has wide repercussions.

A dialectic of education and universal reform is thus formed, a dialectic that will determine Comenius' work until its end.

It seems that in two places in this tremendous, if composite, edifice of thought Comenius was especially guided by the thought of an open soul: in the description of the turning around of the errant person in the *Labyrinth*, and in the design of the previously unrealized projects of an *emendatio rerum humanarum*, projects which aim at the reform of human affairs, i.e., in what has often been called the *utopian* element in Comenius's work. These projects too are "harmoniously" integrated in the eternal ideas, in the *venae rerum*—but here this grounding in what persists recedes into the background: the uni-versality of the projects—human being dedicating itself, applying itself—has become the main issue. This change of perspective and of interest directs human being beyond itself in a much more generous manner than was ever the case in any version of Platonism. Human life offers and expends itself in service to God, to things, to fellow human beings. Here Comenius's urge to outline what is necessary for human being does not come into conflict with his tendency to anchor what has been thus outlined in "nature", in what persists and is to be ascertained.

Let us return to the beginning of this long path of thought in order to trace the initial phase of these thoughts in detail. The *Theatrum universitatis rerum*, a fragment of which was preserved, goes back to the time of his youth, when Alsted's encyclopedianism inspired the young student. At first glance it is a normal encyclopedia, composed in the style of the time. The Middle Ages and the Renaissance knew a large number of such encyclopedias, with depictions of Creation, Fall, and Resurrection as their frame, and Comenius's endeavor seems at first glance only to be distinguished by his wish not to deny the same to his compatriots in their native tongue. But even in this regard his encyclopedia is more than a collection of all that is knowable, solely meant for human being. The work is dedicated to Jesus Christ, and it states in clear terms that the encyclopedia is of relevance *to God himself*, insofar as it reminds human beings of their original duties, which are praising the Lord and turning everything towards God. "From that wellspring of Thine omniscience," reads the text of the dedication, "this little stream too, albeit sullied by the dirt of human incapacity, returns to the righteous path back to Thee, so that Thou beest and remainest who Thou art, the sole beginning and end of all."[1] Such encyclopedic instruction is necessary because human being has fallen out of the right order. "It has pleased Thee to create creatures who should praise Thee, us human beings and the much nobler race of angels . . . The higher ones faithfully fulfill their duty, but *we lower ones spoil Thy harmony* and, gawping at other things, we neglect to do what we are obliged to do . . . and while we remain silent, unreasoning creatures, to our shame, fulfill what we were supposed to do."[2] The harmony that reminds human beings of their duty reigns in nature; the encyclopedia is to remind human beings of this harmony so that they bring about the very same in themselves. The encyclopedia seeks to reveal no mere trivialities, but the triviality of everything insofar as it is detached from God. That is why the composition of the *machina mundi* and the questions that arise from it are always described in such a way that the confused pagan conception is clearly distinguished from the true Christian one. Thus in contrast to antiquity great emphasis is put on the createdness and transience of the world, on its relatively short duration, on its final transfiguration, also on its goodness, beauty and perfection, which mark it out as the work of its creator, while everything evil and negative in creation is attributed to sin, and even the eventual end of the world is explained as corruption by human misdeeds.

The intention, which we can only discern in outline in the remaining fragment of the *Theatrum*, is stated precisely in the *Labyrinth*. That which is treated in a chapter each in the *Theatrum*, namely the false and true view of the world, is presented in two separate parts in the *Labyrinth*: here the bedlam of pure worldliness, there the truth of spirituality. The pilgrim, to whom fell the favorable lot to be allowed to behold and explore the true circumstances of life and its destinies before choosing a profession, that is to say, the seeker, was assigned two strange fellows as companions, Impudence (*Všezvěd*, literally Searchall, who seeks the answer to everything), or Ubiquitous (*Všudybud*, who is always present wherever there is something happening), and Delusion (*Mámení*). (In the former, Schaller thinks he sees—with what seems to me exaggerated subtlety—the image of post-Cartesian subjective reason. But according to Comenius's own interpretation, *Všezvěd* is the brazenness of idle curiosity, as expressed in an encyclopedianism that degenerates into a senseless know-it-all attitude. Its companion (*Mámení*) is the unquestioning seeming and meaning that has succumbed to public idle talk and rumor, formless and nebulous, inconstant and changeable.) These two accompanied the pilgrim before he was allotted the role of seeker. They are innate to human being and want to curb its investigations. They turn truth into mere appearance for human being, like the chains for the prisoners in Plato's allegory of the cave. In Comenius's *Labyrinth*, too, there is something that corresponds to those chains, namely a bridle that enters the seeker's mouth as if of its own accord and that Searchall holds in his hand; and the spectacles of deception that are placed—albeit slightly askance—on the seeker's nose prevent him from seeing the light, like the prisoners in Plato's cave. But despite these commonalities, the role of those two companions is ultimately different from what befuddles and beguiles in the Platonic cave. They trivialize life. They make light of the unavoidable fundamental decisions of life; they allow the burdens and duties of life to appear in a rosy light; through constant novelty, change, and sparkle, they want to captivate and prevent scrutiny in the proper sense. In short, the two companions aim to hinder the whole business of scrutiny that is incumbent upon the seeker. Through the machinations of curiosity, through the bridle of tradition and an anonymous public, through the spectacles of stupefying habituation and delusion, which turn everything into its opposite, the pilgrim is to be entangled in the world and prevented from seeing that wherever he turns, just there what he seeks is not to be found.

The seeker is not passive like Plato's prisoner. But precisely in his mobility, though it seems positive, deception and error are rooted. His mobility is empty and trivial. It is a constant jumping-off, taking-part-in-everything, but never staying-with-anything. This jumping-off makes it impossible for him to encounter the void in the first place; for thereby every opportunity to scrutinize the nature of the thing in question is avoided; and where it comes into view, mere opinion—stupefied by habit and idle talk—sets itself up as authority of explanation and interpretation. The work of both companions is thus complementary: turning-away and fleeing, blinding and playing-down complement each other. Idle curiosity, nosiness, and always-and-everywhere-taking-part are at bottom flight, and interpretation is in truth talking to death and stupefaction.

But the spectacles of delusion sit at an angle in front of the seeker's eyes and that is why he retains something of an undisguised view, which benefits his investigations: he can compare. The mobility of the Searchall, too, is not meaningless for him, since he did not surrender to him freely, but his destiny, which denied him any rest and prevented any attachment, drove him into the arms of *Všezvěd*. He is, after all, the unhappy man who has lost his family, his home, his homeland, the ruler whom he was fond of, as well as the benevolent authority. His unhappiness is what protects the seeker from becoming enslaved to the world, and it gives him the opportunity to investigate and to fathom this enslavement. His pilgrimage through the world is a constant conflict with his two companions, especially with Delusion; the pilgrim is in constant dialogue with her. Delusion is the translator for the queen of the world, Wisdom-Vanity. She can interpret everything in the world, since, after all, the world *is* nothing other than the ambiguity, delusion, and confusion instigated by her in every human being, every estate, every situation, and every vocation. Their common journey through the world is accompanied by Delusion's constant apologies for the fleetingness and delusion stirred up everywhere by the two companions, so that human being should not see the truth of its situation, whatever it may be, but should passively submit to the dominion of evil, triviality, confusion, and negativity. The description of this topsy-turvy world is the description of the work of these demonic powers, which take possession of human being from the very beginning of its life. These powers of the void above all ensure that the void is not perceived, for the emptiness, the nothing, the untrue is what should not be perceived as such, according to their demonic intention. That is why it is above all death that is being concealed by them. One acts as if it did not exist, one turns away, one does not inquire. That is precisely why the revelation of death as the abyss of nothing—viewed from the plenitude of the world, compared to all that is—signifies the end of the two companions' dominion. The disclosure of the nothing is here, we note, the fundamental act of the open soul. For the open soul, things other than what is merely innerworldly exist. At that moment when the pilgrim resolutely throws away the spectacles of delusion and discovers the abyss in which everything worldly, all that is, is grounded, the companions have disappeared, together with their bridle, together with their power of temptation and delusion.

Until this act the open soul is left to its own devices, but now there occurs the saving turn. A voice sounds, which announces a new beginning in the nothingness of the grounding abyss, and leads from out of the nothing of the world to the yes of being. This true being is, for Comenius, at the same time genuine being, supreme being, and the true God. This theologico-metaphysical interpretation of the open soul's fundamental experience is decisive for the further development of Comenian thinking. For him, the open soul does not step outside the circumference of *all* beings, it does not settle outside of everything of which it can be said that it *is*, but in common with the entire metaphysical tradition since Plato it places itself on the terrain of 'what truly is', in contrast to what is merely apparent. However, human being as human being cannot not enter here; mere human power does not allow it to master this path. This transformation into the positive, the founding of a new life, of a new and true world order, the discovery of a sense of life that is at the same time reliable and pleasing—all these are being instigated by a divine guide. Human being can by itself despair of the world, can have insight into its nullity; but to turn this defeat into victory and to see that a completely different true order exists, in which human being is called to participate—this is something of which human being by itself (qua subject) is in principle incapable.

In the *Centrum securitatis*, the fundamental experience of the open soul is interpreted slightly differently than in the *Labyrinth*. Human being's entanglement in the world is here viewed as "differentness" (*jinudost*), as striving to get to the universal center of the unshakably pleasing on different paths than those which alone and truthfully lead to its destination. In this context we would describe *jinudost* as human being's "errancy." In the *Centrum securitatis*, a reason for this errancy is immediately given, and this is human being's "self-singularity" (*samosvojnost*), its tendency of wanting to be the center for itself and for everything else; rebellion against the universal center, separation and revolt. In the *Labyrinth* nothing comparable is described: there, only human being's incapacity to attain what is true by itself was emphasized, but a specific reason for this incapacity was not given. Noting this incapacity together with the open soul's original tendency towards something that is in principle unavailable was there enough to describe its fundamental experience. Only an interpretative account of this fundamental experience in the *Centrum securitatis* reveals the fundamental opposition between the world of Comenian thought and the modern striving for knowledge.

But mastery of the world through knowledge does not necessarily have to be founded in the subjectivist framework of the closed soul; it can also signify participation in the fundamental ambiguity of everything worldly. That is why mastery of the world through knowledge is also absolutely compatible with the open soul, as long as the latter does not lose itself in the former and does not declare itself a power supreme in the world because of its knowledge of the world. It is probably therefore also a one-sided exaggeration to interpret the Cartesian recommencement of philosophy in terms of such a fundamental renewal of the subjectivity of the subject. Unquestionably, figures who were otherwise influenced by Cartesianism, like Pascal, went down a different path in this regard. At any rate, at least since the *Centrum securitatis*, Comenius was treading a path that, though understandable in the context of his polemical intentions, is a dangerous simplification as it fundamentally identifies the modern world picture and the modern mastery of the world with the designs of the closed soul. When, at the end of his career, he writes against Copernicus and Descartes, this is the point of departure for his interpretation of this issue. This path is dangerous because it tempts him to assert the possibility, even the necessity, of a fundamentally different science than mathematical natural science, and to do so in the framework of a metaphysical interpretation of the world process as a whole. This is the path that Comenius actually took; one just has to recall his *Physicae ad lumen divinum reformatae synopsis*. He is not content to cognize and recognize that modern knowledge does not form a whole and is *in this sense* necessary and true. Instead he derives from this the justification for countering this fragmentary picture with a *true* world picture under the guidance of a higher authority. He wants to counter the violent world conception that starts from the methodological grasp of the knowing subject and from the human mastery of the whole with a world conception that starts from the divine and in which "*violentia rebus absit.*"[3] In this endeavor he has to facilitate a connection between what is revealed by God and natural human reason, a manipulation in which he himself is ambushed by arbitrariness, by a *violentia*. This *violentia* is contained in what Schaller calls Comenius's "hypermetaphysics," his "true," holistic world conception that methodologically rests upon the "unification of the three lights": nature, Holy Scripture, and conscience.

It is typical of the seventeenth century—and it is probably related both to the intellectual and historical situation of European humanity at the time— that in those days efforts become vocal that seek to take the troubled *genus humanum* upon a radically new path through a unified, thorough reform of its intellectual light, its reason. Such a vast and violent push towards the radical reversal of "consciousness" must precede any gradual change for the better. Thus Bacon hoped to attain a new science of objective principles by unearthing the "idols" that beguile us, and by the intellect methodically combatting the fateful tendency of indulging in those illusions and deceptions. Thus Descartes hoped to have attained, for the first time in history, a genuine criterion for the certainty of principles and to ground on three very simple foundations the knowledge that would be able to make us—in contrast to our previous impotence—*maîtres et possesseurs de la nature*. For humankind's confusion, its labyrinth, consists after all in not being able to distinguish between what one really knows (and knows with certainty and insight) and what one merely believes one knows. That is why the proposed fundamental reversal is the discipline of reflection, to be taken on by human being, upon the conscious, methodically filtered and cleared up, actively undertaken insight. With Comenius too, this will to reversal, although with him it is fundamentally related to the whole soul, is finally minted and ends up as a *reformatio intellectus*. In this respect he is akin to the Paracelsians, Spagyrics, and Rosicrucians. Although imbued with a conviction that would allow him to go beyond a closed view of all there is as existing on a single intellectual plane, that is paradoxically what he aims for. For he seeks to depict again the sense of what he has experienced in such a way as to form, together with what can be objectively ascertained, the unity of an indivisible knowledge that enlightens human being about everything that its open soul needs to know. It is instructive to compare him with Pascal on this point. Both Comenius and Pascal advocate the open soul. But Pascal does this by distinguishing *different levels*, or "orders," of the true, while Comenius—although like Pascal he protests against elevating geometrical reason to the ultimate measure of being—in the end only knows and recognizes *one* order of things. For this reason, just in regard to human reason, it is not quite right to say of Comenius that he fundamentally endeavors to let things as such be what they are. For not only are his contemporaries' efforts at the cleansing of natural human reason—the *emendatio intellectus*—alien to him, but he constantly interrupts them by trying to make headway with the help of extra-rational, extra-subjective means. For it is especially human reason that he does not let be what it is. On the one hand it is a presumption, on the other hand a risk to attribute to divine guidance the entire harmony of the three sources of knowledge (*mundus, animus, Scriptura*) and the three fundamental human capacities (*sensus, ratio, fides*), based on which a *pansophia christiana* and, as its exponents, a didactic and a universal reform are put to work. The postulate of the "whole" and "harmony" are a *humana violentia*, a human violence, just like the postulate of evidence and certainty as the ultimate, universally sufficient, and ubiquitous standard of knowledge. Not that it is untrue to vindicate God as founding harmony and unity; but to pass off what *we* feel to be harmoniously congruent and in mutual agreement as harmony *as such* is, despite all willingness to theocentrism, arbitrary.

Thus it is not surprising that Comenius was already being interpreted and misinterpreted in terms of modernity by his own time, but even more by posterity, if his fundamental intention was perennially being read anthropologically, his didactic and educational theory paidocentrically, his plans for reform in terms of social pedagogy and social utopia. (This includes the interpretation of his textbooks as mere technical manuals for the strictly limited acquisition of knowledge, e.g., of the *Janua linguarum* as a kind of effective, universally applicable language methodology.) For however strange it may seem to have a plan of a *praxis* and *chresis* as sum and epitome (*medulla et corona*) of knowledge that do not have human being and its centrality as their object—the modern anthropocentric spirit and Comenian reform share the same organizing and managing character; both are anchored in metaphysics becoming practical, and despite the material dissimilarity between such metaphysics, the formal similarities between them cannot be overlooked.

Here there is no space to pursue the origins and the growth of the properly Comenian educational theory further. This theory rests on Comenius's conception of nature, which in turn has its foundations in the divine art, which it imitates and expresses. The divine art is the bringing forth of the Ideas that outline the fundamental plan, the order of the universe on all its levels and in all its regions. This divine art is the matter itself, and when adequate and adapted to it human practice does not need to use any violence, since it then follows the nature of things and relies on the essential impulses of their nature, which spontaneously aim for their actualization. This does not of course mean that here the spontaneous impulses of human nature are ignored: the whole tendency of the didactic, to go from the whole to its parts, keeping the whole constantly in view, to work through it ever anew on different and higher levels in more differentiated and clearer ways is, purely anthropologically, absolutely justifiable and justified. But such a justification—on this point I agree with Schaller's interpretation—is not the Comenian, and, viewed purely anthropocentrically, the universal character of the mature version of the Comenian theory of education—as it shows itself in the late writings, especially in the *Pampaedia*—is not to be justified at all. Viewed anthropologically, the indivisible projects of a reform of knowledge, education, languages, and society may be interesting in some respects. But their inner necessity, from which Comenius could not extricate himself due to the theocentric purpose of his whole endeavor which he truly followed, only comes into view if one takes up and starts from his fundamental metaphysical premises.

Wherein then does the relevance of Comenius studies lie especially today; what does the Comenian œuvre tell us that we are now—only after 300 years—getting to know in its authentic outline and in its concrete form, which is emerging clearly through new discoveries? Although for the age of technology and the science connected with and dominated by it, further successes of its fundamental concepts are yet to come, there are increasing indications that the hegemony of the closed soul no longer satisfies the requirements of the post-European age. It is hardly a coincidence that the conception of the closed soul arose and spread in a historical epoch which could be called "European," the epoch in which Europe monopolized effective knowledge and the ensuing power. This European epoch developed a particular conception of history and spirit which revolved around the autonomous subject and the corresponding philosophy of the State. Nobody expressed this as perfectly as Hegel did in his doctrine of the sovereignty of States. The State is the earthly absolute and at the same time that which is plural for historical reasons and which does not recognize any higher authority above itself. Although against the rest of the world this Europe was defined as a unity, yet internally it was not unified. Its political form was "concerted," an equilibrium based on being able to evade or even resolve those of its differences and opposites that could not be balanced out—a concerted entity that sought to resolve its imbalances by transposing them on to a global scale and that resorted first to parceling out the world and finally, when fear became too general, to the *ultima ratio* of violence. All this—only seeing and recognizing "realities," wanting to master them by means of power and violence, thinking in terms of combinations of forces, to master, possess, assimilate, and partition—belongs to the arsenal of the closed soul. But the procedure of the closed soul exhibits a very pronounced dialectic which manifests itself in the parceling out of the world, which Europe powerfully accomplished in the 1860s, but which led to it being disempowered and a new world appearing, in which Europe no longer played a leading role. Instead it had to pass on almost its entire arsenal of power and skills to its heirs, which historically have completely different origins: demographically of overwhelming strength, unspent and eager to enter the limelight of world events. If the Europe of the closed soul collapsed under far lesser antitheses that ultimately proved unresolvable, in the post-European age far harsher ones await it, which could become disastrous in the face of increased technologies of destruction which aim at the substance of life itself and which perhaps belong to the quintessence of the closed soul.—Hence a new spirituality is sorely needed; a spiritual reversal is necessary if the problems of the dawning day are to be open to a positive solution. Science and technology will not manage this by themselves.

But wish and want alone would not suffice if we were not actually witnessing the birth of a new state of mind, which shows itself in very different contemporary phenomena. There is a new feeling of the inexhaustibility of the universe, which is a positive fact that opens up after the collapse of all historical systems of thought in their pretensions to absoluteness. The positivism of our age is perhaps the mask of a historical consciousness that can recognize manifestations of the depth of being even where a rationalistic ideology of progress practices a skeptical leveling. Our art, which has long since outgrown the narrowly European traditions, is in this respect more advanced than other areas of the humanities. As art it orbits that mystery which must perennially turn to dust in the hands of the closed soul, if it gets to see it at all: it orbits the very nature of appearing, self-showing, self-revealing. But here is the decisive consciousness that the world content, what is in the world, is not enough, and that means: The soul is bound to and dependent on another: it is an open soul. Open of course also means fundamentally finite: although it is rightly being said that trends like existentialism are outmoded, the problem of nihilism, for example, which has dominated European consciousness since Nietzsche, presupposes something that cannot be traced back to things, realities, actualities and that constantly and persistently reminds us that some non-being can be just as insistent as "real" forces and powers.

On the basis of these intimations we can at least begin to develop a sense that in this situation we need a pedagogy of reversal and not just a mere doctrine of the formation of human being that rests on individual scientific foundations. The education for the new age cannot be constructed from human being as thing among things, force among forces, in short, from the closed soul. It will not be a doctrine that empowers whoever is to be educated as the subject of world domination, world assimilation, world exploitation. Instead, it will open them up to dedicate themselves, to expend themselves, to tend and to guard; it will not simply implant knowledge and skills, but will patiently work towards the one point where it is comprehended that the soul has its center outside of things, thus also outside itself—viewed as force and reality—and that it has to exceed itself, give itself away, and expend itself. No complaints!—Instead taking-upon-oneself, resignation as the surrender of closedness, of the *natural* self-enclosing, which is confirmed and enhanced by the *theory* of the closed soul.

In this context the renewed interest in Comenius's doctrine of education— especially in its strange and, from the point of view of modernity, questionable pansophic form—is not only understandable but is a timely inspiration. Standing at the beginning of the epoch of closedness, Comenius has survived it and is making an appearance again at its end.

Notes

1   *Theatrum universitatis rerum*, in Dílo JAK I (Prague: n.p., 1969), 100.

2   *Theatrum universitatis rerum*, 99.

3   "Violence is absent from things" (Ed.).

PART THREE

Phenomenology

Phenomenology at its most basic concerns the relationship of human beings to the world. The phenomenological approach does not lie in dogmatic conceptions of subject and object but in the investigation of phenomena, of "the appearing of what appears." In this way, phenomenology seeks a new beginning for philosophy that is freed from the scaffolding of previous philosophical and scientific conceptions about the world. Patočka's work in this field involves masterful analysis of the philosophy of Edmund Husserl and Martin Heidegger, probing where their projects meet and diverge. But ultimately, phenomenology is for Patočka a living tradition, not defined by any singular figure. Instead, it unfolds as a series of attempts to get to the "things themselves," to step backward from the constructions of "technoscience" to a more primary "natural world" which forms the horizon of all of our activity and the basis for any conceptual accounts of what is. This "way of seeking" means confronting the crises of modernity in their philosophical roots.

In these two texts, Patočka contrasts a phenomenological sense of the whole with the prevailing view that sees the world only as a set of things or beings. He describes his approach to the whole as a "step back from beings" to that which is not of the order of beings, a "no-thing," not available as an object. He draws here from Heidegger's presentation of the nothing in "What is Metaphysics" and maps out its relation to Husserl's epochē and reduction. The notion of being as a whole leads to a renewed understanding of subjectivity, not as an isolated mind or consciousness internally representing the world or projecting a world before itself, but instead as a lived body, oriented between earth and sky, responding to the world and to others in its movements. His analysis supplies the philosophical tools required to rethink the relationship between human beings and the world, and provides the basis for, among other things, a radical ecological responsibility.

CHAPTER SIX

The Natural World and Phenomenology (1967)

Translated from the Czech by Alex Zucker

1

The problem of the "natural world" arose explicitly in the philosophical environment of positivism, that is, in an environment opposed to traditional metaphysics, both outside of science and within it; an environment in which conclusions were drawn based on the empiricist critique of the concepts of substance and causality; in which the positivist conception of a relative, phenomenal knowledge that does not extend beyond what is given by the senses, and the positivist conception of a being as that which is simply given, with nothing added, benefited from the crisis in the mechanistic view of modern natural science that gradually came about, in spite of all its successes, toward the end of the nineteenth century.

The modern mechanistic worldview was of course not mere science, but indeed was of a metaphysical nature. However, the origin of this metaphysics is closely linked to the method of mathematical natural science as elaborated by a succession of mechanistic thinkers, from Galileo to Newton, after the first successful campaign in the natural sciences, the push for heliocentrism from Copernicus to Kepler. To this day, the emergence of this metaphysics, for a long time considered nearly synonymous with the "scientific worldview," has yet to be fully investigated and philosophically clarified. What is certain is that not only is the origin of modern natural science tied to this metaphysics, but also the fortunes of what we call psychology, and of explorations in the humanities and social sciences based on that psychology. Equally certain is that the emergence of this metaphysics also brought about, in response to the audacity and artificiality of its construction, the rise of modern skeptical tendencies in empiricism, and attempts to respond to them in post-Kantian critical and idealist philosophies.

Every critic of mechanistic metaphysics points to its *artificiality*. Within this metaphysics, that which is simply given, in which we naturally live and move on the basis of natural, instinctive automatic behaviors, cannot itself be regarded as a being; for something to be accepted as a being, it must be *constructed by thought*. Mathematics—the study of entities accessible solely in the spontaneity of our mind—is the means we have for conceiving of being in the proper sense. It is mathematics that teaches us to formulate true objective relations, the structural laws of nature. These objective relations will include laws formulated to express the regularity of subjective phenomena, i.e., the occurrence of that which is instinctively given to us. Thus subjectivity itself becomes just an offshoot, an expression, of objectivity.

Another aspect of artificiality is that the mathematical-causal method places us at a single stroke *in the world of things in themselves*, whereas our immediate world is merely a subjective "reflection" of them. So it is that we penetrate to "things in themselves," despite their being essentially unexperienceable. *We are in two different worlds at once*: one in our thinking, the other in our life. This rift is definitive; nothing can overcome it.

Subjectively, the most important aspect of artificiality is that the subject is excluded not only from direct participation in understanding the world, but also from participation in acting in it, because what is really acting now is not the living subject that experiences its own life, but rather its material substrate, which cannot be experienced.

What is important here is that the crossing-over into the physical world of "things in themselves" takes as its starting point what is directly given, and that in turn is subjective, ensured by the self-certainty of consciousness discovered by Descartes. The viability of this crossing-over depends on the reliability of our objective-rational concepts and methods, which are primarily mathematical and metaphysical (substance, causality). Rising up to challenge these three fronts is the skepticism of modern empiricism, a skepticism that calls into question the crossing-over into "things in themselves," rendering it problematic and, on the face of it, weakening the dichotomy of the world. In the same way, physical constructions are reduced to essentially subjective, empirical structures of subjective experience. We live therefore in one world and in fact do not transcend this lived world, not even in our thinking. Meanwhile "the other world" in turn becomes problematic, and mathematical natural science along with it.

Positivism, then, is an attempt to connect the unitary, albeit subjective and (to the subject) relative world, as we experience it, with the methods of mathematical natural science. This connection is to be achieved by giving up the "metaphysical" concepts of substance and causality in favor of a richer usage of the concepts of relation and function. The use of mathematical methods is interpreted differently than in the mechanistic worldview. Rather than opening up another world, they are merely a different way of talking about this world as we experience it, a language of precise prediction. So it is that both the prescientific and the scientific world will be purified of everything that transcends them in any way other than relatively and practically. This leads to a "purification of experience," and, to a large extent, also a return to a "natural" worldview.[1]

So that is how the problem of the "natural" worldview arose, and the problem of the "natural" world along with it. The reason it is a problem is that neither the diagnosis of the illness nor the therapy prescribed is convincing to all those considering it. To illustrate, we will present a range of voices aspiring to a deeper diagnosis.

The metaphysics of mechanism can be defined in various ways, and prominent philosophers have variously described its essential elements. Whitehead speaks of a "dichotomy" between nature and worldview, dating as far back as the atomistic conceptions of the Greeks.[2] Burtt refers to a concurrent shift in the conceptions of 1) reality, 2) causality, and 3) the human mind: reality is understood not as a world of qualitative things presented to us by perception, but rather one of essentially mathematical entities and relations; final causes are excluded from consideration and causality becomes purely efficient; any quality that cannot be expressed in geometrical terms is relegated to subjectivity, the mind reduced to a set of brain processes.[3] Husserl attached the greatest weight to the role played by the autonomization of mathematical idealizations as ostensibly the only true, objective world.[4] Koyré points out the role of Platonism in the origin of this conception already among the first generation of mechanists, from Copernicus to Kepler, emphasizing the Platonism of Galileo himself—his cosmic mathematicism.[5] From a metaphysical standpoint, Heidegger and his followers offer the most multifaceted, but also most expansive, analysis of this period, with their efforts to penetrate to the ultimate ontological foundations. Heidegger sees modern science as not only linked with metaphysics, but as an extreme which all of metaphysics is leading toward. Metaphysics, in his view, is a perverted understanding of being that makes the essential non-objectivity of the primordial foundation of everything into a mere object, a mere thing. The metaphysics of mechanism, for Heidegger, is also an expression of the obscuring, uncomprehending "comprehension" of being that modern technology practices.[6] The central philosophical formulation of this practice of metaphysics is the principium rationis, or principle of sufficient reason, formulated by Leibniz in the seventeenth century, after a 2,000-year incubation: the principle that there must be a reason for everything.[7] Heidegger interprets this principle as one of universal calculability and predictability. Nothing is, nothing exists, unless it conforms to this principle, i.e., unless it meets and is subsumed within the universal requirement that it be secured by calculation. This principle thus amounts to the rigorous, exact objectification of all that is. This objectification transforms all that exists, the *universum*, into an object placed before the subject; the subject, seeking to secure its place in the world, places the object before itself in order to master it. The world becomes a re-presentation in this sense. Thus the entire modern era is the age of the "world picture," if *picture* is understood in the sense of an "objectification," a "representation for the subject," a "counterpart to the explicit reasoning and deliberating activity of the subject," a "structure of re-presenting, of forming, of constructing."

The Anglo-Saxon authors present a diagnosis that offers only one new point against positivism: they are aware that any conception that replaces the mechanistic worldview will once again be an overall philosophical conception of the world and, in that sense, again be a metaphysics. This is something the positivists do not acknowledge, seeking to avoid it through positivism's relativism, its practical conception of truth as that which can be empirically validated. (That this notion of truth cannot apply to the concept of positivism itself, which claims to portray the state of things as they are and not merely as what is validated, escapes them.)

Husserl and Heidegger introduce deeper aspects to the critique of the positivist conception of a return to the natural world. To evaluate them, we must again return to an analysis of the positivist conception.

Positivism seeks to do away with the dichotomy of the world between physical cause and subjective effect (i.e., the image/reflection of true physical reality). Therefore it reduces physical and mental reality to a single level, which[8] it calls the level of "neutral data." This level is the material from which the various types of mutual relatedness are formed, constituting physical objects on the one hand and psychophysiological ones on the other. Physical relations are relations of neutral data, insofar as they are dependent on one another for their occurrence. In Avenarius, psychophysiological relations are those that depend on a certain "System C," which, though in itself constituted by a set of neutral data, also regulates a particular common occurrence of neutral data, which we might term a "private perspective on the whole of the universe," i.e., on the whole of *all* the data, itself included.

This ("natural") picture of the world involves two large, unacknowledged assumptions:

1. The "neutral level" is not actually neutral, but rather subjective, since if it were not subjective, which is to say based in experience, it would make no sense to claim the direct givenness of an object as dependent on System C. In reality this level conceals within it the level of self-certainty of consciousness discovered by Descartes, which was obscured by the way in which it was received by English empiricism.

2. Within this neutral level, two fundamentally different types of aspects of being occur: elements or data, and the functional relations of their occurrence—in essence, mathematical laws.

No less than in mechanism, mathematical laws play a leading role, and therefore are the true reality. These laws are what govern the occurrence of elements. And not only that, but their nature as well. For if these elements are to conform to universal natural laws, they must be components in the functional relations determined by these laws. This means they must be classifiable. Neutral elements are not experiential data, but rather prerequisites for the possibility of mathematical construction. They are a remnant of mechanism at the very core of this "natural" worldview.

The dependence of subjective experience on the object was not in any way diminished by the fact that "System C" itself became a set of elements. The process of the occurrence of elements in the context of a private perspective remained equally dependent on the impersonal process of their occurrence in a purely objective System C.

So what we have is a dual concept of subject, one all-embracing, which overlaps with the "neutral level" on which physical and private-perspective relations are "constituted," and the other one particular, that is, a concept of private perspective that is dependent on the objective System C.

Positivism, then, uncritically adopted some of the fundamental presuppositions of the mechanistic worldview. For one, the presupposition that mathematical relations are the true reality, without examining what they are, how they come to be, and how they arise in experience. With this presupposition, positivism itself alienated the "natural" approach to the world even more from its original nature, introducing an objectively mathematical structure not merely at the level of cause, but directly into lived experience. Thus positivism is an attempt to assure us that our impression of the mechanistic worldview as unnatural is merely a result of our traditionalist, backward interpretation—we need only consistently replace metaphysics with logic and mathematics, and everything will be fine. For another, it adopted the presupposition that all that is must ultimately reveal itself in its being on the level of certainties, that is, on the level of data; and the level of certainties is the level of the subject.

Yet both these presuppositions have been interrogated, in an attempt to arrive at a solution amid the darkness of the crisis of modern objectivist thinking, by philosophers who rehabilitate the "natural world" far more radically than the positivists: the phenomenologists Husserl and Heidegger, albeit each in a different way.

2

Before moving on to *how* these thinkers develop and renew the theme of the "natural world," let us show, in a few strokes, its vital significance: Why in fact is this theme so important, *for what purpose* does it need to be addressed?

In philosophical terms, it is first and foremost an effort to uncover the real questions underneath the surface of seemingly universal certainties. To question again the self-evidence with which our lives are dominated by the metaphysics of science and technology (or better put, technoscience). To liberate our perspective through this problematization of the self-evident. And, with this liberated perspective, to grasp the possibilities in our thinking and our lives that the bias in our vision has previously deprived us of, or covered up from us out of excessive caution: in short, to expose ourselves to the deeper truth obscured by this metaphysics.

Related to this, however, is an aspect that concerns not only philosophy and purely intellectual realms in general. The unprecedented expansion of human power is closely related to the metaphysics of mechanism, and yet, instead of becoming a means for the improvement of human life, this expansion has led to widespread historical and social cataclysms. Only the metaphysics of mechanism has made possible the social phenomena that typify modern times, especially modern capitalism, which grows out of an equally extreme objective stance toward human affairs, subjecting human conditions to an equally lawlike calculus and working with an explicitly mechanistic model of human relations. In a sense, it can be said that German classical philosophy, with dialectics as its highest synthetic method for the restoration of totality, was an attempt to respond to the conceptual and existential situation created both by reality and the ideational structure of modern mechanistic metaphysics. The problem of the natural world could then be defined as the same question on a new level, in a new historical situation. At a time when classical capitalism has devolved into monopoly supercapitalism while its chief rival, socialism, is changing form and critically acknowledging the phenomena of alienation within its own body politic, the question of the natural world—even if it neither promises nor directly reveals any universal cures or sensational reversals in the situation—is a pressing one.

It is significant that the problem of the "natural world" in Husserl's writings actually has the dimensions that we have outlined here: from the outset, his philosophy is a reflection on the foundations of modern science, and especially mathematics, taking a critical stance toward mere pragmatism and the technicism of science. From there he works backward to the Cartesian foundations of this science, and then to a new, deeper Cartesian meditation, which leads to the discovery of a deeper ground underlying the efforts of modern empiricism (and positivism). Here Husserl exposes the central contradiction of Cartesianism, which is the contradiction of modern science in general: the effort to arrive at the absolute foundation, the ultimate basis of all that is meaningful and significant for us, summarily identified with a grounding in mathematics, even as the meaning of mathematical concepts and structures remains unclear, and this lack of clarity affects all of objectivist rationalist metaphysics.

What, then, does it mean really to return to Cartesianism?

It means to persevere where Descartes failed. Rather than remaining at "ego cogito," at the immediate, absolute certainty of the self, Descartes abandoned it for proofs of the existence of God, which he then used as a buttress for objective evidence: the evidence of mathematics and of other material disciplines, particularly physics.

Descartes poses the right question in the right terrain: the question of the origin of all that is and can be meaningful for us. But his aim is to legitimize what he already knows about God, the world, and the soul as quickly and firmly as possible. And because he *already knows*, he uses this knowledge to interpret terrain he has barely discovered, and, as a result, he loses sight of it.

For the self-certainty of consciousness is not to be taken as self-evident, as a field in which the treasures of knowledge lie waiting to be gathered, like the "simplices,"[9] which Descartes saw as the foundation of every science that can be methodically constructed. Before we can arrive at what is certain within this self-certainty—that is, what is given—the terrain must be cleared. Descartes knows this too: he is opposed to all prejudice. But not radically, for he leaves standing the most important one—that when it comes to ourselves, we already know what we are: a thing among things, in a vast network of causal interactions, which contains us like a mustard seed, or one infinitesimal yet ensouled atom of it. Rather than subject this fundamental situation to methodical doubt and suspension of judgment, Descartes treats with skepticism only the world which we are part of, which appears to us as directly given and clearly accessible in the richness of its qualities and living relations. In other words: the natural world is precisely what he excludes, and in its place he installs the world of physics, a mathematical structure causally interconnected with us.

Now if we are to return to the point where Descartes lost his way, we will have to abandon all his metaphysical truths, including the ones he most emphasized: the proofs of God's existence, the proof of the objectivity of the mathematically structured world through *veracitas Dei* ("the truthfulness of God"), the proof of the simple substantiality of the soul. None of this will be valid for us, as we must concentrate solely and exclusively on what is directly given as such, on what is present *in reflection*, yet this is not the case for everything. All such things as God, the world, the soul are merely *objects* which the immediately given processes of life aspire toward and intend, nothing more than that—they are the poles toward which life is directed, but it is this direction, not the objects, that will be the given guaranteed in the cogito. Those objects do pertain to the meaning of the process of life, not in their absolute *existence*, but only in their *significance* as connected to this process.

At this point, it is crucial to note that what we have before us in the reflected ego is not an unquestionable residue of the world, of reality. It is the ground in which everything significant grows, the ground of all possible meaning, whether that meaning is God, the world, or my own self, the I of the human being. It is the ground of meanings in all their meaningful richness, logic, structure, in their mutual references, interlinkage, and dependence, one-sided or mutual. We can observe all this about meanings, merely as meanings, without attributing existence to them. And of course we can do so only insofar as these meanings are correlates of processes typical of our inner lived experience, originally given in reflection: as meanings perceived, imagined, remembered, as correlates of judgments, as results of explicit theorizing, etc.

So now it becomes clear that the terrain discovered by Descartes is not, as he believed, the terrain of the individual human soul as *substantia cogitans* ("thinking substance"). Neither is it the general structure of thinking substance as such, nor the general self of Kantian transcendental apperception. It is the universal meaning-generating field. The error of Descartes was in failing to make a sharp distinction between two subjects: the subject reflected in a radically purified view that admits only what is given to it in this way, what it sees, and the subject as one of the objects that are not given to it in this way (but rather are always in large part beyond reflexive givenness, or even the possibility of such givenness).

Along with this, it also becomes clear that nothing whatsoever is lost *in terms of meaning* with this modified Cartesian doubt (modified in such a way that it is not a negative interest in the world, but rather an exclusive interest in the givenness of reflected lived experience). The whole world is still here—as meaning. But this world, which exists in a constant correlation of meaning with all lived experience, will no longer be the Cartesian world of mathematical natural science. It is originally and at bottom a primordial, pre-given, *natural world*.

So only now, after this purification of the Cartesian cogito, are we able to *really study* the natural world, rather than merely assuming it and discussing it in the abstract. At the same time, we see that the positivists did manage to see the true problem: the unproven metaphysical claim that underpins the self-understanding of mathematical natural science. Likewise we see that their materialist opponents were also not entirely wrong to reproach them for subjectivism and Berkeleyan-Humean idealism: the positivist intention of revealing the "neutral level," consisting of two different arrangements of relations, physical and personal/private (mental), ultimately reduces both to a primary subject that gives rise to all meanings. Yet this subject constitutes them as meanings, not realities. By not adopting the Cartesian suspension of validity, the suspension of faith in the world, positivism inevitably became entangled in complicated problems that make this view of reality, known as "neutral monism," even more incomprehensible than the old dualistic scheme handed down from the seventeenth century. The relationship between the neutral level and the levels derived from it is conceived as real; physical realities are defined by the mutual, real, functional relations between *parts* of this level, while mental realities are given by the fact that certain parts "serve as the condition" for something like a perspective on the whole, that is, a particular arrangement of *all* the givens centered in the image of one's own body; the whole, the neutral level, is therefore both the condition and what is conditioned. Objects themselves must be defined *in their reality* as classes of perspectives; yet these classes, or concepts, must also have the properties of realities, in particular they must *cause an effect*, with that effect taking on the paradoxical appearance of something that is simultaneously and unequivocally given, without contact, in all the various parts of space— the old theory of pre-established harmony.[10] Rather than simplifying reality, the elimination of relatively durable, substantial entities, and of causal effect in the ordinary sense, shatters reality into such a spray of impressionistic fragments that it is impossible to comprehend how it holds together. In its fetishistic fear of introducing a concept not derived from experience, positivism neglected the fundamental *transcensus* that always animates experience, making it an experience *of something*, which, however, can never be placed on the same level of being as the real, reflexively given stream of experience.

3

In its analyses of the correlation between life (the real stream of experience) and meaning (the ideal level of what is experienced), phenomenology as a whole moves within the realm of the "natural world." It studies the composition and logic of its components, for the world is a rich structure that we experience in the original—i.e., even as we perceive it, we also make it present, either as real or only in "as if" mode, observing, analyzing, and so on; and just as the processes of lived experience presuppose and refer to one another, so the ideal correlates connect to and build on one another within that rich structure. This outlines the role of the "constitution" of objects in consciousness or in correlation with it, with constitution as a whole being above all and fundamentally the constitution of the *natural* world.

Yet this very fact, that all phenomenology is actually a phenomenology of the natural world, had the paradoxical consequence that Husserl focused on the natural world as a special problem only rarely, and relatively late in life. For a focus on the natural world presupposes a focus on *the world*, as opposed to a focus on objects in the world, and therefore the question of whether consciousness of the world can be reduced to consciousness of all the objects in it, or whether the world as such need not be accessible first in a special way for which there is no substitute. The *natural world* as a world had to remain undiscovered as long as *the world as a world* remained undisclosed.

The task of grasping the "natural world" is the challenge of grasping those characteristics of humanity that do not depend on historical contingencies of our development—in other words, what can be abstracted by retaining what is common to *all* modalities of human life. This means identifying a fund of possibilities common to both "prehistoric" and historic humankind, to civilized and "primitive" humans alike, those from high cultures as well as those more basic, so as to expose the ground that gives rise to *all* these possibilities. At the same time, it cannot be denied that historicity is a fundamental human characteristic—though historicity and history are two different things. Even a person who has no history is historical, in that they do not live a merely vegetative existence, adhering to a natural rhythm, but must *relate* to their being. Even "ahistoricity," in the sense of a lack of factual history, is a choice for us, one of a range of contingent possibilities, for even an ahistorical person is fundamentally capable of experiencing the vertigo of freedom that comes with the anxiety of confronting the abyss over which their life hovers.

To grasp the variations in what is common, however, does not necessarily mean to grasp some *essence* of humanity, given once and for all. Historicity as essence would then mean nothing but the lack of a substantive characteristic for humans, which could be grasped once and for all as what being for humans *consists* of, what it *persists* in. A "natural person" in the modern sense is always merely a schema, a schema of the *problem* of humanity. A human's being is not finished or complete the way it is for a rock, an animal, or a god. Whether that eo ipso means that we give ourselves our own meaning or whether there is a deeper process of being itself that uses us to materialize itself are two possible interpretations of human freedom. We will not decide between them here. We merely wish to show that the two fundamental possibilities of humanity—to exist "historically" (having a factual history, relating to our own past by denying and retaining it), or to exist "ahistorically" (not denying the past but identifying with it, repeating it in an eternal return of the same)—are both possibilities of a historical being, taking the word *historical* here in an ontological sense, not in the sense of history as fact. These two possibilities become reality in a near-fateful way; humanity occurs in one or the other of these two modalities, and Lévi-Strauss is right to say that humanity has had no greater experience of itself than the encounter of the European modality, the historical modality par excellence (owing to the Christian self-conception, which was already eminently conscious of historicity), with the Neolithic form of humanity after the discovery of the New World in the late fifteenth century.

Only if we do not assume history to be merely a continuation of biology by specifically human biological means (for this may well result in a state of "ahistoricity" that carries on indefinitely, with no explicit tradition, no writing, no "state" in the European sense), can the question be asked: In what sense is *factual history* able to pass on what is essential about human beings?

A proper characterization of the natural world features the following main aspects, which are deserving of closer analysis:

(1) The world is not originally given as the sum total of things, i.e., in the form of a consciousness for which the particulars, both individually and collectively, are intended and given; rather, there is a primordial consciousness of wholes, and of the most comprehensive or all-encompassing whole—a consciousness of the world; this special mode of consciousness must be analyzed in particular, along with the origin of the meaning correlates rooted in it; only in this way can the meaning of "the world" become clear. This is one pole of the relation to the world, the pole of the periphery, of the whole.

(2) Perception and the entire original givenness of the content of the natural world are connected to corporeal life in a fundamental way; life in

the natural world is corporeal life (corporeality in the *phenomenal* sense, not objective and physical); the varied content of the natural world is fundamentally subject-relative; the natural world is fundamentally an oriented, perspectival, situational world. This is the second, internal pole of worldliness.

Re: (1) Let us proceed from the most common notion: The world is the sum total of all things, and we make this totality present in a state of self-givenness, self-presence, i.e., in our perception of things. Under normal conditions, perceived things, in their full state of givenness, are given for us kinesthetically and visually: they are oriented around us with respect to being near or far, within reach or view. Nearness, however, is less a matter of our present perspective on things than it is of our being embedded among them, of our familiarity with them—first individually, then with the recurring style of those things that make up our intimate environment, its material components and our fellow humans alike, a landscape ever presenting something new to do and see. As our present perspective fades into indefinite irrelevance, the outlines of this familiar style are gradually erased, turning into what we already know only in the most general way, while our present perspective takes on alternative forms, which prove to be no longer merely possible but real: a wild, mountainous, foreign landscape; a desert, a sea; enormous, unfamiliar cities; miracles of technology, human anthills, eternal ice and snow ... and beyond, into outer space. Running through it all, however, is a reference to something else even less common. I can never reach the end of possible variants of style, no variant of style is ever absolute. Yet there is always the polarity of that to which I belong, i.e., that which is *essentially* near, as opposed to *actually* near, and of that which is essentially far, foreign, or unfamiliar, so the world is essentially divided between the familiar and the alien or strange.

Now, when we consider these correlations—present–not present, familiar–not familiar, domestic and foreign, near and far—while taking into account the fact that perceptual givenness is always the givenness of the individual (whereas *style* substitutes for the particulars, which *are here for me, but only in an indefinite way*), then it is obvious: the not present, not familiar, foreign, and distant can enter perception only on the condition that the present, familiar, domestic, and near are presupposed, i.e., perception of the not present, not familiar, foreign, and distant takes place against the backdrop of the present, familiar, domestic, and near.

A thing does not disappear when our perception of it ceases; I can return to a previous aspect of it, which means I already know in advance that it is an aspect of something that does not disappear. This idea of non-disappearing is something I have to bring to perception, and that means: perception unfolds within its *horizon*. (So, then, *change* is only possible on the ground of the non-disappearing.) I cannot derive this horizon from my perceptions; it is not merely a "set of perceptions," which have passed over into the actualizable non-present; the fact *that they have passed over* into the non-present but not disappeared is the new, original mode of givenness that horizontal consciousness provides. This non-disappearance of what has once been given is just one instance of the givenness of what is not given, the presence of what is not present; it testifies to the fact that there is far more here than what is presented and shown to us by perception. Our perception of the particular always already takes place in a vast, actualizable non-present. Perception does not happen moving from the givenness of one perception to the next, but from the very beginning in a whole that is present even if not perceived, and this whole is then divided into parts by our perception: given and not given, present and not present, domestic and alien. These structures are intelligible only thanks to the fact that there is first an original, non-sensory presence, and in that sense a givenness of the whole. This primordial presence, even though not *perceptually* present, in the sense of an originally given *perceived particularity*, is nevertheless so intimately here that it *does not need* the guarantee of individual data differentiation, of the situational uniqueness that characterizes perceived particularities.

The primordial non-sensory presence of the whole, someone might object, is the work of memory and thought. Memory, in the sense of remembrance, however, is nothing but the quasi-presence of the particular; thus the presence of the whole cannot be deduced from it. By the same token, thought, in the sense of explicit judgment, cannot be its source, as thought is nothing but a schematization, an idealization, and an eidetically variational operation that presupposes sensory givenness and manipulates it in spontaneous, explicit fashion.

On the contrary, what we have here is a primordial non-perceptual givenness. To say that it is not perceptual and corporeal in the same way as aspects of the particular is not to say that it is an absolutely non-originary givenness, which can be reduced to another mode in which it can be represented in the proper sense. If in anticipation I imagine the other side of the table, I can reduce it to a representation, but I can never reduce to a representation the material thing itself as a whole, in a lasting state of anticipation. The same holds true for the primordial whole. Just as I can never fully relive the past except as the "quasi-present"—in memory—without losing the whole *dimension* of the past, I can never perceive the entire world, i.e., I can never reduce everything in it to actuality at once. *No mind* is capable of that. Horizontal consciousness can never be reduced to non-horizontal consciousness, even if every act is an act within a horizon. *A horizon is not an intention that can be fulfilled*. A horizon is *always equally integral*; what changes is only the relation of the horizon to what stands before it as its backdrop. The horizon is the backdrop to a particular foreground: everything present can and must rise up out of the non-present and sink back into it. All these turns of phrase are figurative, a way of saying, in essence: what constitutes beings are not present perspectives; there are beings before perspectives and independent of them; there are also beings without perspectives; but there is never a perspective without a being.

The total horizon of the world means: the primordial whole is always and in every respect (spatially, temporally, in terms of content) beyond the limits of all that is present. The world is always more than any perspective of it can capture.

The inner horizon of things means: a thing is no less inexhaustible than the world. A thing is not merely the sum of all aspects. I can anticipate and then realize any non-present aspect. In a sense, all aspects are present simultaneously, but the inner horizon of a thing does not consist of the references of one aspect to the others or all of them to one another. *The horizon includes the thing not only as it is seen, but also as it is unseen.* Though what confronts us in a perspective is nothing less than the thing itself in the original, that does not mean the thing is a perspective or a synthesis of purely individual perspectives. The inner horizon, that aspect which cannot be represented, or better put, that necessary counterpart to every perspective which can be represented, shows that even in the present, vividly given representation, there is something present that can never fit into any representation or synthesis of representations. Thus, for example, in our consciousness of things, we are aware not only of an infinite plurality of perspectives referring to one another, but also of the aperspectival nature of things—a thing itself is not a perspective, even though it is always given in one.

The unrepresentable primordial givenness of the whole is what underlies the special modes of human behavior that are not directed at particularities, at resolving individual situations, or at unilaterally oriented measures *in the world*, but rather in which we direct our behavior toward the whole as such. These behaviors are *pointless* in the sense of having no immediate result, unless the point is the consciousness or lived experience of being human in a given situation within the larger whole. What some authors refer to as ritual and representational behavior is only possible on this basis. This is also the basis of a curious dichotomy that is wholly incommensurable with our modern conceptions and has often been observed among peoples living in "primitive" society: namely, that "true reality" is "supernatural," i.e., a reality that cannot be managed or manipulated by technological means. There is a fundamental difference between what can and cannot be manipulated. Of course, in the modern view, *the world in itself* is precisely what can be manipulated, whereas the immediate world cannot. In the archaic view, what cannot be manipulated is the whole, whose way of manifesting is of a completely different order than that of the particulars which every attempt at manipulation must take as its starting point. The fact that this attitude toward the whole, containing a fundamental mystery, may, secondarily, be subject to attempts at manipulation, such as magic, does not prove that its original significance is magical; in the same way, the likelihood that ritual representation led to side effects of tremendous practical significance (e.g., domestication, agriculture, totemism) does not prove that its true, original meaning lies in these consequences.

Re: (2) On the other hand, we must emphasize that perceptual, actual presence, constituting *the whole of the world* only in counteraction with what is not present, is fundamentally an oriented presence, perspectival and situational. Even tactile-kinesthetic perceptions, in which the contrast of holding-and-touching with stepping-and-reaching is a rudimentary givenness of near versus far, are already oriented. The main orientation in the tactile realm, however, is grounded in the subjectivity of touch, in which we feel both things and ourselves, our bodies. Orientation is no less evident in the visual realm, where although there is no moment of experiencing the self through seeing, our perspective always extends outward from the center, which is constituted by a perceptually incomplete manifestation of our own body. In a living context, provided we step beyond pure, actual perceptibility into the flow of time, this orientedness appears as *situatedness*, in which memory, imagination, and verbal expression play as much a part as perception. I must be *in* a situation (not: *above* or *before* it) in order to understand it, and therefore I understand it always only in part.

Orientedness and situatedness point to corporeality; corporeality in this sense means a practical, voluntary corporeality—only by way of a body, and a body over which we have direct control, can we be active in the world, tangibly taking part in the process of changing the things in it. Yet corporeality is still orientation in a different sense: the body, through its *needs*, causes life to take itself as its purpose and objects to serve as a means to that end.

Orientedness thus takes place *through the body* in a subjective sense, through the active body, but that does not mean it is wholly oriented *toward the body*. The center of reference for bodily orientation is outside the body itself: every orientation is an orientation of our action, of the active intervention of our bodies, and that requires a *referent*. The referent of our own acting, realizing stream (i.e., *movement* in the most original sense of the word, movement lived from within) is the stable, *unmoving* ground: the earth. The immobility of the earth is inherent in the world's original orientedness. Oriented and self-orienting action is fundamentally grounded in the earth. It is only resting on this solid foundation of our shared life situation that we are able to act. The earth is not only the indispensable root of our action, but the bedrock of everything: all that we call "things" is grounded in the earth, and even things that float, like a balloon or a cloud, are bound to the earth in some way, overcoming what ties them down. The earth is the prototype of all that is massive, corporeal, material, it is the "universal body," of which all things are in some way a part—as their attraction to the earth, their dependence on it, their origin from it, and their ending in it all indicate. Thus the earth, in the framework of primordial nature that we are analyzing, is not originally a body like other bodies; it is not comparable to anything else, because everything else that might occur and that we might encounter relates to it as the ground that is always presupposed. It is the *natural horizontal* with respect to which we assume every attitude or stance—in every rising to one's feet, every step, every movement, the earth is presupposed, at once energizing and wearying, as well as sustaining and affording peace.

Through the face of the earth as the bearer and referent of all relations, then, the earth manifests also as *force and power*. A force is something that shows itself as the occasion calls for, entering into conflict with other forces and proving itself as either equal, superior, or subordinate. A power is something constant that has its own domain, a realm of its own in which it has no rival. The earth rules the heights and the depths alike. It rules even over the elements, which are forces alongside it, if not against it, but ultimately it is the earth that has power over them. For even a stream of water, even an ocean, is obliged to cling to it, and the air and the weather are like an ocean too: Plato in his day compared us to creatures that dwell at the bottom of the sea. Everything alive takes its power from the earth, including even those living things whose tendency is to go against it. And again in the vertical, in the uprightness of life, it is the earth that rules. It is she, ultimately, she and her elements that nourish life, she that is life as well as something other than life. Holding life, sustaining it, creating and destroying it, covering herself with it and cloaking her ultimate likeness, stark and merciless.

This aspect of the earth as a power is no less *oriented* than the aspect of earth as reference point, the earth as unmoving ground of all movement and activity. For the power of the earth is not the force of an object, which I simply observe or consider, but rather something that rules over me, in whose domain I move along with other things, and which I cannot escape, do not know how to escape, any more than a bird in the air or a cloud—both of which may be freer but are also still bound to earth. And the earth is also a power over life and death as *nourishing earth*. I depend on the nourishing earth through the fundamental rhythm of my bodily needs, for the body is not only that with which I feel and act, but also what dictates my first, most fundamental purposes, that to which feeling and acting return—and if they return, it is always by means of what the earth ultimately provides, what is in one way or another prepared by it, on it, or in it: it is not merely poetic metaphor but captures something essential to speak of humans as "earthlings."

The earth, however, is not the *only reference point*. The earth is the solid ground beneath our feet, and its fundamental, though not exclusive, mode is *nearness*. The earth is *fundamentally near*, albeit immensely vast and difficult to reach in its outlying regions—ultimately we can get close to it everywhere; in one way or another it is accessible. This means that in its massiveness, in its weight and horizontality, the earth corresponds to our tactile-kinesthetic and volitional manipulation of things, to that aspect of our muscular being that exerts *strength*, presents resistance, rises up, overcomes resistance, is active, works. Yet there is still another point of reference, one that is *fundamentally distant*, intangible, and cannot be controlled by bodily contact, no matter how present it appears to be—a referent pertaining to all that is fundamentally untouchable: light, the heavens, celestial bodies, all that encloses our horizon without closing it, all that constitutes the outside as something closing us in; a referent that speaks basically only to our eyesight, to that soundless sense of distance. As distant as the sky is, it is no less oriented a sphere than the earth: whereas the earth primarily gives everything its "where," the sky supplies the "when," for the sky is the sphere of light and darkness, day and night, and their comings and goings. Yet at the same time it is also a giver of "where" in the eminent sense: for the sky is untouched and untouchable—it has signs that always remain in the same place. On earth it is possible to get lost; not so in the sky. And then too, the sky is the giver of all clarity, and with it all knowledge, including the knowledge of what is near as opposed to far: for only in the light can things appear and the earth reveal its inner nature, showing the light only its surface and reluctantly, while inwardly closing itself off to evade the light. In the light, the earth and the sky frolic in colors that reveal things fundamentally not in themselves but at a distance, detached from us, on the surface; that reveal things in a way that is fundamentally impossible to grasp because of its relation to the "heavenly," faraway, distant nature of light, itself impossible to grasp. And so earth and sky are in constant contact and intersection, mutually intertwined in the natural environment of the being that has a world, i.e., a near and a far, control and exposedness, an active will as well as the capacity for distance.

Our coming to terms with inner-worldly things happens only against the backdrop of the earth and the sky—though not necessarily always with the backdrop itself in focus. The earth and the sky never fully enter into the framework of practical dealings and its references. To be sure, the earth and the sky are practical referents, but they are not only that: they have a depth of their own, not exposed to us, which we can always sense. It is clear that the things we deal with, and that we understand by our dealing with them, are *things to satisfy our needs*, things that fit into our bodily functions and our acquisitive skills like teeth into a cog wheel, like a cast fits a mold. And they do not fit into them in isolated form, as individual, self-contained facts, but rather as references to objects: the key in the locksmith's hand refers to the lock, the material, and the lathe; in the hand of the occupant, it refers to the room, its furnishings, its separation from the rest of the building, its contrast with what is outside the occupant's room, the contrast between their private room and the place of their employment, etc. This "whole of how a thing is involved" (*Bewandtnisganzheit*), what it is and what end it serves, is at the same time there in what a thing opens up for us, what we originally understand of it, how we perceive it, what we see in it; the result being that perception as such is not valid as the dominant approach to reality, but is embedded in the functioning relation of how things are involved, what is going on with them. It is a matter of course that the earth and the sky function also in this essentially practical domain: the earth as where things are, what they are on, what they are made of; the sky as light and time to work, time to rest, etc. Yet it would be incorrect to see in them *only* this practical function, or to see this function as primary and fundamental. The earth and the sky, unlike practical things, hold not only the possibility of functioning in relations, but also an eminent possibility of *showing relations*. The earth and the sky are not only "things for," but demand from us and evoke in us an entirely different attitude and behavior than the immediately practical, in which relations disappear, absorbed by the smooth unfolding of action. The earth, with its *significant places*, and the sky, with its immensity and fundamental distance, are likewise the stimulus for a special vertigo in which the world appears as the world in all its strangeness and wonder.

For the most part, behavior that is immediately practical has its teleology in the realm of life: life becomes its own goal, life in its *needs*, which either cyclically repeat or are already detached from the natural rhythms of life. Arising out of this satisfying of needs, then, is a secondary teleology, in which the original means become ends ad infinitum, so that the fulfillment of these ever more complicatedly structured tasks itself takes on intricate forms, even as their fundamental structure is repeated.

All orientational, analytical, and constructive activity springing from practical human intelligence is located in this realm of practical behavior.

Practical relations, the whole of how things are involved, understanding within these relations, which becomes the sole subject of interest, while things in their sensory-perspectival givenness disappear by being overlooked, is one of the reasons why we fail to notice the orientedness of the original givenness of the present. Even though the *objectivity of practical orientation* is the framework within which all functioning of everyday understanding moves, and our life among things is therefore always a life with *oriented* things, that is, with the givenness of their orientation, we overlook this givenness in favor of another aspect, namely, the *significance* of things, their *meaning*, which, as something we do not perceive but *understand*, is perceptually *aperspectival*. Significative perspectivity stands in opposition to perceptual perspectivity, drowning the latter out.

Apart from things, embedded in the nexus of needs and the secondary teleology that grows from them, the center of our world is occupied by our *contact with others*.

Contact with others is the primary, most important component of the *center* of the natural world, whose *ground* is the earth and *periphery* the sky. Contact with others is the very center of our world, giving it not only its ownmost content, but also its main meaning, perhaps even *all* its meaning. It is contact with others that forms the environment proper in which human beings live; our sensory contact with the present reality, our perception, derives its primary significance from bestowing credibility on the reality of others and their presence together with us in the world. The opposite is also true: our sensory contact, our perception, is fundamentally aimed at the sphere of people, not the sphere of things. The entire structure of our space is *human*, from the ground up, for though its entire central and centered structure comes from *me*, it ends in *you*, the other, who is closer to us than we are to ourselves, the *true object* of our fundamentally non-objective view, of our actions, our accommodating orientation, our conversation. Oriented perspective originates from me and terminates in the present object; the present object, the *here* where I actually am, need not be a second I, a second person, but in that case it is less than full, unfulfilled. The object proper is never an it, she, or he, but *you*. You is always a near object, an object within reach; it is the one *with whom* we speak, never the one *about whom* we speak. In this contact, in the mirror of the other, for the first time, embryonically, we *find* ourselves, seeing and experiencing ourselves in the other's reactions, in the other's behavior toward us, which we can see directly. And this structure of the other, closer to us than we are to ourselves, and in the same measure close to themselves through us, is the ground from which the most important part of the drama of life arises. Through this mutual bond, people are connected and relate to one another. Even their biological relations are unthinkable without it. It is this *human* environment in which people grow up and learn to live before they live among things. Not to ignore the existence of orphans and those tossed aside by society, but their case is an anomaly against the backdrop of normality. In the absence of any close human contact *at all*, human life would be physically impossible. Yet this only serves to confirm that life without the other would have no meaning, which is to say, every significance that is constructed or finds resonance in our life is oriented toward contact with others. This follows from what we said earlier: the foundational layer of our experience, sensory perception, is teleologically oriented toward reflecting and expressing the presence of the other. Things vs. others is the original polarity, with things being the deficient mode, that in which *no*-thing except itself appears. Likewise our own experience, although private to begin with, becomes objective through others. The world becomes a real world, something *all*-embracing, by the very fact that my own experience is included in the experience of all others, and by seeing myself a priori only in primordial inclusion among those others who are my objects, so that only with their help and taking the route that leads through them do I arrive at myself.

It is Husserl's profound conviction that the other I, the experience of the other, is nothing but consciousness presenting the other in the mode of actual presence: I can make my *own* life present only once it has already lapsed into the non-present, into the past. If there is therefore such a thing as the presenting of an actual psyche, it can only be the psyche of *the other*.[11] Perhaps, however, the expression *presenting*, or *making present*, needs to be clarified. It is not a matter of reproducing, but of direct perception; I understand myself simply as the object of a significative situation in which the active bearer, the cause, is someone else. A child does not project *its* feelings onto the mother, but experiences her smiles and caresses as a meaningful situation in which both partners are included, under the schema of one sending, one receiving. Originally, we do not have our own lived experience that we can project into the expressive appearances of the other. What we have, rather, is an *overall situation* with poles of its own, interpreted, as in a mirror, from the viewpoint of both participants. Thus at first we do not understand either ourselves or the other as an *I*, but rather as two active *components of a situation*. The realization that the other is a real *I* in the same sense as myself, that they experience, feel, think, that they have an interior of their own, is a *discovery* that requires a long journey. The primordial starting point is a bipolar significative situation, in which two analogous corporeal poles play complementary roles. As an example, take the understanding of a word's meaning: this is possible only in a speech situation in which the child *accepts* what the other *gives*; thus a meaning, once understood, is already and always a meaning transmitted by others, not solipsistically created by me. In the same way, a threat, a frown, a shout is always a bipolar situation in which I see myself as the object and, thus, the other as the originator. This is the reason why we naturally—and rightly—attribute meaning first not to ourselves, but to others, as its transmitters and active authors.

Human life, in its central dimension, is a seeking and discovering of the other within oneself and of oneself within the other. The whole drama of human life is a question of whether what is implicitly contained in that primordial, purely situational contact will or will not be discovered: the interior concealed behind all that manifests itself. The other and the I manifest themselves in the unity of a meaningful situation. The other and the I, insofar as we manifest ourselves, are both objects, something I have before me. What remains hidden is that these objects can appear only because there is an I prior to the objective I of both myself and the other—and because this *primordial I* intends the *other primordial I* as well.

Yet what we have here is not only a dual object, not only two things, but also a relationship and a bond between them. The relationship between a mother and a child is more intimate than merely the mutual presence of two things. The emotion that binds them springs from a depth that is pre-objective, joining two beings, the life of one contained in the life of the other. Each participant has themselves in the other, but in such a way that they have more than simply their own solitude, which always signifies an intention, a lack of fulfillment, an absence, a longing.

Thus, every human, from the onset of life, is immersed, rooted, mainly in the other. This rootedness in the other mediates all our other relationships. Primordially, the other is the one who attends to our *needs* before we can, and before we start attending to them as well.[12] The other acts to ensure that we are fulfilled, that somehow or other we are always already at our goal despite all our individual needs and shortcomings. The other shields us from these shortcomings. *The other*—and in the case of natural and necessary mutual bonding, *the others*—is what shields us, allowing the earth to become the earth for me, the sky the sky—others are our original *home*.

And yet home, the putting-down of roots, is not possible on our own. Home is the place where roots are put down into things, i.e., where needs are met, and this happens through people. But what is needed must be *secured*, obtained, and that happens at home only in part—the securing of needs, labor, takes place *outside* the home, in the workplace, in the realm of objectivity. This objective reality differs with historical and social circumstances; there are differences between what must be managed and what can be lived with, and each provider is at the mercy of different forces. For hunters, this realm is in essence a battle; for farmers, labor and battle are distinct, and they must adapt to the grand cycle of astrobiology; for modern-day humans, it is the mechanized operation of manufacturing and bureaucratic processes. Each of these realms forms and defines people, embedding them in their roles, making what they do who they are. Each realm objectifies humans in a particular way. And each introduces a relation among people as participants in the same exterior, processing the same exterior, aiding or detracting, competing or combining, in differing proportions. Thus our relation to the things in which we root ourselves, in order to get on with the objective situation of life, conditions also our relations to people. Our innermost circle is an anchoring in people, made possible by an anchoring in things as the condition for life as such. Yet that in turn is made possible by assuming an *external* relation to people as the condition of this condition. Ultimately, then, life is grounded in *power relations*, relations of coordination and subordination in solidarity and opposition. Power relations presuppose an external view of humans as a force that is either a helper or an obstacle in our access to the things that are the material means of life. Yet this external relation to *others*, as a force both conditioning and conditioned (in our work and our needs), is by its nature inseparable from our relation to our *own* life through death, in the same way that our original putting-down of roots presupposes a relation to our own life through another. Power relations are no less an internal view of humanity than primordial love—albeit from the other side of life: life is simultaneously an infinite whole, capable of spreading and of renewing itself as a whole in every limb, ever anew. And yet at the same time every limb is a finite individual being that must relate to its own end and live this end, either by deflecting and avoiding it, or by way of active threat, which in essence, in practical terms, means the threatening of oneself by the other, which demands a parallel threatening of the other by oneself.

Thus, at the center of the world, in the realm of the near, we have three basic types of human relations: the infinite relation to oneself through the other, which leads to a view of one's own being as an infinite life; the relation to oneself and to others as finite *forces*, which is the relation that makes possible power, social organization, work discipline, and property relations; and in between, the relation to oneself as a needful being (that is, also finite but *living* amid finiteness) through the nourishing earth, which is the relation in which work, with all its mediated components, and the organization of satisfying needs is rooted. The work of life through life; the work of life bound by itself to the earth and the sky; the work of life through death. In the last, life regards itself as free even with respect to itself; in the second, life sees itself as dependent for its continuation on the sky and the earth, as bound, unfree; in the first, life regards itself as free even with respect to death, as infinite both in spite of all its dependence and in its freedom with respect to itself.

The other, then (and, consequently, also we ourselves), is initially the one in whom and through whom we first put down roots. Though arising from a deep mutuality, this rooting is not yet a revelation of the other in their essence. On the contrary, the other is *hidden* in their function and role, and likewise we ourselves, putting down roots into the nourishing earth, collaborating in the work of satisfying needs, undertake various roles with which, on a surface level, we merge. The needful being, while working in order to satisfy their needs, lives permanently in the shackles of life, that is, in the shackles of death overcome and postponed, but lives *turned away from* this ever-present, ever-possible end. It is a life in shackles: on the one hand, dependent on the nourishing earth, and on the other, in servitude to the powerful, those who organize life and determine the satisfying of needs. In this regard, every being with needs is an objectified being who lives in the world as a thing among things.

In a deeper sense, however, we are never things, as already testified to by the priority of putting down roots in others, which is possible only by virtue of the fact that humans are by origin something beyond their own particular center, something transcending their own self-contained person, their corporeality and needfulness. (As are animals, but only out of instinctive necessity, whereas in humans there is always an element of free consent; we *co*-create this relationship with others and thus are simultaneously identical to and at a remove from it; as a result, we are able to understand, to *see*, this infinity in the other.) Even where I am living my role and in others see only their role, there is a dissatisfaction, a seeking for a deeper relation, that comes with this symmetry. Dissatisfaction is the rejection of every objective finite form. It is an emotional and practical detaching from finitude, it is the will to risk, to the death of everything definite. Yet even this will to overcome is something I can be only through the other; only when the other, who is my object, performs the same movement as I do, but in such a way that I am an object for them in the same way as they are for me. This overcoming of finite form may take place through struggle; in fact it requires the other as the reality of a threat. Hegel analyzed this situation dialectically as a struggle to the death.[13] Yet no positive awareness of the self comes of it, since the other here is as destructive and negative as I am. A deeper overcoming of finitude, which would in contrast have positive content, takes place where I invest my life in the other, not undergoing a movement of return from them to myself, but surrendering myself to them; I constitute myself by creating the other, just as they create me, and at no stage in this process of overcoming is there not a path from one to the other and back. In struggle, I gain no greater self-awareness than the negative one that I am not any thing and, in general, not any objectivity; in surrender, I gain awareness of myself as *essentially infinite*, reproducing the whole in every part, producing another being outside of myself, one which is non-objective rather than merely finite. I stimulate the other to the same movement, and they in turn remain free and non-objective by doing the same for their own other, me. I manifest my not being finite by giving up my finite being, giving it entirely to the other, who returns to me their own, in which mine is contained.

At the center of our world, then, the aim is to move from the merely given life to the manifestation of a genuine life, and this is achieved by the movement of shaking off the objective rootedness and alienation that are inherent in a role, in objectification—a movement that is at first purely negative, shaking loose our attachment to life, freeing us with no further revelations, and then positive, manifesting what is essential—as universal life, bringing forth everything in everything, inciting life in the other, transcending ourselves in the direction of the other and then, in turn, with them, toward infinity.

The fundamental proto-relations at the center of the world have a clear relationship not only to the basic components of the world, but also to the originally temporal, and thus historical, nature of human existence. The relation of anchoring is a relation of the past, a relation to what is always already here; it is a penetration through human structures to the earth and the sky, to the primordial whole, and its domain is therefore horizontal; it is a primordial awareness and originally an overall self-relating similar to mood, as in "how we are," "how we feel." Attending to needs, undertaking and fulfilling a role, identifying with a role—all these are in close relation to the present, to givenness and its objectification. The confrontation with finitude, with death and nothingness, shakes every role, even though originally associated with one role in particular—that of the warrior. This role has the unique quality of shifting a person to the periphery of humanity, out of the warmth of everyday being at home into the freezing cold of non-being. Yet in this confrontation, a disconnect occurs between the person and the role. An urgent question is posed here, a question that cannot be answered by the social consequences of the threat represented by the organization of power, the structuring of humanity as a constellation of forces. The *view of the whole* still remains, answering the question that deflated the role and brought about freedom, but failed to fill that freedom with substance and give it definition.

So human life in relation to others has certain basic forms that are simultaneously dimensions of the world and of time. Before all doing, orienting, and acting, there must first be *an anchoring*, a rooting, that takes place in the dimension of passivity, of surrender. What opens here above all is the whole that is prior to the parts, fundamentally inexhaustible, and our relation to it, or rather, its relation to us in terms of affect, the type of mood it puts us in, *the way* we are exposed to it, how we are open and sensitive to it—here, most originally present, is that unindividuated component of the world which never entirely breaks through to the light. That it is all closely related to one dimension of personal life is obvious: the whole world may be a mother's lap; it may be a warm, cheerful, affectionate, safe chamber, or the cosmic winds may blow through it with their icy, deadening breath, and both are closely related to whether or not someone in the world smiles out of the world at us and greets us with goodwill. The possibility of life is the possibility of this warmth, this reciprocated smile, this primordial acceptance into protection, which is the placing of our own being into the hands of another, a nearness that assumes nothing alien or strange despite difference. That means life is possible only as a state of *already* entering into the warmth that has been prepared, in the passivity of being penetrated by *acceptance*, and therefore only on the basis of a past that enables us to drop anchor and put down roots.

This vital warmth is not just a "feeling," allowing life to unfold in such a way that it may someday become a life of activity, something that we personally take over and perform for ourselves. It is also a repetition, in which the vital or life-sustaining warmth that we originally experienced with our mother is now experienced from a romantic partner, in a relationship that is all the more alive and necessary in proportion to how much our "personal" life was mechanized and "depersonalized" beforehand, sometimes to the point of complete self-absence (i.e., a total losing of ourselves into the presence of things). In the eyes of the other, who is also a person awakening from the concealment of the instrumental body, I begin to live anew, to feel my life, in every way that up until then had escaped me, present but hidden—yet without life becoming an object, detached from me and placed before me; instead taking on a novel attractiveness and intensity, while losing none of its impenetrable quality, its unsounded depths and untouchable mystery, losing none of the *distance* that indicates it to be the past. In an erotic relation, I am given to myself not in what I make myself, what I strive for, what I do, but in what I am, that is, what I *already* am— therein lies the passivity, inseparable from the charm, the magic, of this entire realm. Life is *returned* to me, given back—in that here again, a past trait is "repeated," something that was never really actual is directly present as a gift, something given to us, aimed at us, which we could never give to ourselves, arrange, procure *ourselves*. This is why the immediacy of discovery is integral to the authenticity of the erotic—any manipulation, any effort to gain control of it inevitably violates it, pollutes it, makes it ordinary, objectified, "dirty."

If putting down roots is a matter of the past—not of the past that has passed, but the past that is always unavoidably with us—then it must manifest itself in a state of constant exposure to those powers into which our original rooting has enabled us to grow. Yet even this exposure is not solitude with the earth and the sky, for the earth is always the earth of people because it is the *nourishing* earth. The earth wants to be forced into its nourishing role, and that is a matter of *shared* participation, *shared* work, *shared* consumption. Here the other is an indispensable co-participating force, a particularity, a thing among other things, as I too am in this realm. And because the realm of how things are done, in which humans are interchangeable, stems from doing, from dealing with the fragmented state of powers in each individual circumstance, on each occasion, it is therefore the realm of the present, of the function and the role. Every "intervention" or "trick," all technical subject matter, essentially boils down to *how it is enacted*, i.e., in the present, in the "here." To carry out these actions means to identify with them, being swept up in the constant nearness of living moment to moment, and from those moments piecing together the whole, a "life program" within which there is "time to . . ." Likewise, the objectivity and objectification of this entire sphere is impossible except in a specific type of human relations, as nothing here is mere nature, instinct, a ready-made construction; rather, everything is *traditionality*. This traditionality, however, is not related to the past, but is the necessary presence of others, their *partnership* with me. They are here in the tools, the equipment, I use; if they are actually with me, they are the presence of utility, as in their absence they are the utility of presence, and I myself am the same for them. *This* realm of shared being, however, is not merely an indifferent coexistence, as when we are together with tools, equipment, machinery, etc. There is always at least a hidden "against" that comes into play. Co-participants are always in some sense rivals, even if they help one another, share among themselves, etc. Individual centers, in their "personal" interest (meaning the most general interest on which everyone agrees), turn out to be another set of forces, fragmented realities in constant motion, running up against, influencing, obstructing one another, *now* and time and time *again*. This shared presence of one with the other is at the same time a presence *against each other*; rather than seeking destruction, though, this against-each-other seeks only subordination and exploitation of the other. The entire realm is one of diffusion, atomization. Yet atoms in "against" mode orient themselves toward equalization with one another, arriving at the same level of energy. This leads to the paradox of atomicity based in relation to others, a repetition of the same without continuity. It is through this repetition of the same, same actions, same procedures, that life goes on, that it is always here anew and able to repeat the same again—the "reproduction," individually and as a species, of the same life.

That the third fundamental relation to the other is also temporal follows from its relation to the future, to non-being, to death (this relation being given and present in the form of things and forces). A free relation is always necessarily a relation of mutual threat—against oneself by the other, and against the other by oneself. The fact that this relation is an individualizing one, not splintering the self into atoms but deepening it into a more profound selfhood that rejects "the norm," does not mean we can conclude that it does not include the other; the other is absent only as *a norm of oneself*, as an exterior imposing itself on an interior. The other is here precisely as this possible individuality, on the hearing end of a silent, unaddressed appeal, and as a selfhood alienated in those necessary forms of life lived in a function, diffused throughout those functions and their objective meaning. Every free relation comes in with the aim of disrupting this objective diffusion, threatening both the diffusion and itself. Every free relation is necessarily a conflict. Free life is necessarily a struggle. Struggle, in the most primordial sense, as something so indispensable that life would be unthinkable without it, does not emerge from functioning life and its instincts, from the necessity of reproduction of life, from its constant state of returning to itself, but rather from the fact that life is not merely a state of persistence, but already exists in the instinctively vital sphere as a project of itself. Understood in this way, struggle is a form of self-reproduction, part and parcel of the earthliness of life, of its relation to the nourishing earth, of which all life is a part. Eventually this struggle may be replaced by something different, which is capable of accomplishing the project of self-reproduction more fully and effectively by transposing it to human means and possibilities. But that does not make struggle in the deeper sense futile. *Struggle is necessary as the struggle of awakening.* Struggle in this sense is not primarily an attack, but a *provocation to counterattack*, to repression, obliteration. Only defense against this initial repression, against a power only now becoming what it is, leads to *revolt*. Revolt need not manifest always as physical violence; here violence is a secondary phenomenon, a consequence, albeit closely tied to the fact that *awakening is always finite*. Awakening is a *renewal*, an authentic unveiling of life, not in its past depth and passive givenness as a gift, but in the appeal to take on, to claim as our ultimate destiny, what cannot be escaped, what inescapably *comes*, but therefore is precisely what does not allow us to squander ourselves, to diffuse ourselves in turning away from ourselves.

One could say that struggle and the practice of struggle, in the external sense, offer an opportunity for humans to grasp and understand struggle in the true, profound sense of the word. Struggle in this second sense is first of all the conquest of what is deadening within oneself, of distraction into repeated moments of alienating presence (into an exterior always present, always surrounding us). Being deadened is death that has taken hold of our life behind our backs and emptied it under the pretext of making it last, repeating its moments. Paradoxically, this deadness can be conquered only by claiming mortality, by claiming the very thing deadness seeks to escape and yet through doing so repeatedly confirms. There is no other way to come to terms with and overcome this escapism except by making this claim. Once harnessed, the power of this claim is such that life is no longer an eternal recurrence, an ongoing repetition of always the same. In every recurrence, what endures is only what can be *seen*, viewed, observed, but not lived, not what we can be. *To be* means to be in absolute uniqueness, exposed to the absolute threat. A threat is absolute when it threatens *everything*, when *nothing* remains beyond the threat. Under absolute threat, however, the earth has summoned a courage far beyond itself, surrendering itself to the abyss. It is not the firm *hedos asphales aiei*, the "ever-unshakeable seat,"[14] that it originally presents itself to be. There "is" something here other than the play of its appearances and repetitions, something wholly other than all that is.

This is why the earth and the sky are, but only humans *exist*. Only through humans is it possible that all there is, the entire universal whole, is a whole, and that it has a terminus, a telos, an end. That also means it is all transcended, called into doubt; a question is posed to it. Yet to pose a question to the earth and the sky means to sacrifice oneself so that something other can "be," so that the earth and the sky may not only reveal themselves, but also become the manifestation of something "higher." This primordial turn is the only means by which something "higher" is even possible. Only if humans are capable of it, only if it takes place within them, does this "higher" exist. It can never be "objectively" proven and demonstrated precisely because it is higher in comparison to the objective, to the primordial, to "the whole."

In *claiming* finitude, what takes place is something other than a proclamation of nothingness and nihilism. What takes place is the overcoming of finitude, a true overcoming in the sense of *sublation, i.e., both abolishing and preserving*. Life is capable not only of prolonging itself through self-renunciation, but also of substantiating itself through self-surrender. It succeeds in proclaiming itself not as the highest power, but as a powerlessness that surrenders itself to the power of the highest, primordial meaning. Only here does life gain the negative strength of self-dedication, self-surrender. To surrender oneself, however, a living being needs an other to surrender to. The power of the transubstantiation of a life is the power of a new love, a love that surrenders to others without condition. In this love alone is selfhood itself without keeping the other in a state of self-renunciation. Only here is the distraction of atomized life replaced by an inner continuity for which the other is not alien but a living I, not only abstractly, as a fiction I am not, but rooted in the power of my own self-surrender—similarly as in biological, life-sustaining love, but now free, unconfined, universal. This is not love as sympathy, as sharing in a fate of the same suffering, but a sharing of the same glory, the same victory—victory over self-renouncing self-centeredness. Biological love is merely an incomplete and inconsistent metaphor for this true and ultimate love.

So we see that the fundamental relations to the world are also temporal relations, i.e., *movements*—movements through which we *encounter* the other, our neighbor. The natural world, the world in which human beings live their unfinished, episodic day, is from the outset an apparent whole, not open to us like a theater, where we sit looking on and the director lets us take control, but rather a whole *in which* we are always like an embedded component that is never permitted to stand above it and never will. All our consciousness of the whole is therefore primordial; we can never reduce it to an objective perspective and place ourselves in front of and above it. At the same time, it is the whole within which we carry out our own life's movement, which as a movement within the whole is related to the whole—therefore this movement is never "absolute," but rather a movement of standpoint—a movement that sees the whole from within itself and sees itself against the backdrop of the whole, therefore a movement that is a continuum of perspectives, with all paths from it leading only to more perspectives, never out of them. This is just another way of stating the fact of corporeality, which is the framework within which this movement and all its orientation take place. The powers within which this movement unfolds are the referents of this movement. Its character as movement is revealed in the fact that it takes place in the modalities of anchoring, self-renouncing self-prolongation, and self-threatening self-acquisition, all of which are, throughout, temporal modalities and related to an other. Thus, ultimately, in the process of self-acquisition, the acquisition of the other in oneself and of oneself in the other also takes place, under the condition of the ultimate self-transcending movement of declaring our finitude.

4

In the preceding, we have tried to show that the primordial world of our pre-theoretical life is originally a world in which we *move*, in which we are active, not a world that we discover and observe. The world and human beings are *in mutual movement*—the world includes us in such a way that together with others we can carry out within it *the movement of anchoring, self-renunciation through self-prolongation, and self-finding through self-surrender*. This movement is movement in the most original, strongest sense of the word; every one of *our* "physical movements" is in fact part of the all-encompassing overall movement that we ourselves are—our movements are fundamentally the movements of a "subject body," or are indelibly marked by that body in their meaning—and likewise all givenness is part of an "orientation" whose whole essence is corporeal, and so it too can be designated as movement. Our birth is a movement, our acceptance, our encounter with things through perceptions, our instinctive reactions, our self-reproduction in dependence on others, as well as in our own feats, in work. Our parting with our original home on reaching adulthood is movement, as is the attempt to rediscover our own life in physical love, the return to a home of our own, and other typical recurring movements. Work and struggle are movement, struggle revealing within us a dimension in which it is possible to renounce self-renunciation—movement, then, is that in which, ultimately, we can encounter ourselves and others not as a mere thing, but as a living self-transcending I, reaching beyond itself, as opposed to an I acquiring a lifeless infinity of repetition.

All space and all that fills it, the states and transitions that we observe within it, are originally referents of our primordial movement; they have meaning only in correlation to it, and are open to us only because the movement of a being that is not worldless but has a world cannot simply *take place*, cannot be merely a gradual unfolding of a state, but must be *performed*, and so this movement has its own real where from/where to, its own in-the-midst-of, its own growth, its own encounters.

The natural world is a world of movement; the key to it is *movement in the world*, the movement of a worldly being. But that now gives us at least the start of an answer to how the natural world can collapse into its exact opposite. Indeed, we see that in the movement of a worldly being there is unavoidably a phase or mode whose nature lies in turning life against itself: in self-prolongation through self-renunciation, in the focus on things, and in the loss of self through distraction amid these things.

In *Crisis*, Husserl showed us how a process of objectification inevitably follows from the everyday practice of human life and its handling of things, an objectification that leads first to the origin of measuring practices, of prescriptions and measures, then to the rise of geometry as the *art* of objectification; how, next, the objectification and rationalization of individual provinces of successful mathematization little by little penetrate every branch of reality, setting the task of an endless praxis of rationalizing and objectifying; the emerging ideal of modern science and its resultant consequence—technoscience—do not manipulate individual objects, but rather seek to manipulate reality in the broadest possible sense. This rationalizing, objectifying praxis, this art, is then understood as access to true reality itself, as it lacks a rear-facing view of the life it grew out of, being wholly absorbed, fascinated, with the mathematically idealized objects in front of it, which it can use to orient itself, employing its skills to analyze them and develop methods for calculated control over them—and so it is that human life becomes entangled in the nets of its own creation.[15]

The objectification Husserl traced as a fundamental development for human beings, an integral component of human history, must therefore be connected to a fundamental movement of human existence. Husserl himself does not do so, as the problem of the overall movement that is human life in the world is absent from his philosophical analyses. For that same reason, though for Husserl the advance of objectification is in harmony with the principle of the immobilizing of movement (which objectified being is everywhere full of), it is hard to grasp why—and how a gradual loss of the world goes hand in hand with that (given that the world as an integral primordial whole is inseparably linked with that vital movement). Husserl merely revealed that the method technoscience uses to interpret the objectification it performs is perverted, and that objectification in fact takes place on the ground of the natural world, rather than the natural world taking place on the ground of the objective entities ostensibly revealed by the technoscience behind it; likewise he established that objectification is a movement whose meaning is inseparable from shared being with others in a world where we have to communicate and cooperate, finding connections and intermediate links among and for ourselves.

It was Heidegger who revealed the movement of self-renunciation through self-prolongation and the movement of self-acquisition through self-surrender. Yet, because the two movements stand in sharp opposition for him, involving two fundamentally differing conceptions of the being of what is (one metaphysically timeless, the other historical), and given that for him this conception is not a human creation, but a primordial mode of openness in which humans already inevitably move, Heidegger views the objectification of metaphysics as not merely an incorrect, because incomplete, self-interpretation of life, but a particular metaphysical fate to which we have fallen victim, a danger we must outlast. There can be no mediating between the two. Although he emphasizes that the movement of self-renunciation is necessary, he does not analyze the ultimate foundation of this necessity: corporeality, the naturalness of the human being. Husserl, with his analyses of the body and bodily movement, came much closer to revealing this naturalness. Also, his emphasis on the interpenetration of human coexistence, on intersubjectivity as the dimension without which we cannot grasp the movement of human existence in its proper sense, points to one direction in which we may extend the analysis of self-acquisition through self-surrender.

In the preceding, we have attempted to outline how it might be possible to unpack the entire problematic of the natural world and its objectification; in doing so, we have sought to avoid lapsing either into a subjectivism that at bottom views humankind as the absolute itself (meaning humans are regarded as internally infinite beings), or into the irrationalism of the primordial being, with the meaning of humanness left at its mercy. In the first case, we would need to deepen the movement of existence in the world into a movement by which the world is first created—but the world, as we have seen, is always already primordial, as we have presented above. In the second case, this movement would have no human closure, no practical value, but would be merely a dialogue between the highest and the earth, mediated by humans—and meanwhile what a human is and can be to another would be completely left out of the process.

* * *

Objectification—Husserl does not deny its legitimacy, but he is opposed to its metaphysical hypostatization, for which mathematically conceived objectivity *is* reality, and the *sole* one at that.

In contrast, Husserl proposes his *absolute subjectivity* as the reality that includes objectification and is the ground from which it develops.

Yet if not only subjectivity exists, but also the world, with equal absoluteness, then objectification must really be a process of apprehending the world "in itself"—mathematics, laws, structure will be the poles toward which the experiences of all subjects converge. On the other hand, *that toward which subjects converge* cannot exist in itself. Since these are relations requiring termini, it is inconceivable.

And yet there *are* mathematical laws no less than, for example, there are limits: a limit conditions the process of approaching a limit, and in that sense it *is*. Limits are the conditions of possibility for all that converges toward them—i.e., they are *causal* laws; yet their objectivity is not identical with any approximation that our objectification could achieve.

On the other hand, these laws, this purely objective *structure* of the world, cannot be regarded merely as the limits of constitutive acts in the transcendental ego, or in a transcendental intersubjectivity. If we must accept the thesis of the primordial world as a whole within which the subject is always integrated and which always transcends the subject with its *meaning of the whole* (and is guaranteed simultaneously with the cogito); if *subject-transcendence* is guaranteed by the *presentational immanence* of the whole in the same way as the subject-immanence of a reflected experience, then we cannot deny that objectivity in itself has meaning.

However, nothing can be posited as being "in itself" that is merely an abstraction from subjectivity—for example, visual objects stripped of certain so-called primary qualities, as they are in mechanistic materialism. No perspective or perspectival component is possible in itself.

Therefore what is "in itself" can be only an analog of transcendental subjectivity, *sleeping monads* or dynamic unities, perhaps ephemeral. Not even that which converges toward the limit of absolute objectivity can exist by itself alone (and still less can some component of it); nor, for that matter, can the limit. Limits and converging aspects are correlative, and converging aspects cannot be confined to transcendental subjects alone, but must also be represented by "bare monads."

Husserl's protest against absolutization, against the hypostatization of objectification, is thus not wholly tenable. We must resort to a metaphysical conception of objectification. Yet in doing so we cannot objectify either mere perspectival givens, as if they did not imply a perspective (i.e., a subject), or pure structural limits, which are eo ipso mere forms (by their very meaning, they cannot exist in themselves). Instead we must resort to a monadology that will recognize not only transcendental subjects, but bare and sleeping monads as well.

Notes

1   The crisis of the mechanistic view comes about in connection with the development of modern physics—in the confrontation of this development with the positivist conception of knowledge as merely an exact description of empirical reality that fundamentally does not transcend it. The mechanistic

worldview in its classical form is a combination of corpuscular theory with Newton's absolute space and time: these are the main representatives of the "things in themselves" of mechanistic metaphysics. Dynamics and the theory of gravitation, these two non-identical theories of force, corpuscular theory combined with the theory of forces residing in material elements, the mechanics of points, rigid bodies, perfect fluids, the theory of internal friction, the theory of elasticity, and analytical mechanics have all since joined these ideas. Celestial mechanics is the grand application of them.

The development of other branches of physics, no less mathematical but independent of the corpuscular conceptions of classical mechanics (that is, of their "metaphysical" concepts of substance) and of the concept of mutual interaction (see the second law of thermodynamics), leads then to the quest for a unitary method in the physical disciplines, and for their interdependence and mutual deducibility. Thus, for example, thermodynamics, in its generalized form as energetics, seeks to establish itself as a universal science, free of "metaphysical" concepts and models. (That the concept of energy is itself substantive, which is to say conservative, escaped the notice of proponents of energism.) In addition to classical mechanics, optics and the theory of electromagnetism established themselves without corpuscular concepts. While corpuscular concepts celebrated their entry into thermodynamics with the kinetic theory of heat, the development of that theory in statistical mechanics again took the path of unrepresentable abstractions. Classical ideas about the motion of material bodies in absolute space and time then ran up against the Michelson–Morley experiment [Albert A. Michelson and Edward W. Morley, "On the Relative Motion of the Earth and the Luminiferous Ether," *American Journal of Science* 34, no. 203 (November 1887): 333–45. Ed.), while classical notions about the continuity of the process of electromagnetic wave propagation ran up against the puzzle of energy distribution in the black-body spectrum; this led to an acute crisis of the mechanistic worldview. On the development and crisis of physics in the nineteenth century, see Olivier Costa de Beauregard, *La notion de temps: équivalence avec l'espace* (Paris: Hermann, 1963), 17–28.

2   Alfred North Whitehead, *Science and the Modern World* (New York: Macmillan Company, 1925), 1–20 (Ed.).

3   Edwin Arthur Burtt, *The Metaphysical Foundations of Modern Physical Science: A Historical and Critical Essay* (London: Kegan Paul; New York: Harcourt, Brace, 1924), 303ff. A second issue of the book, in 1932, by Columbia University, in New York, bore the title *The Metaphysics of Sir Isaac Newton: An Essay on the Metaphysical Foundations of Modern Science*; later it was published under the abridged title *The Metaphysical Foundations of Modern Science* (Ed.).

4   Edmund Husserl, *Die Krisis der europäischen Wissenschaften und die transzendentale Phänomenologie*, in *Husserliana*, vol. 6, ed. Walter Biemel (The Hague: Martinus Nijhoff, 1954), 48–54 (Ed.).

5   Alexandre Koyré, *From the Closed World to the Infinite Universe* (Baltimore, MD: Johns Hopkins University Press, 1957), 28–99 (Ed.).

6   Martin Heidegger, *Die Frage nach der Technik*, in *Die Technik und die Kehre* (Pfullingen: Neske, 1962), 5–36 (Ed.).

7   Gottfried Wilhelm Leibniz, *Discours de métaphysique* (1686), § XIII (Ed.).

8   In the author's typewritten manuscript, corrected by Patočka's hand, there is an insertion here that reads, "in [Ernst] Mach, [Richard] Avenarius, B. Russell, etc." (Ed.).

9   "simple things," i.e., those which the mind is incapable of subdividing into a larger number of clearly identified things. See René Descartes, "Regulae ad directionem ingenii," in *Oeuvres de Descartes*, vol. 10, ed. Charles Adam and Paul Tannery (Paris: Léopold Cerf, 1913), 419 (Ed.).

10 See the critique of "neutral monism" according to Arthur O. Lovejoy et al. in Raymond Ruyer, *La conscience et le corps* (Paris: Félix Alcan, 1937), 10–19.

11 Edmund Husserl, *Cartesianische Meditationen und Pariser Vorträge*, in *Husserliana*, vol. 1 (The Hague: Martinus Nijhoff, 1963), 148 (Ed.).

12 At first glance, it would seem to be the same situation in nidicolous animals (the Nesthocker, or "nest squatters," described by Adolf Portmann), although here it is simply a matter of the uterine role reaching completion, coming to an end. There is no extended period of a conscious taking charge of oneself and the world, as there is for humans, where, therefore, *internal contact* is presupposed. For animals, the mere hint of contact is enough; it is not an enduring atmosphere in which an *individuum* is formed, i.e., a being for someone and therefore unique *in the world*.

13 Georg Wilhelm Friedrich Hegel, *Phänomenologie des Geistes*, IV, A, in *Werke*, vol. 3 (Frankfurt am Main: Suhrkamp, 1970), 149 (Ed.).

14 "forever firm ground"—Hesiod, *Theogony*, 2,117, 3,128; see also Plato, *Symposium*, 178b5 (Ed.).

15 Edmund Husserl, *Die Krisis*, 20–54 (Ed.).

CHAPTER SEVEN

What is Phenomenology? (1975)

Translation from the German
by David Charlston[1]

Introduction

With the beginning of this century there arose a new philosophy, one which
attempted to bring about a style of thinking different from all that came
before. As true philosophy, it is not meant to operate in the tradition of
the special sciences, their methods and their familiar lines of enquiry.
Rather, it is meant above all to see through the prevailing prejudices both in
daily life and in natural cognition, and with this perspicuity to work out
both its proper methodology and its original lines of inquiry and to establish
a completely autonomous field of knowledge. In doing so, phenomenology
wants neither to be nor to renew a formal-abstract discipline, but rather, for
all its generality, it wants to be a very concrete discipline. Phenomenology
concedes to positivism that philosophy cannot be an isolated science, and
that there would be no place for it if it wanted to concern itself with
exploring the material structures and lawfulness of things. But
phenomenology is also not an a priori discipline reflecting with logical
formality on presuppositions and conditions of possibility. It does not
want to presuppose even logic but rather seeks to investigate its ground
and basis. Phenomenology does not want to investigate material reality,
but the appearing of everything that appears. Since phenomenology
understands this task as a philosophical and foundational one, it cannot
accept the subordination of the problem of appearance to psychology, which
proceeds as a natural science and is rooted in the natural sciences.
Phenomenology must thematize appearing as such, wherever and however
it may be found; it must owe its procedure only to appearing as such and not
yield to any of the current prejudices about the appearing of what appears,

prejudices that sprouted from the traditions of metaphysics and of the individual sciences.

Accordingly, phenomenology was and still is the most original philosophical direction of this century, one that has made and continues to make the greatest demands: to provide a new grounding for the autonomy of philosophy; to bring about philosophy as a rigorous science; finally to create a universally acknowledged metaphysics; to pose anew the fundamental philosophical problem, the question of being; to trace the whole of metaphysics for the first time back to its ground; and to penetrate this ground, freeing the question of truth from its traditional sclerosis, opening another beginning for the whole of philosophy. That these great ambitions contradict one another in part arises from the fact that the fundamental problematic of phenomenology—the question of the ultimate ground of the appearance of that which appears—received two radically different answers from two great thinkers, even though both were committed to drawing out appearances just as they give themselves from the "things themselves," and to realizing a method which alone is suited to define the subject matter of phenomenology.

Phenomenology would be poor indeed if it were not possible to bridge oppositions between the two fundamental doctrines in a way that uncovers the ground of their difference—indeed phenomenologically—in the things themselves, and if the thing itself could not decide any points of dispute. For this purpose, we must seek in both thinkers the common motives; we must attempt to work out the unifying element behind and beneath their opposition. This unifying approach ought not lead to an eclecticism, but rather to a critical response to both doctrines.

In what sense does the more recent phenomenological doctrine follow through on motives that had been abandoned in the older doctrine? In what sense can adhering to the older doctrine on certain positions illuminate the difficulties of the more recent doctrine? These are examples of some of the lines of inquiry to be attempted here. But above all, the present attempt seeks to renew the effort to get "to the things themselves."[2] We shall attempt actually to begin with things just as they show themselves and as they appear, and to remain with this self-showing without succumbing to speculation.

Husserl's late work *Crisis*[3] has shown that science and traditional metaphysical philosophy start out from constructed concepts and never encounter anything like pure, unrefracted experience. What defines the approach of the phenomenological method is not the phenomenological reduction but rather this unveiling of the *modus procedendi* of science and traditional philosophy. When construction is unveiled as the way of proceeding in the disciplines that use mathematical projection and experiment, an almost self-evident task follows: to return, regressively questioning and critiquing, to the genuinely original experience upon which every construction must ultimately rest.

This task is not a purely reflexive one, as Husserl thought when he took the primordial "givenness" of the present thing as guaranteed in the intentionality of consciousness. The prejudice that the primordially given could be seized in "immanent perception" is rejected along with the associated method of objective clues. One discovers the self-showing of things by interrogating the appearing things about what allows them to appear as they appear and by attempting, by way of inquiry-driven distinctions, to break through to this ground of what appears.

Of course, the dismantling of constructions can in no sense be carried out without anticipation, without the guidance of a fundamental idea. The diversity of phenomenological projects, the very differences among concrete descriptions and analyses of phenomena, depend upon the guiding idea which directs the great progression of phenomenological work, i.e., upon the progress toward concrete experience. It is clear that one will catch sight of other phenomena if one adheres to intentionality as the ground of the appearance of what appears—that is, to the thought of the primordial binding of all experience to an objective correlate and therefore to the concept of consciousness—than if one begins from the fundamental experience of the relatedness to being and the nihilation that occurs in the ground of Dasein and relinquishes the concept of consciousness and intentionality as the ultimate ground of experience. But it is nevertheless the advance toward the phenomena, their fullness and their interconnection, which then decides the guiding ideas. These must then be tested in their relationship with one another; one must be mindful of where they deviate from one another, where they are in conflict; the sources of the conflict must be considered more exactly. But above all else, one must discern where the streams of original experience and their unimpeded course flow freely and where these have been impeded or even obstructed by the remnants of constructions. Husserl believed that a pure view of phenomena could be obtained with the single procedure of reduction. That was indeed an illusion, for we must inquire time and again into the historical sedimentation of the concepts of being. But the attempt to lay bare the original structures of experience must be undertaken continuously even on a provisional level, for only in this way can one, questioning further, penetrate deeper.

This conquest of construction, initiated in phenomenologically oriented philosophy, is no mere theoretical concern, pertaining only to philosophers in their professional interest.

Construction, as such, is indispensable and not dangerous. Its danger only becomes evident where it is recoined as an abstract ontology, as an understanding of the essence of what is. This, however, as the history of modern science and philosophy testifies, has been taking place for 300 years, and this whole period down to the present day can be designated as a triumph of construction. Again and again, modernity has repeated the foundational process called subject-object division: the mathematical outline of being, the progressive specialization from the point of view of an "objective" structure, and the reduction [*Zurückführung*] of every as yet "non-objective" remnant to an objective ground. Technical civilization is nothing other than the putting to work of this project, which gradually appears self-evident, because it has become important, yes, even indispensable, to life.

We spoke of repeated advances because the procedure was interrupted by interludes of reflection; by the spiritual movement in Germany between 1770 and 1830, by the philosophical turn in the first decades of the present century. Soon enough, however, the triumph of unreflective construction continued and achieved ever new successes.

Reflection becomes ever more difficult because the successes are ever greater. Only today is it possible to see that the most constructivist sciences, having endured crises, are beginning to reflect upon their own constructivist character, and this is a completely new factor which must be regarded as an important step along this path.

Among the reasons which make reflection so difficult: there is no counter position of similar coherence to oppose construction. Wherever practical success is the goal, wherever human beings are to be helped, the starting point is always construction. The "self-evidence" of construction makes those who oppose it, who draw attention to its danger to humanity, seem like malicious enemies of humanity and its supposedly evident aim of "progress."

Perhaps it should be pointed out in this context that today significant attempts are being made to ground scientific and practical methods on a "human-oriented" observation of anthropological matters, i.e., on a fundamentally phenomenological manner of observation. One such field seems to be psychotherapy. The possibility of a similar approach to the problems of education and pedagogy is evident. As a philosophically worked field, theology seems, through all the obfuscations of modern experimentation, to establish itself as a purely theonomic discipline and yet—*contradictio in adiecto*—a discipline legitimated by an appeal to human experience, and accordingly, it seems to establish the possibility of giving back to humanity the fundamental experience of the divine. There might also be occasion to consider a similar critical reflection in the political field and thereby to sketch in a positive way a humanization of the most important arena of human action (not a "humanizing" in the sense of the familiar "ideal of humanity," but rather a phenomenology of doing, action, and creation, including work, following roughly the ideas of Hannah Arendt).

It should perhaps also be remarked: these latter observations may agree with Edmund Husserl in his *Crisis* to the extent that the facts and possibilities suggest that the present crisis of humanity is not curable unless a new science comes into view, whose outlines of being no longer start out from constructions. Admittedly, it is questionable whether today we are already in a position to create this new science, whether the new outline will not be a long time in coming, whether we are not still condemned to remain in the provisional, in the critical preliminary phase. However, as suggested above, there are early signs that indicate a transformation, and even the conflict between phenomenological interpretations and systems seems to show the following: phenomenology cannot be replaced by a constructivist approach, but only by a more deeply phenomenological approach.

What is Phenomenology?

In §7 of *Being and Time*, Heidegger says:

> The expression "phenomenology" signifies primarily a concept of method. It does not characterize the "what" of the objects of philosophical research in terms of their content, but the "how" of such research.[4]
>
> The term "phenomenology" differs in meaning from such expressions as "theology" and the like. Such titles designate the objects of the respective disciplines in terms of their content ... The word "phenomenology" only tells us something about the "how" of the demonstration and treatment of *what* this discipline considers. Science "of" the phenomena means that it grasps its objects *in such a way* that everything about them to be discussed must be directly indicated and directly demonstrated.[5]
>
> As far as content goes, phenomenology is the science of the being of beings—ontology.[6]

This implies: *with regard to its object*, phenomenology is not a new science, but rather, since its fundamental concerns coincide with those of philosophy (which, as ontology, is the oldest science and the origin of all remaining sciences), it is the oldest of all sciences.

Husserl's first sentence in the introduction to *Ideas I* reads as follows:

> Pure phenomenology, the way to which we seek here, and the unique position of which relative to all other sciences we shall characterize and show to be the science fundamental to philosophy, is an essentially new science which, in consequence of its fundamental peculiarity, is remote from natural thinking and therefore only in our day presses toward development.[7]

The "fundamental peculiarity" of this science of "phenomena" is that its phenomena, the same phenomena which also underlie the other sciences, emerge in an attitude that has only recently been defined, an attitude that modifies the sense of the phenomena of these sciences in a determinate way.

Therefore it is really like this: in the case of Husserl, we have an entirely new science with phenomena as its object. In the case of Heidegger, we have a method of that science which is oldest of all with respect to its subject matter. "The fundamental feature," the new attitude, could admittedly be approached just as a method, and then it would rightfully read, "*primarily the method.*" But "primary" would then only amount to "by way of introduction," "functioning as access to the authentic." For Heidegger, "primary" designates the primordial, that upon which everything depends and in which the essence of the thing consists. For Husserl, however, the essential is the acquired ground of the modified phenomena themselves, upon which the *entirely new* science arises. This is, for him, the *proper* theme of phenomenology. Thus, he continues:

> To understand these modifications or, to speak more precisely, to bring about the phenomenological attitude and, by reflecting, to elevate its specific peculiarity and that of the natural attitudes into the scientific consciousness—this is the first and by no means easy task whose demands we must perfectly satisfy.

The first, but not the central task: the center is the ground itself, and thus Husserl adds:

> . . . if we are to achieve the ground of phenomenology and scientifically assure ourselves of the essence proper to phenomenology.[8]

We see here a looming opposition, and, as might be suspected from what has been said already, it will be no easy task to comprehend the scope and background of this opposition. One senses commonalities, yet what clearly emerges in the end is a contrast.

Husserl made inroads toward a pure phenomenology by seeking an appropriate subjective access to his "idea of pure logic." He could not find this in the empirical psychology of his contemporaries. More suitable was Brentano's *Psychology from an Empirical Point of View*, with its idea of the certainty of being and the intentional relation as fundamental characteristics of psychic phenomena (both fundamentally refer back to Descartes; although he never elaborated the idea of intentionality in a subjective direction, this was suggested by him). This, however, was not sufficient to arrive at "elements for a clarification of cognition." Here it was a matter of epistemological—i.e., philosophical—problems, more specifically a matter of philosophical methodology. The discovery of the dynamic character of the intentional relation (intention-fulfillment with the identical relation to the object in question) and its analysis turned this relation into intentionality and intentionality into the essence of the mental [*des Geistigen*]. At the same time, this meant that the dynamic-intentional has a universal meaning: there is intention-fulfillment not only in the domain of individual being, in the sensible, but also in the domain of the ideal, the categorial, and so forth. A philosophical-methodological project thereby became possible which allowed the advantages of empiricism and an "intuitive" rationalism to be

)

united. This project shared with empiricism the direct, intuitive access to phenomena; the attempt to turn the philosophical problematic into an intuitive one resting on direct manifestation [*Aufweisung*]; and an aversion to construction from abstract principles. However, it now became possible, with the help of categorial fulfillment and eidetic intuition, to overcome empiricism's one-sidedness, its adherence to that which is individual and contingent. The same principle of dynamic intention also offered the prospect of a purely structural consideration of everything mental while excluding external influences, above all those of the mathematical projection of nature; for the subject–object relation (*res cogitans–res extensa*) no longer had to be treated causally, but rather it sufficed to conceive and analyze it purely intentionally-structurally. To that end, an elimination of every causal manner of consideration was required, the naturalistic (i.e., Cartesian) one as well as the theological-transcendent one (that Descartes himself employed). The solution was arrived at through a highly astute and original analysis of Descartes's methodological skepticism, which distinguished two independent components in his procedure: a suspension of judgment or bracketing of theses—the so-called *epochē*—a limbo that refrains from decision; and the actual application of doubt. For the purposes of the exclusion of a causal consideration, one does not need to go as far as doubt; the limbo—the exclusion or bracketing—suffices. Of course, this must not be limited to individual theses, but rather must apply to the "general thesis of the natural attitude," that is, the conviction, preceding (instinctively) all individual theses, that the totality of beings exists in an absolute way independently of every thesis. This "general thesis" therefore relates above all else to nature, i.e., to the totality of physical things and processes, upon which in natural succession living things and the mental also depend. If I place this general thesis out of action, then the belief in such an independent being of the world totality and therefore also in everything transcendent to consciousness, is suspended. These transcendent beings can then be "reduced to the purely immanent," for the objective world is not canceled or weakened through doubt, but rather preserved in the form of objective correlates of intentional acts with all their phenomenal character. They now acquire the sense of phenomena, and the subjective acquires the sense of pure phenomena, that is, purified from the objective thesis of being. Appearances form a realm of objects the researcher can thematize in a pure, inner intuition and subject to eidetic abstraction and insight [*Wesenerschauung*] in order to capture their pure essence. In this way, a previously unknown research field is discovered; in each of its fields, it is as infinite as nature; yet it is the field of a wholly different, undreamt-of science, where the meaning of the research as dependent upon the meaning of that which is researched is entirely reversed. For if up until now the research project of "natural science" was directed by the thought of the absolute being of the world and by the dependence of mind, now by contrast the objective is seen and investigated in its non-causal but rather essential-structural dependence upon subjective correlates (that is, in its structural constitution). Instead of comprehending the structure of the universe on the basis of the mathematical-constructivist projection of a *res extensa*, one builds up intuitively (in the sense of intentionality) from the *ego cogito cogitatum*.

With Walter Biemel's publication of the "Five Lectures" as the second volume of *Husserliana*,[9] we know that the thought of this reversal and methodological alteration of sense [i.e., the objective correlates of intentional acts now acquire the sense of phenomena, and the subjective acquires the sense of pure phenomena] in the reduction to pure immanence, an alteration which does not conflict with transcendence in self-givenness, was there earlier than a methodologically mature working out of the reductive procedure.

The *Five Lectures* contain neither the idea of a general thesis nor a clear distinction of *epochē* and skepticism; however there is the thought of a building up of objectivity in pure immanence, that is, constitution.[10] If, then, the *epochē* appears in its purity as an act of freedom capable of suspending all theses regarding beings, then the question naturally arises whether the suspension here characterized is actually carried far enough, so that it would be able to show its full import. Specifically, it becomes clear that the suspending of this suspension prior to the entrance into subjectivity is motivated by something that can have no ground in the *epochē* itself. Husserl says:

> ... with good reason we *limit* the universality of [this *epochē*]. Since if it were as comprehensive as possible—as we are completely free to modify every positing and every judgment and to bracket every objectivity about which a judgment can be made—then no region would be left for unmodified judgments, let alone for science.[11]

The restriction is therefore imposed for the sake of providing a foundation for a science. This science quite clearly bears features of a *positive* science, of a *science of beings* as such. Pure phenomena are admittedly designated as irreal,[12] but they are irreal only insofar as they are devoid of the thesis concerning everything transcendent, that is to say, insofar as they do not belong to the real-transcendent world. The sense of their being is modified; it is no longer being in the world [*Weltsein*]. Nonetheless, *they are*; it makes sense to say of them that they are. The suspension of positing [i.e., of their thesis] stops before them, i.e., precisely the justification to posit them as being is explicitly declared and emphasized. They are not real, but not all beings need to be real, i.e., dependent upon the world. On the contrary, we are poised to discover a mode of being of beings [*Seinsweise des Seienden*] which are neither real nor ideal—and yet, they are beings all the same.

The science of pure phenomena is therefore a science of beings, a positive science. As such, it has an infinite field, one to be cultivated through progressive research, though it is inexhaustible. It even bears an unmistakable characteristic unique to the ideal of individual positive sciences, namely, the accumulation of knowledge through progressive research across the continuity of generations. Indeed, it also bears certain features that show it to be related to the *episteme* of antiquity, namely, absoluteness, the incontrovertibility of the truths established through it. Modern science, by contrast, has an essentially hypothetical character. However, Plato's episteme (and so too Aristotle's) is not a science of beings (beings in our sense are for Plato the objects of *doxa*), but rather one of ideas, which the moderns designated as unreal and non-actual. Husserl's ideal of science is in fact quite clearly informed by its relation to psychology. In the treatise *Philosophy as Rigorous Science*,[13] this philosophy [i.e., the science of pure phenomena] is claimed as the groundwork of a psychology that is scientific in the true sense (and also as the groundwork of a true critique of reason), which, to be sure, must not mean that it is a science *like* psychology. Its relationship to psychology is better conceived of as analogous, *mutatis mutandis*, to that of mathematics to natural science, that is to say as a relationship of one positive science in the modern sense to another, where each science grows and progresses by itself and has its particular object as well as its own characteristic method. For phenomenology, this is the priority of intuition, in the sense of the originality of reflection and eidetic seeing, over the deductive-constructivist procedure that predominates in the mathematical disciplines.

Admittedly there are explanations, both in the treatise *Philosophy as Rigorous Science* as well as in *Ideas I*, that testify that Husserl assigns to phenomenology first the task of investigating the essence of the *being* of the psychic in the form of pure phenomena. While he asserts that one can never approach the essence of the psychic through contingent experience and experimentation, he combats naturalism on the strength of the fundamental difference between judgments concerning the essence of the being of physical things [*des dinglichen Seins*] and those concerning the essence of the psychic: physical things have their identical "nature" in the manifold of their aspects and effects, while the psychic has its essence without existing as identical in the manifold of appearances.

By way of summary, one could perhaps interpret the beginning of the introduction to *Ideas I* as follows: Husserl seeks a new fundamental science of philosophy called pure phenomenology.[14] This new fundamental science, in its systematically rigorous grounding and execution, is the first of all philosophies and the indispensable precondition for every metaphysics and any other philosophy[15] (Husserl understands metaphysics as the science of facts [*Wissenschaft vom Faktum*]). Its first task is to determine in a rigorously scientific way the sense of the modification that phenomena (physical, psychic, historical, etc.) undergo when they become pure phenomena. That is to say, the task is to distinguish the phenomenological attitude from the natural attitude.

But what does it mean to distinguish the phenomenological attitude from the natural attitude? Is the alteration of attitude merely subjective, to be defined through an act of the subject? If that were so, then one would not yet understand the point of this attitude. *With respect to their content* the phenomena themselves remain afterwards what they are. In this they are not modified. What pertains to them, insofar as one can say of it that "it is," remains what it was. What is modified, however, is this "is," the meaning of their being. What is at stake in this attitude, then, is the *meaning of the being* of pure phenomena in comparison to the meaning of the being of what is given in the natural attitude.

The sought-after science (and to seek means to question), then, is on the way toward the *question* of the being of pure phenomena (and with that also toward the question of the being of consciousness and of the object of consciousness). It inquires about being, for the result—which arose in questioning—of the fundamental operations of the *epochē* and reduction is to ascertain how the being of the world and the being of consciousness can be delineated and how they relate to one another. Husserl, however, believed he could achieve this result with a science of the same type as the modern positive sciences, the sciences which always have *a being* as their object, one that they seek to evaluate in their infinite progress over the course of generations and through the continuous accumulation of the results of research.

If one looks at the situation in this way, then what Husserl *asks for* here is certainly something profoundly different from the systematic collection and articulation of experiences on the basis of pure immanence, and accordingly something profoundly different from what he himself *answers*. The Husserlian questions go *toward being* [*Sein*], toward something that determines the fundamental meaning of beings in the mode of the contents of the world and, on the other hand, in the mode of consciousness, while answers make statements in which this meaning is already presupposed and which thus fundamentally cannot further determine this being [*Sein*]. The answers given by the object of the desired science thus fundamentally can*not* answer the questions that arise in the conception of the *epochē* and in the idea of a reduction of worldly beings.

In this way Husserl seeks *one* science and finds *two*. He seeks the fundamental science of philosophy. Metaphysics has long been viewed as such a science. As is generally known, however, metaphysics has fallen into disrepute in modern times because it cannot demonstrate itself to be a positive science in the sense of constant, apodictic progression on the firm ground of a secured object. That toward which Husserl strives coincides to a great extent with what Kant imagined when he spoke of a metaphysics that will be able to come forward as science.[16] Even Kant, in the famous paragraphs of the second Introduction to the *Critique of Pure Reason* where he describes the evolution of a science, measures philosophy by the yardstick of positive science.[17] However, while Kant had logic, mathematics, and mathematical natural science in mind as models, Husserl had a scientific psychology, a science of mind. And while Kant saw the turn to the objective a priori (instead of empirical fumbling about) that must lie ready in the human mind as the foundational move for a science, Husserl finds the decisive act for the grounding of his *philosophical* science in the *epoché* as suspension of all validity of the world, indeed of every objective validity whatsoever. He spoke not so much of metaphysics as science, but rather of a new critique of reason.[18] Pure phenomenology, we see, takes the place of traditional metaphysics.

If that is the case, then it would perhaps be obvious to pose the following problems: does what Husserl imagines as an answer (i.e., as a genuine science of phenomenology) actually suit the fundamental question? And might it be necessary, in order for the answer to properly appear, to ask a suitable question?

Is the *epoché* a stance [*Haltung*] that is meant to serve as an introduction into the realm of pure phenomena, and thereby something with an as yet unexamined meaning of being; or is it in essence an act that, conducted in its full universality, allows our gaze to be conducted away from beings in general and toward being—and not merely toward the being of "pure phenomena," but rather toward the meaning of being in general?

And then again, does one obtain a being whose mode of being is different from that of the *res* (for the *res cogitans*, too, is still a *res*, even if it lacks the attribute of *extensio*) simply by suspending the thesis of the transcendent in order to be able to view the purely immanent in absolute presence? Is the reflective having of the self something that is given in the original? Is what is glimpsed in this having the essence of the self? Is this reflective having of the self not just then above all to be approached and conceived as the weightiest, the fundamental accomplishment of the subject, when ontic truth is seen as certainty, as a fundamental accomplishment of the "subject"? Has there not become visible at the being commonly designated as "subject" and precisely through the *epoché*, what must necessarily be respected when "subject" has to be grasped in the original: that the "subject" is not only able to re-present *beings*, but prior to that, is able to understand *being*?

With this Husserlian version of the problem, was the project to lay the foundation of philosophy as a science not essentially bound to come up short? What emerged from Husserl's way of asking as an answer to the question about the meaning of the transcendental position? What is the meaning of the being of pure phenomena? They are "absolute being," which "*nulla 're' indiget ad existendum*,"[19] because they *are* themselves surely the fundamental *res*:

> The realm of transcendental consciousness as the realm of what is, in a determined sense, "absolute" being, has been provided us by the phenomenological reduction. It is the primal category of all being (or, in our terminology, the primal region), the one in which all other regions of being are rooted, to which, according to their *essence*, they are relative and on which they are therefore all essentially dependent.[20]

The sense of this primal region, then, is to be the foundation, the substratum of all other being:

> The theory of categories must start entirely from this most radical of all ontological distinctions—being *as consciousness* and being as something which becomes "*manifested*" in consciousness, "transcendent" being.[21]

It is clear: in the ontological line of inquiry, not much new has been achieved in comparison to Descartes. The fundamental division of finite modes of being is Cartesian. Only the immanence [of *res cogitans*] was emphasized; the sense of the *res extensa* faded into being an object, and the relation of the two, rather than being causal-objective, is turned into one of intentionality. But the regions of being are not the only concepts of being that arise in this context. There is also talk of essence, of categories and a primal category, of ground and the grounded. These concepts surely demand a systematic treatise concerning their meaning. But that task was omitted because of the rush to construct a science of the pure phenomena, a wholly *new* science.

Does this mean that the Husserlian idea—the possibility of a doctrine of "purified subjectivity," of an original kind of conception of the "subject"—was groundless? Simply asserting this, too, would be one-sided. It is only necessary not to regard this subjectivity as that toward which the way is exclusively and originally opened in the *epochē*. The *epochē*, more radically conceived, opens the way to the being of beings of every mode of being. But what is required for the "purification of subjectivity" is not only the *epochē*, but also insight into a historical nexus of conceptions of being. The *epochē* is in a position to guide our view from beings to being. It can breach the prejudice of the absolute mode of being of the transcendent, of beings in the mode of *res extensa*. But is it capable of remedying the prejudices in the conception of being that have resulted from a murky tradition, from the confounding of being with beings, and from the lack of points of orientation when dealing with the problem of being? The *epochē* warns us not to regard beings as the only possible theme of knowledge, and it explodes the corresponding prejudice. But it is insufficient to reveal the disguises, concealments, and coverings-over that occur in being itself. Only a historical procedure is capable of that, one that exposes traditional interconnections, opaque assumptions, and uninterrogated components in the current representations and conceptions of being. These must then be seen through in their supposed obviousness, and their dogmatic inertia is, so to speak, to be rooted out. "Purified subjectivity" can only be targeted when the roots of the prejudice of the genuine grasping of the self in a reflective gaze (which can grasp nothing but the *res cogitans*), and the ground upon which these roots grow, have been uncovered. The theoretical stance of a pure gaze is, however, fundamentally a comportment which presupposes that the "subject" is taking it "for the sake of itself" (and that, as such, it is more than a "pure" gaze, which would be just a present gaze), and that the "for the sake of oneself" presupposes a "non-indifference" of the "subject," i.e., that the subject has "something at stake." And these are all structures which are, of course, to be grasped reflectively, but which allude to an essentially responsible and active being that therefore is to count as original and takes priority over the representing comportment with which the Cartesian approach is predominately, if not exclusively, concerned. In this way there comes into view not only the more original temporality of human experience, i.e., looking ahead, and being in a situation in which we already find ourselves, but so too the phenomenon of responsibility [*Verantwortung*] as giving over [*Über-antwortung*] and with that also the task of grasping the "subjective" being as *free*, ethical, ontologically one with understanding.

If this is a dogmatic-metaphysical formulation of the problem, then, admittedly, the whole of German idealism, beginning with Fichte, and even Kant, too, with their efforts to overcome the dualism of the representing and the freely acting I, must also be called dogmatic—this should be taken as a comment on a critical statement by one contemporary philosopher, who suspects that the agenda of a dogmatic metaphysics lies in the critique of the primacy of consciousness and reflection.[22]

The conception of phenomenology as a method of ontology thus gives rise to *two* sciences, both of which admittedly cannot be called new, but are instead renewed through this method: ontology as the search for the answer to the question of the meaning of being and ontology of human life, which one could also call the theory of the soul. The theory of the soul is a new science in the sense that it stands in fundamental opposition to the Cartesian ontology of the *res cogitans* and seeks the theory of a mode of being that is fundamentally not that of the *res*. This "fundamental ontology" is made possible by unfolding anew the question of being, for this is where human Da-sein, as the site of being (in the understanding of being), must naturally be targeted. Thus, human life must not be conceived as a "present-at-hand" *res cogitans*, to be viewed from the distance of reflection—as a conscious being present-at-hand—but rather as something that comports itself to itself in its understanding of being. This means, further, that grasping the self is not a pure seeing of a being by the same being, a "pure intellectual intuition," but rather it is itself conditioned and guided by an a priori. Neither the naive nor the reflective, philosophical grasping of the self is ever without an interpretation, without an a priori preliminary understanding, as one can see best in the example of the Cartesian *cogito*, which admittedly possesses the absolute certainty of self-grasping, but only for the present moment. As such, it presupposes a mathematical conception of time, that of the tradition. The concept of reflection itself is profoundly modified in the moment where one sees that "consciousness" is not the fundamental concept of all understanding taken as comportment toward beings [*zum Seienden*], but is rather before all else an understanding of being [*des Seins*]. This understanding, itself unthematic, allows beings to be presented thematically. Self-consciousness then can be nothing other than the turning-toward this being [i.e., to itself] as far as its relation to being [*Sein*] is concerned, a turning that is itself guided by an understanding of being. If this understanding is not an original understanding which has, on the basis of the critical dismantling of inherited prejudices, become for the first time really seeing, but rather remains an "average" and leveled understanding, then the turning-toward itself can by no means show the mode of being which is truly appropriate to the targeted being [i.e., to consciousness].

To presuppose the concept of consciousness as something ultimate behind which it is impossible to go further belongs, of course, to those attempts to establish ultimate limits of philosophical interpretation. Such attempts take as a basis a certain way of interpreting being in order to absolutize that way of interpreting (e.g., the impossibility, but also the superfluity, of ontology, because being cannot be defined and is moreover a self-evident concept, one that is not to be further analyzed).

It is thus a vain struggle to attempt to reach consciousness in pure reflection. For grasping this being [i.e., consciousness] depends upon how far the horizon of its understanding has been cleared. However, this we can never achieve on our own as those who are projecting the knowledge-project because we do not have the presuppositions of our life at our command. On the contrary, they command our life. We have only historical experience, which teaches us that these presuppositions are, in a certain sense, variable, i.e., that being "clears" itself in different ways. Thus we can never maintain that we have reached the limits of the knowable, a definitive grasp of the a priori of our understanding.

One can thus characterize the Husserlian standpoint in the following way: it is the continuation of the metaphysical pursuit of the concept of being without a clear, explicit differentiation of the ontological difference between being and beings. In this difference, however, lies the proper sense of the *epochē*, when conceived generally. While the question of metaphysics concerns being, its answer offers beings, as was already the case with the Presocratics: Thales inquired into the being of things, what they "really" are, and he answered: "water," a being[23] that can be employed as a "model" for the variability of being. With the *epochē*, Husserl too performs the step back from beings; he seeks (inquires into, questions) being, and he answers with a being, the *cogitatio* of a *cogitatum*. He renews Cartesian metaphysics with the Kantian concept of the transcendental.

With the clarification of phenomenology as a methodological concept, one does not need to abandon the concept of a philosophy as rigorous science, understood in opposition to *Weltanschauung*-philosophy, which purports to be a doctrine of beings.[24] Admittedly, phenomenology is not a *positive* science. That follows from the fact that it does not *posit* beings to carry out its research within the field of beings so posited—that is to say, it follows from the fact that phenomenology stands fundamentally within the *epochē*, and indeed not in a restricted one, but a general one. For that reason, it can also be called, albeit paradoxically, a science *of nothing*. For the object of philosophy *is* indeed nothing of which one can say "it is" or "there is" this object; rather, the object of philosophy is this "there is" itself.[25]

With such a conception, one is certainly capable of something that the Husserlian conception of the ground of the "new, unheard-of science" of phenomenology was not capable of: finding a justification in life itself for the fact that something like the *epoché* is possible. For Husserl, this act of freedom comes "as though shot from a pistol" and is itself a grounding ground, one that cannot be further grounded. Heidegger's treatise "What Is Metaphysics?" sought to accomplish this [further] grounding.

The *epoché* may not be a negation, a denial. All the same, it belongs to those attitudes that are of a negative nature. It is a non-affirming and a non-denying, a limbo, a mode of comportment grounded in *nihilating*.

To what extent is the *epoché* a nihilating comportment? To the extent that it is a *non-use* of theses. A freedom, a not-being-bound by beings, is experienced. *Prior to* the unfree judgment-comportment, which is dependent upon beings, a sphere is discovered where beings *do not* rule, where they *compel* neither affirmation nor denial. But how would such a comportment, a freedom of this kind, be possible were it not based on an experience of the fundamental possibility of distance from every activity, even judging? The *epoché* starts with a characteristic of the thesis, with its non-obligatory character. The possibility of an *epoché* and its limbo is inherent in the experience of nihilation. Only on the basis of this limbo can a new interest awaken, an interest in that which is precisely not a being.

One could summarize in the following way: It is not the *epoché* that establishes the limbo upon which the phenomenological reduction is built up, but rather the *epoché* presupposes the experience of the limbo, the nihilation, to which every *repelling* (negative) attitude refers as its origin.

On the other hand, the limbo of the *epoché* must remind us of the transcendence of Dasein and of that which must not be spoken of as a being [*seiend*] in a usual sense (and thus must be called a non-being [*nichtseiend*]).

Like logical denial, the *epoché* is also native to the sphere of logical acts and comportments. For that reason, it cannot count as the proper origin of what it pretends to unveil. What it does unveil, however, is a "region," a "plane," which stands outside of that which is the object of a thesis and which can accordingly be called a *being* [*seiend*]. Husserl himself called this region "pre-being" [*Vorsein*] and identified it with transcendental consciousness because he did not bring the *epoché* to its conclusion and believed he had to insist upon a subjective basis because otherwise there would be no object for a theory that could be called rigorous science.

In fact, however, the *epoché* is only evidence of nihilation and the possibility, even in the theoretical realm, of proceeding through the presence of nihilation up to the brink where one can and must leave the territory of beings. The *epoché* tends toward the purely theoretical performance of a "step back" behind beings.

The origin of this "step back," however, cannot be grounded in the *epochē* itself, for the *epochē* presupposes the dominance of logic in the "general thesis," that is, in the interpretation of the original relation to beings as *thesis*, and as such as a logical positing, as assertion. Phenomenologically viewed, however, the "thesis" of the *world as universe* of beings is not a possible act, since the universe of beings would first have to be conceived, which is however totally impossible; and the *world as horizon* is precisely not an object and therefore cannot be an object of a judgment thesis either.

The "general thesis" is thus a problematic concept: it means either a *logical* thesis, in which case it cannot be carried out; or it means a disclosure presented as a mood or feeling, in which case it is not a thesis. By way of contrast, the situation is clarified if one does not insist that the primary relation to the world is a thesis, something theoretical involving objects, but rather sees instead that it is contained in an affective finding oneself so [*Sich-Befinden*], i.e., in the "sphere of feeling," and that this is where the disclosure of beings as such and *as a whole* originally takes place.

This limbo brought about by the *epochē* suffers from the difficulties introduced above: (1) it is not allowed to be performed without restriction, or else it leads *in nihil*; (2) as theoretical, it cannot be initiated, since one never reaches "the whole" as an object. The difficulty with the *epochē*—that it is a *theoretical* act capable of bringing beings into limbo—can be remedied by revealing the limbo brought about by the *epochē* as a nihilating comportment. This nihilating comportment is grounded in the original "nihilation" and opens access not to a being (of whatever sort), but to an "open region" of what has been cleared, of what can "withstand" Dasein who understands being. Thus what Husserl intended as transcendental, as absolute consciousness, is, in the proper sense, no such thing but rather something perfectly distinct from every objective (present-at-hand) as well as subjective being [*des Seienden*].

From these considerations, if they are cogent, it seems to follow that an interpretation of *What is Metaphysics?*[26] is possible that can *implicitly* be characterized as a confrontation with the Husserlian *epochē* as the core of the reduction. Or it can be interpreted as, *among other things*, containing such a confrontation. Husserl's attendance at [Heidegger's] inaugural lecture makes it probable that questions ought to have been addressed there that most profoundly concern both phenomenological philosophies. Husserl's fundamental problem, however, was to ground philosophy upon the *epochē* and reduction as a phenomenologically rigorous, but positive, science. Husserl claims to ground phenomenological philosophy, as a positive science that justifies all the theories of the individual sciences, upon said methodological procedure, and in this way also to arrive at a metaphysics (metaphysics of mind) that will finally be able to come forward as science. To this claim Heidegger opposes his conception of phenomenology grounded upon the nihilation of the nothing. This conception cannot accept the traditional dominance of logic in philosophy (philosophy as doctrine of reason), which begins in modern times with Descartes. The Husserlian *epochē* certainly initiates the surmounting of this dominance, but cannot radically and consistently execute it, instead coming to a halt at the indeterminacy of the thought of the natural attitude's "general thesis." By contrast, Heidegger attempts an all-out attack on the dominance of the logical by attempting to show that one of the presuppositions of logic—negation—is grounded in the pre-logical, in Dasein's openness to being, specifically in nihilation. The idea of philosophy as a positive science proves to be a vestige of Cartesianism in phenomenology.

Already the starting point of Heidegger's lecture shows that the horizon of Husserl's entire investigation is philosophy in its relationship to positive science, and thus also the concept of philosophy as rigorous science. According to Husserl, philosophy as rigorous science should become a metaphysics that is able to come forward as science. Metaphysics is thus that which is initially asked about. As proper philosophy, metaphysics ought not be presented by talking *about* [Be*sprechen*] its subject matter, but rather *giving voice* to [*Aussprechen*] it. It is characterized (provisionally) by the fact that each of its questions encompasses the whole of its "field" and that the questioner is herself put into question at the same time. This putting-into-question of the questioner turns into the putting-into-question of the scientist, which, of course, Husserl's "Philosophy as Rigorous Science" also considered. It was Husserl himself who strove to anchor the sciences in their essential ground at a time when their fields had diverged widely through specialization. It is established in agreement with him that this anchoring is today "dead." (Phenomenology wanted precisely to renew this anchoring. The entrance into phenomenology was nonetheless the reduction and its core, the *epochē*—a much more "negative" attitude than every negation, a way into the philosophical beyond every science of the world, beyond every science of actual beings.) The sciences are without exception primarily characterized through this relation to the world: whether exact or historical sciences, they pursue beings in order to approach the essence of the things in question. Science approaches the thing [*Sache*] itself (one of Husserl's requirements, which he also demands of philosophy), and, in bondage and subordinate exclusively to the thing in question, it wants to help the thing come into its own [*zu ihr selbst verhelfen*]. For the thing is not capable, as it were, of *being* itself on its own. In short, there is talk of an "irruption" of the being "human" into the whole of beings (into the universe) in order "to allow beings to emerge" as what they are and how they are. The things as such need this irruption and emergence [*Einbruch und Aufbruch*], which cannot come to them from themselves, for so far as things are not akin to Dasein's type of being, they are *not* capable of coming into a relationship to their own being, and so far as they are only *akin* to Dasein's type, they are not capable of coming into an *explicit* relationship to their own being. This irruption can occur, however, only on the basis of what exists as an original relationship not toward beings but toward being—i.e., toward something that is not of the order of beings and for that reason also precisely *is not*. But this relationship is the ground of the appearing of what appears. Appearing is thus, in its *ground*, to be sought outside of beings. This ground, being, is, however, the object of metaphysics. Since it is not of the order of beings, it must be, regarded from the point of view of beings, nothing. This now mobilizes the question of the lecture: What about this nothing?

Upon first glance this characterization (science wants to know all beings in the world a*nd nothing further*; the scientific attitude takes its lead from beings *and nothing further*; it grapples with beings *and nothing further*)[27] seems to be something superfluous and gratuitously added. In actuality, that which lends to science the power of the irrupting emergence of beings is expressed in this "nothing." The discussion of the concept of the nothing that then follows is at one and the same time a confrontation with logic. Is it an accident that this took place in the presence of the great phenomenologist, who in his most radical endeavor of thought (the reflection on the *epochē* in *Ideas I*) remains subject to the dominance of this logic to such an extent that he downright recoiled before the nothing? In the face of the thinker, that is, who for this reason remains a prisoner of the subject-object relation (in a transcendental version) and a transcendental idealism?

In any event the investigation now takes a detour where it is shown how logic fails when faced with the concept of nothing, how it is incapable of formulating this concept and *for that reason* can only repudiate it. Yet is this repudiation proof that there is nothing of issue with the nothing? Certainly the nothing is not a being to which a concept in the proper sense always refers within a context that must have already been illuminated. In the case of the nothing there is nothing of the sort, and the concept itself says as much. What, then, is the use of the concept? Logic certainly cannot use it, but is that a proof against the nothing? "The nothing" is after all a logical objectification. Logic is capable of circumscribing the nothing in no other way than by such an objectifying operation. For it, the nothing is the utter *negation* of the totality of beings. With that, the nothing is subordinated to a logical operation; it derives from negation. Such an operation, however, is not at all achievable; it is an empty intention. It conflicts with the essence of fulfillment, which in canceling [a thesis] always presupposes a partially positive thesis. One can "realize" a negation only on the basis of something positive. Moreover, the totality of beings can never be positively realized— that conflicts with the necessarily horizonal givenness of the individual.

In spite of this, the information provided by logic, the negation of the totality of beings is not entirely devoid of sense. It suggests a confusion of two concepts of wholeness: wholeness as the sum of beings (something unrealizable), and a whole as the phenomenon without which appearing as such is not possible, the condition of the possibility of appearing. This whole is what is open in appearing, the "world" in the sense of a region that must already be opened to Dasein if Dasein is to understand and perceive beings. This whole is thus no being, but it goes beyond beings. It is felt as a whole, opened up in an attuned feeling: This feeling holds together even that which is most disparate and fragmented in our activities and makes them always into something derived from, and first disclosed by, a whole.

That implies, however, that what appears in any given case can address us only if we relate to it through a prior disclosedness, if we find ourselves *attuned* within it [*in ihr uns befinden*]. There is, however, also a fundamental feeling [*Grundbefindlichkeit*] that refuses and closes off any address whatsoever; nevertheless, this feeling still bears the characteristic of the "as a whole." No open comportment, no pursuit of something [*Besorgen*], and no care for others [*Fürsorge*] is here possible, nor a pure looking at and taking up in an intuition that is interested in the pure look. Everything that turns up in this "disclosedness" has the characteristic of *repulsion* [*Abweisung*]: one can strike up *nothing* with it. No possibility presents itself. This feeling offers the experience of the nothing, of not being addressed by anything, of *no* possibility. While the negation of beings can only be performed through a replacement, there is here no alternative, no replacing, but rather an absolute disappearing. It can also be put like this: beings offer here *no* possibility of a "hold," no surface to grip; they slip away as soon as the attempt is made to get hold of them. One learns through this experience that our customary being-in-the-world is a matter of supporting ourselves upon things we have grasped—a supporting that here fails.

The negation of the totality of beings is impossible; the slipping away of beings as a whole, by contrast, is a fundamental experience of Dasein. What is this slipping away more specifically? Nothing other than the unveiling of Da-sein as such. Da-sein is not a being that is simply there, but rather a being that understands others and itself, that is, a being to whom beings appear. In the slipping away of beings, which repel us and say nothing, the following becomes clear: only on the basis of something that is not a being [*etwas Nichtseiendes*] could beings appear to us. Only by "transcending," by taking the "step back" beyond beings, does Dasein understand beings; things appear to it, and it itself appears to itself. In the "step back," then, Dasein learns that it is fundamentally "uncanny" [*unheimlich*], that it is "not at home among things." It experiences that which is strange [*die Fremde*], the strangeness [*Befremdlichkeit*] of beings as such, that is, the strangeness of their being. In this way, in the presence of the nothing, Dasein gains experience of being, and without the possibility of this experience it is precisely not Dasein, not understanding, not something to which beings stand open, to which beings reveal themselves.

It is thus the nothing of beings, as the experience *of the being* of what is experienced, that forms the constant point of relation out of which the lucid comportment toward beings that stand in the open can unfold. What is not a being [*das Nichtseiende*], being [itself], is that point of support around which a light, open region forms itself within which the appearing of beings is possible. This region is the *how and what* of beings that can address us; yet being itself is only present in refusing itself, and that means that being withdraws itself by indicating beings to us and referring us to them. The region of the open, within which beings open up, is thus necessarily linked with the self-withdrawal of being that intrudes in the form of the nothing.

Since, however, being is the condition of the possibility of understanding, of the projection of possibilities and thus also of appearing, the human being or its "mind" can never be grasped as something purely "positive," as a light that approaches things and illuminates them with its rays. Nor can it be grasped as a light that "confirms" objectivity. Thus one fundamentally cannot get by with the concepts of "consciousness," even when it is defined through intentionality. Even when we disregard the fact that the kind of being of consciousness remains undetermined or is even (when it is grasped in pure, inner reflection) something confirmed, present-at-hand, "consciousness" remains a thoroughly positive being, incapable of any transcendence and so also incapable of yielding an appearance, the emergence of the "there is" [*es ist*] in its fundamental strangeness. Or, more precisely, either "consciousness" implies, without itself suspecting it, the transcending toward that which is not a being [*zum Nicht-Seienden*], in which case it is, in its positivity, a misleading concept (and it is in this way that, for example, even Husserl's transcendental subjectivity seems to vacillate between a transcending and a traditional-positive concept of consciousness). Or consciousness is (as it was, for example, for Brentano) a being without transcendence, in which case, however, the problem of the appearing of beings has not even been posed, much less solved.

And now, the question must also be broached, why Heidegger did not go the way of an explicit confrontation with *epochē* and reduction but chose instead this indirect one which is so difficult to penetrate.

The answer is contained in part, I believe, in the lectures *The Basic Problems of Phenomenology*, which have now been made available.[28] Here, *three* components of the phenomenological method are distinguished which we can now clearly understand, specifically from the perspective of a confrontation with Husserl: (1) the reduction, concerning which it is stated:

> We call this basic component of phenomenological method—the leading back or reducing of investigative vision from naively apprehended beings to being—*phenomenological reduction*. We are thus adopting a central term of Husserl's phenomenology in its literal wording though not in its substantive intent. *For Husserl*, phenomenological reduction ... is the method of leading phenomenological vision ... back to the transcendental life of consciousness and its noetic-noematic experiences, in which objects are constituted as correlates of consciousness. *For us* phenomenological reduction means leading phenomenological vision back from the apprehension of beings, whatever may be the character of that apprehension, to the understanding of the being of these beings (projecting upon the way they are unconcealed).[29]

(2) *construction*, the projection just mentioned; and (3) the *destruction* that belongs to the reductive construction, that is, a "process in which the traditional concepts, which at first must necessarily be employed, are deconstructed down to the sources from which they were drawn."[30]

But why did Heidegger retain the title "reduction," when it could have led to disastrous confusion? In light of what has been presented above, were there not *two* decisive reasons for this choice? (1) In spite of what is ultimately the starkest of material differences, there is nonetheless in both procedures something common, namely that which we designated as the "step back beyond beings," the limbo of the non-employment of theses of beings. (2) Since at the time of *Basic Problems*, which is also the time of *Being and Time*, the hope of a common procedure still existed, Heidegger sought an ontological interpretation of the material achievements of phenomenology. This is probably also the meaning to be found in the remark in *Being and Time*,[31] which, Heidegger would later explain, was the proper justification for the dedication of the work to Edmund Husserl.[32] There is talk there of how Heidegger's own investigation should be seen as "steps forward in disclosing 'the things [*Sachen*] themselves'"[33] and how this is owed above all to Husserl himself. Does that not hint clearly enough at the fact that Heidegger's own standpoint (of ontology as the *matter* of phenomenology) was acquired in a reflective confrontation with the Husserlian approach? Here we have simply endeavored to discover the path this reflection could have taken.

We have commented above concerning "construction" and "destruction" when we spoke of the "fundamental ontology" of human Dasein.

Followers of Husserl are sometimes reproached for having interpreted Husserl by way of Heidegger, without respecting the former's *own* scientific intention; this, so the charge goes, did not consist in establishing a new metaphysics (this is maintained in spite of Husserl's numerous statements to the contrary), but rather in developing the method of a historically bound, "topical" reflection on the conditions of the possibility of naively objective approaches. It is, however, curious that precisely Heidegger emphasizes so strongly the methodological characteristic of phenomenology and connects this with a fundamentally historical reflection. A critique of Heidegger's procedure must before all else be oriented toward his relationship to Husserl's fundamental concepts and the manner in which they have resulted from thinking through Husserl's fundamental starting point with the concepts of the general thesis, the *epochē* and the reduction.

Perhaps now a question which has caused considerable confusion can also be clarified: Is there in Heidegger a reduction or at least the *epochē*? The Heideggerian concept of construction, of the projection of the being of beings in view of these beings, presupposes, we believe, an *epochē*, but not a reduction in the Husserlian sense. That Heidegger does not explicitly mention the *epochē*, however, stems from the fact that he saw it as a nihilating comportment grounded in something that lies deeper, namely, nihilation, which delivers itself originally before the being of beings as a whole.

Now would be an opportune moment briefly to go into the following question in a positive way: what does phenomenology mean *for us*? What has lifted it to the singular position that distinguishes it in the thinking of the present? Phenomenology is neither an academic philosophy, dedicated to fostering a scholarly tradition, nor is it a philosophy that wants to assert its vitality by helping to change the world, that is, a philosophy that is or wants to be revolutionary. It is a reflection, specifically a reflection on crisis. It must investigate the crisis of humanity down to its first origins, for it wants to expose positive science and scientificity generally in their roots. That demands, however, a path to origins of a radical kind and a striving for impartiality that also must remove the prejudices of the positive sciences from the path of its reflection. In this radicality there is nothing else to match phenomenology, and it goes in the opposite direction of everything else that has occurred—in obfuscated naivety—in science and philosophy. The discoveries that offer themselves up along this way are manifold, but there is one that is of paramount importance, and both luminaries, Husserl as well as Heidegger, have worked on it in common: the discovery of the essential Cartesianism of our entire epoch, if one—to employ the Heideggerian terminology—views Cartesianism as the aggregate of the ontic consequences of the ontological approach of substance dualism, that is, Descartes' doctrine of the two thingly modes of being. The attempt to offer a way of *seeking*, in opposition to the fundamental concept of modernity that has here been laid bare—that is phenomenology.

Notes

1   Based on an existing translation by Hayden Kee. See *Husserl: German Perspectives*, ed. John J. Drummond and Otfried Höffe (New York: Fordham University Press, 2019), 84–109.

2   Edmund Husserl, *Logische Untersuchungen*, vol. 2:1: *Untersuchungen zur Phänomenologie und Theorie der Erkenntnis, Husserliana*, vol. 19/1 (The Hague: Martinus Nijhoff, 1984), S. 10 (English: Edmund Husserl, *Logical Investigations*, 2nd edn, vol. 2, trans. John Niemeyer Findlay, ed. Dermot Moran (London: Routledge, 2001), 168).

3   Edmund Husserl, *Die Krisis der europäischen Wissenschaften und die transzendentale Phänomenologie: Eine Einleitung in die phänomenologische Philosophie*, HUA 6, 1976 (English: *Crisis of the European Sciences,* trans. David Carr (Evanston, IL: Northwestern University Press, 1970)).

4   Martin Heidegger, *Sein und Zeit* (Tübingen: Max Niemeyer Verlag, 1927), 27 (English: *Being and Time*, trans. Joan Stambaugh (Albany, NY: SUNY Press, 2010), 26).

5   Heidegger, *Sein und Zeit,* 34f. (32f.).

6   Heidegger, *Sein und Zeit*, 37 (35).

7   Edmund Husserl, *Ideen zu einer reinen Phänomenologie und phänomenologischen Philosophie. Erstes Buch: Allgemeine Einführung in die reine Phänomenologie*, ed. Karl Schuhmann (The Hague: Martinus Nijhoff, 1976), 3 (English: *Ideas Pertaining to a Pure Phenomenology and to a Phenomenological Philosophy. First Book: General Introduction to a Pure Phenomenology*, trans. Fred Kersten (The Hague: Martinus Nijhoff, 1983), xvii).

8   Husserl, *Ideen I*, 3 (xvii).

9   Edmund Husserl, *Die Idee der Phänomenologie: Fünf Vorlesungen,* ed. Walter Biemel, HUA 2, reprint of the second edition, 1973.

10 Jan Patočka, "*Epoché* und Reduktion: Einige Bemerkungen," in *Bewusst sein: Gerhard Funke zu eigen*, ed. A. J. Bucher, Hermann Drüe, and Thomas Mulvany Seebohm (Bonn: Bouvier Verlag Herbert Grundmann, 1975), 76ff.

11 Husserl, *Ideen I*, 65 (60—Patočka's citation corrected and Kersten translation modified—HK).

12 Husserl, *Ideen I*, HUA III, 6–7.

13 Edmund Husserl, *Die Philosophie als strenge Wissenschaft*, in *Logos* 1 (1911): 289–341. Reprinted in HUA 25, *Aufsätze und Vorträge* (1911–21), ed. Thomas Nenon and H. R. Sepp (The Hague: Martinus Nijhoff, 1987), S. 2–62 (English: "Philosophy as Rigorous Science," in *Phenomenology and the Crisis of Philosophy*, trans. Quentin Lauer (New York: Harper and Row, 1965)).

14 Husserl, *Ideen I*, 3 (xvii).

15 Husserl, *Ideen I*, 8 (xxii).

16 Immanuel Kant, *Prolegomena to Any Future Metaphysics That Will Be Able to Come Forward as Science,* ed. and trans. Gary Hatfield (Cambridge: Cambridge University Press, 2004).

17 Immanuel Kant, *Kritik der reinen Vernunft*, B VII–XV (English: *Critique of Pure Reason,* ed. and trans. Paul Guyer and Allen W. Wood (Cambridge: Cambridge University Press, 1998), 106-10).

18 Edmund Husserl, *Philosophie als strenge Wissenschaft*; Naturalistische Philosophie, Abteilung IV. Cf. Edmund Husserl, "Philosophie als strenge Wissenschaft," *Logos* 1 (1910–11): 289–341 (English: *Phenomenology and the Crisis of Philosophy*, trans. Quentin Lauer (New York: Harper, 1965)).

19 "which does not need any 'thing' to exist" (Ed.)

20 Husserl, *Ideen I*, 174 (171). Cf. Martin Heidegger, *Grundprobleme der Phänomenologie,* ed. F. W. von Hermann (Frankfurt am Main: Vittorio Klostermann, 1975), 175 (English: *Basic Problems of Phenomenology*, trans. Albert Hofstadter (Bloomington: Indiana University Press, 1982), 124ff.).

21 Husserl, *Ideen I*, 171 (174).

22 Gerhard Funke, *Phänomenologie: Metaphysik oder Methode* (Bonn: H Bouvier Verlag, 1966), 176 (English: *Phenomenology: Metaphysics or Method*, trans. David J. Parent (Athens: Ohio University Press, 1987)).

23 Heidegger, *Grundprobleme der Phänomenologie*, 453 (318ff.).

24 Heidegger, *Grundprobleme der Phänomenologie*, 17 (12ff.).

25   Heidegger, *Grundprobleme der Phänomenologie*, 13ff., 18 (10, 13ff.).

26   Martin Heidegger, *Was ist Metaphysik?* in M. Heidegger, *Wegmarken*, GA 9
     (Frankfurt am Main: Vittorio Klostermann, 1976), 103–22 (English: "What Is
     Metaphysics?" in *Heidegger: Basic Writings*, 2nd edn, ed. David F. Krell (New
     York: HarperCollins, 1993), 89–110).

27   Heidegger, *Was ist Metaphysik?*, 105.

28   Martin Heidegger, *Grundprobleme der Phänomenologie*, §5: "The character
     of ontological method; The three basic components of phenomenological
     method."

29   Heidegger, *Grundprobleme der Phänomenologie*, 29 (21).

30   Heidegger, *Grundprobleme der Phänomenologie*, 31 (23).

31   Martin Heidegger, *Being and Time*, trans. Joan Stambaugh (Albany, NY:
     SUNY Press, 1996), 400 (Ed.).

32   *Der Spiegel* interview with Martin Heidegger, May 31, 1976, 199. See Martin
     Heidegger, *Reden und andere Zeugnisse eines Lebensweges (1910–1976)*, ed.
     Hermann Heidegger (Frankfurt am Main: Vittorio Klostermann, 2000), 652ff.
     (English: "Only a God Can Save Us: The Spiegel Interview," in *Heidegger: The
     Man and the Thinker*, trans. William J. Richardson (Piscataway, NJ:
     Transaction Publishers, 1981), 45–67).

33   Heidegger, *Being and Time*, 400 (Ed.).

PART FOUR

Arts and Culture

Patočka's writings in this section show the depth of his engagement with the arts, particularly literature and poetry. His novel insights on language, temporality, fantasy, and world-disclosure within literary writing affirm the philosophical value of literary texts, especially in a social context that is dominated by instrumental reason and by the increasing specialization of knowledge. The phenomenological analysis of time in "Time, Myth, Faith" and "Time, Eternity, and Temporality in the Work of Karel Hynek Mácha" moves away from our pragmatic and our formal senses of time and asks about the relationship of time to an outside-of-time, and about the significance of past and future in human time. His vivid and discerning readings of Sophocles, Thomas Mann, Chekhov, and others are stirring works of literary criticism that serve as a reminder of the importance of aesthetic experience in our understanding of ourselves.

The nature of myth and the mythical is a recurring theme in these texts. Patočka seeks to recover the meaning of myth in an age that has lost touch with the notion of myth as a ritual comportment toward the world. The importance of myth is twofold: on the one hand, it speaks to us about all that is accepted as the necessary background of human life, of the world into which we are accepted and for which we paradoxically become responsible; on the other hand, myth stands in for a non-instrumental relationship to what is, a recognition of the *mysterium tremendum*; as such it serves to counter the comportment that prevails in modern life.

CHAPTER EIGHT

Time, Myth, Faith (1952)

Translated from the Czech by Alex Zucker

Problems of time, its essence, its objective meaning, its structure, our awareness of it, are recognized as important issues in modern philosophy. It is sometimes said that modern philosophy differs from ancient metaphysics in that time exists for it; the increasingly pronounced historicization of the modern image of the world would seem to attest to that. Yet, to an extent, the problematic of time also has relevance for some issues of religion.

We do not intend here to articulate a solution to the question of the nature of time. We simply wish to differentiate certain temporal structures and lay out a schema of the most important temporal phenomena.

We distinguish primarily the temporal world, that is, the set of all realities in the temporal dimension, in temporal order. Every event has a certain positioning within it and every reality a certain extensity. We may conceive of the temporal world in and of itself without any succession. Relations within it are relations of order (same or different date). What we see in the temporal world is fully analogous to the three dimensions of space with which we are familiar. Thus relations of order are transitive and it makes no difference in which direction we pass through them.

Another important phenomenon that accounts for the specificity of time as we come to know it experientially is successiveness. This successiveness may be seen as consisting in a clear cut (i.e., the present) slicing continually, without leaving out any dates, through the temporal world conceived as a set of ordered positions. This cut divides the entire band, in every moment, into two parts: a class of dates that have already taken place (i.e., the past) and a class of those that have yet to take place (i.e., the future). Therefore every cut has its two classes; a past and a future of its own. Successiveness is fundamentally asymmetrical (this asymmetricality is usually what people are getting at when talking about the so-called "irreversibility" of time; in fact, time is more than irreversible; the relation of succession is essentially asymmetrical, in one direction). What fundamentally distinguishes the phenomenon of time from the phenomenon of space is successiveness.

The laws of physics may be formulated as laws of the temporal world; if we see unidirectional phenomena in a physical process, such as for example an increase in entropy, this unidirectionality pertains to the content, not to the temporal form itself.

However, succession is necessary for the consciousness of time to come into being. Without real successiveness there would be no consciousness of change and consciousness would remain in an eternal now. On the other hand, successiveness alone is not sufficient for time-consciousness to come into being; it alone is not enough for consciousness itself to become successive. The successiveness of consciousness is something different from the consciousness of this successiveness. To have a different cut through the temporal world at every moment already implies succession, but only if the consciousness of all the other preceding cuts were related to it could a temporal consciousness, i.e., a consciousness of succession, come into being. No wonder, then, that the study of time-consciousness has for so long been concentrated on the study of the consciousness of succession. All kinds of observations and speculations have cropped up regarding how past experiences (past presents) are preserved into the current present. In connection with this, there was discussion of the "creative character" of internal, lived time, which contains both past and present in a particular indivisible unity, and in that way constantly enriches itself. At one point, it was countered that the past is not preserved without modification, but rather the character of its givenness changes; at another point, these reflections gave rise to a two-dimensional schema of time-consciousness, in which one axis contains a series of present moments in progress, while the other contains a series of present awarenesses of the current present and non-current presents, gradually sinking into the indefinite. Only such a series of "retentions" and "protentions" surrounding the current present creates the "temporal horizon" to which conscious recollection can then turn and choose from it what it needs.

But is what we have here really a fully developed consciousness of time as we know it in human experience, as presented to us in some of the greatest and most momentous phenomena of life? A constant and particular consciousness of time is characteristic of human life: we plan our lives in terms of time; for every day, every period of time, we have a sort of schedule. This schedule is embedded into the outlook of our life cycles. The seasons of life are like the rhythmic lapping of waves against the background of great historical interests and the fates of human societies, both individually and as a whole. Against this backdrop the life of an individual human, that finite stretch of time, takes form as something capable of fulfillment or failure, of overall "success" or catastrophe, at once shaped by these great events even as it shapes them. Thus human time-consciousness proper has been characterized by its historicity from the very beginning. But is historical time a mere consciousness of succession, or alternatively, of succession with a maintaining, a retaining of the past within reach of our conscious view? Or is there still another, deeper temporal structure?

Doubtless, not only humans but also animals possess both successive consciousness and an awareness of succession. Yet animals do not live in terms of time—they do not plan, do not schedule time, do not live by temporal tasks, have no real fate. They live in the narrow present. Not that this present does not contain its own outlook into "the past" and "the future," but the here-and-now, the present, absorbs animals completely. Where there is no untethering from this bondage to the here-and-now, there can be no deeper relation to time in its broader scope: there can be, for example, no critical, disapproving attitude toward what already is (i.e., what has been), nor can there be any building on the past. So it is understandable if some thinkers consider the essence of time-consciousness in the human, historical sense to be a negative relation toward what is finished, given; the present negation of the past through a program, a project for the future, is characteristic of historical time (though insofar as the past was at one point also the future, which it denied in the same way, it is possible to build on those moments of the past that are associated with the current negation). Thus the current conflict between future and past contained in the present becomes the true source of human historicity, and the future, the moment of newness, becomes the true generator of human, historical time. Historical time is presented here as essentially creative; historical time is the creation of the new. For us to arrive at a specifically human time-consciousness, more than succession and its continuity are needed; there must also be discontinuity, represented by that radical "no" to what is merely given and received, mediated by tradition.

Here, however, another question must be posed: Is our consciousness of time, especially our consciousness of the future, grounded in human need and the ability to create something new, or, on the contrary, is the possibility of creating something new grounded in our having a consciousness of the future?

In the concept we have been describing, while the future is the negation of the past and the driving force of a forked present, it is not obvious that this negating future is itself in fact a secondary phenomenon. The primary phenomenon from which it derives is the future "in its entirety"; the negating future can be understood on the basis of the entire future, but not vice versa—the entire future cannot be understood on the basis of the negating future.

The whole of temporal succession, its course through the temporal world, can be understood in two ways: one is that the whole current is nothing but one alteration, form, modification after another of what is already here; in this conception there is no choice but to passively accept the course of events, at most with curiosity about the ever-new forms it takes. Curiosity and unrest are, however, indications of the dissatisfaction that binds this overall attitude toward time to its opposite counterpart.

The other fundamental form of overall understanding of temporal progression is grounded in the fact that, resisting this powerlessness, resisting this surrender to an inaccessible past, we assert with deep certainty that what is most essential, the main thing, is never contained within this flow. The main thing, what is most important, always lies ahead of us, however far we go. And yet its very absence may shape what comes next for us, our concrete future.

These two fundamentally important phenomena are among the characteristics of consciousness that extend beyond the animal's bond to the present. Even if we do not happen to adopt one understanding or the other in our current experience, it holds true that they are internally linked to each other, and in a particular way: consciousness of the true future is *the overcoming* of a mere awareness of the past.

Thus a truly human consciousness of time is not possible without contact with, or better put, an appeal to, something that lies beyond the contents of our experience, that is, the temporal succession through which all reality passes. It may be paradoxical to say, but human consciousness of time essentially entails a relationship to something beyond any temporal world or temporal flow. Contact with and connection to this entirely other is characteristic of human time. This explains some of the features typical of historical time, of the time of our life as human, social beings, in particular its heterogeneity. Historical time does not flow *aequabiliter*, i.e., uniformly, like biological succession or the absolute time of Newton. There are moments of contact with what is ultimate and defining that time will never contain, yet nevertheless they may shape time and give it meaning. As a result, historical time is preparation for "the right time," "the right moment," "the fullness of time." Only in this historical time do we live with an awareness of human meaning, in the fullness of human life (whether true or illusive).

Since time immemorial, humans have had an awareness of the entirely other, τὸ ἕτερόν. Doubtless, it is already true of mythical humans, but the passivity that typifies mythical experience means that it is interpreted and neutralized in a particular way. Mythical humans are passive and powerless; they understand their lives as the work of powerful outside forces that operate or cooperate in a determining way wherever humans appear; life is accepted as a gift from the hands of these outside forces, a waiting for favor or disfavor; to live is to be weighed on their scales. Accordingly, mythical life is a living out of the past, out of what already is; all events are determined by the past. However, it also follows from this that ἕτερόν cannot be understood in its true character as waiting for us in the future. On the contrary, being extraordinary and defining, it is situated at a mythical beginning as an event, a fate, a decision that has put its imprint on everything that follows, interpreting and giving meaning to it. The mythical ancient times, an entirely different period, a fundamentally different era, the youth (old age viewed from another perspective) of the world, contains the key to everything that has actually happened since. States and mythical palaces flourished and fell based on what happened in the counsels and battles of the gods. If there was an order that reigned in the world and a "law" along with it, it was because Zeus put an end to the primordial anarchic era of chaotic gods and events, and tamed the primordial chaos. In contrast to mythical ancient times, when everything was decided, we live in a sphere of repetition and imitation, in a fallen world, lacking autonomy. Continued decline is held back by the occasional restoration of contact with the primeval world, reviving the scope of its meaning for us, renewing assurance of its favor and beneficial import; in these moments the world is restored to spring in more than memory alone; celebrations blossom, heroes are born to rival the heroes of myth, great historical events erupt . . .

Where, then, does the essential shortcoming lie, the essential defect in mythical consciousness? Not primarily in the fact that it distinguishes qualitative differences in time, and substantial breaks; nor in the fact that it lifts itself out of the deathly gray, out of the senseless continuation and repetition of what is commonly and without question considered irrevocably real; nor in the fact that it is fully resigned, like those who suffer from an utter lack of faith in the possibility of renewing life, whether their resignation comes across as blasé or impassioned. This false repetition, false perpetuity, is a state that lacks a true eternity; it is an avoidance of the challenge of the true future.

But neither does the defect in mythical consciousness lie in placing the future in the wrong position within the temporal world; for with a mere shift of accent, mythical consciousness can replace the past primeval world, which is of course the most characteristic aspect of mythical consciousness, with a future, eschatological world, a world in which human, often all too human, desires find fulfillment, in which mythical ancient times, the primeval world, assumes the role of its symmetrical counterpart.

Should we not see the shortcoming of mythical consciousness in the fact that it places in time something other than our human response to the unconditional appeal, that it tries to make commensurable (by placing it in time) what is by its very nature incommensurable (because it is beyond time)? And does true human experience of time then, in fact, not lie in an act of faith, which sees reality in its sober vestment, free of all idealization and illusions about our ability to grasp it in its entirety, while at the same time not losing sight of this categorical appeal and its incommensurability?

CHAPTER NINE

Art and Time (1966)

Translated from the Czech by Alex Zucker

If the ultimate goal of our educational work is to lead to an understanding of works of art, then for specialists such as us to reflect on the essence and possible ways of approaching a work of art is not only theoretically legitimate, but also promises practical results. Any such reflection would be merely theoretical if artistic creation and its achievements did not require us to make decisions and evaluate our position; but the universe of artworks is not a peaceful museum in which the masterpieces lead a life of peaceful coexistence, like so many isolated atoms; it is a universe of seeking and struggles. These conflicts result from the way in which humanity has understood the essence and function of art throughout history, a matter on which clearly no educator is or can be indifferent. Neither immediate adoption of a combative position, nor instinctive taste, nor a sense for the essential is the solution; it is only by drawing on a combination of philosophical, historical, and aesthetic positions that we can more or less adequately address the issue. So forgive me if in my opening lecture I attempt to speak on these rather abstract and surely difficult questions.

I will attempt to explain the problem using the example of the visual arts. In the twentieth century, these art forms underwent a true revolution, turning against every artistic norm that had been regarded as valid from the fifteenth century up until the nineteenth. Whether we like it or not, whether we consider this revolution a valuable gain or a scandal, the phenomenon of this revolution exists, and along with it the fact that this revolution, long regarded by many as an aberrant, passing phenomenon, has succeeded in convincing the audience of experts in a wide range of countries. On the other hand, the organized opposition to this revolution within certain social milieus is also worthy of consideration. Although this phenomenon cannot be understood simply by way of such catchphrases as "fashion," "perversion," "decadence," or other psycho-sociological categories, neither can it be reduced to mere conservatism or the ostensibly healthy instinct for social equilibrium. In order to comprehend this whole complex of phenomena, we must recognize that the meaning of works of art, the way in which we understand them, has itself been subject to change over the course of history, and that we have reached a turning point along this path. What we have before us is not merely an interesting sociological phenomenon, but a fundamental aesthetic development. In my own interpretation, which follows, I will attempt to trace this change. One might add that there have been parallel developments in the fields of music and poetry, and we could just as well take them as our starting point. However, the visual arts have the advantage that they more clearly show the unique nature of this modern evolution, including both what it shares with attitudes of the past and what separates it from them.

One could attempt to interpret modern art as a return to *style* as an element of artistic creation after centuries of the primacy of imitation, a period initiated by Leonardo da Vinci. Style—that is, a system of forms created intentionally to express that which has no real-world equivalent— prevails over imitation, for example, in primitive art, Assyrian-Babylonian art, Romanesque art, and early Gothic art; it is subordinate to imitation in the era inaugurated by the Renaissance, and then returns to dominance again in the twentieth century. This perspective gives us an understanding of what modern art has in common with the great tendencies of the past, yet it fails to emphasize the difference, which to me seems no less important. We will try to clarify this difference based on some of the teachings of Hegel's *Aesthetics*.

At first glance, it may seem paradoxical that we are attempting to shed light on the significance of the modern attitude to art by referring to an author whose whole conception, however magnificent it may be, revolves around the classical ideal, an ideal that modern art rejects with utmost vehemence. Yet our reliance on Hegel will be only indirect. Hegel's *Aesthetics* is the first modern treatise on art that is based on a consideration of the artistic universe, which, although far from complete, circling around the "Greco-Roman antiquity–Renaissance" axis, is nonetheless historically oriented. Hegel takes as the main subjects of his reflections Greek and so-called romantic art, i.e., art that is in a broad sense Christian, with an emphasis on the strongly rationalized Christianity of the modern age. Yet, beneath the surface of their shared humanist ideal, Hegel discovers an opposition, which in his view consists in the function of art in the overall development of spirit. Like religion and science, art is a specific *way* in which spirit apprehends itself, while at the same time representing a *stage* in the return of spirit to itself. The essential function of art, then, is to express truth. The truth of art is truth itself, spirit as the substance of being. Art, however, expresses this truth by confronting the perspective of spirit on objectivity with an ideal that expresses the absolute, the infinity of spirit, in finite, sensory form. Art is the self-contradictory miracle of reconciling the infinite with the finite, the intelligible with the sensory. This reconciliation itself, however, is only a tentative, unstable equilibrium. The depth and richness of spirit cannot be exhausted through art; spirituality, pure spirit as spirit, cannot be expressed by external means. Be that as it may, there does exist a period of historical progress when humanity is aware of the most important, defining spiritual matters only through art: At this point, art discovers the world, apprehending the truth with a depth that, for example, conceptual science, still in its beginnings, was not yet capable of. Greek sculpture, then, is not merely sculpture but religion, in the same way as Homer's epic, the tragedies of Aeschylus, and the Olympic games are. Certainly art is still capable of continuing after the fall of Greek antiquity. In modern painting and modern music, art turns inward, with the emphasis increasingly on spirituality, but this spirituality is no longer invented by art, the way that art invented the Olympian gods—although art here goes beyond the equilibrium between finite and infinite, it has lost its role as the spiritual leader of humanity. Next it falls to faith, soon it will fall to science, to formulate a clearer revelation of the absolute. And this whole evolution culminates in what Hegel calls the past character of art; when art has exhausted every domain of sensory and finite expression, when art no longer has anything substantial to say, it ceases to be a problem of the living spirit fighting for its expression—instead it becomes a splendid museum of our past efforts, which we may comprehend and take pleasure in forever, but we no longer expect from it any new enlightenment, either about the world or ourselves.

There is something extremely courageous and radical in this vision, so fully committed to the classical ideal—an understanding of the limitations of this ideal and of the inability to continue with it. One hundred years before the artistic revolution, Hegel sees a crisis in the art of his day that no one else suspects. At the same time, this vision shows us that a certain way of negating the traditional attitude to art can also be seen in the highly conservative approach, if art is judged historically. The revolution in art, then, is not an inorganic event with no relation to the themes of the previous era. Hegel is conscious of the profound difference between an art that creates gods and reveals the world, between the imperative and binding art of ancient times, and an art that no longer binds anyone, that revolves around itself and culminates in itself as created by its contemporaries. His one mistake is in identifying "humanistic" art, which pursues the expression of beauty and an idealized, transformed imitation of nature, with art in general. As a result he fails to see that the subjective, private, noncommittal nature of modern art could lead not to a pushing of art into the past, but to the coming of an age of *subjective style*.

To be clear, we do not share the premises of Hegel's system. No one today dares to defend his central theses. An absolute spirit that comprehends itself and whose dialectics does not merely reflect being but creates it; art as a contradictory adequation, a balancing, between the finite and the infinite—

that is not what concerns us here. Our focus is on the contrast between traditional art, which refers to something outside of art, where a work of art is transparent and open, so that its function is to reveal something other than art, and modern art, which ultimately resulted in the twentieth-century revolution, where a work is seen as such, as a *work of art*, and the world refers to the work, rather than the other way around, and therefore the work is an object complete in and of itself, in which the intentions of both artist and viewer alike are fulfilled. Yet by the same token we agree with Hegel that there are different ways in which we relate not only to things but also to being, these ways can be described as different forms of truth, and all these forms are interrelated in different ways at different times. Thus, for example, our culture is utterly dominated by conceptual cognition, as represented by mathematical natural science, the radical objectification of reality. It permeates our schooling from the elementary level up. Aided by technology it penetrates everywhere, and it is inconceivable that scientific methods and procedures would not also have some effect even on an activity as radically different as art. Whereas art once served as an incubator for the emerging fields of science and philosophy, now it must be newly conquered as a realm of abstract conceptuality by the weapon of intellectual reflection, employed with great intensity. So we see that the approach to works of art is not the same in every era; it depends largely on the constellation of intellectual activities in a given period, on their dominance or subordination—in short, it is not time-independent.

We can therefore modify Hegel's thesis that the function of art depends on time, in the sense that we set aside absolute knowledge and consider only finite truth in the form of science, philosophy, and art. However, we cannot elaborate on their relationships here with the depth and detail required, so rather than analyze these relationships we will illustrate them. So, for example, it is striking that the only spiritual expression of being that humans knew initially was ritual action. This was later expressed through art, and this evolution reached a point of incomparable richness and vigor as religion, science, and philosophy expanded within the scope of expressive possibilities it provided, without entirely breaking its predominance; on the other hand, the absolute supremacy of truth as the correct arbiter in modern times forces us to take an indirect, mediated approach to art; art is no longer the very air we breathe, as it was for Greek science, which *saw* ideas and whose proofs were works of architecture; for us, abstraction is the natural attitude of the mind, and this is plain to see in the art of our era.

Perhaps it might be possible to divide the spiritual history of humankind into two great epochs with a transitional stage in between: the era in which art dominates, and the era in which the abstract and formal concept dominates. In the first, art, that is, thinking through creation, through the seeing and representing of concrete shapes, is the natural medium for approaching the world, offering access to something other than art; a work of art is not seen in and of itself; our intention passes through it, directed toward the essence of all things; the people of the Stone Age taking in the paintings in Lascaux Cave, Athenian citizens before the Parthenon, medieval Christians gazing up at a Romanesque tympanum—none of them considered these works of art. The culture of this period is more artistic than aesthetic. In the second period, culture is essentially intellectual and volitional; it grasps hold of every object in order to analyze and master it, then it discovers among all these objects those that are artistic, works of art, and concentrates on them, thinking in a specific way that is historical and aesthetic. While an *aesthetic* attitude is certainly one component of this culture, the culture is not itself artistic in nature. Aesthetic culture is exemplified by the discovery of art as a specific activity, distinct from those that are purely technical, and by the collecting of artwork for purely theoretical purposes. The museum; the history of art and of literature (as long as they are not purely philological); aesthetics as a discrete branch of philosophy that strives to be scientific— these are characteristic inventions of this period. The culture of aesthetics spreads worldwide, conducting extensive research, making one discovery after another. But confronted with the concrete problems of artistic creation—for example, in the applied arts—it can only address them on the basis of factual analysis, through laws and the determination of abstract relations.[1]

One distinctive trait of this first system, in which art dominates, is that art here refers to something else. It is a method for experiencing, feeling, and thinking through religious, ceremonial, and other similar issues, something that gives access to a solemn, extraordinary, overpowering, divine facet or aspect of the world. However stylized it may be, however great the rift between its formal language and everyday reality, this art is inevitably an interpretation of the independent world. Employing the useful distinction of Arnold Gehlen, who identifies three layers of meaning in a work of art—the layer of formal elements, the layer of primary objects representing those elements, and the layer of ideal representations, which we arrive at through the first two layers—we observe that none of these layers may be missing in this type of art. The third layer in particular, the last in the hierarchy, brings the structure as a whole to completion. It is the most important layer, and its existence is conceived as independent of art and the work, neither synonymous with the existence of the work nor inextricably connected to it. This alone makes possible the strange captivation, the fascination that takes hold of us on seeing these creations.

For works of the reflective period, it is entirely different. Over the course of the nineteenth century, we see a decline in the importance of the ideal layer, first in favor of the layer of objects, then in favor of the layer of formal elements. By the time of modern landscape paintings, the center of gravity shifts, and we can hardly speak of three layers anymore. In Cézanne, for example, the object layer is merely a pretext for the creation of a grand pictorial style that plays out entirely in the most fundamental layer. And even if there is an ideal layer, as in the abstract compositions of Kandinsky or Mondrian, it does not lay claim to any existence other than in the painting; if the artist has other pretensions, we may refuse to give them credence and still the painting loses nothing in terms of meaning, depth, and content.

Another crucial point: In the period when art is dominant, it communicates "metaphysical qualities" to the viewer, corresponding with the essential transcendence of the work, which points to something else that illuminates the festive, ceremonial aspects of the world. "Metaphysical quality" is the term that the famous Polish philosopher Roman Ingarden uses to describe the "guiding idea" of an artwork.[2] Metaphysical quality is not identical with a painting's layer of ideal content. It is not the fact that male and female figures gathered around a well "represent" the meeting between Rebekah and Jacob.[3] It is the emotional dominant of a work, which acts as an integrating factor around which all the other elements crystallize. One might say that metaphysical quality is an artwork's overall meaning, explicated or developed in every element of the work; as in Bergson's model the simple act of movement is externalized, projected in space in an immeasurable number of body positions. This metaphysical quality, then, in the period when art dominates, relates to what is numinous, divine, miraculous. It varies depending on the way in which this numinosity manifests; often it is a *mysterium tremendum*, a fascinating horror, or an alien majesty, haughty and inaccessible; but whatever the case, the particular elements of the work, its formal and material constituents, to which this quality relates by way of its overall general meaning, are necessarily in accordance with this metaphysical quality. Ancient Greece and its artistic tradition foregrounded the fact that this metaphysical numinous element, on Mt. Olympus, turned into a *harmonious majesty*, and this tradition of harmony endures wherever the harmonizing influence of Greek art is felt. Harmony between the elements of a work of art and its overall meaning constitute what Hegel calls beauty—in the formal sense; the Greek contribution lies in the discovery that *consonance*, harmoniousness, a noble sense of proportion, is also an essential metaphysical quality, and therefore constitutes beauty in a material sense, in terms of content; so we can claim, at least to some extent, that a tendency to material beauty asserts itself in periods when art predominates. This creates a bridge between the periods of stylization and the period of imitation. In imitative art, "idealization," ennobling the transfiguration of sensuality, replaces the absolute transcendence of periods of zealous faith and religious ecstasy. And yet it is logical that art in an intellectual era would lose this harmonious dominant, with all metaphysical qualities equally permitted, no matter how diverse and divergent; they are all basically on the same level. Again, the "beauty" of a work becomes a formal matter, defined by the consonance of its elements with its overall meaning. This springs from the fact that metaphysical qualities themselves are now understood differently. It is no longer the work that proposes to say what dominates the world—rather, the world ultimately crystallizes into a world of meaning that exists only in and through the work. We may characterize this difference using the words of Mallarmé, who declared that the purpose of the world is to be contained in a "beautiful" book.[4] A diversity of worlds of meaning blossoms forth from modern art, with each world at a great distance from the others, and harmony being merely one value in a range of indefinite multiplicity, this multiplication of meaning in modern art inevitably leads to disharmony, unrest, even pain. The result being that the more it finds its own essence, the less accessible it is to a broad audience. Yet if art is not attractive by virtue of its metaphysical quality; if, on the contrary, it demands considerable intellectual effort, only to plunge us into a state of mind that is the opposite of harmony, pleasure, and reassurance, then the inexperienced mind may easily wonder what good it is.

This feature of modern art is nevertheless very closely connected with the relationship that ties the art of the modern era to the historical reality from which it springs, that is, the present day. We have proceeded from the thesis that the dominant spiritual trait of contemporary art is abstract intellectual knowledge; mathematical natural science, merged with technology in our current era, is the most perfect model of this that we have. This type of knowledge has become indispensable to the existence of society today. An industrial society in which production relies on artificial energy sources in ever-increasing quantities cannot do without predictive, constructive knowledge. Scientific-technological knowledge constructs "phenomena" based on current data, using formulas that allow for formal transformations, which we then interpret as predictions. This knowledge is superbly adapted to the task of not only the objectification of lived experience, but an objectification formalized to the extreme, in order to take maximum advantage of this knowledge. The reality to which this knowledge corresponds thus becomes the "natural" environment of a human race seeking vast resources of energy for a level of production that can only be sustained by expansion. It is no coincidence that the law of conservation of energy, essentially stating that energy is the very foundation of nature, the essence of nature in durable form, was discovered soon after the first wave of the Industrial Revolution. If we agree with those sociologists who maintain that the human "environment" has changed over the course of history—our first environment having been animals, who were our main partner in the days when we lived chiefly by hunting, after which our life came to center on that of plants, determined by large-scale astronomical rhythms corresponding to those of the sedentary farmer, creator of great civilizations and history in the proper sense—then we must also acknowledge that modern humanity is now undergoing yet another transition: to a world of inorganic nature, albeit inorganic nature in its abstract, non-representational form. This is a world less of "forces"—a word still evoking physiological associations that would be out of place here—than of formulas. Present-day humanity is increasingly under pressure from this fact; although the small-scale rhythm of private life may not exhibit this influence at every step, it is clearly evident in the underlying conditions: nuclear energy and its repercussions on society, the science and technology of human space travel, the mass production of energy and its impact on the landscape and the environment overall—in all these phenomena we are faced with the increasing effects of this new "environment" on the smallest aspects of our circumstances and interests in life. Ultimately, the world at large, the environment in which our life plays out, determining it day to day, is accessible only to a way of thinking that is highly abstract, formalized, calculating, and constructive.

The start of this fundamental transformation of the human environment can be traced back to the origins of the industrial era. Production maintained only through expansion is production in the capitalist mode. The unavoidable encounter of modern capitalism with abstract and formal rationality launches a process that ultimately transforms the very nature of present-day production. We see the appearance of a phenomenon described by one contemporary thinker as "unchained production," that is, a production whose main outcome is production itself, its efficiency, its organization, its ability to modernize and improve its facilities and supply chain.

This establishes a new concept of wealth: no longer does it consist of owning individual products, but of owning a "general product," i.e., production capacity itself. In order to seize the wealth produced by labor, therefore, it is not enough to take possession of its solid, reified products. It is no longer even possible to seize production once and for all; at best it can be organized, and the only way to do that is to be part of the process. Power and labor, then, show a tendency to merge; production absorbs distribution, government intervention in the economy increases, and organized labor becomes a factor in the power structure. The traditional shackles on production—the opposition between working labor and indolent power, active work and passive consumption—fall away one after the other. And, above all, production no longer encounters any external limit in a "nature" capable of transformation only insofar as that transformation is compatible with its eternal essence. This eternal essence, ostensibly expressed in the laws of nature, is something we no longer take into account, as any transformations we need are invented, with science at hand to seek and find new degrees of freedom for creative will; in the modern age of technoscience, nature is elastic as never before. No longer is there any definitive "given," either for an object or a human subject. Possibility no longer *precedes* reality but, in the course of reality's creative process, becomes reality itself.

At first glance, this perspective is a highly attractive one, giving cause for enthusiasm. All the bonds of traditional humanity seem to be broken or on their way to it. But upon closer examination, we see that the liberation we have described benefits not so much humans as human production. Production is not human, but an objective process in the third person; if humans are indispensable to it, it is only as a force of production, as an essential cog in the machine. Viewed in this way, "unchained production" is in fact the imprisonment of humanity, insofar as we consider humans to be the original subjective source of activity. One of the major phenomena of our times serves to illustrate this, a modern-day Prometheus in new chains: the consumer. Unchained production, inventing new products to anticipate the demand determined by pre-defined human needs, keeps us enthralled with the variety of goods on offer, exciting us at the prospect of being able to enjoy them even as new products are constantly produced in their place— thereby turning humanity into the instrument of an objective process of unchained production, which is to say, a process of ever-increasing power.

This may be a good place to define what we believe could be called a crisis of our planetary civilization, or—if we wish to reserve the term *civilization* for those historical-cultural complexes that are durable and extensive yet not all-embracing—a crisis of our rational supercivilization. This supercivilization is unquestionably rational, in the sense that it is based on the human capacity to deliberate and the effective rationality underlying that. Yet we may ask if this is still rationality in the traditional sense, where reason is the mark of human freedom, transforming an alien world into a human one. Or better put, this raises the pressing question: Is this still true of the technoscientific reason of our day? In becoming more efficient by comparison with antiquity and the Middle Ages, has reason become a prisoner of efficiency? It seems that reason no longer knows anything absolute, nothing capable of dominating life in its totality, nothing transcending the bad infinity produced by our creative realizations because they are still relative. This reasoning capacity is immanent in character rather than transcendent. Immanent in the process of production, it is an instrument of ever-increasing power. A curious teleology manifests itself here, a purpose-driven anti-teleology: the only being we know of that can knowingly transform things and processes into means toward an end, thereby giving meaning to things, itself becomes part of a process in the third person, a process of ever-increasing accumulation of power to which every human meaning ultimately succumbs, turning into nonsense. It is tempting to interpret the rift in today's world, too, its schism, into two systems, which originated in the passionate yearning for human emancipation, through the demonic accomplishments of this inverted finality. Two or even multiple worlds in confrontation, each threatening the others with extinction, living in fear that the others may overtake us—what an unrivalled instrument for the accumulation of power!

And this is also why scientific reasoning, no matter how dazzling its feats, no matter how innovative its inventions, cannot serve as an argument in the debate on freedom, on the autonomy of the human being. As for philosophy, which strives to move beyond the perspective of technical considerations, it is divided within itself—how many philosophers have put themselves at the service of this idea of efficiency and power!—and further, it must reconsider its categories in light of the new facts that we have presented here, a task with which it has yet to come to grips. Granted, some great thinkers have meditated on the plight of our world; one of them has identified the origin of the crisis as European science, which has convinced itself and us alike that the methodological approach it employs—abstraction, idealization, formalization, and construction with the assistance of idealized concepts—defines the very reality of things. Others, however, feel that there is a profound transformation of the relation to being itself at work in our technoscience—a forgetting of the essential that may act as preparation for a new revelation of the essential by radically setting it apart from all relative content, which always concerns individual existing things. But this all merely points to the fact that philosophy has scarcely taken the first few steps toward defining this problem, and cannot yet determine with convincing clarity the locus of freedom and autonomy, the original source of humanity. Yet there is one essential activity of present-day humanity that we dare assert is integral and by definition authentic proof of our freedom of spirit. This activity is none other than art—assuming art is the creation of works whose viewing *possesses meaning in itself as a lived experience that does not refer to anything other or beyond itself*. And it is the art of the *aesthetic epoch*, as we have attempted to define it here, that most strongly exhibits this characteristic, even in the case of art "engagé"—even then, it still incorporates the value that it is supposed "to serve" and around which it crystallizes, embedding it in the framework of what it gives us to experience, what it presents us with. Thus contemporary art, like all art, is an assertion of interiority, and therefore of freedom. In art, human creativity does not serve as a pretext for anything else. The moment a person embarks on the adventure that is art, they assert themselves as a fundamentally inalienable being, protesting against the invasion of exteriority. To be sure, art, like every other contemporary human activity, can be exploited by the unchained production and consumption of artistic works; this is symptomatic of our era; art as a social reality is powerless in the face of the social forces that seize hold of it in that reality; but the *meaning* of art, its inner significance, is unaffected. If contemporary art adheres as closely as possible to the sources of contemporary life, it is not a challenge to lose ourselves in its labyrinths, but on the contrary a call for us to wake up, to make us see and feel what we are no longer capable of seeing and feeling in everyday life, penetrated to the core as we are by forces that bring us into conflict with ourselves.

This is not to say that the art of our time has no internal tension, that there are no ruptures which require resolution. The main such division now is the contradiction between the heritage of the past and the problems of the present. Our past heritage is one of halfway measures, of compromise suggesting that we continue in the ways of the nineteenth century without subjecting them to reconsideration. The art of the pre-Renaissance period exhibits an artificial expressive style, making evident the solemn, superhuman aspect of the world, whereas the last great periods, the Renaissance and

Baroque, seek to achieve the same result by different means, with imitation prevailing over style. The nineteenth century realizes that art is a universe of self-contained meaning, independent and self-sufficient, yet preserves imitation, description, and analysis of the given as indispensable components of a work. It is also the nineteenth century that creates the concept of subjective art, or rather that allows the blossoming of long-existing tendencies in that direction. One consequence of this development, which had been underway since the Renaissance, is that the layer of ideal representations, the "content" of a work of art, becomes fictitious and the imitation of sensorially given forms thus loses its original meaning. At this point one could attempt to replace the old ideal contents with new ones, but these contents, drawn from everyday life, rather than from the sphere that transcends it and gives it the fullness of being, turn out to be alien to the art, a mere additive, extraneous and utilitarian. The other possibility is to strip away all the fictions and conventions, upheld until now for extrinsic reasons; in this way the artist's undertaking may be conceived as the attempt at a radical foundation for a concretely lived meaning—and this puts us the on the path to the art of our time.

As is evident from the previous, then, there is a continuity between the art of the nineteenth century and the art of the present day. We may even say that the great artistic gains of the nineteenth century laid the foundations for those of the twentieth. Painting not only definitively parted ways with architecture—Dutch painting saw to that—but also gradually freed itself of ideological conventions. The canvas became a window onto a world that was exclusively pictorial. Instrumental music created a self-contained musical space, with the ability to conceive imaginary events, rather than being merely an element in the creation of real space. In this regard, Wagner's decision to hide the orchestra from view of the audience, eliminating the bridge between reality and theatrical illusion, was symbolic. Parallel phenomena appeared in every branch of art, based on the same principle: art is a universe of particular, concretely lived meanings; we can understand and identify with them, but they are not binding, and in that sense may be viewed as "subjective." Many of those involved in the production of art during this subjective, romantic period believed that this allowed them to draw a conclusion very much of the era: namely, that art is not only a universe unto itself, but something more—it is salvation, delivering us from the ordinary world, a land where we can live in safety, undisturbed by vulgar reality.

This is precisely where the art of our time draws a line between itself and the art of the nineteenth century. Contemporary art does not seek to be an artificial paradise, which humans create so that they no longer have to live. If the art of our time *does not represent*, does not describe, the ordinary world, that is not to say it *does not express* it. It expresses it through the artist. This is what sets it apart from all the art for art's sake experimentation (*l'art pour l'art*). We can go even so far as to say that the attitude of artists today still implies certain theses about our shared everyday world—although negative, to be sure. There is no "salvation," no single focal point of meaning to which everything else ultimately relates. Nor do the formal practices of contemporary art stand in the way of the work being considered from the standpoint of ordinary reality. This is why modern drama goes beyond the boundaries of the stage, attempting to bridge the "theater–spectator" divide; this is why sculpture is coming down from the pedestal and painting is returning the pictorial surface to visibility after its disappearance since Giotto's time. Contemporary art is a part of our reality, and in the framework of that reality it fulfills an irreplaceable function. This art demands to be seen not only in itself, but also in light of this function, which is not one of escape. As we have seen, art is an irrefutable manifestation of human freedom, bearing the indelible seal of that freedom even in this age of unchained production, which subordinates humanity to a process of objectification through the ideal of Homo consumens. The inner meaning of art is a powerful protest against this abdication of self. For the very reason that it is rooted within its time, that it is not an artificial paradise, it can express the internal impoverishment and hardship of our times more effectively than any other form of cultural activity. There are critics who believe that this art necessarily leads to our being reconciled to the present, with its prevailing tendencies to habituate us to the current state of affairs, so that we feel comfortable, but I believe they are wrong about what this art seeks to be and in fact is. The profound sense of freedom that permeates modern art is especially clear in the formal means that it employs: to be sure, by concentrating on the underlying layer of meaning that *signifies*, it sacrifices the metaphysical layer of *signified* in the sense of what is told, but this allows the work to concentrate not on what it tells, but what it *is*. Art in its current process of liberation is the world, the outpouring of being, the concrete meaning that emerges from elements that are in themselves mute; it is pure creation in which we take part by taking part in the work: yet at the same time it is also practical evidence that humanity is not merely an accumulator and transformer of the energy produced by the interplay of cosmic forces, but rather a genuine source of creation, a freedom.

Here I conclude my tentative reflections on art and time. We have seen that, historically, art was at first a method of expressing all of spiritual life, a medium itself invisible, yet making visible the solemn, ritual, superhuman element of the universe. In an essentially intellectual world, art has become a particular activity, the production of objects of a certain type, distinguishable among other things by traits unique to them alone; objects that express a world of concrete meanings, which can not only be thought but directly lived, and are organized based on the principles of a meaning that originates in human spirit and is therefore comprehensible but not binding and, in that sense, is "subjective." This is the perspective that we are obliged to take now when looking at every creative work, including those of the past, which were viewed entirely differently in their own times. It is especially important for educators to adopt this point of view, given that it is their task to deepen the understanding of works of art, and I believe there are undeniable implications to what we have attempted to demonstrate here: the paramount importance of contemporary art for the *entire* task with which the educator is charged; the art of the past cannot be understood unless we see it in the light of the present; art for us cannot be a method, an element of a feat of magic, or of a ritual or religious act. Art for us today is a style, a language at once both formal and concrete, expressing the creative power of humanity, i.e., the capacity to make Being manifest. Yet if humans are the place where Being manifests itself, it follows that we are not a cybernetic machine powered by cosmic energy. This means that art educators have a unique and essential role to play in the current crisis of humanity, a role which they can carry out only if they are mindful of the significance of this moment that we are now living.

In the past, there have been several grand ideas about the importance of art education. First, the idea of Shaftesbury, adopted by Herder, that art is an indispensable instrument of humanization, by virtue of the fact that it alone among human activities cultivates sentiment. Then there is the idea, advanced mainly by Konrad Fiedler, that art, being a form of intuitive knowledge, differs from knowledge that is solely intellectual in that it is an indispensable exploration of the sensory world that humans inhabit, and it is impossible to imagine a truly human culture without it. Even more profound was Schiller's idea that the educational significance of art lies in the fact that it prepares us for a period in history when a truly human and humane freedom will reign, neither arbitrary nor cruel. Finally, let us once more cite Hegel, who, counter to all this, asserts that the essential role of art education is an *aesthetic* education turned toward the past, that the meaning of art has undergone a profound change over the course of history, and that art itself no longer represents the living apex of spirit. Each of these ideas contains a grain of truth that we can retain without lapsing into tendentiousness, and that is what we have attempted here: for us too, art is an exploration of the visible world (treating "visibility" in the broad sense of everything accessible either directly or through the senses) that refines our affective life, the life that opens new horizons; although Fiedler was surely mistaken in emphasizing sensory *knowledge* as opposed to the active *creation* of style.

Finally, with regard to Hegel, we should note: it is probably true that the significance of art has changed in the radically intellectualized world of today; yet, in spite of this profound change, art remains the most eloquent, least ambiguous testimony to free creative power, to the profound autonomy of the spirit. Those educators who succeed in firmly anchoring and deepening our understanding of art perform a task without parallel: basing their work on the solid rock of authentic art, they prepare the way for what we might call, with Hegel, a new inroad of the spirit.

Notes

1   In the first version of this essay, written in French, the following sentence appears here: "On connaît bien la fameuse histoire de Gottfried Semper, critique de l'exposition mondiale de Londres en 1850: il reconnaît loyalement que les peuples européens, supérieurs aux autres par le savoir et la technique, sont absolument aveugles en ce qui concerne les principes du style de leurs produits, et sont battus dans tout ce domaine par ceux qu'ils osent appeler des sous-développés ou primitifs—qui manifestent au contraire un sentiment infaillible de ce qu'il faut faire."

"The story of Gottfried Semper, a critic of the Great Exhibition in London in 1851, is well known: he faithfully acknowledged that the European nations, superior to others in matters of knowledge and technology, were entirely blind concerning the principles of style in what they produced, and were bested in every area of this domain by those whom they dare to call underdeveloped or primitive—yet who, on the other hand, demonstrate an infallible sense of what needs to be done."

2   Roman Ingarden, *Das Literarische Kunstwerk: Eine Untersuchung aus dem Grenzgebiet der Ontologie, Logik und Literaturwissenschaft* (Halle: Max Niemeyer, 1931) (Ed.).

3   There are two important meetings at a well in the Old Testament: Rebekah with Eliezer (Genesis 24), and Rachel with Jacob, son of Rebekah (Genesis 26). Both meetings have served as inspiration to countless artists. It is impossible to determine which meeting and which picture Patočka had in mind when writing this sentence (Ed.).

4   What Mallarmé actually wrote was "tout, au monde, existe pour aboutir à un livre" ("everything in the world exists in order to end up in a book"). See Stéphane Mallarmé, *Œuvres complètes* (Paris: Gallimard/Bibliothèque de la Pléiade, 1945), 378. Probably what Patočka had in mind was the version reported by Paul Valéry, in a speech delivered at the fourth international congress of the P.E.N. Club in Berlin, in 1926: "Le monde, disait-il, est fait pour aboutir à un beau livre" ("The world, he said, is made in order to end up in a beautiful book") (Ed.).

CHAPTER TEN

Time, Eternity, and Temporality in the Work of Karel Hynek Mácha (1967)

Translated from the Czech by Alex Zucker

These few brief remarks do not purport to be a literary-scientific study of the themes of time and eternity in Mácha.[1] Rather, this is an attempt at a philosophical *interpretation* of Mácha's poetry, guided by two questions:

1. Is Mácha's melancholy, as a typical feeling of fleeing, of the extinction of everything individual, a mere personal sentiment, or is there a coherent view behind it on the nature of time, eternity, their mutual relationship, and the consequences that flow from it?

If it turns out to be possible to find or construct a thought schema that Mácha's statements conform to, then there is a strong presumption for the second alternative.

2. If we wish to understand the poet, is not the way to do so by construction of a unitary schema based on the striking, contrary, self-contradictory features in his formulations and by attempting to introduce unity to these contradictions? It is quite unlikely that *every* contradiction could be explained by way of a *different* schema. Therefore is it not the first requirement to identify these dark, at first glance problematic and unintelligible passages and statements? Should we succeed in finding the key to these contradictions, presumably it will also serve as a key to the poetry as a whole, exposing its core and essence, even if the poet himself never conceived of or presented such a schema constructed in abstract form.

I

The observations from which we proceed are:

1. Mácha's characterization of childhood as evening—in contradiction to the most common, natural parallels and schemas ("Večer na Bezdězu");[2] this characterization is temporospatial;

2. His characterization of eternity as apprehensible only in the negative, as emptiness, "nothingness";[3]

3. His characterization of his own *future* in *Máj* is the image of a pilgrim, whom we never see again *once he passes*—in other words, something that is essentially characterized by the *past*. The future as something past.[4]

Let us now take a closer, clearer look at the relevant texts.

> . . . in the same way, whenever I have read a comparison of human life to the different stages of the day, I have concluded that it would not do to compare the time of childhood and early youth to morning, just as the years of adolescence should not be called midday, just as it would not do to liken the manful age to afternoon and old age to evening; but rather it has always seemed to me that childhood should be called evening, the adolescent years night, and so on.
>
> For man enters this world a child; in evening's embrace the land is ablaze with rosy-red like a beautiful tranquil painting; *only the landscape nearest is clear*, only it can be seen; the distant mountains before and behind us glimmer, mere dusky shadows in the evening sky. So tranquil do the earth and its creatures appear to the child's bright eyes and innocent soul; *it sees only what is nearest, not knowing the past, not guessing at the future*; life, tranquil and beautiful, promises the child everything . . . the child's years pass quickly, more quickly than a spring evening."[5]

Highlighted here is the temporal characteristic of childhood—the concentration on the living present with no long-range perspective, i.e., without entering into the horizon of future and past; these stand only on the distant edge like shadows, attracting no reflective gaze. Each moment is lived fully and trustingly—every moment is a *promise*, that is, the present is open to the future with no misgivings, no differentiation even: this present is naturally trusting and believing. It is the domain of every original positive attitude—faith, hope, love, trust—intrinsic to life in its original naive form. If Mácha in *Versuche*[6] sings the praises of these "virtues," it is not a matter of Christian morality, but a characteristic of this primal naiveté. For the spilling of the present into the future is a self-evident faith that is not at all aware of itself, and in its stepping out of itself it is eager hope (that the future present will be in essence the same as the one here now, that is, the one the child accepts and feels itself to be in quiet agreement and harmony with), love—i.e., abiding harmony; and all of these attitudes as a whole signify *trust*. Minor sorrows and displeasures cannot ruin the fundamental, overall attitude of trust, in which the living present spills into the future; thus, given over to itself, this feeling might last with no end: the first reflection perceives duration as a form of permanence that seeks endless repetition of itself—into infinity. It does not yet apprehend infinitude as *mere* repetition, as *bad* infinitude, but sees it as self-evident that it is eternal life—it is not yet clear that this is a *contradictio in adiecto*. If faith, hope, love are seen as *sequential* leaders along the road of life,[7] then all these leaders together are but nuances of a single fundamental trust that does not wane and lasts beyond the grave. Affiliated with this first self-sense and self-understanding of life, therefore, is *eternity in time*, eternity understood as *life eternal*. Yet at the same time it is apparent that with this temporal projection, with the above-mentioned "virtues" successively replacing one another in the lead, the original self-evident trust becomes strained, shaky; the distance between the present and the future becomes perceptible; and as a result, faith no longer appears as a naive spilling over, but rather as an act of mighty courage. This is the subject of the poem "Columbus"[8]—a celebration of this bravery, which at the last moment is rewarded and fulfilled—because to discover a land that already exists, it suffices to hope and believe long enough. Yet it is hard to keep from asking, What if the land had been too distant for the patience of his shipmates? What if it had been out of reach for any *human life* at all? The act of faith renders eternity finite, making it as close as the moon that a child's hand reaches out to touch. The crew gave Columbus a deadline of three days; where is the guarantee that land will appear *within that time*? A new land, a destination, where one can come to rest, where everything is headed—is all that within reach of human life? Is life, as life itself naively and naturally believes, life eternal?

It is of course possible to respond to this lack of trust, on the contrary, with trust and faith. We can hope ad infinitum, as long as some dark horizon of the future lies before us—maybe the land will appear a minute after death and not as it did for Columbus, but that does not disturb the original childish happiness of life, as the date is sheerly arbitrary. The real crisis occurs as soon as we ask eternity itself about its essence and its relationship to time.

The time of life when this question arises, when a person is fundamentally alienated from the close, the given, the present, "the earth," is adolescence—in Czech, *jinošství*, "otherhood." Mácha: "Our tongue has titled this age outstandingly; a young man of this age is an alien, an other to our land, wandering in other realms, rearing up in the flight of his thoughts; he stands alone, seeing nothing but phantoms of his own images of himself."[9] Adolescence is a time of distance as well as solitude. Distance, however, is always *from* something, and what the adolescent here is distancing himself from is not merely things in space or in time. The greatest distance is from that which precedes any thing, and that is none other than time. Only this distance makes it possible to glimpse time in its essence. Yet the poem says also that the adolescent "sees only phantoms of his own images." The adolescent fundamentally, inherently yearns—for something beyond appearances. What is this unreality? This yearning is directed upward, toward the stars, toward ideals, toward the place "where the homeland is," "the fatherland,"[10] toward the "realm of light,"[11] where the "form of beauty" resides, that is, ideas, eternal archetypes—hence toward eternity. But eternity cannot be seen, eternity cannot appear; we can only darkly sense it in the depths of our soul,[12] the sight of something eternal cannot be reconciled with our physical, manifest actuality. The more the adolescent distances himself from the earth in the direction of eternity, the clearer it becomes that time is incommensurable with eternity, that eternity does not exist in time. Thus he sees also his childhood now in a different form: it is both ideal and real at once, an unachievable, utopian unity of the two—childhood is therefore fundamentally lapsed, past, irretrievable. It can never be brought back to life. *Therefore* it is not only passing, but wholly past in the sense that it is unrevivable. As long as a note is resounding, as long as any single phase of it is given, the whole note is alive; as long as we hear any note of a melody, the whole melody is present; any conflict, concern, or drama that we are living through is here in its *entirety*, not only in its current phase; yet childhood, once past, is never brought back to life in this way, and never can be. This is expressed in the famous metaphors of cantos III and IV of *Máj*, about the towns reflected in the water, the final thoughts of the dead, the faded northern lights . . .[13] The adolescent sees at the same time both the true reality of time and the false idealization of it, which he enacts, which *is* childhood. The distance he has reached enables him to see both at once—time in its reality as well as in its illusory form. We already know what its illusory form is like. But what do we know of the "reality" of time? It is strange, it is twofold: On one hand, nothing can appear except in time, therefore time is the phenomenon of all phenomena, truer than any individual, finite truth; on the other hand, it is a passing, a lapsing, a fading away into the irretrievable, a dissipation of every phenomenon to the point of nonexistence. Eternity can never be drawn into this nullifying, annihilating realm, it is absolutely incommensurable with it, and for us who are temporal beings it is absolutely unattainable, no matter that we may have a "dark affection" for it. The essence of time, then, is the finishing of the given, or better put: its *finishedness*. The essence of time is the *triumph of the past*. Time is the "brother of death."[14] The ability to see this essence of time is tied to distance, to a detachment from time and nature, and this detachment (this "jinošství," i.e., "otherness," i.e., adolescence), which is the outbreak of *freedom*, is at the same time the origin, the enablement, of all evil—of which, of all that exists, only humans are capable. Therefore time, understood in this way, is "the son of loathsome sin,"[15] the fruit of distance and alienation. The adolescent therefore lives in an impossible double longing: longing for a childhood that he knows is irretrievably gone, because it is an illusion; and longing for an eternity that he knows is not an illusion—as his dark affection gives away—but which he knows is incommensurable with him, the living phenomenon, the subjectivity of a being to which the world appears.

Is there any way to express this "dark affection" in fuller, nuanced fashion? Is not this idea in and of itself self-contradictory? We cannot *know* eternity, it is not accessible to us in a positive way, by *determining* it; but there does exist something like negative access to it. Access by way of "nothing." For us, eternity is "nothing," it is "that which we *call* nothing,"[16] but that does not mean it is nothing *in its essence*. It is not that eternity is nothing, but that nothing is eternity announcing itself to us. In "nothing" the finitude of appearances announces itself, and that means also the finitude of time. The attempt to gain this intuition of eternity, to achieve the state of ecstasy that leads toward it, are the subject of the second canto of *Máj*.

The ecstasy of eternity in *Máj* is presented in three sections with a prelude.

The prelude is the first column of verse, which, without a paragraph break, first describes a fallen star, then a fallen man. A fallen star and a fallen man—is this a parallel or a contrast? Both. The fallen star, whose "weeping resounds from the grave of all," the universal grave, is earth. ("Unhappy land, unhappy mother! You deeply feel the immense grief of your innumerable creatures, and yet you see no end in sight, no deliverance.")[17] The earth's life lies within us, our serenity lies within it, therefore our grief is its grief, and since the earth is a universal, therefore immortal being, there is no ending or deliverance to its grief, whereas ours comes to an end. The criminal awaiting his death the next day is a piece of the earth; his anxiety, dread, and pain are the earth's. Inside the prison there is "sheer darkness,"[18] as in the earth's interior. Thus the omnitemporality of earth and the temporality of humanity stand opposite each other; eternity makes its appearance in opposition to both.

The appearance of eternity takes place in three sections. The first is devoted to themes of the past: ranging from the prisoner's recollection of his native village—his childhood landscape—to the illusion of an eternal life of bliss, which we will see repeated again later, despite that it is revealed for the illusion that it is, despite that it goes hand in hand with the tragedy it conceals—and embracing the main feature of the past, *guilt*, a terrible fall into the greatest and typically human crime, Oedipus's offense: the murder of the father in revenge for the mistress-mother, the perversion of every natural relationship, of all "humanity" in the common sense of the word, of everything that embeds us in reality, everything that binds us to it. *Guilt* is the vanishing point of this section of the poem. But what is, ultimately, the essence of guilt? Is it not that which underlies and enables every guilt? And is what enables it not that very distancing from nature and the bliss of childhood, from childish innocence, that isolation, that otherness, that freedom and distance which is nothing else but the way in which the abandonment of the earth by eternity is reflected in humans, revealing the age-old illusion that is eternity in time, the illusion of childhood? Earth seduced, is that not the illusion of childhood?

Yet most importantly, while guilt is associated with a freedom that feels out, with an instinctive, near-somnambulistic assurance, what *it wants to do*, what is necessary for it to do, its true mission—the moment it *experiences humiliation*, it *must* immediately compensate by "getting even," taking revenge—at the same time this obvious, clear resolve amounts to the *acceptance* of a mission. And this mission then forces a concentration on the act, a *detection* of everything that provides an opportunity for it —resolve, acceptance, and detection, although by their nature regarding different dimensions of time, are inseparable from one another. While this whole act is characterized by a peculiar *necessity* that leaves no room for Hamletizing— no deliberations, indecision, hesitation—and under any circumstances, even with the utmost deliberateness, would always proceed in essentially the same way, it is clear that this resolve is freedom *without clarity*, a freedom in some sense blinded, unseeing, and in this inability to see *overcoming* the situation's problematicity.

As a result, the act is always a disruption of a boundless web of relationships and interests, tearing them apart even as it weaves new ones at the same time, thoughtlessly upsetting the equilibrium with no clarity about the boundless consequences. That means the act is always one of opposition, something not in symmetry with what is given, standing opposed to it as alien, always in a position of part *non-understanding, non-comprehending*, in part *wrongdoing* (crime, rebellion, negation). The status quo, which of course was itself also created by an act such as this, was also a solidified sedimentation of guilt—thus guilt begets guilt, the father's guilt the son's— to the point that one may ask whether the guilt is really *my guilt*, or whether it is not just punishment for an older guilt, whether we are not just "lured into the dream of life"[19] only so that we may punish the guilt of our fathers. To right a wrong always means—from another viewpoint—to commit a wrong. There can never be freedom without an act, but an act is always finite and guilty. There is always an act in Oedipus's situation—originally he sees *before him* only redress, only a mission, but inevitably he drags the guilt *behind him*.

To punish another's guilt and in so doing to become guilty oneself—is that not then the end of the idea of guilt? Is not the punishment of guilt, conceived of as a metaphysical mission, a document of the colossal metaphysical injustice that has toyed with human life by cursing it to a never-ending chain of culpability—which injustice itself has wrought and for which therefore it itself is ultimately responsible? Punishing a person both in time and in eternity for something of which, ultimately, it itself is the cause, this injustice that merely pretends to be just?

With this metaphysical meditation, this attempt to blunt the point of guilt, the meditation on the past comes to a close. Resolution comes only in the third canto, with the criminal's humiliation and acceptance of guilt—to say *yes* to my freedom means also to agree that I am guilty, with all the consequences, including the sword that comes down on my neck—for only then can I be that free being that exists in relation not merely to a time emptied of its essence, but also to what stands above time, what Mácha terms eternity. Although evil is in a sense "hereditary," handed down from one generation to the next, guilt is always *my* fault, and only at the cost of guilt am I what I am—the *other*, the adolescent who discovers the emptiness of dead, worldly time. The *beginning* of the answer is therefore the next section of the second canto with its theme of the future and eternity.

A metaphysical meditation on guilt as revenge for past guilt, a response to it that continues it, has from this perspective a different function: it shows the acceptance of his mission as an act of *repetition*. Under new circumstances, the free being *repeatedly* takes up a mission of the *same* formal structure, a mission that existed already before and that exists in every historical struggle.

Toward the end of section one, the prisoner's fate is forecast as the grand theme of section two: the future and, with it, the antithesis of eternity and time. This theme ignites in the antithesis of two nights. A springtime night in nature is undoubtedly a moment, i.e., time, and, to an extent, time is night too—the present emerges from the dark, then sinks back into darkness, like the stars in the sky. The night in nature, time, is an interrupted darkness, broken by the brightly shining courtyard of the present. There is nothing like that in the second, deeper night of eternity: no interruption, no shape or boundary, nothing finite. To be sure, what melts away without shape, like music, like an emotion, offering us a moment of communion and forgetfulness—and is only part of the first night, while absent from the severity of the second—even that is nothing but a "vain yearning for a vanished world."[20] Any attempt at a bridging unity, neglecting the differences between the two, brings us no closer to an understanding of eternity. This meditation on time transitions naturally into the theme of the life-dream; after all, time is an emerging of the present from the dark into the dark, an interrupted appearing—like a dream—and as a "form of inner sense"[21] time is the requirement for all revealing, for all experience in general. The dream in life and the life-dream, continuing beyond death itself, repeating subjectivity in new forms—this is the first theme that emerges; this is how life looks from the viewpoint of the universal being, from the viewpoint of omnitemporality, from the viewpoint of earth. But eternity is something else; it is much closer to "sleeping without dreaming,"[22] a notion that emerges in the prisoner's mind at first only at random. He then abandons it in order to exhaust the subject of life-dream, then again abandons the subject with a skeptical "no one knows."[23] And when at last the stars go out, and instead of music the only sound is time itself in drops of water falling from the ceiling, counting the moments disappearing, one by one, with a mechanistic monotony, the theme that is the heaviest, evading both eye and mind the longest, is urgently drawing near, the theme of the second night: eternity.

Eternity has nothing in common with time: If time is at once expanding and contracting, if it is a border constantly crossed, a dividing line constantly breaking down the whole, then the negative of this aspect of time is the key to eternity. The infinity of eternity is boundless both *ad extra* and *ad intra*; there is nothing in it to grab hold of, no radiance, no differentiation—therefore also no "from where—to where" and thus no destination or movement. Without the possibility to determine a thing or event, all that is left is sheer negation, sheer emptiness; our idea has no foundation, no support for its finite activity, and so falls asleep—forever. Dies. It is—for us—sheer nothing, "that which we call nothing,"[24] in fact true infinity, eternity. *For us* this most positive quality is the most negative, absolutely incommensurable with humans as beings of mere appearance.

The fourth section is made up of the prisoner's ecstatic vision and the scene with the guard. Gaze fixed on infinity, the prisoner sees nothing, or rather *he sees* nothing, thrashing about in an "ecstatic"[25] dream; the prisoner whispers words the guard can glean only by placing his ear to the prisoner's lips, and what they make clear is a struggle for his spirit and his soul, his own individual existence, which is disintegrating in infinity. The content of his communication, though not explicitly stated in Mácha's poem, is plain from the outcome—the guard never smiles again in his life—the "otherness" of the convict is passed on to him. What is the motif of this change? Is this just a trite Romantic image, or is there some deeper connection here to the whole issue of time and eternity?

This would be an appropriate place to move to our third observation: the characterization of the future by way of the past, of the future as past. This image, which we find at the end of *Máj* ("Do you see the pilgrim . . . Never again will you set eyes on that pilgrim once he disappears"[26]—in which the relationship to the future is the same as to what has passed: nevermore, etc.), occurs also at the end of "Pouť krkonošská": The future, preceding us in our youth in the form of a pale-skinned woman, turns into a gray-haired old man who strides ahead of the pilgrim, leading him into a dark underground passage, where he will sleep the eternal dream.[27] The understanding that eternity is incommensurable with time, that forever is beyond time, exhibits its main characteristic in relation to the future. Even the future itself is marked by the past; it too is lost in a way, having lapsed into the past, even before birth unavoidably sinking toward and destined to extinction. The future is no longer that promising time into which the present imperceptibly spills, but that which signals disappointment in advance. Nothing true or ultimate, in the strong sense of the word "real," can be expected of it; no encounter with what *is* in its full meaning. Not only the poet who has grasped it, but also the "guard" to whom the prisoner has conveyed it, live a changed life from that moment on: "Who will give comfort to such a heart?"[28] Nothing positive can be expected from sober experience; it has no ultimate, passionate bond to offer, the way we are bound by a dark, indissoluble bond to eternity; it offers nothing that could be loved in the way the naive gaze of a child loves the illusion of eternity in time. This love is betrayed in advance; it is more compassion than love.

In essence, then, in this approach to time there is still a clear predominance, a triumph of the past—even if the past is the quasi-present, the present may be seen as the here and now of the past, and likewise the future as the emerging, nascent here and now of the past. The emerging here and now is always a nascent not-here-and-now, and what time in its monotonous way begets is, in the end, always the not-here-and-now. Without the present there is no past, yet the present does not stop at itself, but transfers its contents into the past, which is definitive, from which nothing returns, in which everything finds its final place and destination. For even if, from an objective standpoint, the time line, with all its points, flows ever steadily into the past, from the standpoint of the original appearing in our lives, the past is an abyss of forgetting, from which we can summon into the present individual shadows, yet the shadows called forth are incomplete, not fully alive, and so overwhelmed by the dead that the living fades away under its weight.

Given these assumptions, how are we to understand the project of "celebrat[ing] the beauty of nature in May"?[29] For, according to the poet himself, this is *Máj*'s main purpose. Nature is beautiful as an illusion that has been unmasked, as something past and unreal, a mere sensory image of an idea (of eternity). Beauty is not an inherent property of nature; its beauty is in its manifestation, and nature's manifestation, persisting in spite of its being seen through, has, in contrast to the ultimate truth itself and in its ironic counterpoint, an undying charm. Despite its essentially dead and prosaic substrate, nature time and again takes on the countenance of eternity in its manifestation, of eternity in time. (Schiller's theory of aesthetic semblance may not be entirely alien to this concept.) Nature itself does not know that it is beautiful, and beauty is not its objective purpose, but rather our approach and judgment, and this approach presupposes both the givenness of illusion and its shattering. The givenness of illusion is not yet in and of itself beautiful—a child does not experience beauty; that comes only with adolescence. And so only when time times itself from the past, from its "prior" dimension, from what *already* is here and finished, when the uncovered deeper nature of time enables us to see the nature of time with our own eyes, does this illusion stand before us as a whole—as *beauty*, as "freedom manifested," as a contradiction that nevertheless "is," a contradiction that is a persistent phenomenon.

In his own interpretation of *Máj*, Mácha writes that in the first canto he sets "the quiet, solemn, etc. love found in nature against the wild, passionate, unbridled love of man; likewise other qualities of May nature are set against similar seasons of human life in the other cantos."[30] Love in nature, however, is only an *image*, a symbol, an illusion of eternity in time; similarly, in the second canto, night is just an illusory symbol of eternity, of the second night, and in the third canto, the splendor of the day is likewise a veil through which the truth of the tragic fate is illuminated and thereby somewhat softened.

We may use the viewpoint indicated above to interpret not only *Máj*, but also Mácha's other, equally enigmatic poems. For example, the masterpieces "Těžkomyslnost" ("Melancholy"), "Budoucí vlast'" ("The Future Homeland"), "Jaroslavna," "Vzor krásy" ("The Form of Beauty"), and the fragment "Duše nesmrtelná, která bydlíš . . ." ("Immortal soul, you who reside . . ."). This same point of view also enables us to understand the tension between Mácha's "nihilistic" and theistic subject matter.

In spite of Mácha's "nihilism," consisting in an awareness of the incommensurability of time with eternity, and therefore negating the commonplace conception of individual immortality, there is undoubtedly a theological theme that appears in *Máj* as well as in his other poems. God here appears as lord of the realm of eternity, as he who created the world along with its forms, and therefore as inaccessible and hidden to us as eternity. Yet we are bound to God by dark affection in the same way we are to eternity, and in the same act with which we liberate ourselves from nature; the exposing of its illusion, its "seducedness," is at the same time a revolt against God, because it is also a discovery of our cruel fate, our hopeless situation in the world. God is the lord of the page boy in the "future homeland"; the page seeks here, in life, in life's manifestations and beyond them, the true being for which he yearns, "his homeland," and in vain are the words of warning that he has no homeland; his lord gives him the only possible consolation of dreamers—namely, the eternal dream, death, eternity, and perhaps even transformation. God as lord has ambivalent traits; he is certainly not the benevolent father of common imagination, but rather the giver of crushing eternity, ruler over the world of appearances. The alternative, in which humanity stands before God, is this: either there is me, who longs for the eternal, but cannot attain it in time, or there is eternity, but then there is not me.—That any revolt against the lord of eternity is futile is attested to in *Máj* by the criminal who is humbled before being put to death.—Is this "theological" version not merely an inconsequential relic, which Mácha might easily have disposed of had he more thoroughly thought through his concept? For God as lord is only a symbolic expression of the fact that eternity is not merely the other in contrast to time and appearance, but it is the lord over appearing in general: eternity is a precondition of time; without it time is impossible, time is in essence only a symbol of eternity, as evidenced by time's relationship with death, the gateway to eternity.

II

Now we must pose the question about the actual nature of the phenomena of time and eternity outlined here and their relationship to each other. We assume that Mácha, under the notion of "time," does not imagine any particular entity, anything existing, of which it would make sense to ask in what way it exists, but rather that time for him—similar to Kant—is the "form" of inner sense, a basic framework of life without which a phenomenon cannot be a phenomenon.

So what does this proto-phenomenon look like, how to describe it? Mácha once wrote, "More and more, past and future are colliding in a heap,—at the point of impact, there is nothing, time is extinguished; life has no present, one can say only 'will be' and 'has been,' in life there is no break."[31] That means: the present as experienced—which takes the form of a span, such that experientially it is not a mere point—is what is most fundamental *in time as a phenomenon*. As long as this moving divider between future and past exists, time exists too.

If Mácha's time is truly analogous to Kant's conception, then a closer analysis of Kant's notion of time may shed helpful light on Mácha's views. This would allow us to transpose them to the philosophical level and compare them with other conceptually definable approaches.

Kant's notion of time is originally infinite—any temporal quantity is possible simply by limitation of this original limitlessness. That means that every time period is part of a single linear, unlimited sequence of succession. A time period is either a period of real time, or the notion of time in general. Every period of real time is conditional on the givenness of something sensory, whereas the notion of time in general is not conditional on *real* sensory givens at all; for that it is enough to be aware only of the *relationships* that hold between arbitrary, *possible* givens. This relational consciousness, i.e., the consciousness of permanence, succession, and simultaneity, is the prerequisite for us to comprehend the temporal relationships of concrete, real events and to determine when they took place.

Perhaps one might say: We have a notion of concrete temporal relationships within the framework of the notion of time in general—every real time period is embedded within some duration in general, some simultaneity and sequence in general, within the horizon of "and so on." Both the notion of concrete temporal relationships as well as the notion of these relationships in their purely formal form, of "before that and before that, etc.," are possible only through the particular activity that our mind performs when it posits its ideas. The way in which this activity—the synthesis of apprehension, i.e., passing through a manifold and summarizing it in an intuition—acts on us ourselves, the way in which it manifests to us, is time. In other words: time is *created*, time is a *performance* that "objectifies," that projects before us our own interior activity of representing, that is, placing phenomena before our eyes, transitioning from one to the next, and retaining them. That in turn means: the consciousness of time, automatic and passive, nonetheless presupposes the *activity of positing, retaining, and synthesizing*, which delivers a performance that is a temporal schema. This schema is linear, but it is not a line whose parts all exist at once—still, a line is the most accurate objective *image* of time.[32]

The infinitude of time is therefore not simultaneous, infinitude within the present, but rather a successive infinitude, the interminableness of the "course" that arranges our representing in a creative manner, thereby creating a stage on which any impression, any sensorially given reality, can appear before us. This stage is the *only one*, it is not personal or private. *Awareness of time* is personal, it is *my* retaining, positing, etc., but there is only one time as a schema of relations. Each time period is part of this single time, so, as Kant says, any time period is a "limitation"[33] of it. How does this limitation happen? One boundary is the current present, another is the present past. Each present, however, is *in the same* infinite horizon of the preceding, the forthcoming, and the contemporary.

So much for Kant, and in this Mácha agrees with him; it does not contradict the fact that the present for him is not experientially a mere point with no dimensions. The punctal presence is merely an idealization: in the present, if we pay careful attention, there is also transition taking place—a note lasts, though *as a whole* it is ever present—and thus the living present is already a continuum of phases. Therefore likewise there may be different attitudes toward time: we may concentrate on a living present (childhood); or we may emphasize and concentrate on a purely formal structure and, again, convert it to a linear schema in its indifferent form (adolescence, the manful age), with all difference ultimately reduced to punctal succession; and, finally, we may imagine the disappearance of boundary itself, the absolute continuity of all succession, seen in *uno intuitu*, all at once—and that is the disappearance of time in eternity. *From the standpoint of eternity* there is no present in life, and it is indifferent to the past or the future, there is just a temporal continuum; time is a *phenomenon* and is bound to the phenomenon of presence.

Mácha's pessimistic, disillusioned approach to time, then, springs from the fact that he considers time in its objective form, time as a form of succession. Conceived in this way, time is a mere form of appearing of sensory existence; true being, which is non-phenomenal in nature, is incommensurable with it—time collapses under the gaze of supratemporality, i.e., eternity. The emptiness of Mácha's time stems from his concentration on the linear continuum of successive presents. Yet time as a succession of presents is nothing but a formalization of the conception of time that intrinsically falls within a framework of self-understanding which is fundamentally based on objecthood and classifies itself as an object, that is, a thing among things.

If this concept is truly valid, however, then it becomes impossible to comprehend how a *purely temporal being* can have anything like a relation to eternity, how one could distance oneself from time extended in this way. If eternity is to have any meaning for human beings, they cannot be mere phenomena, i.e., situated within objective time, but must be free, i.e., not defined as mere objects in time, but rather as that which is defined by temporal existence and thus far stands above time. This is how Kant himself understands the matter. Humans as practically reasonable and therefore free beings cannot be beings in time. We may pose the question: Is that so *in no time*, or only in that time which is a form of intuition, without which experiential objectivity and the determination of it are not possible?

In fact we have seen that time, as the only objective frame of all objectivity, presupposes the subjective activity of apprehension, which is in fact "intuition"; the activity of apprehension itself creates in us the impression of time; it appears before us as time. Activity itself as objective is associated with the creating and arranging of the objectively relational frame that is time; the activity of apprehension terminates, ends with that. So how is it with this activity itself, with the subjective course that this activity presupposes? This activity itself can also be captured; not in the transcendentally analytical, regressive approach of Kant, but in Husserl's reflexive approach. Husserl attempted to analyze what stands subjectively behind the act of apprehension that Kant observes. He pinpoints apprehension in original temporal consciousness. This original temporal consciousness enables access to what is not here and now, and does so in a dual original direction: as retentionality into the past and as protentionality into the future. Original temporal consciousness itself, however, cannot be situated within objective time, and yet it "flows" like time. This "flow," this synthesis of what is temporally spread out, is never in linear time and cannot be converted into it, because it presupposes objective time. Objective time, time as a form of intuition, thus refers to a *different time*, a time of subjective continuity of flow. For us to step out of vulgar time and its nothingness, its lack of all essentiality, there is thus no need to rise suddenly to a completely different plane than the plane of objective determining of the sensorially given by the faculty of understanding, as Kant concludes. Yet the real attainment of this new plane remains forever objectively undecidable. It is possible to move from the plane of common time to the one that is more original.

The discovery of "dual" time, derivative and original, was the great philosophical impulse of the first half of our century. In its name, Bergson placed time as duration in opposition to space, the original creativeness of the interior as opposed to the repetition of matter, true "creative" evolution as opposed to mechanical. William James discovered in it what he called the "stream of consciousness." Along with the previous two, Husserl placed it in opposition to the continuum of objective time with its identical moments to which one can return in memory, whereas with the inner continuum, the original temporal stream, something of this sort makes no sense.

Husserl, however, more consistently than his predecessors, linked the idea of dual time with another grand theme of his—that of the intentionality of consciousness. Time as an objective continuum is the *object* of the more original flow, whose stream offers primary access to the immediate past and immediate future, to retention and protention: i.e., the flow, in spite of all its varied content, has a fixed structure of anticipating–retaining, which then "makes" it so that something like an objective temporal continuum can stand *before us*, be a representation of ours—and be so in such a way that within its framework certain relationships and laws always apply—the same ones that Kant discussed: the laws of duration, of succession, of the present.

Husserl focused his study of internal temporal consciousness mainly on the past, on memory, to show that in original temporal consciousness we not only *have* consciousness of the past, but we *are* consciousness of that past. In some passages there are indications that Husserl was likewise aware that we are equally originally *anticipating* consciousness as consciousness of the immediate past, and that therefore making present, retention, and protention are with equal originality inseparable dimensions of temporal consciousness. The irreversibility of original time, its orientation, is connected with the fact that every retention is a retention of a past present along with the horizon of what is retained, and that therefore any and all temporal past is always included in the present, albeit only "implicitly."

Heidegger created a new theory of the essence of original time—in his view not merely a theory of *consciousness* of time, but a theory of the *essence* of time—through a synthesis of the varied themes of more recent philosophical concepts of time, among which Husserl's theory of original temporal consciousness is of first-rank significance.

Heidegger calls the essence of time "temporality" (*Zeitlichkeit*). Temporality is inextricably tied to the nature of beings that are human, beings whose intrinsic structure is fundamentally different from objective beings in every form, from things in any sense—those with which we are in everyday contact, as well as those which the scientific approach to reality discovers and constructs through artificial objectification. Humans are by their nature *Existenz*. By *Existenz*, Heidegger means beings that in their being are concerned with their own being, and that by virtue of existing also already understand Being in some sense, even if not explicitly, conceptually. *Existenz* for Heidegger therefore is not a shading of *subjectivity* in the modern sense of the word, derived from Descartes and his successors, that is, a shading of the problem of *knowing* the world. Heidegger intends to leave behind this whole issue from Descartes to Kant and Fichte. The point is not to grasp how a knowledge of things is possible, à la Descartes, Locke, or Kant, but rather to comprehend *being*, and above all the being of that in which knowledge plays a role and which knowledge makes possible. Although not in the way the great post-Kantian systematists took on this task—as a theory of absolute spirit, which understands the universe, because the universe is nothing other than a moment in its own procession toward itself through self-alienation. What this difference consists in is hard to express, and Heidegger himself had to rethink his philosophy radically to be able to give an answer satisfactory to himself. What it likely consists in is this: humans are not the return of the absolute spirit to itself, but rather a "place" that *Being itself*—that "Is" without which there is no clarity about anything, no revelation, no truth (because truth always consists in the discovery that something *is*)—has chosen, so that with the help of this "place," anything may be both revealed and concealed at the same time. And

Being has chosen humans for this, because of all beings, it is only humans who "are" in such a way that in their being they are concerned with Being— of course primarily with their own being, which they may grasp or fail to grasp, but this grasping is inseparable from the mission of Being itself; it is the response to the challenge of Being. To be clear, this is not a matter of being, whether one's own or another's, but of the Being for which humans, through their existence, provide a place for its independent, original manifestation. This manifestation is the original *story* that is the ground of all of European *history*. Yet it also happens in such a way that Being is hidden, veiling itself in the form of beings whose being it is—so that ultimately it may reveal itself all the more clearly in its difference with respect to everything that is. The hiddenness of Being would thus be the path to its most radical revelation. Our era of radical technicism and positivism, in which it seems every ray of meaning of the miracle of Being has vanished in the radical manageability of everything, is perhaps the epoch when the greatest danger also brings closer the "saving power," which in its distinct difference from everything manageable and calculable ultimately enables also this calculability. If the people of today, as always in the past, keep this mission in mind, they can *be* concentrated on their lot, which does not tolerate any distractions or deviations: to consume themselves, to squander their finite being on the ultimate task, which is the truest there is, because in this task truth itself is created and takes place.

However, the way to comprehend what history is about (that is, the story of Being itself, of the original truth) is to analyze the being of a being *that can actually be concerned with something*, that is capable of having, or better put, taking on or failing a mission, and on the basis of that, be what it truly is at its core, originally, or not be that. Only a being such as this, that is, *Existenz*, can be the bearer of a mission, can rise to the challenge of the mission or ignore it, so that it is wholly imbued with the impossibility of objective fixation: this *Existenz* is never apprehensible as an objective thing. The concept of *Existenz*—contrary to Hegel's absolute idealism, which fixes the historical meaning of individuals and epochs in the dialectical laws of a strictly logical evolution—was formulated by Kierkegaard in the nineteenth century and introduced to German philosophy by the "Referat Kierkegaards" ("Report on Kierkegaard") that Karl Jaspers included in his 1919 *Psychologie der Weltanschauungen* (Psychology of Worldviews).[34] Although Kierkegaard intuitively discovered on his own the concept of *Existenz* and the other "existentialia"—i.e., the basic concepts that in his view, unlike objectivity, characterize *Existenz* (anxiety, freedom, choice of oneself, the moment, repetition, etc.)—he did not manage to give a unitary interpretation of all the existential phenomena resulting from realization of the fundamental ontological difference between the being of *Existenz* and the being of objectivity, material and spiritual.[35] Heidegger claims that therefore *nolens volens*, "like it or not," he remained in thrall to Hegel's dialectic, but modified it by making it a way of thinking in antinomies that lacked synthesis.

Heidegger himself seeks to apply such a unitary ontological viewpoint, using phenomenological methods in the footsteps of Husserl and Scheler. The concept of *Existenz* thus becomes—paradoxically—the beginning of a new ontologically oriented philosophy. (Whether such a ground is even possible, by what method the ontological structures here are obtained, whether this method can be reconciled with the very concept of *Existenz*—these questions will merely be mentioned here.)

If an existing being is actually to exist, that is, if it is to be capable of being concerned with its existence, its being, then it must "understand" this being; though of course not only the being of what it itself is, but also the being of what it is not—for *Existenz* lives and plays out among things, in a merely material environment, the dwelling of *Existenz* is always a *dwelling in the world*. The world in which *Existenz* lives is not originally the sum of all that is, but rather the *human world*, a meaningful context that practically active beings understand based on ends and means, that is, based on the *possibilities* that are open to them and in which they live. It is within these contexts that we understand "things": here Heidegger has assimilated some themes common to the various modern philosophies of praxis, whether Marxist or pragmatist. Possibilities are always something anticipated, something not yet fully decided, and so living in them we are always "ahead of ourselves"; but they are always at the same time possibilities in whose light the given world is always already comprehensible to us, so that it is obviously the world of a child, a worker, a farmer or a writer, and in this light then we also discover what presents itself to us in the moment as present and topical. Thus the overall structure of dwelling in the world becomes visible for the first time: being ahead of oneself (*Sich-vorweg*) in a world *already* comprehended (*Schon-sein-in-einer-Welt*), where we are concerned with (*als Sein-bei*) something that is part of the context of this world and is something that we encounter (*bei innerweltlich begegnendem Seienden*).[36] These three moments—which Heidegger calls the moments of existence (to be ahead of oneself), facticity or self-finding (to be in a world *already* comprehended), and fallenness (to be concerned with what we encounter in the world)—form a unitary structure, and this in turn in its unity he calls "care" (*Sorge*): the essence of dwelling in the world is thus care. This is not meant to imply anything gloomy, but rather the essential temporal character of human dwelling in joy and pain, depression and vigor: leaning forward, but always already dragging behind it its own situation, in which it can only carry out the active procurement and arrangement of anything.

Yet we can only comprehend the temporal character of this dwelling when we compare it to Husserl's structure of original temporal consciousness. Original temporal consciousness for Husserl is not spread out in objective time, but rather every living present contains the future and the past, or better put, it contains that which enables access to the future and the past as parts of the objective continuum. The living present contains a solid structure of original temporal consciousness: temporal consciousness is a stream, a passing, which itself cannot be situated within objective time, that is, within a zone of "suspense" in which life force flows in a single direction, from present to past, and if unavoidably we *lead* the present with anticipation of the future, then from future to past. Meanwhile, though, in the original structure of temporal consciousness, anticipation and retention open a horizon that is in a sense *contemporary* with living presencing. The triple horizon of temporal consciousness *in its structure* does not flow by, but rather stands still.

In Husserl there is no emphasis on the primacy or originality of any one moment in the structure of temporal consciousness, or on the undividedness of this structure. Hegel, however, during his Jena period, in his dialectical analysis of time, emphasized this moment of wholeness in the temporal structure and the primacy of the future as the original dimension of time, without highlighting the difference between the two types of time (objective and original). Heidegger is familiar with and cites Hegel's analysis; yet, strangely, he does not clearly realize that the dialectic of time as a point in its being for itself, a point *not yet* the next and *no longer* the one preceding, presupposes elevation above the level of objective time and attainment of the dimension of "temporality," if we are to use this term for the original consciousness of time that Husserl discusses (he does not call it this).

For *temporality* in Heidegger's view is the very essence of care. It is nothing other than the true meaning of care—that is, the presence of the future embedded in the past (i.e., in what is already here). "The future" means anticipation, the coming of what is to be, of an as yet unrealized possible that is returning to what is *already* here (i.e., the past), and impacting it in the presence of what we are encountering now (i.e., the present) (and what allows and forces us to realize our possibilities). These dimensions— "ahead" (the present future), "already" (the present past), "during" (the present)—are not successive but simultaneous, and go together in such a way that none of them can be what it is without the others. The original past is no more "behind us" than the present or the future, but rather "we are past" in the same way that we are future and present. Temporality, the essence of time, is therefore identical with the essence of the being of human *Existenz*.

This needs to be made still more precise. *Existenz* is a way of being for a being that *may or may not* be realizing a mission. Accordingly, there are also two different ways in which temporality manifests itself, or, as Heidegger says, "temporalizes" itself. *Existenz* may take up its mission, concentrate on it, be consumed by it; or it may avoid it, become distracted, forget about it and thereby about itself, flee both it and itself.

Now, how can we recognize the "genuineness" of *Existenz*, the temporalizing of life that makes it possible for humans to take up their genuine mission? We can recognize it in the fact that *Existenz* "grasps" the intrinsic nature of its temporality. It understands that what makes temporality the "tension" between beginning and end is the fact that *death* is at the root of temporality; authenticity, the genuineness of existence, is measured by how *Existenz manages* to live moving toward death, looking it in the face. The tension of *Existenz* stems not from the fact that "everything perishes in time," but rather from the fact that *Existenz* is originally finite, that it is hastening to an end. We may expose ourselves to this self-understanding or run away from it. We are called on to expose ourselves to it by the phenomenon of *conscience*. If we expose ourselves to the self-understanding of our finitude, *if we get ahead of ourselves* to meet this ultimate unbeatable deadline, then we can open ourselves up and *resolve ourselves* to doing the one thing that makes it worth it for us to "have time"—and that is taking on, *repeating* the mission to which we devote ourselves, in which we invest our lives. The acceptance of this mission is at the same time an admission of original insufficiency, of guilt. Without resolve we just run away, avoiding, only ever "intending," living in nothing but provisional circumstances, where one possibility is like the other, all equally flattened and none truly chosen, deeply connected to us—everything external, only *expected* and only "intended." And so although *formally* temporality may be *described* as "the presence of the future embedded in the past," concretely this form covers two entirely different ways of temporalizing time: a way in which time is temporalized "from within," from itself, from "the end," i.e., from the finite future—*anticipation (of the future), repetition (of past possibilities), and* Augenblick, *the blink of an eye, the moment* (i.e., a moment of clarity about my *own* possibilities, choosing what within "the given" points the way for me, and with insight into what, right here and now, is uniquely possible and necessary to do)—or in constant *expectation of resolve, in forgetfulness and presencing*, procrastination, where time is not timed from the inside but from the outside, from what we come into contact with, what we deviate toward in flight from ourselves, from our ownmost being; therefore in an authentic way the *future* dimension predominates in temporality, while in an inauthentic way the *present* dominates, but it is a present so oddly flattened that it is in fact indistinguishable from the past (or the future, seen from its point of view): an "eternal yesterday," everything essentially still the same as what it was, despite the constant alternation— nothing new under the sun. It is, in short, this inauthentic temporalizing of time in which we are able to look at the usual, objective, passing temporal continuum with the feeling of disillusion that Mácha conveyed—a disenchanted time that has lost what kept it "in suspense," the true future dimension.

Heidegger's analyses of temporality, however, culminate not in the discovery of this dual fundamental way of temporalizing time, but in the attempt to show the origin of "vulgar," commonly objective, measured time from the inauthentic way of temporalizing. Vulgar time is not, as Bergson thought, a simple "spatializing" of the original duration. Nor is vulgar time simply space. It originates, of course, from the fact that we treat time—the most authentic essence of us ourselves—as if it were a thing, not something we are, but something we "have." And thus what we "have" is not original, but derived, adopted time, and it is the only time we can "count on." This counting of originally *significant* (albeit significant only in a derivative way) *world* time, which is not *originally ours*, takes place by our *dating the present*, i.e., by determining *with what* it is contemporary, present. Dating is at once flattening and publicizing. These both then always lead to the discovery of something like a *clock*, i.e., a thing on which I can observe the dated time, with the aid of which I can count various "nows" in the horizon of "before–after" and perform systematic dating. These "nows" are then separated in their purely formal structure from what is originally dated as significant in the world, creating a purely formal series of "before–afters," a line of entirely equal "nows," all on the same level, following one another— and these "nows" are understood as something *given*, that has already existed somewhere before and moved from the future to the past. So it is in vulgar time that this strange duality originates, to which Aristotle alluded when he asked whether "now" was ever the same or always new—it is both, because in the "now" that is understood as a "*thing*," one "now" ceases to be even as another comes into being. And so the awareness of time (in full agreement with Mácha) is *essentially the awareness of a disappointing, empty time*, as Aristotle already observed—time is negative, causing decay, the state in which things *mainly perish*.[37] From this standpoint, this surprising aspect, brought to the fore by Aristotle in the first and forever classic analysis of vulgar time, is neither an arbitrary one nor uniquely Greek, but is rooted in the essence of vulgar time and inextricably bound to it.

In the above, we in part related Mácha's experience of time to the coordinates of Heidegger's temporality. Now let us try to make this comparison as a whole.

Original temporality—that is, anticipation, repetition, moment of vision—manifests in Mácha in the breaking through of time by "eternity." Eternity is the end of vulgar time that assumes the possibility of breaking free of it, of looking at vulgar time and seeing through it; as in all of tradition to now, Mácha knows no time other than vulgar and no opposition to it other than eternity. But if we abstract from the concept of eternity as *nunc stans*, in which we find nothing of what makes time a form of appearing in general, and if all we take of the opposition to the vulgar conception of time is that it precipitates the flattening of the regular series of countable moments, then in Mácha too we find the essential past as *guilt*, i.e., freedom in its unavoidable situatedness, partialness, blindness, and prejudice; *resoluteness and anticipation* concentrated into a mission (revenge) and a *moment of vision* in its effectuation, which is self-fulfillment and self-abandonment, self-consumption, bearing within it both end and punishment. Resoluteness and anticipation are reflected in the prisoner's meditation on eternity, no less than guilt is in his meditation on fate; on the other hand, it means nothing that the prisoner meditates on eternity only after the deed—it is not a matter of *chronological* time, but of intrinsic time, the opening of its depths, which have nothing to do with temporal sequence. Eternity, i.e., death, from which original temporality is born, has prepared a mission for the "prisoner," cast into the fate of finitude; it has determined for him his guilt, resolve, and moment of vision (his opportunity and deed). Mácha resurrects the image of human life as a prison, which has an extensive tradition, and he does so from the standpoint of his own experience of time. Human beings are ground up between time and eternity; cast into a mission that in the finitude of the situation makes them unavoidably guilty. Human authenticity, humanity itself, consists in not blaming this guilt on anyone or anything, but accepting it along with the mission that they have set out to pursue, on which they have squandered themselves, as a part of that mission. Time is a void of melancholy, if passively lived; once actively accepted, it is an abyss of appalling fate. Reconciliation exists only in an eternity incommensurable with humanity, and is anticipatorily contained within the awareness of this incommensurability, in the prisoner's final humiliation before death.

III

Apart from the occasional reflection, Mácha did not explicitly philosophize; to the extent that one observes any philosophical concepts about time in his writing, they are, in my judgment, essentially of Kantian mint. What, then, is the meaning of this curious congruence that we observe between the treatment of time in *Máj* and the concept of Heidegger's temporality, which are philosophically otherwise quite different?

Philosophers more recently have at times drawn attention to the curious fact of congruence between poetically expressed experience and certain philosophical concepts. Thus Walter Biemel, in his interpretation of the Franz Kafka short story "Der Bau" (The Burrow),[38] points to the congruence of meaning between what Kafka says there and the content of Heidegger's treatise "Die Zeit des Weltbildes" (The Age of the World Picture);[39] he concludes from this an essential congruence of poetic and philosophical intention of meaning.

One can agree with this conclusion only in a very qualified way. A congruence demonstrated by way of detailed, convincing interpretation, i.e., an interpretation that clarifies any murky or contradictory passages, is of course an argument in favor of the thesis of a *certain* congruence of intention of meaning; surely there is more here than mere randomness. But we cannot consider this congruence uncritically, without asking *how far it extends*, which aspect of philosophical intention it touches on. And, further, asking likewise what is the *scope and significance* of this congruence, that is, what poetic experience might mean in relation to philosophy, whether there might be a terrain for philosophy within poetic experience where metaphysics could come into contact with a type of experience that is closer to generally human attitudes than a philosophical attitude is, owing to the fact that the poetic approach is not reflexive but "sensory," that is, direct.

It is worth noting that the structures to which our interpretation has drawn attention are quite evident in Mácha's meditation on time: the difference between, on one hand, vulgar time, the "eternal yesterday," and, on the other, the breaking through of this time (in Mácha, "eternity," which announces itself as a "nothing," which must be come to terms with, which we must "get ahead of"). This breakthrough opens up a realm of fate, guilt, resolve, and action; an acceptance of finitude, fate, freedom accompanies this act. Thus the structures of temporality emerge quite distinctly after the overcoming of vulgar time. Heidegger's temporality thus finds some support in poetic experience, whose meaning it has helped to perceive and unlock.

On the other hand, we must not construe this as confirmation of Heidegger's philosophy as a whole, but rather only as far as the evidence of these phenomena reaches. And this evidence relates to the original temporal *structures*; it does not relate either to the overall concept of Heidegger's philosophy as ontology, or to the specific concept of existence on which Heidegger builds his analysis of temporality.

Heidegger conceives his analysis as the introduction to a reprise of ontological philosophy, which aspires to be successful where Aristotle and Hegel foundered—which seeks not merely to observe and to analyze the structures of possible human experience, but rather to penetrate to Being itself—not, this time, to the being of eternal existence, like Aristotle, not to the being of the spirit, as Hegel sought, but to Being *in its distinctiveness* from anything that is, to Being in the process of understanding what makes it distinct, a process that has chosen to make its home in humans amid the heavy seas of historical events.

The *Existenz* Heidegger chose as the starting point for his analyses, however, is a fundamentally non-objective way of being. Nevertheless, an analysis of *Existenz* makes no sense when the being of *Existenz* is conceived of as something independent, on which a gaze of reflection can be directed as it is on subjectivity in the phenomenological approach. It does have meaning when it is conceived hypothetically as an analysis of the conditions of possibility of such a being. That, however, means: it should not be an analysis of observed structures, arrived at *by defining them*, but of structures of another, postulated sort, an analysis of the conditions of possibility of human, i.e., finite, freedom.

Perhaps, then, it is not a "fundamental ontology" that could discover the variety of fundamental features of the *essence* of a particular being, i.e., of a human being as such, but rather a structural analysis of the conditions for the possibility of a free act, i.e., of an objectively unclassifiable and undeterminable act—a structural analysis that in itself remains no less hypothetical and ontologically unprovable than Kant's analysis of the conditions of possibility for reason to become practical. However, Kant's analysis relies on the postulate of moral life, on the unconditionality of the moral imperative; the moral imperative here serves as a guarantee of the reality (although not knowability for us) of an intelligible world, unclassifiable in sensory reality. Yet where is the proof of reality for Heidegger's reflections on finite freedom? On what can they be based so they will not be reduced to a mere idea, a conceivability, a mere hypothetical construction, exploiting the immediate feeling of personally subjective freedom?

To be sure, on the one hand, analyses of *Existenz* and its freedom are based on moral postulates. *Existenz* is something that falls under the obligation "you should," as opposed to submitting to the determination of what is. If not for obligation, if not for its appeal to concentration, if not for the concept of *conscience*, which Heidegger only interprets in a unique way, while confirming its formal character, no retrieval from the scattering of moments in time would be possible, no overcoming of the "aesthetic stage of life" that Kierkegaard cites as the starting point of his whole existential dialectic. The question, however, is whether existence can be reduced to a moral stage, and Kierkegaard and Heidegger both answer this question in the negative. *Existenz* for Kierkegaard is not confined to morality, because while morality may concentrate our attention, it can never satisfy us. Morality never extends beyond the borders of "you should," whereas *Existenz* wants more; *Existenz* places demands on reality, on the world, on what does not depend in the final analysis on me. *Existenz* claims and postulates that we have our roots in the ungiven and the ungivable, which we are not and yet which in some way is still there.

To this last, internally unguaranteeable postulate we may impart a kind of objectivity through its *objectification in poetic experience*. Philosophers, for that matter, have adopted it from poetic experience—Kierkegaard's. But the fact that we encounter the concepts and structures that this postulate entails in other quite different authors too—as we do for instance in Mácha—signifies a sort of confirmation of them, an indication of more than private validity, of something more than a fanciful construction.

If we look at things this way, however, we cannot make *Existenz* the gateway to a new ontology. Existential structures are not the opening of the path to the being that is humans, as these structures are not knowledge in the full sense of the word, but merely structures of the conditions for the possibility of finite freedom; they are no less conceptual, that is, no less aspiring to universal comprehensibility and obligatoriness, than any other philosophical structures, and the mystery of Being manifests in them neither more nor less than in any other philosophical spheres; except that this attempt by Heidegger to introduce conceptual order into realms that can never be transformed into knowledge in an objective sense, just as in Kant the moral realm, however important and obligatory it may be, cannot be made a realm of objectively determining science.

III [version two][40]

Mácha did not explicitly philosophize. He penetrated to the essential, fundamental structures and questions as a poet, as an artist: through the power of imaginary world-building and poetic expression, he introduces us to the process of the phenomenalization of being.

During his lifetime, Mácha's concentration on questions of time, eternity, and temporality struck his audience as an enthralling, unique apprehension of the essential outlines of human finitude. Mácha was ahead of the thinking of philosophers of his day on death and its significance for human life, such as Feuerbach's "Todesgedanken" (thoughts of death).[41] That is apparent from the way in which the themes on which he concentrates—guilt, revolt, reconciliation—are illuminated through confrontation with much later ideas about the nature of time and temporality.

This is not to claim that Mácha *thinks* time in the same way as Husserl and Heidegger. What it does mean is that in probing the sources of the phenomenalization of being he touches on the structures, hints, and references illuminated by these more recent philosophical concepts, and that these structures, on the other hand, represent a sort of phenomenal confirmation for the philosophical concepts themselves; they mean that some of the new understanding of the self as a finite, temporal being was already preconceptually glimpsed in the poet's phenomenalization.

We also therefore do not intend to present Mácha's probing as any sort of *system*. This is not possible, if only because more recent philosophical concepts of time, temporality, etc., do not in themselves constitute a system and are merely philosophizing along the way. Neither Husserl's theory of internal time-consciousness nor Heidegger's concept of temporality reached beyond the border of a subjective *understanding* of time. However, Heidegger aims beyond this border, in which case all revealed structures must be revised and modified. For, ultimately, it will not be human subjectivity that shapes the nature of time, but rather time, that primordial happening, deeper and earlier than any movement, process, action, or change, will be the foundation for each appearing, every phenomenon, for each clarity of everything that is and for everything that such a clarity presupposes. Philosophical inquiry possesses no more definitive, no more comprehensive key than does the poet's descent to the foundations of phenomenalization in creative imagination. Yet the parallels are like flashes of lightning that can aid in concentrating on these foundations and, to an extent, perhaps even move the inquiry forward.

Thus an analysis of *Sich-vorweg*, "being ahead of oneself," and of the call to acknowledge our own guilt can draw our attention to the temporalizing of temporality in Mácha, to the historicity at the foundation of his story, to the temporal-ontological foundation of human passion and the "unbridledness" that distinguishes human love from the "quiet love found in nature"—and show that, in one regard, the meaning of *Máj* lies in this revelation of the primordial distinction between human and natural being. On the other hand, Mácha's emphasis on eternity at the foundation of temporality points out the fact that time, even when it speaks to humans and sets up the camp of phenomenalization within them, has a deeper than human origin, that it does not dwell in the human self and its activities and passivities, but rather somewhere at the very center, where things and their appearing are one and the same, where the world is more than a collection of existing things and processes, where it precedes and enables them; its temporal character is, however, already contained in this *precedence and enabling*.

Where did this concentration on questions of time and eternity in Mácha come from? Not from the poetry of his day, none of whose great representatives recognized time as a central theme of contemplation, as a fundamental plane of poetry. But it is proof that contemporaries who had a sense of the intellectual atmosphere to which Mácha belonged were not wrong to label him a Hegelian. Although it is true in a somewhat different sense that Sabina[42] and his ilk were Hegelian—meaning Left Hegelian. It is, after all, highly surprising not only that Mácha, writing poetry in an atmosphere of subjectivism, put his finger on what Hegel believed to constitute the essence of the subject, of the self, of the concept, of absolute negativity, that is, time. No less surprising is that Mácha's concept of time issued, like Hegel's, from Kant's idea of time as a form of inner sense— meaning a concept of time in which the future and the past are separated by the present, and in this form constitute the framework of life, of experience, whereas in the "moment" when they "merge," that is, cease to form a succession, when, as in a panoramic vision, they tend to appear before us all at once, "time has perished," eternity has arrived, and with its arrival our self ceases, the distinguishing of our self from things and processes, from their externality, the juxtaposition of mere *partes extra partes* disappears. But similarly as in Hegel, Mácha too reaches beyond the form of succession, beyond the temporal line of successive "nows" to time as fundamentally internal, non-extensive, at most perhaps (as in Husserl) a polydimensionally imaginable structure of temporality in which the drama of human life plays out, of homelessness in the world ("you have no home, boy!"),[43] of the basis of all guilt and the point of departure for a rebellious decision that absorbs life and for which one pays with one's life. In Mácha too, then, it is the future whose project strips the present of reality, rendering it past, and this derealization is not merely an external storyline, following on from the present, but a moment of vision, a moment of seeing one's ownmost possibilities, and in seeing them, identifying with them; a creative intrusion of the future into the present, which in its given form is thus derealized, transformed, overcome. But what is particularly similar to Hegel's concept in Mácha specifically is the emphasis on the past character of time as a whole, on the fact that the past, negativity, derealization penetrates through all dimensions of time, i.e., it is time in its totality. This similarity is all the more remarkable given that, in the writings of Hegel published at that time, there is no mention of this past character of time; it was only elaborated with great force as an axis of the whole dialectics of time in "Jena Real Philosophy." And the fact that Mácha actually fathomed this concept is testified to not only by the image in "Pouť krkonošská" of the future that precedes us, changing from a female figure into a gray-haired old man, but also by the scene with the guard in *Máj*, as well as by numerous other images and turns of phrase as mentioned above.

It has long been recognized that Mácha is a poet of time, but I do not think it has been sufficiently emphasized what a variety of temporal phenomena, what a quantity of explorations into the essence of time, is contained and suggested within the scope of his relatively small oeuvre. The continuity with Hegel's conception is clear, yet that is not in any way to take away from Mácha's depth and originality. Under the influence of nothing more than a few allusions to the relation between time and the Absolute Idea (the "fulfilled concept"), to the destructive-constructive power of time, which he was able to glean from whatever books by Hegel were available to him, Mácha must have arrived at the initial starting point of the German thinker's investigations of time.

Analyses of Hegel's early reflections on time on the one hand, and Mácha's temporal images and phenomena on the other, seem to demonstrate that the parallels are not mere speculation, but rather that in Mácha there is an actual internal relationship to the modern problematic of time, and this in turn suggests as well the conjecture that the depth and power of Mácha's temporal intuitions have yet to be exhausted, and calls for our contemplative persistence in this pursuit.

Notes

1   We cite from *Dílo Karla Hynka Máchy* (The work of Karel Hynek Mácha), vols 1–3 (Prague: František Krčma, 1928–9), hereinafter cited as *Dílo*. (We supplement also with reference to *Knihovna Klasiků: Spisy K. H. Máchy* (Library of classics: The works of K. H. Mácha), vols 1–3 (Prague: Karel Janský, Karel Dvořák, and Rudolf Skřeček,1959, 1961, 1972), hereinafter cited as *Spisy*) (Ed.).

2   K. H. Mácha, "Večer na Bezdězu" (Evening at Bezděz), in *Dílo*, vol. 2, 167ff.; *Spisy*, vol. 2, 133ff. (Ed.).

3   K. H. Mácha, *Máj* (May), in *Dílo*, vol. 1, 28; *Spisy*, vol. 1, 32 (Ed.).

4   Mácha, *Máj*, 47; *Spisy*, vol. 1, 50ff. (Ed.).

5   K. H. Mácha, "Večer na Bezdězu" (Evening at Bezděz), in *Dílo*, vol. 2, 167; *Spisy*, vol. 2, 133 (emphasis added) (Ed.).

6   K. H. Mácha, "Glaube, Hoffnung, Liebe, Vertrauen" (Faith, hope, love, trust), in *Dílo*, vol. 1, 51ff.; *Spisy*, vol. 1, 283ff. (Ed.). *Versuche des Ignaz Mácha* (The essays of Ignaz Mácha) was Mácha's first book of poems, written in German and published in 1829 (Trans.).

7 K. H. Mácha, "Die Führer durchs Leben" (The leaders through life), in *Dílo*, vol. 1, 53; *Spisy*, vol. 1, 285 (Ed.).

8 K. H. Mácha, "Columbus," in *Dílo*, vol. 1, 62–6; *Spisy*, vol. 1, 296–300 (Ed.).

9 Mácha, "Večer na Bezdězu," in *Dílo*, vol. 2, 168; *Spisy*, vol. 2, 134 (Ed.).

10 K. H. Mácha, "Královič" (The crown prince), in *Dílo*, vol. 1, 154ff.; *Spisy*, vol. 1, 115ff. (Ed.).

11 K. H. Mácha, "Noc" (Night), in *Dílo*, vol. 1, 150; Spisy, vol. 1, 203 (Ed.).

12 K. H. Mácha, "Vzor krásy" (The form of beauty), in *Dílo*, vol. 1, 148; *Spisy*, vol. 1, 120 (Ed.).

13 Mácha, *Máj*, in *Dílo*, vol. 1, 40, 46; *Spisy*, vol. 1, 45, 50 (Ed.).

14 K. H. Mácha, "Duše nesmrtelná . . ." (Immortal Soul . . .), in *Dílo*, vol. 1, 249; *Spisy*, vol. 1, 222. "Návrat" (The return), in *Dílo*, vol. 2, 143; *Spisy*, vol. 2, 123 (Ed.).

15 Mácha, "Návrat," in *Dílo*, vol. 2, 143; *Spisy*, vol. 2, 123 (Ed.).

16 Mácha, *Máj*, in *Dílo*, vol. 1, 28; *Spisy*, vol. 1, 32 (Ed.).

17 Mácha, "Návrat," in *Dílo*, vol. 2, 148; *Spisy*, vol. 2, 126 (Ed.).

18 Mácha, *Máj*, in *Dílo*, vol. 1, 22; *Spisy*, vol. 1, 26 (Ed.).

19 Mácha, *Máj*, in *Dílo*, vol. 1, 24; *Spisy*, vol. 1, 28 (Ed.).

20 Mácha, *Máj*, in *Dílo*, vol. 1, 23; *Spisy*, vol. 1, 27 (Ed.).

21 Immanuel Kant, *Kritik der reinen Vernunft*, A33 (Ed.).

22 Mácha, *Máj*, in *Dílo*, vol. 1, 26; *Spisy*, vol. 1, 30 (Ed.).

23 Mácha, *Máj*, in *Dílo*, vol. 1, 26; *Spisy*, vol. 1, 30 (Ed.).

24 Mácha, *Máj*, in *Dílo*, vol. 1, 28; *Spisy*, vol. 1, 32 (Ed.).

25 *trapný*: in Old Czech, *otrap*, meaning "suffering," also meant "ecstasy" or "vision" (Trans.).

26 Mácha, *Máj*, in *Dílo*, vol. 1, 47; *Spisy*, vol. 1, 51 (Ed.).

27 K. H. Mácha, "Pouť krkonošská" (Krkonoše pilgrimage), in *Dílo*, vol. 2, 163ff.; *Spisy*, vol. 2, 114ff. (Ed.).

28 Mácha, *Máj*, in *Dílo*, vol. 1, 47; *Spisy*, vol. 1, 51 (Ed.).

29 Mácha's own interpretation of *Máj*, in *Dílo*, vol. 1, 301; *Spisy*, vol. 1, 53 (Ed.).

30 Mácha's own interpretation of *Máj*, in *Dílo*, vol. 1, 301; *Spisy*, vol. 1, 53 (Ed.).

31 "Dodatky k literárním zápisníkům—autografy" (Addenda to literary notebooks—handwritten manuscripts), in *Dílo*, vol. 3, 326; *Spisy*, vol. 3, 251 (Ed.).

32 Immanuel Kant, *Kritik der reinen Vernunft*, A33 (Ed.).

33 Kant, *Kritik der reinen Vernunft*, A32 (Ed.).

34 Karl Jaspers, *Psychologie der Weltanschauungen* (Berlin: Julius Springer, 1919), 370–80 (Ed.).

35 There is a footnote in the manuscript here: "It is interesting that Kierkegaard himself sees the specific temporal character of *Existenz*, but attempts to cope with it by traditional means—through opposition and synthesis of the

concepts of time and eternity (similarly as so often before, see for example our Mácha)" (Ed.).

36 Martin Heidegger, *Sein und Zeit* (Halle an der Saale: Max Niemeyer Verlag, 1927), 327; GA 2, 433.

37 Cf. Aristotle, *Physics*, Book IV, 221a30ff., 222b19ff. (Ed.).

38 On February 6, 1964, Biemel delivered the lecture "Die philosophische Interpretation der Prosa von Franz Kafka 'Der Bau'" (The philosophical interpretation of the Franz Kafka prose "The Burrow") to the Kruh moderních filologů (Circle of Modern Philologists), at the Czechoslovak Academy of Sciences, in Prague. On February 7, 1964, he delivered the same lecture to the Brno branch of the Jednota filosofická (Philosophical Society). See the Kafka short story "Der Bau," in Franz Kafka, *Gesammelte Schriften*, vol. 5, ed. Max Brod (New York: Schocken Books, 1946), 172ff. Bieml's lecture was published, under the title "Der Bau," in Walter Biemel, *Philosophische Analysen zur Kunstwerk der Gegenwart* (Philosophical analyses on the artwork of the present) (The Hague: Martinus Nijhoff, 1968), 66–140. See also "Die Wahrheit der Metaphysik: Die Wahrheit der Kunst" (The truth of metaphysics: The truth of art), a lecture Biemel delivered at the University of Geneva, in 1984, in Walter Biemel, *Gesammelte Schriften*, vol. 2 (Stuttgart: Frommann-Holzboog, 1996), 7–28, especially 15ff., and his lecture "Kunst und Übersetzung" (Art and translation), in *Gesammelte Schriften*, vol. 2, 265–85, especially 279ff. (Ed.).

39 Martin Heidegger, "Die Zeit des Weltbildes" (The Age of the World Picture), in *Holzwege* (Frankfurt am Main: Vittorio Klostermann, 1977) (Ed.).

40 A different version of Part III of this essay was found in the author's belongings after his death. We present it here in full, edited in accordance with the preserved handwritten manuscript and the author's typescript (sign. 3000/105) (Ed.).

41 Ludwig Feuerbach, *Gedanken über Tod und Unsterblichkeit* (Nuremberg: Johann Adam Stein, 1830) (Ed.).

42 Translator's note: Karel Sabina, "the most emblematic figure of Czech radicalism." See Balázs Trencsényi, Maciej Janowski, Monika Baar, Maria Falina, and Michal Kopecek, *A History of Modern Political Thought in East Central Europe: Volume I: Negotiating Modernity in the "Long Nineteenth Century,"* (Oxford: Oxford University Press, 2016), 252.

43 See K. H. Mácha, "Budoucí vlast'" (The future homeland), in *Dílo*, vol. 1, 145; *Spisy*, vol. 1, 180 (Ed.).

CHAPTER ELEVEN

On the Principle of Scientific Conscience (1968)

Translated from the Czech by Alex Zucker

Opinions on the essence of science, on its meaning and value, differ profoundly depending on philosophical orientation.[1] These questions are related to the most profound, eternal, and probably forever unsolvable questions about the nature of knowledge and the meaning of truth, questions revisited throughout history as humankind becomes aware of itself, the contingency of its existence, and its possibilities for freedom. However, if the point is to consider the role of science in society, then fortunately there is no need to descend too far into these depths. For that, we need not concern ourselves so much with what science is as with what it does and how it proceeds.

What is characteristic of science today, in contrast to the situation in the nineteenth century, is that it impinges on the lives of us all. Highly specialized knowledge, in the natural sciences especially, but to an ever greater extent in the social sciences too, affects the life of every individual, as evidenced in the waging of modern industrialized wars, the role of the atomic bomb in the division of the world, and the influence of public opinion research in politics. As "value of goods manufactured" gives way to "manufacturing potential" as the means of assessing nations' wealth, science itself, in its technical form, is becoming the decisive productive force. As a result, the governing and organizing of science is becoming of primary importance. This in turn has led to the emergence of the colossal institutions we now encounter everywhere, to some extent or other, under the name of institutes and academies. Spending on science in developed countries is rising, and is even considered one of the criteria of civilizational achievement. Yet, at the same time, this has led to an unprecedented onslaught on science from the outside, which likewise has no analogy in history.

From the beginning of the modern period until the nineteenth century, the pressure exerted on science, from Galileo to Darwinism, was essentially ideological: a religious-ideological defense against dangerous *views*. Today's onslaught is not merely ideological, but also and above all practical—economic and political—while the ideological onslaught only serves to support these two. For example, one could see in the well-known debates concerning biology[2] and linguistics[3] that the content of the officially enforced theses was less important than internally paralyzing and breaking scientific researchers, thereby rendering them compliant, malleable, and disposable. The form of external control that arises in the name of and under the aegis of the motto "scientifically managed society" is particularly insidious. For this motto obscures the ambiguity of the words *scientific management*, which may mean either management guided by external scientific results or management guided by the internal principle of science. Yet results may be applied without any criticism or factual understanding, whereas the internal process of science is synonymous with criticality and factual understanding. And here is the place where we must talk about the principles of this internal process.

The scientific approach is, at its core, one of conscious, active objectification. In the sciences, we divest ourselves of the subjective, perspectival, private element that attaches to our situation in the world and to our original practical orientation within it. This opposition to the private situational element is most radical in the natural sciences, whereas in the historical and social sciences certain limits to this opposition are defined from the outset: the historical world, generally speaking, is human; the scientific seeks to be purely objective, even if that is likely a never-ending and unattainable task. The process of objectification is transpersonal, presupposing cooperation and tradition, the passing of objective knowledge from individual to individual and from generation to generation. Even while striving to attain objectivity, scientists are aware of their subjectivity and choose to sacrifice it, putting it at risk, rendering it problematic. This questioning of one's own self, the permanent state of provisionality in which one lives, is the spirit of scientific work, the air without which science is not science and will perish.

From this flows the corollary that science is not *results*, but rather *a process* in which every result is subjected to criticism anew. The deciding authority is neither personal nor societal, but the object of science, the *thing itself*. Yet the thing itself, in pure form, lies only at the end of an asymptotic process of constant self-criticism. This *necessity* of ceaseless self-examination is integral to the nature of science. The scientist confronts this necessity constantly. Hence we can say that performing the work of science depends on the *principle of scientific conscience*—if by "conscience" we understand that which imposes on us the necessity of correct conduct and of examining whether our actual conduct conforms to the standard of correctness. The principle of scientific conscience may be formulated simply: the only authority that scientists can and must recognize in arriving at their conclusions is debate among those with knowledge of the subject, guided by the principle of pure objectivity.

Scientific conscience is something other than the principle of free scientific inquiry, assuming this freedom entails the free and individual defining of subject matter, the freedom to proclaim one's results, and so forth. Whether a matter of basic theory or the application of theory, whether the problem is externally given or discovered independently through scientific genius, the principle of scientific conscience applies in equal measure. By the same token, it does not depend on the scientific field, historical stage of development, or degree of objectification within a given science, so that it applies as much to disciplines where subjective influence is minimal, such as mathematics, as it does to those where the personality of the scientist is perforce relevant, such as history and philosophy. The principle of scientific conscience has other far-reaching implications as well, such as the essential internationality of science, its incompatibility with religious and political dogmatism, etc. As a principle it is both formal, meaning it holds true regardless of subject matter, and hypothetical, meaning it holds only for those who recognize scientific work and scientifically established truths as being of binding value, so that the principle cannot itself serve to justify these values. On the other hand, it serves well for the purposes of *defining* a true scientist. Anyone who does not acknowledge this principle cannot be a scientist, even if that person appears to have been "working scientifically" for a time and for a definite purpose, i.e., performing certain mental tasks in accordance with their talent and training, achieving concrete results, and so on. In this way one may become or be a *scientific bureaucrat*, but not a *person of science*, accountable for their actions.

One characteristic of such a person is an awareness of the *indivisibility* of the principle of scientific conscience. For even though this principle constitutes the basis of *scientific individuality*, it is also the foundation of scientific *solidarity*. It unites scientific workers as free personalities.

A scientific bureaucrat may be more talented, and therefore more successful in obtaining results, than a person of science. Yet results may obscure the difference between true science and science that is potentially or actually corrupt. Potential corruption manifests, for example, in confining oneself to the interests of one's own particular science: a worker in natural science, say, who feels no solidarity with those in the human sciences subjected to pressure to stay in their lane. If meanwhile the natural science worker basks in the favor of the powerful, providing them with the means for their power while failing to realize that their own indifference and abetment implicates them in the pressure being put on their fellow scientists, then there is a crossover from potential corruption to real, actual corruption. There may still be external successes and results, yet internally this type of science is already dead, awaiting the coup de grâce, which may come whenever the deforming external intervention happens to choose the field worked by the successful "scientist" as the site for a demonstration of its omnipotence. Outward success, authority, and status are then no guarantee of scientific conscience; on the contrary, they in themselves arouse suspicion. Suspicion is especially appropriate when the institution in question was created not by a spontaneous internal act of scientific initiative, but through an act of will by scientifically incompetent organs of power. So when the public demands that officials account for their scientific morals, and officials defend themselves by pointing to the good functioning of institutions, to various sorts of international recognition and so on, they are acting out of blind naivete. In doing so, they only demonstrate how utterly insensitive they are to the problem and how fundamentally incapable they are of doing what they claim to do.

On the other hand, it seems to me, the conclusion we may draw from the above is *that scientific workers must join forces for the expression, protection and expansion of scientific conscience*; in order for them to do their work, it is not enough for society to give them jobs, institutes, schools, etc. On the contrary, they must also be guaranteed the possibility to associate as *individuals*, for the protection of their own moral interests as well as the interests of others that follow from this morality and are related to theirs. The only way this guarantee can be granted is by legally reserving the right for scientists to associate in this manner, as well as an equally legal commitment to hearing and respecting the voice of this organization of scientific figures in all matters related to science.

This, as I see it, is the deeper meaning of the association of scientists whose preparatory and programmatic committees have recently begun their work. Our scientists have realized not only that the scientific institutions and activities organized within them do not represent them, but that on the contrary they prevent scientific workers from freely exercising their voice at a historical crossroads in our life; likewise they have realized that, without an initiative for the defense of their own rights as individual scientists, for the defense of their own moral interests, the very essence of their work is suspended in thin air, exposed to dangers similar to those whose well-documented and unsightly results everyone still remembers. The participants in this undertaking do not wish, as some may imagine, a simple rearrangement in leading positions. They do not want to exchange one bureaucracy for another. They want to eliminate the bureaucratization of science in general.[4]

Notes

1 At this point in the handwritten manuscript, the following passage is lightly crossed out:

"In the tradition of classical Greek metaphysics, science was conceived as the observation of ideas, an activity that was an end in itself, allowing humans to approach the eternal and the divine. Another classical tradition describes science as part of *paideia*, the cultivation of humanity, a free development of our intellectual powers and talents, appropriate to the dignity of a free individual. The modern conception sees science as power, placing it at the service of the kingdom of man. Science conceived in this way is essentially an instrument, characterized more by its efficiency than by its ability to capture the nature of things, and its purpose lies outside itself. It is technical in nature, dependent on technical apparatuses, in essence organized and realized on a transindividual level.

"These different conceptions are probably related to the fact that different types of knowledge share in the construction of science to different degrees, and to different extents in the construction of different sciences. Scheler [in *Versuche zu einer Soziologie des Wissens*, 1924] made a distinction between controlling knowledge, educational knowledge, and saving knowledge. Perhaps his classification does not correspond to reality, but the idea of different types of knowledge (and of truth as a correlate of knowledge) is by all indications indispensable" (Ed.).

2   Referring to the interventions in biological science carried out under the aegis of the theories of Trofim Lysenko and his collaborators. See Valery N. Soyfer, *Rudá biologie: pseudověda v SSSR*, trans. Klára Hladilová (Stilus: Brno, 2005). In Russian: Валерий Сойфер, *Красная биология. Псевдонаука в СССР*, 2nd edn (Flinta: Moskva, 1998) (Ed.).

3   See Joseph V. Stalin, *Marxism and Problems of Linguistics* (Moscow: Foreign Languages Publishing House, 1955) (Ed.).

4   In the handwritten manuscript, one additional sentence follows: "The practices of those who seek at all costs to remain in charge of our institutions, despite that they clearly fall under the heading of scientific managers associated with the worst phase in potential and actual corruption of the scientific conscience, elicit not only pity but outrage at their insensitivity to the central question of the existence or nonexistence of science in our country."

Either the author himself or the editors of the publication apparently felt the sentence was too strong a statement to include for publication. Although the text was written during the time of Communist Party reform in Czechoslovakia known as the Prague Spring, the booklet containing this text was ready for print only after reform was brought to a stop by the Warsaw Pact armies' occupation of the country in 1968, and was not printed until 1969, after difficult negotiations with censors. Ultimately, it was forbidden to be distributed publicly. Only a few copies were secretly passed to friends of the editor, and the rest were destroyed (Ed.).

CHAPTER TWELVE

The Writer's Concern (Toward a Philosophy of Literature) (1969)

Translated from the Czech by Alex Zucker

Whether the new epoch, whose first signs are now taking shape in the dissatisfaction of the intelligentsia, in its new self-confidence and its demands, in its tight-knit community and solidarity, will be the one in which we overcome the crisis that has been marked nearly everywhere by the powerlessness of reason in the face of the present reality of stubborn absurdity, we do not yet know; many are inclined to notice the aspects of these new phenomena that suggest to them aggressive irrationality, unwarranted passions, in general the riffraff in the traditional sense, and let their judgment be swayed primarily by them. If we seek a criterion that would allow us to distinguish between a stubbornness that is decadent and a stubbornness that is hopeful, one possibility that presents itself is a return to normality, i.e., to the elevation of reason over mere fact, and the criterion of reason is an attentiveness to things. Any development that aims not only to make forward strides but also to be meaningful should therefore be an advance toward greater attentiveness to things, and because in the history of the mind a state of attention to things has more often been not merely intended but in part achieved, we must speak of a *return* to attentiveness to things.

An attentiveness to things assumes that we are aware it is necessary and that we are working toward achieving it. A conscious attentiveness to things, on the other hand, requires that we know which thing is at issue. The intelligentsia now making their entrance are, however, concerned with various things. The creative intelligentsia—those whose task is not πρᾶξις [praxis], but ποίησις [poeisis]—may be roughly divided into technical, artistic, and scientific. Technology, science, and art all create new human possibilities. The other areas in which the intelligentsia are active—politics, economics, administration, law, education, medicine—are also imbued with these possibilities and in constant exchange with them, but once these possibilities are discovered and unlocked, they are exploited by conversion into permanent functions.

In this essay we pose the question, What is the essential concern of the artist? and we seek to do so concretely in the case of writing as a particularly important art form. Our question comes at a turning point in time, when the rule of reason is taking shape as a universal possibility, capable of reworking the world in a groundbreaking manner, overturning the existing inert traditions, insofar as they oppose this new rule, and reintegrating them, insofar as they can be brought into harmony with it. This possibility is what the intelligentsia are going to have to fight for in the coming decades, applying their energy to the effort, and perhaps even more.

Yet, in order for us to capture the writer's thing at its core, we must begin far away, in abstraction. The writer's work is literature, verbal expression captured in writing. Writing is the result of a process of gradual objectification of the word, and the impact of this on humans and their possibilities. Therefore we need to begin from an analysis of this process.

Language, this human characteristic (no other animal has language in the sense of a *meaningful* medium of communication), crystallizes originally from speech, from the activity of speaking, and that activity is inseparable from a speech situation. The speech situation is what determines the meaning of what is spoken, localizing meaning in place and time, relating it to those individuals whose presence is understood from the context. Speech is originally part of a situation and comprehensible only from it; apart from objective expressions, which are not localized, any conversation or utterance from one to the many necessarily also contains expressions whose meaning requires supplementation from the situation they are referring to: only the situation tells us who is "I," "you," "this one," what is "today," "just now," "this," "near," "far," etc. These occasional meanings (to use Husserl's term) are in themselves essentially incomplete notions that, unlike generic notions, signify not abstract features of the concrete, but formal features of the situation in which we are denoting things and speaking about them. Occasional expressions are speech embedded in the world, such that only the world makes it fully meaningful and intelligible. Speech is thus both part of our life and situated in the world as a part of it.

The whole objective component of language is in practice usable only by relating it to our concrete surroundings, to our specific conditions, through the situational component. In a speech situation we appropriate the historically elaborated linguistic system of our society and era. Also the understanding of individual meanings for a given language takes place in a speech situation. Language, however, is conditioned by the situational nature of speech not only in formal terms; the manner in which we appropriate objective meanings in a situation, the manner in which we phrase reality in terms of meaning, is also historically relative. In Czech I segment the human body differently than in German; in German I cannot use *Hand* as a synonym for *Arm*; in Czech there is no equivalent for the distinction between *Schenkel* and *Bein*.[1] Through speech praxis the French person comes to know the difference between *rivière* and *fleuve*, which has no correlate in either Czech or German. Rilke used to complain that German had no corresponding term for *paume* and *dlaň*.[2] The perspectives on articulation of a given object, semantic perspectives on the same object, are different in different languages. One cannot designate objects either outside of a situation or directly, but only in the context of a situation and perspective, and perspective means choosing a viewpoint that is largely arbitrary. To return to our example: limbs may be "seen" either as fundamentally segmented or as a single unit— Czech "sees" the upper limbs as whole, therefore the *paže–ruka* distinction is secondary, whereas German, French, and English see the upper limbs as divided, therefore *Arm–Hand* and *arm–hand* are non-interchangeable, in the same way as *bras–main*; some concept, some principle of division *must* be adopted in every language, for *things themselves* are never given, but rather are always only intended through our meanings; semantic viewpoints themselves, however, depend on the attitude we take, that is, on the subjective principle of choice.

What is remarkable and important is that we fail to see, fail to notice the situational and arbitrary nature of language from the outset, even if, on reflection, it is so fundamental and striking. This is because it is through language that we arrive at things. Language is not an end in itself, but gestures outward from itself, toward something objective. In ordinary life, language is never our subject. Thus the orientation toward objectivity is established in language from the outset. Already this primary performance of language—namely, that in the process of linguistic communication the one having an experience (e.g., the patient in pain) thinks the same thing as the one not having the experience, but with whom it is being shared (the doctor asking questions)—demonstrates the objectivizing tendency of language: through language we penetrate deep beyond the narrow realm of what we ourselves can experience in the original, yet without our being solely in the realm of subjective fantasy.

In an original speech situation, however, in its generic structure the possibility is also contained of rising above it. The original structure of an individual speech situation is the speaking self, the you or plural you to whom the self is addressing itself, and a third party, which is spoken of without being a direct partner in the conversation; these three moments are inevitable and inseparable. A normal speech situation is a dual situation, in which every I is at the same time you and every you is another I, engaged in mutual exchange and symmetrical reflection: what from the viewpoint of one is activity is for the other receptivity, what is here for one is for the other there, and both I's are also in relation to a third, commonly contemplated and conceived member, who although therefore differently seen is in this difference the same. In news, information, and reports, this commonality becomes the only subject, while the particularity of the actual situation fades from notice in a way analogous to how a change in our perceptual field fades from notice as we move through a landscape that we perceive to be motionless. This commonality also includes the self in the "they" form, into which every expression of "I" (both for oneself as well as others) is automatically translated; and this gives rise to the impression of purely objective information that we aim to achieve in a speech situation.

Hence also the possibility of expressing oneself in such a way that our relation to a speech situation drops from notice entirely and speech becomes intelligible internally all on its own. This is the quality of a coherent narrative that can be understood by any person who hears it. We do not need to be present in order to understand it, as we do in a live conversation. Speech itself provides the references to the relations that it wishes to call attention to, speech itself guides us. Relations originally bound to the speech situation become independent; references to things become themselves references to words, clauses, whole literary works. Each sentence containing a relative or demonstrative pronoun is a potential link in a chain of purely verbal relationship.

Thus a verbal structure may expand to the point that it begins to take on a universal character. The possibility emerges of capturing in objective terms whole processes, relations, events, experiences, subject domains. Linguistic structure, originally a mere part of the world, a fragment of the human reaction to the living environment, becomes the frame within which, on the contrary, it is possible to capture and portray large parts, whole structures, of the world. Little by little, it even reaches the point that through narrative we can express not only particulars, but an overall sense of things, a functionally purposeful connectedness that expresses for us, or seems to express, how things are interrelated for us, how they mutually presuppose one another, what fates and conflicts follow from these interconnections— the subject of this narrative may be wholly divorced from all given reality, it may be wholly or partly fantasy and yet still express the real, or what is believed to be real, overall meaning. This is the case in myth, the first great objective literary expression, in which the original situation of the speaking creature is reversed—speech as a unique phenomenon in the world becomes verbal expression capturing and therefore, in a sense, containing the world.

Another level of the same dialectic through which humans come to live explicitly spiritual lives, i.e., in *explicitly* conscious relation to the world, is writing, the fixing in place of verbal expression. The urge to fix in place is ancient, primordial: it is evident in the stereotypology of early spoken narrative, in the ritual precision with which myths are told, in the figures of speech that make recitation and memorization easier. Through writing, i.e., the word, becoming a preservable thing, the objectification of the word develops, and with it the possibilities for humans to develop to a level where they are capable of accumulation, control, revision, in general of life in the realm of objective memory. The realm of actuality, as well as the realm of accessible non-actuality, expand and solidify to a tremendous extent. Here is where we see how the human path inward, into the interior, is originally a way out. Without the fixing in place of the word, without the external technology of writing, without the transformation of the word into a solid thing, without its incarnation, humans would have no past that they could live in; no history; no poetry in the sense of an extensive, formally skilled composition, in which the parts and the whole mutually presuppose one another; and of course no science, not even in the sense of a fairly comprehensive book of prescriptions, a collection of practices and techniques pertaining to a certain subject.

With the emergence of writing and the possibilities offered by it to manage verbal expression and the meaning fixed within it, three different ways to exploit this fixed, objective meaning open up.

The first is one originally seen in letters, documents, acts, reports, and today mainly in newspapers. This is the tendency to reach an audience, the tendency to preserve and reproduce a document, to expand and accelerate documentation. In all these manifestations, their situational character and subjectivity is retained; they all deal in what is relevant for the announcer and for the audience—what is changing about them, however, is the means by which these tendencies are realized; they are becoming increasingly more thing-oriented and mechanical, increasingly more technical, reliable, rapid, accessible, enabling us to enjoy the virtually instantaneous presence of relevant parts of the world, as well as contact, the exchange of views, conversation on a technically new level, *a level of artificial presence and technologically mediated contact*. Meanwhile linguistic, verbal expression retains the thing-oriented impetus that is characteristic of a speech situation—language fades into inconspicuousness in the face of what is being discussed.

The second way is the one arrived at through the mutual efforts of science and philosophy in Greek antiquity: the defining of expressions used in ordinary life and in specialized praxis. Philosophy soon revealed that we use words even when we do not know their precise meaning and are not able to use them to formulate anything more than unstable ideas and opinions that are at variance with other, equally plausible ones; philosophy provided the impulse to search for the indisputable; in geometry the first fundamental object was discovered, simple flat figures, which could be discussed without dispute and in such a way that every word had its own precisely determined meaning, to which it was always possible to return and on which all thinking people agreed; it even turned out that on the basis of a few meanings, concepts, and sentences, it was possible to exhaust every valid statement about a given object in geometry. The tendency toward the determination of meanings, toward defining them and determining their place in the system, thus became possible and continued onward. Thus a new language was created, distinct from the language of ordinary life, a language of unambiguousness, of ideally precise meanings, not only divorced from the situation, but free of all arbitrary, subjective viewpoints and attitudes. If this tendency to objectivity through the exclusion of subjective components characterizes the science of antiquity, it characterizes modern science even more so, especially mathematical natural science; thus classical science deals with individual islands of reality (planar and spatial shapes, the equilibrium of bodies, the reflection of light), while modern science endeavors to deal with nature as a whole.

The last and for us here most interesting path is the effort to arrive at life's meaning, to capture it explicitly by means of natural language. There is a basic difference between a meaning merely lived and a meaning explicitly captured, because formulated. We experience much more than we are able to capture, formulate, express. Nonetheless it is also true that an experience unformulated is half an experience, a halfway experience, for the original direction of our lives is not toward ourselves but toward that with which life is engaged, toward the things that interest us, the things with which we engage, into which we embody and divert our lives. Original life is a life in self-forgetfulness. Escaping ourselves consists in not reflecting on ourselves, not regarding ourselves, not putting ourselves at the center of our own attention, and therefore it also means that the connectedness of meaning which our activity effectively brings about is only in our lives; it does not stand before us as an object, as a theme. In ordinary life we are fully occupied with *addressing the situation*, even when we cannot see the situation as such; all that is visible is what it demands of us, that alone is a phenomenon. Through our own situation, then, we are imprisoned in the world as a set of particular realities and events, for it is always through the immediate situation that we relate to the particular: to this school assignment, to this classroom where my task is to teach these children this particular lesson, to these buildings and bus stops on this particular street in this particular city where I live and make my home and am employed, etc.

Now we have seen that through the objectification of language, this situation may take a marked change in direction. With the creation of objectified, reified, stable linguistic architectures we create something that is not merely a thing in the world, but at the same time is able to "contain" the world within itself, to be an expression of it, and which enables us to see it in front of us, to objectivize it. The objectification of language is thus an especially forceful example of *human transcendence*, of the fact that humans at every phase of life have always already taken a step beyond the world as a set of individual things.

We have adopted the view that the first fruit of this change in direction is the myth, the fable, the fairy tale—as already noted above. Yet there is a unitary meaning that holds together the myth and the fairy tale: unitary in that the storyline, the plot, the life situation, the task must be brought to a successful or tragic conclusion, but always in such a way that the ending is an answer, resolving the meaning of the storyline. Thus life's interconnectedness is objectified, its internal references, its form and content. Here all of life's original tendencies are expressed—the dreams that life revolves around, the problems that pose a threat to it, the obstacles that it avoids or runs up against—in the form of a material narrative. Here we find the son who, having disposed of his father, becomes his mother's husband; here we find the aged patriarch bound with ropes, castrated by his conspiring descendants; here the eternal seduction of power, which brings the victor to catastrophe with its allure and compels all those who know its favor to overstep the bounds. Conveyed here is the original powerlessness of humans in the face of the true powers, the kinship between naiveté and good fortune, and all this provides an opportunity and an impulse for the true individual creator to integrate it all into a comprehensive whole that, within a mythical framework, depicts the entire world in an ideal image, in a way intelligible to humans of a certain time.

Myth, however, is an eminently collective creation, and as such does not present the world of an individual person (in the sense of the complete meaningful content of any single individual's life), but rather the meaning of life for a certain *we*. In the oldest phases of true written literature, which naturally retains contact with myth, this theme is expressed in the fact that literature is oriented toward the generic. Not only for example in Greek epic poetry, but in lyric poetry and drama too, there is an equal impulse to capture what is generic, giving rise to not only the impression of, but a pronounced tendency toward, essentiality. In Sappho, amorous stupors and emotional ecstasy are expressed in this way. Then again elsewhere, vengeance, the first expression of triumph, has the power of that embryonic state which succeeds in its attempt to capture the essential, becoming the basis as well for every subsequent creation of that period, with poets and writers now speaking only for themselves.

For the emergence of writing in the proper sense, writing by writers, the breakdown of mythical consciousness and its unity is of particular significance, as is the influence of other trends in the written objectification of the word on the formulation of life's meaning. For our civilizational sphere, this breakdown took place in Greece from the late sixth century onward; at that time a new possibility for our relationship to the universe emerges, modifying our originally unreflected-upon, instinctive relationship via an explicit *thought* act: philosophy. Amid the atmosphere of emerging philosophy, systematic science was established on the basis of technical books of prescriptions. The seeds of history sprout from the news report, the document, the official record, and narrative technique. All of these forms are individual; the individuals in them, originators (of evidence or systemization, of an idea or theory, of an insight or news report), speak for themselves and take responsibility for what they say; but it is *objective* meaning, not *life's*, that is being pursued. What we have before us in classical antiquity is not writing proper, in our modern sense, at least not in any reliable way. Classical writing shifts constantly between myth and objective meaning, and retains this character even when myth becomes a mere convention. The Middle

Ages replaced myth with theology and a mythology stripped of gods and degraded to mere moralizing or allegorizing subject matter. Yet the characteristic feature of modern development, which cannot be summarized here, is that increasingly it takes the form of an *individual* capturing of *life's* meaning, i.e., a rendering for which the authors themselves vouch—naturally, in the context of society, but not in relation to an automatically functioning *we* that is anonymous and bound to anonymity.

For the modern writer, whether they write poetry or prose, this individual capturing of life's meaning is crucial. What we value in the writer-artist is what they are able to reveal of *life's* meaning with the help of ordinary language, as it comes from everyday practical usage, joined with an orientation toward the matter-of-fact and what we know (in an objective sense). Their ability to employ language to uncommon ends, in a seemingly new direction, to make language an expression of life instead of things, to express life as it springs ceaselessly from the living presence within us, creatively integrating this outpouring into all our previous achievements— this is the task that sets the writer-artist apart from other types of writer, from the philosopher, the scientist, the scholar, the rhetorician, the historian. As such the writer-artist is not merely a person with an imagination and "ideas," who creates literary forms, stories, and incarnations of ideological concepts; the writer is a *revealer of life*, of life's meaning as a whole as well as in its particulars.

Apart from the objective approach, apart from psychology, sociology, history, etc., there exists still another, entirely different method for capturing life in its concrete functioning, in its concrete phenomena. In this method what matters is the essential, not the real or reality. Therefore it grows out of the soil of fantasy. What matters is the essential, not the essence, therefore it grows out of the presentation of the unique, not of generalities. The essential is not defined, but suggested and presented, shown. Therefore the fundamental element is not unambiguous conceptual speech, but ordinary language with its metaphorics, its ability to demonstrate, to expand, to specify meaning through its suggestive power.

From the writer's point of view, the reader is placed in a quasi-present, with quasi-reality presented to them in such a way that they pass through it as if it were real. However, what is presented to them is not their own life's reality, but rather one on which they are only looking in, yet in such a way that they are not looking in from outside, but rather as if it were taking place inside of them—a reality lived yet seen, and therefore *reflected upon*. This is reflection not in a form that is truly introspective, but in the form of fantasy, a fantastical variant of reality, *along with an appeal to our own experience of the essential*. Under the influence of the poet's words we imagine a fantastical reflection, we see life unfold into the position required to address the designated situation under the specified conditions, however unique they may be—these situations do not always repeat, they may be unique and yet there are relations here we can grasp, not simply from habit or because they are familiar: who has not had the experience of something within them crying out at a poetic description of the solution of a psychological entanglement, a complicated situation that they themselves have never actually, in reality, lived through: that's it, that's exactly how it must have been? Long before the psychological theory of existential psychoanalysis and the libido was elucidated, writers presented internal conflicts and their solution in an "internally" truthful way. Tolstoy presented a whole phenomenology of being toward death, which contains such extreme situations that one cannot imagine actually living through them, and yet they are still "internally" truthful.

Let us attempt to determine still further, by way of contrast with other views, what is this "life's meaning" that we are discussing, which properly should be the content and secret of a writer's work, that something for which there is no substitute and which cannot be displaced by any other intellectual activity—science, philosophy, religion. So often is this phenomenon skirted that the trail of avoidance indicates almost precisely where it lies on the map of the intellect without setting foot on it. There is an age-old feeling that poetry enriches not only our sensitivity and our subjective relationship to things, but our knowledge directly, what we know *about the world*, and this has led to a search for that specific method of coming to know that is unique to the poet. We speak of "intuitive knowledge" of the singular in contrast to abstract knowledge of the generic; of an "expression" as opposed to a concept; of knowing imagination and intuition as opposed to concepts and laws. In all of this there is something truthful intended, but who can fail to see the vagueness of these assessments? Where is the *object* of all these "methods of knowing"? Is knowledge here still what it is in its normal disposition, the capturing of an object with which intellectual activity is engaged? What does it mean to speak of "knowledge" of Hamlet? On the other hand there doubtless is an object in poetic activity: the object of it is Hamlet. The question is whether or not it is the object of poetic, writerly *knowledge*. Psychological aesthetics of fifty or sixty years ago spoke of empathy, understood as the projection of one's subjective experiences and states of mind into an object. Thomas Mann, in an outstanding essay,[3] speaks of *Beseelung*, meaning "ensouling" or "animation," a breathing to life: poets for him are not primarily inventors, but adhere to given reality. The inventing of characters and stories is an inferior activity, but what is entirely their own, what causes a yawning chasm between their creation and the given reality is the soul they impart to what is found. Mann's "ensouling" bears some resemblance to empathy when he goes on to say that poets insert themselves into their own creations, it is they themselves who are captured in them, and yet my judgment is that in essence Mann is far *beyond* the theory of empathy, that he is expressing through means unique to him an idea of life's meaning, an idea about the reflection of life in fantasy. There are also others with views close to this idea, including our own Václav Černý, who, in touching on motifs of German idealist aesthetics, discusses the way in which a literary work shapes meaning, making real what is unspoken in the world. With respect to "knowledge," then, a poetic work would have the value of a personal hypothesis or philosophical creed, a declaration that we in this field, driven out from everywhere else, would tolerate. However, a poetic work does not seek to express and capture what *might* be, but rather what *is*, and not only that, but what is before everything else.

Here I believe Husserl's notion of the lifeworld yields a solution. The world in which we originally live is not a "world in itself," to which we work our way through an arduous process of gradually eliminating all "anthropomorphism," but rather a lifeworld whose meaning is constantly elaborated and enriched by the "anonymous" functions of life. I call these functions anonymous because we receive their results on a constant basis but there is never any sender. The object of life is not originally life itself, but a world that is given meaning by life, elaborated, ensouled, the world as a constant echo (in which we hear also our own voice from outside, from a distance). In living praxis, which is primarily concerned with things in their independent state, this echoing does not interest us: what matters is to arrive on time at our workplace, feed the boiler the correct amount, follow the correct procedures on the lathe, etc. The writer-poet, however, constantly reveals and shows us the echoing of the world. They do not add to, complete, or insert meaning, but simply gather and reveal it. They do not do so as a reflective philosopher, who works their way backward from the meaningful world to the subjectivity that is the performance of this meaning, but instead they leave anonymity anonymity and merely emphasize its results, the "ensouling" of the world, which constantly plays out anew and never comes to an end. The writer reveals the creative process of reality itself, that part of reality which is not an aspect of "substance" and yet undeniably exists. The writer's relationship to the world stands between life praxis and philosophical reflection somewhere in the middle. Therefore every true writer's or poet's performance is at the same time a summoning of the world in its essence and yet full of mystery, of what has not yet been resolved and yet is here at every step. By what method does the writer achieve this result? By none other than *underscoring* those life echoes with the help of that medium in which the world is naturally reflected and expressed: language. Linguistic structures, originally directed toward praxis, yet also bearing the indelible traces of life's origin, are thus put to use in a new way. *This is why*, without linguistic genius, which can *reverse* the previous direction of linguistic usage, directing it inward from the outside, there is no writing performance. Formal analyses may certainly confirm this new function of poetic speech, yet rather than understanding it from the perspective of final intent, they understand it only in the result, as a fait accompli, not in the drama of human transcendence, flinging itself into reality, becoming a part of it, only to once again reclaim its status superior to things, its worldliness.

The "ensouling" or "echoingness" of the world cannot be psychologically explained away as a set of associations, projections, etc. Associations, etc., is a title for something *subjective*, a story of experience that itself merely points to something objective, to a relation; ensouling is not association, but at best a result, a performance of it. Therefore one cannot say that poets in their metaphorical, figurative, expanding, emphasizing, highlighting speech *create* the reality of their work; in reality the point is—and herein lies the *knowledge-based* character of the writer's work—to *capture the world* in its living form, the world of a specific life, using every possible figment of imagination, linguistic and conceptual structure, character, and plot scheme. Thus the object of the poet's work is not Hamlet, but a world of a certain type and style is *captured* with the help of and through the means of Hamlet. For the living world is the world of a particular life. Granted, every life and world shares features in common, but in each one they are spun together in a particular way, depending on their fate and the way that it unravels. Through empathy and understanding we can immerse ourselves in different worlds, yet we do not identify with them and therefore do not make them our own. What is integral to Hamlet's world does not apply to us—namely, Hamlet's fate. Therefore we also cannot speak of *knowledge* (which is always objective, i.e., intersubjectively identical and binding), but rather of understanding as the basis of and prerequisite for all objectification, in the sense of a methodical *elimination* of all subjectivity.

The world in its lived form is *a whole*. It is undivided in nature, i.e., it always comes before the particulars, it transcends them and contains them within itself, so that in each particular the whole is co-intended, and yet at the same time the world does not stand as a finished thing, but rather as a framework of possibilities for the free being, which is constantly crossing out certain of its possibilities and embracing and mapping out others, grasping some and casting off others, until it fulfills itself entirely in its own way, such that this being is a being of this world and the world is through and through a world of its possibilities. The world is a whole because it is the correlate of something that as a whole is always both given and not given, in the dual sense of both completed and also not yet actualized; the world is a whole essentially characterized by time, with original time at its foundation.

The world is a world of possibilities. All its contents are but correlates of the possibilities to endure and do something, and these in turn exist in relation to how the initial, immediate possibilities are oriented, in relation to the *overall* making-of-meaning that manifests in them. This overall making-of-meaning is an aspect of each individual life program, of its extent and the fortunes related to it. So the world is still a world of *generic* possibilities, and therefore comprehensible to everyone, yet it possesses a "that-whichness," which means the world is not even possible without subjectivity, and *discovery*, the uncovering of things, which is the world's work, cannot happen otherwise. And yet in spite of this individual *key*, the *universal totality* of things is always revealed both implicitly and in covert fashion. Because, however, the writer is the primary, original revealer of these connections in life's meaning, it can also be said that the writer is the unique and original manager of life's undividedness and along with it of universal totality. While all other intellectual activity is increasingly subject to the law of specialization and individual fragmentation, which can be opposed only through the social division of labor and the organizing of specialized cooperation, writing is still the custodian of individual totality, of an unfragmented, personally achievable life's meaning, and consequently writing is also the unmistakable spiritual authority that proves the *individual spiritual existence of humans* as the *ens realissimum*, the most real being. Nowadays even philosophy, which in the field of conceptual knowledge for a long time represented the cohesion of the spiritual view of the whole, in opposition to the specialized sciences, is not *effectively* capable of anything other than a merely formal upholding of this claim. Today art, and most directly writing, represents the claim for the undividedness of life and individuality itself, as every other type of art is made up of objects, inevitably accompanied by a verbal interpretation, whereas in a writer's work verbal expression is the very element in which it lives.

The significance of literary work, therefore, in the future will grow to the extent that other intellectual fields, especially today's science and technology centers, continue to strengthen in their power to penetrate things, controlling and shaping them, which is the power of specialization and segmentation. The greater the segmentation, the greater the need for compensation and a reminder of the wholeness of life, of the undivided relationship to the universe. Literature defends this undividedness above all else. For this same reason, its place is wherever there is a confrontation of the major tendencies arising from the character of society today, in both West and East alike.

This is due primarily to the industrialization of culture, and especially of the traffic in writing, which makes the writer into a cog in the complex machinery of supply and demand. If that is permitted here, there is a risk that writers will cease to be themselves and become merely the object of external demands.

This happens also due to pressure from organized society, which recruits writers for external goals, to engage in society for reasons that do not come from within, from their own decision, but rather from something external with respect to their function as writers.

Lastly there is the influence of the mass media, which are attractive to writers not only for economic reasons, but also because it offers influence on the public and access to broad strata otherwise unreachable. Yet the mass media also imposes strict requirements, stereotyping expression, stripping it of differentiation, flexibility, depth. Not that writers should cede the field to mere journalistic routine, but they must be conscious of the *risk of being public*, which always means mutual influence, seducing the writer to conformity even in situations where they feel seemingly free.

All these reasons lead any writer conscious of their fundamental interests quite naturally to the heart of the movement of present-day intellectuals. It is *the very fact of their individuality* that must drive them to feel solidarity with the conception of common interest that is the pre-eminent sign of the times, as this tendency is no longer merely a powerless moral protest, but the force that will lead society to a new future.

Notes

1   Here the author is referring to the fact that, in German, *Schenkel* is typically understood to mean "thigh," whereas *Bein* signifies the entire leg (Trans.).

2   The French and Czech words for "palm" (of the hand) (Trans.).

3   Thomas Mann, "Bilse und ich" (1906, in *Gesammelte Werke*, vol. 11 (Berlin: Aufbau-Verlag, 1955), 7–18).

CHAPTER THIRTEEN

Ivanov (1970)

Translated from the Czech by Alex Zucker

In spite of indifference and skepticism, people in our societies are still the descendants of Christianity. Living for us is not only a problem of economics, prestige, and health, but also, and above all, morality: we want to be "decent," "honest," "upright" people, and recognized as such. The form of spirit that makes this possible is "conscientiousness," conscience, as Hegel already knew 160 years ago. Conscience, which is to say: having within oneself one's own internal compass, a standard of behavior. Do nothing ill-considered, know always what action to take. Judge not by abstract rules, but be the rule oneself. Live only according to universal principles and projects; live for others yet also know how to put oneself, one's own talent, to use; awaken interest and in doing so encourage others. Yet, taking a closer look, what is the content of a conscientious person's actions? What is it that the conscientious person always has handy, what does it really mean to be conscientious? What they have handy is what is immediately given to them, and that is their interests. So in their case conscience means: framing interests in terms of the collective, in terms of duty or obligation, the good of all. This type of conscience, a moral brilliance that emerges from its chrysalis as two-facedness, always manages to satisfy itself and win for itself recognition. It wins recognition by constantly speaking up, advocating for its convictions, but another reason its statements are recognized is that they spring less from internal sources than external; they are *accepted* as much as expressed. A fiery look in the eyes, a pounding heart, magnanimous plans, self-sacrificing designs are the seductive signs by which such a sanguine good conscience may be recognized.

There is an extreme form of this mindset toward life that begins with "turning inward." This extreme form differs from the norm in that it senses the two-facedness lurking behind the facade, and knows that it will be impossible to avoid the moment one gets down to actual action. It cannot be avoided because action consists in putting one's interests into practice, actualizing something that I am invested in, which means actualizing *myself*, not the collective, and actualizing my own interest *instead of* the collective means to sin, to sully oneself. So the delicate-natured take no action at all, staying in the realm of their dreams, preferably those that are completely unachievable, just so long as their souls can remain internally beautiful. One feature in common to a good conscience and a beautiful soul—both want to seize hold of their content and acquire it *immediately*, one as a given, the other as a dream, imagined.

But non-action is also action of a kind; it is hard to maintain the beauty of a beautiful soul, especially once it has begun to act. Once having moved into action, taken a swing at reality, then it has accepted commitments, expressed convictions, engaged and fixed its position; but being a beautiful soul, it has also felt the danger of this fixation and the two-facedness lurking behind it. A beautiful soul in such a person therefore develops an aversion to its own reality, which at this point is so fixed that the soul cannot simply go back. Since it is not two-faced, it cannot indulge in any of the numerous illusions of good conscience, such as the smug presumption of those who identify with the standard and are the very epitomes of honor and openness and directness, walking yardsticks, nothing more. So it is aware of its own responsibility for what it is. Yet it feels that it is nothing. For it cannot acknowledge what it has decided for and what it has fixated on as its own, and what it immediately is, is nothing but emptiness. It is thus responsible for this emptiness, therefore it has a sense of *guilt*. The good conscience has turned into its opposite. A beautiful soul that has developed an aversion to itself does not blame the "higher" principle that it has pursued, it does not become a cynic; but this higher principle is not its own, and what is its own lacks all higher principle.

This emptiness and the responsibility for it, this guilt, now becomes the sole content of the beautiful soul with an aversion to itself. Its initial enthusiasm ended in emptiness, and was accepted as an ending, instead of being understood as an authentic beginning. The disappointed beautiful soul maintains from the period previous its faith in immediacy, the unambiguousness of the good and the obligatory that was intrinsic to the good conscience and the beautiful soul that is so pleased with itself. Unambiguousness is the source of two-facedness: for then the other, guilty side must be glossed over, covered up, imagined or argued away. The disappointed beautiful soul still does not want to know that our self, our soul in the true sense, is not anything immediate but rather is *uncovered*, unlocked by a process of negating whatever is not ours, whatever does not correspond to the situation we are in and to the unique order of love, that order being the one thing which enables us to manage this always hard and tough situation in a cohesive, consistent way. Our management of the situation must be strict toward both our own possibilities as well as those of others, and therefore can never be guilt-free. Yet guilt here is not the end, but rather a starting point; it is not the subject, but rather the basis of our action, driving us forward like a wind at our backs. This negative experience, this work and exertion, is what the beautiful soul in its self-aversion seeks to spare itself, the slow, patient dying of that which seems to be, which is simultaneously the birth of what is. And because it seeks to spare itself what is essential, confronted with any plan it feels weariness or rather a lack of strength. This weariness is not weariness from too much action, but weariness *at the prospect of* all one's own actions. Actions that it knows are merely the immediate adoption of whatever is being offered, whatever may be inspiring, carry us away, intoxicate us, provide a momentary uplift for our new beginning: improvisation. These actions as such then lead only to a new, *alien* conception of the higher, and therefore to the same exercise in disappointment. Only this disappointment does not then just fall back into the same situation, but exacerbates the situation by heightening awareness of the vicious circle within which the whole exercise takes place. Guilt begins to obstruct the entire horizon, the same thing constantly repeats itself in the future, there is no possibility of getting through to oneself, and so life, despite being in the middle of its journey, comes to an end with this movement of improvisation.—That the beautiful soul cannot find a relationship with *others* amid the whirl of improvisation is the result of its not being able to find a positive relationship with itself. Life is completely swallowed up by the whirl, with no aspect of it remaining free to allow anything positive to get through to it. Loneliness in this situation is substantial and is bound to manifest itself especially acutely wherever one is externally together with others, in relationships such as marriage, love, friendship, of which all that remains is a mere husk with no substance.

Chekhov's *Ivanov* is in our view a word-for-word description and analysis of a beautiful soul that has developed an aversion to itself. He begins his life's undertaking with the great vitality of a good conscience—taking on every obligation and project at once; the more extraordinary, the more rash his decisions, the more vitality they arouse in him, as if he felt his strength grow with every task. He plunges into a socially proscribed marriage, economic reforms, pedagogy and teaching, he "writes to the minister," makes speeches. Yet all of a sudden he feels he is losing his vitality, that he does not in fact love the woman for whom he once felt such fiery passion and who has sacrificed everything for him, that he could not care less for pedagogy, that farming bores him, that all talk is but empty words. *To him* they were all someone else's projects that momentarily excited him because the collective commitment they represented also represented a possibility *for him*. He is too honest not to admit what he is, and yet he does not apologize, make excuses, or malign the ideals he once believed in; still they are not his, they are someone else's, spoken like lines, borrowed. Not for one moment does he cynically diminish what he believed in; not for one moment does he try to convince himself that he is carrying out his obligations conscientiously, that he does what he does in the interest of others. He is not a base hypocrite.

He feels only emptiness, boredom, weariness. If he condemns anything, it is himself—hence the indefinite feeling of guilt, unrelated to any single deed or event, but overwhelming everything and provoking idleness. All of this has taken place deep inside of him while he has been busy with his projects, getting married, pondering on scientific farming, serving in the district administration, etc. In the district administration, there has been a silent coup, an event he notes with surprise and horror and does not understand. This lack of understanding stuns and paralyzes him. He is incapable of processing this first real event in his life, the first authentic experience with himself. Failing to understand, he weeps, immobilized in all his external zealousness, in activity not truly his but merely adopted as his own. His wife no longer recognizes him, he no longer recognizes himself. He is seized with anxiety: at times when he should be alone with his wife, that eloquent testimony of what he once believed himself to be but turned out he is not, he cannot stand the view of this empty void and flees only to return each time with an awareness of the same void. His escape is nothing but running in a circle: to lose himself in enthusiasm and passion for some thing or project is tempting but impossible. And so the difficulties pile up: weariness breeds inactivity, inactivity boredom, and both increase the difficulties in which, slowly but surely, the external situation is drowning. Unable to bear the change that has taken place in the man to whom she is attached, who has also, externally, become the axis of her life, Ivanov's wife, Anna, is wasting away. For the main character, however, the only route open is improvisation. Thus the fictitious relief of the outings to the Lebedevs', which lead to the improvisation of Sasha's project to rescue Ivanov. It is a project as superficial as Ivanov's initial nobility, a project that first and foremost deals a death blow to his wife, as well as causing even her, despite her better intuition, to start believing the insinuations of those vulgar owners of good conscience, who each for their own reasons explain the matter away—as a marriage of convenience, for money. This is what Sasha's parents believe, as well as everyone else who keeps company with the Lebedevs, and especially Dr. Lvov, the model of good conscience. It is an act of vulgarity that provokes Ivanov to an equally vulgar act, causing him to reveal his vengefulness toward the cause of his own suffering ... And so the decline continues further with each attempt to get out of it. That these are all false caprices becomes clear even to Sasha herself after Anna's death. As Ivanov remains internally dead, she herself begins to doubt whether her love is love or just another project. However, her stubborn pursuit brings nothing except an exacerbation of her anxiety and feeling of guilt, to the point that all it takes is a slight knock, a clumsy act by Lvov, to cause the powder keg to explode.

Thus the plot of *Ivanov* is an unfurling of the logic of improvisation, which is rooted in the main character's internal break—in the beautiful soul's developing an aversion to itself. The logic of improvisation requires an absolute sobriety of means, eschewing all flashy effects or extravagance. Thus every character that appears is either a principal or a foil of the tragic improvisation that hastens whirling toward its end. Lebedev and Shabelsky are former good consciences too, disappointed in themselves and surviving their disappointments in a state of indolence, one a drunkard, the other a sardonic commentator and cynical misanthrope. Ivanov beholds in them both the future that awaits him the moment he is engulfed by the outbreak of vulgarity. In both he sees what he escapes by taking his own life. Dr. Lvov meanwhile has chosen his own type of escape: he lives by comparing, judging others by external, accepted and recognized, standards, yet in the end he and his good conscience become a stumbling block to them.

We believe that one of Chekhov's letters to Suvorin (dated December 30, 1888)[1] provides extensive confirmation of our interpretation. The actors and the director initially understood the play as a demonstration of "good conscience": Ivanov the villain, Lvov the hero, an excellent, honest man. Chekhov replies: the play cannot be performed under these assumptions, and he tries to show why the two women love Ivanov in spite of everything, and why everyone else (except Lvov) respects him. He tries to show, assuming that it is possible to do so at all (since the play takes place on two levels, one of which is fundamentally inaccessible to the "good conscience," Chekhov does not say so directly), that what has happened to Ivanov, his "boredom," "weariness," and so forth, is in fact positive, or inseparably linked to what is positive in him. Yet, at the same time, he also tries to demonstrate the elements of the process that estranges Ivanov from lofty ideals, summarizing them in four points: weariness, boredom, guilt, loneliness. These terms are all ambiguous; they may be interpreted externally, physiologically, or socially. What is really meant, though, is the process of turning the good conscience into an evil conscience, external ideals into estranged ideals, an enthusiasm for people into the impossibility of a relationship. Ivanov does not betray the "higher," but he abandons the higher that *is not his*, that is merely accepted from outside himself, rather than being created and wrestled with internally. Boredom is the awareness of this otherness, this nothingness so arbitrarily accepted. Guilt lies in the knowledge that responsibility cannot be pinned either on the "higher" itself or on conditions, or on others, that the entire process comes from inside of him. It is the nothingness of the accepted, which Ivanov cannot see in any other than a negative light. Loneliness springs from the inability to reach himself, let alone being able to reach another person, given that guilt impedes any prospects of doing so.

Ivanov is loved by a woman because she is a beautiful soul, sincere and free of pretense. In him, the "higher" is seemingly palpable, and so an equally beautiful soul, left to rely on improvisation, attaches herself to him with a desperate ardor. He is loved also by Sasha—much more actively, since she sees him as a suitable object of self-sacrifice, of self-renunciation, which Sasha masks as fulfillment. Chekhov, in the second half of the letter, draws a diagram of Ivanov's gradual decline, which is similarly incomplete, being an external representation of his interior. The diagram itself is a *spiral* that contracts, disappearing at the point where its movement can only cease.

Is Chekhov's Ivanov as typically Russian as Chekhov himself believes? I wonder if Chekhov is not mistaken about the Russianness of his main character, or at least mistaken in part. There are certainly deeply Russian parallels to *Ivanov*; for example, Tolstoy's *The Death of Ivan Ilyich*. But that is not to say that a subject viewed in the particular Russian case is not deeply universal, human. Ivanov is a person on the path from the exterior to the interior, but the path he follows is the false path of enthusiasm for what is already here, what society, the people whom he encounters, his circumstances, education, reading and dreaming provide as an opportunity to develop the beauty of his own soul. Everything that gives a person a good conscience, that allows the mutual recognition of decent and honest people to thrive, is sincerely dear to him, but he cannot find *his own* way to it. He is at the start of the journey, yet believes himself to be at the end. He is deeper than the society in which he lives, and yet he lives only on the basis of its impulses and contents, unable to free himself of them internally. His depth comes from the fact that he is sobering up from the intoxication of what he has attached himself to in the field of the external and foreign. His inadequacy in being unable to find his heart. Not a card player, nor a good-hearted swindler and con man, nor a husband and a weakling, nor a bitter cynic and caustic misanthrope of lost honor—yet also not a hero, explorer, or martyr. A man of little faith and no hope, who is facing his own destruction and cannot see that he has robbed himself of both, and especially the open horizon of a future, without which life is not possible.

Examples of Ivanovs can be found today in abundance. This is the form that depth takes nowadays, a form of powerless testimony to the fact that in our present-day world of surfaces the soul has not died out, but is decaying all on its own. The more widespread the impression that we live our lives in "the lonely crowd," the more it obscures the problem that the internal regulation of our lives is steadily being replaced by our radar for what is externally accepted. The Ivanovs who crowd the streets today, in great number and myriad forms, are tragic evidence that radar is not the solution.

Notes

1   Anton Chekhov, *Korespondence*, trans. Karolína Dušková (Prague: Státní nakladatelství krásné literatury, hudby a umění, 1960), 120–7. Excerpts of this letter were printed also in the program notes to *Ivanov* by Anton Chekhov, directed by Otomar Krejča, Divadlo Za branou (Theater Beyond the Gate), Prague, 1970 (Ed.). In English: Anton Chekhov, *Letters of Anton Chekhov to His Family and Friends*, trans. Constance Garnett (New York: Macmillan, 1920), 111–19 (Trans.).

CHAPTER FOURTEEN

The Truth of Myth in Sophocles' Theban Plays (1971)

Translated from the Czech by Alex Zucker

We are accustomed to abusing words to the point that they are reduced to their tritest meaning, worn like an old coin to a mere bit of metal devoid of any value. So it is with the word *myth*, which signifies to us both deception and self-deception, an anonymous, self-emergent idea, an opinion or rumor, which we regard not as a creation of the mind with real implications, but rather as a mere subjective symptom. It is in this sense that we speak of national, social, and political myths, which some take issue with on rational grounds, while others irrationally cultivate them, such as the myth of race, the "myth of the twentieth century," the myth of the general strike, and so on. No one thinks to use the word in the modern world in any other than this decadent, degraded sense, which corresponds to its stunted role in our spiritual life. However, myth originally is not the subjectivism of "autistic thinking," but *truth in the strong sense; it both treats truth and contains truth*, and needs to be approached *with the utmost solemnity*, as befits all things primordial and originary.

How could myth not sink into decline in our present day, when the very life context in which myth has meaning and from which it takes meaning is detached from the world of rational civilization and dying out? For myth originally was not separate from life, and its original form was not fairy tales for children. *Myth belongs to the context of a certain type of human comportment and action*, which, as we say, any primitive can grasp, and to which we still owe a debt, albeit somewhat depreciated, even if our main comportment and all our practice dissuades us from it, causing us to lose the habit of that practice. We still know, even if only from unquestioned tradition, the difference between everyday life and holidays; the names of our parents and of our family relationships still stir a feeling akin to *mysterium tremendum*[1] in all our joints, on every level; fortune, good and bad—fate, unforeseeable to us and yet meaningful—still awaits us at the crossroads of life. Like the limestone shells that coral reef builders leave behind when they die, the rationalizations of once-living myth remain within us. The comportment I am referring to may be termed *ritual*, and the context in which it occurs, but also what makes it distinct from other human comportment, especially *pragmatic comportment*, is obvious. Ritual comportment does not have at its center any instrument or instrumental action; it is not work, it is not managing and procuring, accumulating, securing and providing for the immediate and intermediary means of life in the material sense of the word. In rites, dances, ceremonies, initiations, sacrifices, we comport ourselves not with regard to particulars, entering into the possibilities of maintaining ourselves amid the pulsing rhythm of the needs of life and the satiation of those needs, but with regard to *the whole of all possibilities in which the world addresses us*. And just as there is no more original way to access the things around us than the way we make practical contact with them—meaning that we handle them and work with them as the means and appurtenances of a life for which metal is that which can be forged; stone is that which stabilizes the road; matter, hyle, *silva*, is the material from which a thing, a product, is created—so ritual comportment provides *original access to certain aspects and dimensions of the world*. We are well aware that *this original contact cannot be replaced by anything*. Just as no conceptual reconstruction can explain, interpret, and offer us living contact with our rich, resonant, resistant and permissive, suitable and unsuitable, exhausted and exhausting surroundings, by the same token *nothing but original ritual comportment opens the gate to that dimension of the world which we call sacred, numinous, "supernatural," divine*. And just as no one can explain the original natural world of our surroundings with its order of appurtenances on the basis of the atoms and their eternal movements, a world that is nonetheless independent and a thing in itself with respect to us, so no one starting from the standpoint of our objectified, physical world of realized mathematical formulas can reach *the world of sacred contact* into which *the spontaneity of the rite* is built, suddenly, naturally, and with all the power of originality.

Myth, then, belongs to this context as *language that originates in rite*. And *given that in language the world is duplicated and thereby reflected, in myth we have also the first onset of reflection, the original instance of human reflection on humanity's overall relationship to the world*. This is not to say that in myth humanity *exhausts* the possibilities of its original relationship to the world as a whole. Myth contains an oddly *one-sided* relationship to this whole: the basis of myth is what always and forever constitutes the primordial situation of humans in the world—our positionality, the situatedness of random ephemera in the ruthless and yet somehow merciful supremacy of the immeasurable. But the framework of every human understanding of anything, whether within or outside of oneself, as Kant first discovered, is time. Time is a complex structure related to "a hidden art in the depths of the human soul, whose true operations we can divine from nature and lay unveiled before our eyes only with difficulty."[2] Yet if time in the original sense is indeed the gateway to any understanding, then some essential feature of original human temporality will be the key to ritual comportment too. The temporality of myth is suggested by the essential character of myth itself, the fact that it *narrates an event that has already taken place in the past,* not in such a way that it is gone once and for all, swallowed up irretrievably, but so that it shines a light, so that it illuminates what is right now, in the present. The past, however, illuminates what is if the present *is* past. The essential frame of everything past is what we are always already confronted with as human beings, with our primordial situatedness within the merciful-merciless whole. That which has been and is—through which a temporality opens, deeper than the irretrievably disappearing sequence of moments, ultimately fragmented into instants— the essential "already" of human life, is the basis of mythical understanding of ourselves and things alike. This "already" is itself an occurrence, the dawn of life, the dawn of light in the darkness of the immeasurable. This dawn is what has happened and is happening, through which the closed core of the universe can open. This cut, this deviation from ages of isolation and concealment is a theme to which myth repeatedly returns in the related themes of theogony, cosmogony, and anthropogony. This cut, this break, this deviation from the general order of supremacy, this special privilege yet simultaneous weakness of human beings, is the inexhaustible source and "subject" of the language of myth. A human life, viewed in its light, does not contain only guilt, but is itself a deviation, a cut, a blow and a "transgression." This transgression impinges on every aspect of human beings' unique standing between clay and spirit, as well as on shame and the entire realm of passionate but disciplined instinctive corporeality, which brings with it a constant threat of chaos and danger to humanity; it also impinges on human ability and curiosity, human action with regard to good and evil—these are all part of the deep probing that is always present in any true myth, constituting its specific profound truth. Greek tragedy grew out of ritual comportment and at its high point was a ritual comportment associated with the creation of language, with poetry based in the true spirit of myth. Tragedy was originally the rite of reincarnating the hero to whom a mythical cult was dedicated, the forefather who through his own history is rooted in the primordial world that constitutes the structure and lasting core of all that is and is present. Only because what is is that which was can the hero come to life in the person of the *choregus.* Nor can the subject be anything other than that primordial story, the *mysterium tremendum* of human existence in its "primordial transgression," which gives rise to every essential feature and dimension of human life. Assuming we understand tragedy as the original ceremony, then we can say, paradoxically, that it originates neither in the spirit of music nor in myth, but that it is itself the source, the very hotbed, of myth. In this, then, lies also the immense and vital significance of tragedy, that sovereign creation of the world of morality, as Hegel puts it, of the world of the Greek *polis*, which was not merely a factual cult community but a sacred cult community. Tragedy is a sovereign, original, and never-repeatable form of human self-understanding, in which the entire community publicly demonstrates to itself what humanity is and means. It is not theater, it is not the performance of a colorful and entertaining story; what is performed here is what everyone *is*. And the reason why they *are* what they are performing is because they are mythical people, people who grasp the truthfulness of myth, its original, underivative nature. This is the same reason why we cannot perform Greek tragedy in the true sense: Hamlet can be played in a dress suit and ordinary clothes nowadays, this being the modern world where plot is nothing more than the history of an individual, interesting to us as such, whereas to play Sophocles in modern clothes would be impossible. It would be a caricature, with us ourselves caricatured most of all, in our inability to adopt the point of view of rite and myth.

The idea of performing the Labdacid tragedies as a unit seems to make sense in terms of the mythic history of the house of Labdacus, in terms of the judgment being passed down the line from father to son and then to the children of the son. But to do so presents a unique problem: if *Antigone*, which was the first work, conceived independently, is placed at the end, in accordance with the chronology, the viewer may be under the impression that this demonstration of fate is the purpose. In fact, if *Oedipus Rex* and *Oedipus at Colonus* are inextricably linked as the opening of a gap and the healing, amicable settlement that subsequently bridges it, *Antigone* has a fundamentally different intent. The subject of the Oedipus tragedies is guilt, not as an act we commit, but as what we *are*. The Oedipus tragedies present a mature form of the primordial myth of humans as creatures possessing a clarity that deviates from the rest of the universe and that becomes human destiny, a path that must be traveled to the bitter end. The subject of *Antigone* is the power of myth and its standing in relation to the world of human ability, foresight, rationality, in relation to the world of the day. Thus the Oedipal tragedies and the tragedy of Antigone are profoundly different from each other; yet, in the event that we do place *Antigone* at the end, it is not against the *inner logic of* Sophocles' works. We just have to be aware that this logic does not coincide with the logic of the chronology and that it is not a tragedy of "fate."

Sophocles' Oedipus shows how clarity, understanding, insight are in the nature of human beings; they are our destiny, a path that must be traveled to the end, and we must comprehend ourselves as a deviation, as a rupture and ruining, unless we can find a way to reintegrate ourselves under the supremacy of law and a higher meaning that rules even over our own finite meaning. Something higher than human meaning does exist—that which has held true through the ages, which is simultaneously primordial and contemporary, and which therefore the vision of a seer can see even before it has appeared. Human meaning may rebel against it, but it cannot resist or override it, for it itself is included within it and overridden by it. We fulfill it even when we avoid it, believing ourselves triumphant; indeed it may even be said that the whole essence of humanity is contained in this attempt to avoid, override, and assert our own meaning, to forget that it is not the *whole* meaning. As Heraclitus says, "We should let ourselves be guided by what is common to all. Yet, although the Logos is common to all, most men live as if each of them had a private intelligence of his own."[3] Humanity *is this idia phronesis*, reliance on self; this reliance on one's own insight or understanding is at the same time both the essence of humanity and its deviation from the whole, and this is confirmed by the fortunes of Oedipus; for it is private insight that brought him to the pinnacle of glory and power and gave him the appearance of savior of the whole community; it is this that made him a transgressor who violated the foundation of all humanity, and it is this that distinguishes humans, in spite of our corporeal and carnal nature, from animal promiscuity; it is the familial code and respect, obedient subservience to the father and the prohibition of incest, so that the putative ruler and sage is in fact secretly the one who undermines the foundation of society, an outcast who is to be shunned and banished from every hearth and home. The whole drama lies in the fact that Oedipus, with merciless rigor, unswervingly, follows his destiny as a human seeing and wanting to see, unearthing and assembling piece by piece the edifice of evidence that will place him in the most terrible light. The wife-mother then has no choice but to take leave of the human world, while Oedipus is destined for a harder lot: to expunge and deny the power of *idia phronesis*, private understanding, to thwart his merciless vision with his own hands and accept his fate as exile and fugitive; his role is not yet fulfilled by the catastrophe that swallows up Jocasta.

For Oedipus is not only a transgressor who through the strength of his vision overrides himself and declares himself guilty. As a transgressor, he is taboo in the double-edged sense of the word: both a cursed man and a sacred being. He is not simply an outcast, but a *chosen* outcast. He is "chosen" so that, in him, more than anyone else in the family, the essential danger threatening us from within, from our essence, may be revealed, made apparent. He is not an intentional transgressor; he is guilty yet blameless. The community that persecutes him commits the same wrong by failing to see and acknowledge this other side of the matter; and in failing to see the sanctity of the sufferer, the community itself renounces its claim to the reward of grace, which lies in the immeasurable suffering that he has taken on for the sake of the many, in fact for the sake of all. This favor rightly falls to that community which comprehends the *whole of this fate*, a truly communal community, which to prove its understanding grants the fugitive asylum and gives him a home. Neither his native community nor its mortal enemy, Oedipus's son, now overcome with devastating rage, see heaven and earth as communal, shared, connecting mortals and immortals in a single whole; both must therefore yield to a community that is entirely based on this unity. This is the type of "ideal" community that Sophocles wants to have, and he sees Athens, his birthplace, as cast in that image, presenting and bequeathing his mythical wisdom to it.

Antigone, too, is a sacred sufferer, in this respect a successor to the fate of Oedipus. The paradox is that this daughter of stigma is destined to be the one in whom the law of family piety, "divine law," from which all human laws take their sustenance, reveals itself in all its force. Antigone is the very model of familial love and piety: it is she who takes on the burden of Oedipus's wandering life after his expulsion from his birthplace, and it is with her that her ill-fated renegade brother, felled by his own brother's hand, finds his final refuge. But Sophocles also presents in this tragedy a unique version of hubris that entails *idia phronesis*, a personal, self-contained understanding. Creon represents the original form of enlightenment, which Sophocles saw gaining ground in the political reality around him. It makes no difference that, by his own estimate, this *idia phronesis* is channeled toward the wellbeing and power of the community as a whole; its manner of implementation, relying on the judgment of the man who rules and on the requirement of absolute obedience, demonstrates its autocratic, tyrannical tendency. In contrast to this claim of proto-enlightenment, whereby a single man takes into his own hands every aspect of life both for himself and the community, allowing the *law of the day* to rule, Antigone demonstrates the *supremacy* of myth, the supremacy of *the whole*, from which the law of the day too takes its sustenance, the law which is only a part of the whole, annulled whenever and wherever it seeks to *be* the whole.

It is not the intention of these few lines to call attention to the greatness of Sophocles' *poetic* act. Undoubtedly Sophocles ranks among those creators whom only a scant few are fit to judge, captivating and delighting anyone who is at all open to what is great and pure. No one has characterized the poetic figure of Sophocles as simply and aptly as Hölderlin, when he wrote, "Just as Aeschylus wrote in the style of his belligerent decade, so Sophocles wrote in the spirit of his more cultured age. A mixture of proud masculinity and feminine softness: a clean, thoughtful, yet warm and captivating form of address, characteristic of the age of Pericles."[4] And no one has undertaken such a profound attempt to gauge the full breadth of Sophocles' myth and his characters in *Antigone* as Hegel in the famous chapters of *Phenomenology of Spirit* and *Lectures on Aesthetics*.[5]

In *Phenomenology*, Sophocles' work—in the section titled "The Ethical World: Human and Divine Law, Man and Woman"—becomes one of the fundamental forms of spirit, whose development, conflict, and resolution reflect the full meaning of the world of free citizens that was the Ancient Greek and in particular the Athenian *polis*, that *polis* which lies beneath the surface of the whole historic edifice of European spirituality like a hidden cornerstone. Sophocles made it possible for Hegel to drop a philosophical probe into the depths of classical Greek myth, whose power he grasped because he approached it in all seriousness, not as a mere creation of fantasy but as a whole and in its details as the profound *truth* about fundamental human relations in general, the truth about the strength and the weakness of the ancient world and its humanity, the truth about humanity's relation to all that is superhuman, to the earth and the heavens. If Sophocles was such a monument of truth and profundity to the greatest thinker of modern times, what an urgent warning to us more recent thinkers, who live amid the tumult and clamor of a one-dimensional age, and dare to decide what is and is not by the application of a dry objectivist measure. In fact the question Sophocles poses to us today might sound like this: Is not the vision of the world that today we take as self-evident, a vision of the sober absurdity of all that is, which willingly bends itself in service to our arbitrary ephemeral goals, being in fact merely that same *idia phronesis*, human law as opposed to divine law, "private understanding" projected into the cosmos and conceived as absolute? Is not our world the ultimate consequence and result of the same hubris whose internal contradiction is expressed by the fate of the Labdacids? Are not the catastrophes of our century in fact a repetition of the same collapse below the threshold of humanity that Sophocles demonstrated in Oedipus to the humans of every era?

Notes

1   "awe-inspiring mystery" (Trans.).

2   Imannuel Kant, *Kritik der reinen Vernunft*, B 180–1. English: *Critique of Pure Reason*, ed. and trans. Paul Guyer and Allen W. Wood (Cambridge: Cambridge University Press, 1998), 273 (Ed.).

3   Heraclitus, B 2, in Hermann Diels and Walther Kranz, *Die Fragmente der Vorsokratiker* (Berlin: Weidmann, 1974), 151 (Ed.). English: *Heraclitus: The Complete Fragments. Translation and Commentary and The Greek Text*, trans. William Harris, Fragment 2, 4, https://fliphtml5.com/jmfd/opdc/basic.

4   Friedrich Hölderlin, "Geschichte der schönen Künste unter den Griechen," in *Sämtliche Werke*, ed. Friedrich Beißner, vol. 4/1 (Stuttgart: Kohlhammer, 1961), 204 (Ed.).

5   G. W. F. Hegel, *Phenomenology of Spirit*, trans. Terry Pinkard (Cambridge: Cambridge University Press, 2018), 251ff., and *Aesthetics: Lectures on Fine Art*, trans. T. M. Knox, 2 vols (Oxford: Clarendon Press, 1975), vol. 1, 221ff.; vol 2, 464ff. (Ed.).

CHAPTER FIFTEEN

On Faust: The Myth of the Pact with the Devil—Observation on the Variants of the Faust Legend[1] (1973)

Translated from the German by David Charlston

Myths do not just die out as the rationalists and their kin used to think; they merely transform themselves. For there is not only the contingent content of the world and scientific knowledge of this content; there is also the heart of the world, which is elevated above contingency and non-contingency in their usual sense. And this heart can be *known* not only in a philosophical way; *we enact ourselves toward it with our entire essence,* and it is this that we narrate to ourselves, allowing it entry into language as if into another, wider world, which is nevertheless a component of the *one* great world; and this is myth in its authentic sense. That is why myths have not been discarded by philosophy and science; indeed, it is often precisely the philosophers and scientists who continue to work with them. Nevertheless, the most important shapers of myths are admittedly the poets.

We speak here of shapers rather than creators because the question of who creates a myth in the original sense is a dark problem, like the more general question of primordial beginnings. The Faust legend is a good example. Its motifs merged, meandering along remote secular paths, finally crystallizing around a remarkable but otherwise obscure historical figure and sucking up the sap of the great hearts and lives of the late Middle Ages, until eventually—in the age of the printing press—someone arrived to offer the ripe, thrilling fruit to posterity. But almost immediately, the poets seized on it, drawing out an intensity of living content initially present only in the germ. Specifically, a myth is a question communicated from humanity to humanity, a question originating from a depth within us which is prior to the logos. This radical question—which we do not ask, but which puts us into question—summons the poet to formulate it expressly and to deal with it.

What, therefore, is the question which captivates us in the Faust legend and haunts poets, thinkers, and their public, so that creative minds have reached out time and again for the Faust theme? Where does the fascination come from? It is bold to formulate an answer which, in its unambiguousness, threatens to curtail the living complexity of the myth. But, in attempting to interpret this Faust question as the sale of the immortal soul, risk must be taken.

With a non-object like the soul, what does "sale" mean? We must start out with a clarification of the tensions inherent in the concept of the immortal soul. Since Plato, the immortal soul has been the supreme good of Western humanity, but this only applies under the condition that immortality is not taken as a passive, de facto state, but rather as the supreme intensification of existence. For precisely when immortality is understood as securing the duration of existence (Dasein) beyond the empirical, it can become a support for every kind of weakness and depravity; it can mean a slavish bondage of the spirit to life. Immortality of the soul in the genuine sense is obtained by those who choose non-being in preference to the corruption of the soul. To them, immortality means the supreme importance of the present life, its complete seriousness, for eternity is decided in the *hic et nunc*, the here and now: eternity of the *me on* (non-genuine, inauthentic being) or of the fully authentic *einai* (being) of the self. The actuality of this decision arises in view of the two basic possibilities mentioned; it is full of potential, and for that reason, it is completely free self-realization, which includes the empirical task of the self, in that it chooses non-being over the loss of genuineness. By contrast, non-genuine immortality of the soul is anxiety and unease, a not-being-able-to-give-oneself-up, a weakness, which means decay down to the vital roots. Perhaps an excusable weakness, but unworthy of the spirit, the soul of the soul, which is characterized by insight—namely the insight into being and non-being. Genuine immortality exists for those who have overcome the terror of physical death with the terror of absolutely negative existence in order to attain what is attainable at the pinnacle of this mortal life, its finite absoluteness.

For Faust, the man at the dwindling of the Middle Ages, the choice is admittedly presented differently than for Socrates, who stands before the alternative of "potential annihilation, associated with the preservation of genuineness" or "prolongation of life, paired with denial of the self." Regardless of his choice, Faust anticipates a prolongation of life beyond the threshold of death. *His* alternative is: "eternal expectation of salvation through acquiescence to the traditional" or "temporary exaltation of being and eternal fall." But, under these circumstances, how is it possible to choose as Faust does? How can a lofty spirit make such a contradictory choice to sell the expectation of eternal salvation for a short period of earthly omnipotence? The legend has been interpreted as a warning against the dangers of the *vita contemplativa*. The contemplative life is said to have detached Faust from the context of human society in which he would have been able to exercise his freedom in a manner both human and spiritual, seducing him to excess and wantonness. But this explanation does not make the choice more understandable—because, after all, a contemplative person must be capable of measuring, calculating, and evaluating. The legend retains its profundity only on the presupposition that Faust can see an advantage in the choice he makes and is not a mere victim of seduction and bedazzlement. For him, what is at stake is not earthly power. The advantage he seeks is a self-chosen, self-enacted, but short-lived transformation of his being, as against an eternity of passive acceptance. Here, he can *realize himself*, this is a possibility only *in this life*; later, he will merely resign himself. Faust is deceived not *in* the choice, but *after* it. He is too weak for his choice and therefore fails to attain the desired higher level of being for which he strives; instead of becoming a pure intelligence, he becomes a common magician. The Faust legend is not just a moral warning—it is a prophetic legend about human freedom, about its labyrinth, its tragedy, and its damnation.

The ethical importance of the idea of a life after death is to increase the decisiveness of present action and awareness of responsibility, because future destiny is decided in the present, or, in other words, eternity is decided in time (for Plato, until we are faced with the next choice of destiny, in Christianity once and for all time).

In Christianity, however, the freedom of this decision is a fully valid act of one's own only in the negative, for the choice of the good requires the free grace of God and therefore rests upon an external condition. The freedom which qualifies humans in contrast to higher spirits themselves is therefore the freedom of self-damnation. Indeed, it may be inferred that this is no longer an authentic freedom because it *lacks* choice. But the choice is made precisely by preventing the *possibility* of grace and denying it. In this respect, Faust realizes the full extent of human freedom.

The bad infinity of everlasting possession can therefore be resisted with a certain justification; this may contain a genuine motivation, for example, to confront it with the *inward* infinity of a thirst for knowledge. Admittedly, the difficulty here is that, alongside this inward infinity, the individual, finite life possibilities resulting from it appear equally enticing, because, with the will toward a genuine inward transformation, one has, at the same time, in fact remained the same old person; so that one misappropriates one's own genuineness, and in striving for being, once again, one only snatches at some arbitrary finite possession. Indeed, the inward infinity of knowledge is ambiguous; it also contains within itself the ambiguity of *Verstand* and *Vernunft*, understanding and reason.

Above all, the sale of the immortal soul probably means that anxious self-preservation along the traditional lines of bad infinity has become obsolete for Faust and is something he wishes to renounce. What is more, he finds the buyer eager to please, indeed duping him with the inward infinity of an all-encompassing understanding, but only as the bait for a great deception. First, he gets Faust to grasp at active, effective knowledge instead of insight into the secret of the world; then he gets him to reach out for the fruits of this knowledge, which can satisfy the immediacy of life, and this initiates the move from the superhuman, from the transformation of existence to average existence and triviality; the secret has been overpowered, but, for all this, it has still not been penetrated by opening an eye to infinity; instead, it has been done away with. The secret is no longer there. One has become knowledgeable and capable of a great deal, but insight and therefore knowledge as the activation of existence has been abandoned. In the end, what was purchased for bad infinity is not nothing, but—like all immediacy which lacks absolute insight, the insight into the good—it comprises relative and problematic goods. In principle, Faust misses out nothing of what can be offered in this context: he overcomes space, overcomes need, he has food for the eyes and sensuousness, he acquires power and basks in the favor of the respectable. But the extraordinary means by which this was achieved are shown to be only a cloak of triviality, because, ultimately, they achieve only what is achievable on the ordinary path of common experience, but with greater difficulty. Although he began with a heroic soaring—*eroico furore*—of generous, noble existence, he allowed himself to be deceived by the ambiguity in the sale and lost the true immortal soul, which was his actual concern, the deepening of existence toward spirit. It is therefore not surprising that he finishes up with what appears in Plato as a symbol for the loss of the self—practical jokes with cloaks of invisibility, the analogue of Gyges' ring, this symbol of the wildly sensuous, and therefore lost, life; Faust, the dupe,[2] becomes a half-comical figure, suitable for the puppet theatre. Nevertheless, there is a deep meaning in the tragicomical character of the Faust character which was recently underscored by Edmund Husserl's book *Crisis*, which recounts the history of modern science in a remarkably similar narrative:[3] both stories involve self-deception about being arising from confusion between success and insight, or, in traditional philosophical language, *Verstand* and *Vernunft*, understanding and reason, and associated with that, a loss of the sense of one's own action and one's own being.

As a chapbook and in its first literary rendering by Marlowe, the Faust legend is very German. Time and place in the world are clearly inscribed in it. The unity of Christendom has collapsed; countries at the periphery of the Western world are forthrightly asserting their emancipation from bondage under spiritual power and authority; the Holy Roman Empire, itself experiencing the inner turmoil of reform and full-scale confusion, remains what it always was. Of course, the Ghibelline motive of traditional anti-papism is given new energy by the Reformation, but even this testifies that the bonds with this ancient center of action, spiritual power, and authority remain in place. The threat to the ancient, universalist form of life and the political organization of Europe is of course strongly felt, and it could perhaps be said that, in this respect also, something like a sale of the immortal soul in exchange for new worldly possibilities has taken place. And here also, the change was originally prompted by genuine universalist motives, which are completely abandoned in retrospect.[4] The ancient, universalist political organization of Europe was certainly not sustainable in the long term; founded on authority (*auctoritas*) more than on power (*potestas*), it was fitted together too loosely to withstand the new concentrations of political and economic power; but it was nevertheless an actualization of the immortal, holy Empire, an organization of humanity founded on spiritual power and authority. The immortal soul had its socio-political expression in the idea of a spiritual power, and this idea took on its outer form in an admittedly precarious, but nevertheless actual, holy Empire. It is no surprise that the most extreme threat to this former refuge of European humanity invented the legend of the sale of the immortal soul. But it must also be asked whether precisely *this* sale concerned the immortal soul in its genuine form or in its fallen form—because one cannot shield oneself from the suspicion that authority based on spirituality, that is, insight and inner persuasiveness, is undermined as soon as the persuasiveness fails. The idea of a spiritual empire was conceived with the aim that a completely truthful, that is, truth-seeking person, a person living in truth, can live in the State. At the moment when the previous organization of authority—perhaps corresponding to the level of a quest for truth but resulting in self-preservation—ceases to correspond to its idea, it is then lost, and because it has been hollowed out, there is a risk of forgetting its genuine form and its necessity.

Goethe took up the idea of Faust at a time when an attempt was being made to integrate the Germanic components of the holy Empire (*sacrum imperium*) into a new Western Empire, which was holy and spiritual only in the memory of the Messianists. His poem seems to us to belong in the same frame which characterizes the spiritual life of this time, especially German spiritual life: it is an attempt to interpret the most recent flowering of the German spirit in poetry and thought as harbingers of a universal spiritualization of the age. Following the outward turn of the Enlightenment, time now allegedly seeks a path back into the interior which it will find signposted by this movement. Applied to the Faust legend, this means an attitude of reconciliation. No sale of the soul takes place, but instead a wager. The immortal soul is sure of itself, it cannot become lost; at most it grows weary, it can be taken in and lulled by things which are beneath it. Between Enlightenment and universal spiritualization, between understanding and reason, between external and internal, there is now not only opposition but also continuity. The immortal soul, the spiritual content of life, eternity, stands firm as in ancient times; the wager is about the present, this-worldly life and its justification from the spiritual standpoint. This justification must be possible, for in a spiritual universe, everything must ultimately be capable of being understood spiritually. Now, earthly life is threatened with exclusion from the spiritual only if it closes itself off within itself and does not find a way out; that is, if it stands still and is not capable of completing an upward movement of existence—then it falls toward the *me on*, toward an inauthentic being which is not only indifferent, but, from the standpoint of the living soul, worse than non-being. Even before life's descent into an unbounded immediacy which will draw it into complete recklessness about what exists and is accepted as valid, that is to say, from the very outset, Faust paradoxically already bears the guilt that he will heap upon himself as a result of this descent; it is a guilt which proves that the life of immediacy is inseparable from the context of what is factually accepted as valid. The proof is seen in that, where life should be grasped, death is the result. Sensuous life is thus revealed as an aspect of the ethical; awareness of guilt is its legitimate result, and when Faust himself also protests and perseveres in opposition to prejudice and tradition, Gretchen's acceptance of the awareness of guilt is deeper than his individualistic defiance. Her refusal to "save" herself through flight, becomes, through her death, that which continues to act and to transform itself within Faust himself. Guilt, the immutable destiny of death heaped upon himself, becomes the secret thrust behind Faust's continuing forward urge. As a result, even sensuous action has become ethical; it was an ethical action, namely an evil action, and Faust can therefore set out on the path to purification, which passes through aesthetic education and active life, and completes itself in the afterworld. In Goethe's version of Faust, Gretchen's tragedy is authentically tragic and thus forms the backbone of the whole poem: here, in an entirely Platonic manner, punishment is experienced as a purification of the soul, external help is rejected as appearance over against being.

What separates us from Goethe's version of Faust is not so much his advocacy for Faust—the guilt-laden figure, always storming ahead—as his idealistic interpretation of the world, his image of a spiritual universe where everything is a spiritual and ethical symbol. A profound relationship exists between this interpretation and Hegel's dialectic of the spirit. In Hegel's view of the world as light and Idea, immortality of the soul and eternity of the spirit are not a problem or a wager, not the objects of a potential metaphysical action, but simply a starting point. We feel that this view of the world weakens the seriousness of the question of the soul which can still sell itself where it strives for higher genuineness, instead of presenting it in its fullness. With Goethe (as with Hegel), the soul *cannot* sell itself; the "pan-tragic" is a foreground; reconciliation, albeit through negativity, is the presupposition here. Even in its most degenerate form, the soul passes through self-estrangement toward self-renewal. That explains why it is a matter of activity, of continuing. Storming ahead and self-overcoming become the key words, and from there onward, it must be understood that the authentic internal note, namely that guilt is the motive power in this movement, is misheard. Faust is increasingly understood as a person of energy, a superman in the modern, post-idealistic sense.

Goethe's solution to the Faust question, rejecting the sale of the immortal soul as impossible, thus leads to the third form of the legend, which belongs almost to our own age. It has been just twenty-five years since the publication of Thomas Mann's *Doktor Faustus*, which we attempt to place alongside the two previous versions as the third basic variant. Once again, the historical situation, which is reflected in the new version, is taken as a starting point.

Once again, there is a "German Reich," but in a form completely different from the German classical version. Spiritual power and authority are now completely out of the question. Looking at its political structure, this "Reich" is an inheritor of the Prussian, pre-revolutionary century; after its failed attempt at world dominance, it is finally transformed, in Plato's catalogue of superseded polities, into an unprecedented tyranny, which was made into a waking reality by unleashing forces otherwise daring to appear only in the nightmares of madness. Confusion among intellectuals, who were initially still trying to build a bridge back to the age of Goethe, is expressed in stultified followership. They awaken all too slowly from their entanglement in its finely spun delusions, but ultimately, it gives way to a most rigorous distancing. However, it really was too late; the madness had buried forever not only the German Reich but, at the same time, the 2,000-year-old edifice of Europe. In this situation, the poet, who had wandered the entire labyrinth of illusions of his own age, reached out again for the Faust legend.

Once more, the question of the soul is painfully serious. It is now no longer merely a question of how long a pedestrian, vulgar, and obscene evil, vainly trying to justify itself, can deceive a profound human spirit about the meaning of the spiritual-divine world. For the world has unveiled itself as soulless. There is no longer any sense in asking the Faust question in the manner of Goethe. On the one hand, the wager remains, on the other, there is a return to the pact with the devil, to the sale. But we believe the meaning of this sale has been reversed in comparison with the old Faust legend: a human gives himself, his life, to gain the immortal soul—a ransom enacted with the appearance of a sale.

The wager or the pact with the devil for the immortal soul in the soulless world—what does this mean? Long ago, this poet familiarized himself with the "great sin of the nineteenth century," Schopenhauer's discovery of the irrational based on rational appearance. Like Richard Wagner, he became inebriated with it and watched as its metaphysical shuddering was transfigured into musical mysticism. But now, actuality, devoid of any world beyond, came along in turn. The poet learned from Nietzsche that there is no "true world," no further ground behind the one, actual world. The entire reality of the bourgeois age, whose interpreter he was from the beginning, emerged further and further from its chrysalis like a Penelope, who wove and unraveled the veil between this world and the other world but finally lost all confidence in this weaving. An unprecedentedly hard, disenchanted, soulless world rose up. And in this soulless world, there is no superhuman ear to which one could entrust one's loneliest thoughts, no heart which might resonate with one's own. There is only the world, and everything there is—both actual and possible—is only in this *one* world. Even God and gods, should they be there, could be sought only inside it, never outside; and initially, the spiritual is present only in finite, material, slavish form, subjected to chance. Indeed, dreams and fantasies, conjectures and world variations are contained only within this *one* world, however much they might seem to repeat it, even infinitely often, as a quasi-world.

For all its inhumanity, this world has something like a heart, a core, an essence—not, of course, a sentient one. It can be called a heart, because it is this which lets the world be a world. It determines every object in it; it is the structure of the whole, which binds everything together and—itself presupposed by everything—presupposes nothing further. A remarkable necessity not comparable with any other, either abstract or factual, holds it firmly within its bonds. And if we compare ourselves, the thinking bits of straw which are its products, with it, then we say: there is within it an "irrational," something blind, factual, without therefore and wherefore, and this is disposed somewhere directly at its ground. One need not travel out into the world of things in themselves, into the world of the will in itself, to discover the abyss of this wonderful and wondrous groundlessness—that of the world itself. But the "irrational" is a name, an aspect of evil, evil in principle, the first and most all-encompassing evil, that which precedes every destruction and makes it possible, not only because it cares about nothing, but because its essence is such that it cannot ever even have cared about "caring" itself. That is the "cold evil" in itself, the ruthless wind which blows bitingly toward us, scorching us from the distance and depth of the world. But there is also the "red-hot" evil: in principle, nothing other than the coldness within us, the passionate and reckless, the unlimited and unchained bad infinity within the human.[5]

In principle, the soulless world is the same world that was always there, only "disenchanted," so extensively objectified by us that we not only no longer want and dare to measure it against our own scale, but there is even a risk that we completely fail to notice ourselves in it. Nevertheless, in precisely this world, the question must be asked whether humanity itself has now also become a thing, an indifferent existent, or whether it has remained in principle the same as the humanity which implored the gods for protection, which knew of guilt, purity, atonement, obligated itself inwardly, felt responsible and free. In other words, if by immortality of the soul, we do not understand the "bad infinity" of an everlasting duration, but rather authentic being (*Sein*) attained in contact with the never-dying, the never-submerging, then the question is: must the immortal soul be shaken off with the other illusions of the age, the subjective experiences and dreams regarded as real, or, by contrast, is this the era where the reality of the soul is subjected to its most searching test (*Bewahrheitung*)—the era of which Socrates would say, as he said to Callicles, if I had a soul made of gold, would I not reach out to you as the true touchstone?[6]

In one important respect, the pact with evil, with the devil, no doubt means a turning away from the idealism of the age of Goethe: whoever looks at the world unadorned cannot fail to recognize, and in this sense, show solidarity with the world evil. But, from the standpoint of this world evil, the offer contained in the pact is something more. It contains a suggestion to superior humans, to the Faustian genius, to realize himself as a Dionysian through the ruthless unchaining of his superiority; in him, the world evil, boasting and overacting in anything and everything it does, will attain one of its most extreme and most refined forms. Evil, the demon, attempts to chain the high-minded person to the dimension of limitlessness, to the abyss. From the standpoint of world evil, Adrian Leverkühn's story appears as the development of an extreme spiritual will to dominance, a self-overreaching, in which everything other is also proudly overcome and discarded in sovereign scorn, in coolly transparent heartlessness. Adrian Leverkühn's entire impetus is an impossible wager: to create a work of art in an impoverished time, in which all opportunities and means seem depleted and must first be renewed with extreme intellectual rigor, but must then also be melted down again in an all-consuming blaze which is inseparable from the work of art. In its own essence, the world evil offers this Dionysian alliance of the heat and cold of the world to the approaching artist, who does not hesitate to attempt the impossible. And, indeed, since it has chance and even capriciousness at its disposal, evil can intensify the natural genius of the uniquely gifted person in a manner which befits it alone, by poisoning him with spirochete and preventing a timely cure. And it adheres faithfully to this course: anything and everything which might interfere, such as warming and sustaining family relationships, friendship, love, one's own family life, tenderness toward a child—all that is held back with a rigor necessitated by the consistency of an evil asserting its ownership.

But, now, there is another aspect of the same process which largely reverses the situation. As an artist, Leverkühn is a seeker and a prophet of truth. And it is no abstract conceptual truth, although in his youth he did abandon himself to academic studies—characteristically to theology, which, however, captivated him primarily as a path to world evil. The artist's search for truth renounces propositions, and can therefore never say anything directly, but, in return for this, it is also not bound by the limits of language. Like every original truth, the artist's truth is an unveiling of the world. The world is not unveiled like an object, like something inner-worldly, by standing in front of and beside it; that is impossible in principle. The only way to proceed (and this is the way the artist proceeds), is to try to let the world itself come toward him by excluding everything which is *our* addition, *our* perspective, *our* meaning mediated through our interests. By transforming oneself in this manner into a pure milieu, pure existence, and letting go of everything which is not the world itself in its core, one can create a work in which the world itself is refracted. Only in this way can one experience it as the monstrously wonderful, eternally un-past and mysterious, and find means as unique as the concealed which has been revealed.

From this perspective, Leverkühn's isolation appears quite different. The artist's isolation, his solitary life, his escape from all relationships of human warmth is not a self-aggrandizing furor of unchained hubris; it is conditioned by service to the truth. Accordingly, an element has been inserted between the world evil and the artist, which is in principle different from the world evil itself. Moreover, the artist now no longer stands before the world as this talented, ambitious individual greedy for success. He has left this behind, because something completely new and different—the world itself as appearing—has placed itself before his gaze. He is nothing but the one who makes possible this appearing; he is not a unique self. In this office, he can be substituted by and in solidarity with all who are capable of it. His reclusiveness is therefore no longer arrogance. Seen from this point of view, even his exclusion from basic human movements and relationships in work, love, friendship, conflict, looks different from before. There is no damnation in it; it is the inescapable condition of his service to the truth. Once he has consecrated himself to artistic truth, this "curse" is no more than logical consistency.

However, just because world evil, in the form of blind chance and capricious fate, itself collaborates with this new event does not mean that it is simply a "flower of evil." No doubt, the devil would welcome it with a double rejoicing: first, because the most glorious fruit of world-being, the artist and his work, has shown itself to be just a result of his roll of the dice; and secondly, because fallenness and decay lurk behind this pinnacle. But in fact, the power of blind chance has been broken precisely because the cold chaos of the world has cooperated with meaningful destiny. In the long episode reporting this conversation, the devil argues demonically but ultimately against himself, when he draws Leverkühn's attention to the fact that the diseased focus in Leverkühn's brain is certainly not a factory of illusion, which merely generates demonic hallucinations; it is rather an appropriate means of making the demonic voice visible. For with the same justification, the entire world of the evil, chaotic, hyper-indifferent and boundless bad infinite could be regarded as a means and an opportunity, allowing truly soulful happenings, i.e., truth, art, but also other "ethical" phenomena such as guilt, conscience, responsibility, to step into actuality. Much as this might indicate a tempting attack of madness, just by appearing as the devil, world evil has already reduced itself, because the devil has been transformed from a purely neutral being into an ethical one; he has moved over into a sphere which is no longer his own.

In the soulless world, starting out from the world evil is, of course, unavoidable. Even in traditional, "animistic" world traditions, the acquisition of genuineness always began with decay. But something more than this is meant here: as the world evil, evil participates in weaving the emergence of the immortal soul; it transforms inner determination to outer necessity, to destiny, to something immutable. Whoever has been bound *in this way*, like Leverkühn through his "pact" and his disease, has bound himself irreversibly: he has abandoned himself irrevocably to the highest purposes of life, mutilated himself, and become guilty in himself. And whoever is guilty, has experienced a new kind of evil, allowing it to enter the world: the evil for which we bear responsibility, which is *our* evil, which must be borne and suffered.

One's own determination has become destiny, inescapable as death. One has damned oneself—but to what end? In the demonic view, it is for a boundless, unbridled, irresponsibly playful frenzy of creativity. But in this act, the experience of guilt has also been created. No hubris grows. This destiny is not carried as a privilege but in the awareness of guilt. Indeed, at every opportunity, where the inability to enter a human, inner-worldly relationship shows itself anew and more painfully, the capacity to meet the world itself becomes greater and more thrilling, and new works mature within it. But it is no longer a Dionysian existence which manifests itself there, but rather a yearning for purification. Guilt is at the same time the appearing of purity, and what purifies is atonement, punishment. The guilty one does not bear his destiny as a privilege, but as judgment and justice.

By creating the artwork, which is the truth of a soulless epoch, Leverkühn creates something epochal, and he no longer merely exists locked up within himself. Although he seems to live remote from every human relationship, condemned to defy tradition, even in this solitude, the immortal human soul has come back to life. It has become immortal through service to the immortal, the all-determining and all-encompassing, through service to the world itself. It is now a soul that wants to resonate with others within the essential, so that its solitude is not exclusive but authentically generates universality. But for this reason, the new musical work is, at the same time, the dream of a new community, which does not yet exist and "which does not need to be the Church."[7] Something different from the bustle and "culture" industry is sought there. "The future will see in her [music], she herself will once more see in herself, the servant of a community which will comprise far more than education and will not have culture but will perhaps be a culture."[8] If the warmly personal is out of bounds for Leverkühn because it generates interests and would therefore be alien to artistic truth, that does not yet mean that artistic truth cannot be generative of society. The discussion here is about sublating the divide between art and accessibility, between high and low, about the repetition of the romantic enterprise of a folk music without its sentimentality, with new means, probably in conjunction with satire and irony, without pathos and prophecy, auditory inebriation and literature. No blessed ode to joy will resound, there will be no universal embrace in the face of the benevolent father. Renunciation of the universal spiritualization of Beethoven's age is definitive, the reawakened soul is not a redeemed soul, but a soul marked by the will to judgment.

And yet, it is an inwardly matured soul, grounded in being and, in this sense, an indestructible soul, which, here, through loss of the most beloved, is only strengthened in its universal awareness of responsibility. His own vocation as artist to become a servant of truth has indeed solidified into destiny; but the destiny is an irrevocable choice, the paradoxical unity of freedom and necessity, into which the randomness of the world enters, which may not be assessable, but which is also indivisible; whoever knows themselves and wants to follow this vocation, at the same time chooses the world evil; it links them inseparably, and as co-intending, they are complicit and co-responsible for everything that the evil contrives. Leverkühn is justified in feeling *this* responsibility, when, in his Faustian leaving speech to the invited acquaintances (and the society that they represent), he declares himself responsible for things no one knows how to bring into a normal causal relationship with him. This universal responsibility and the will toward it—universal accountability—is also Leverkühn's ultimate legacy, both of his person and of his musical work, to the grave time at the beginning of which he knows himself to be living.

The universal feeling of responsibility is therefore not mysticism, not a feeling of unity, not a lapsing and collapsing of everything in universal sympathy. It is a feeling of solidarity in participation with the truth and with what makes truth possible: human destiny. What does this responsibility mean in a universal sense? Nothing other than: accepting judgment and therefore the security of the law and the universal, true community; wanting to be condemned in the knowledge of complicity with everything: wanting to bear and to work off one's part in the universal hardship, not wanting to escape from it into the private, the playful, the aesthetic—wanting to participate in universal justice as the only condition in which the soul can exist as such, as a being soaring out of the fall.

Summary

The first, popular version of the legend by Marlowe portrayed a fall in the sense of understanding what the immortal soul means, a fall which is grounded in the fact that Faust exaggerates the will to freedom and, instead of attaining at least temporarily a higher level of being, for which Faust sacrifices salvation, he only becomes the master and possessor of nature. In Goethe's version, the magnificent will to self-sacrifice which inspires Gretchen, causing her to reject earthly "salvation," leads Faust to believe in a higher sense of the world, contrasting with cynically trivial appearance, and to set out on the path to purification. But his ideal, spiritual interpretation of the world has become incredible to us; evil must be taken much more seriously; reconciliation must not be allowed to sink down to an event played out before us, a spectacle. Accordingly, Thomas Mann also presented the Faust legend to us as the story of an artist who sells himself to evil, to the cold evil of the world, and falls prey to it from a will to power, which he, the genius, feels as the essence of the world and to which, as an artist, he sacrifices everything "human," every inner and intimate enthusiasm. But precisely in his unlimited will to truth, the soullessness of the world is broken, and in his self-sacrifice and will to be judged before a court, the pact with the devil is also broken—not as theatre or history, but as a rediscovered will to responsibility for the world and its people.

Notes

1   The title of this work has been amended by the editors. Patočka's original title is "Der Sinn des Mythus vom Teufelspakt" (The Meaning of the Myth of the Pact with the Devil) (Ed.).

2   Patočka uses the German term *Der Betrogene* here, which literally means "the dupe." But Thomas Mann also wrote a story with this title to which Patočka no doubt refers. Helen Lowe-Porter translated the title of this story as "The Black Swan" (Ed.)

3   Edmund Husserl, *Die Krisis der europäischen Wissenschaften und die transzendentale Phänomenologie: Eine Einleitung in die phänomenologische Philosophie*, HUA 6, 1954. English: *Crisis of the European Sciences,* trans. David Carr (Evanston, IL: Northwestern University Press, 1970).

4   The European-Christian sense of mission is older than *auri sacra fames*, which dominated the first planetary beginning of the world (*auri sacra fames*: phrase from Virgil, *Aeneid*, Book 3, 57. Later quoted by Seneca as *quod non mortalia pectora coges, auri sacra fames* ("what do not you force mortal hearts [to do], accursed hunger for gold")).

5   See in this context Leverkühn's philosophising about life, humankind, the good as the *Blüte des Bösen*, the "flower of evil," in Chapter 27 of Thomas Mann's *Doktor Faustus* (Ed.).

6   Plato, *Gorgias*, 486.

7   Thomas Mann, *Doctor Faustus*, trans. J. E. Woods (London: Vintage, 2015), 86.

8   Mann, *Doctor Faustus*, 465–6.

PART FIVE

Philosophy of History

In Patočka, history is not a mere series of events that can be understood apart from wider philosophical questions. History, in the sense outlined in these texts and elsewhere in Patočka's writings, is a distinctive human achievement that begins in self-questioning, in the recognition of finitude and radical uncertainty. Patočka's philosophy of history was forged in a bleak time, in a context of global polarization, and, at the same time, the implosion of the European project. Perhaps the direct reckoning with uncertainty and catastrophe is what gives these texts an enduring appeal.

Additionally, these texts introduce Patočka's views on both the distinctive source of Europe in the self-questioning of the ancient Greek experiment, and the self-destruction of Europe in two world wars, leading to the need to articulate a post-Europe based on a recognition of the collapse of the European project and a simultaneous need to continue the project of living together in truth.

"The Spiritual Person and the Intellectual" explores the possibility of living meaningfully in the face of a cultural and existential nihilism. Looking, as Patočka often does, to Socrates as an exemplar of spiritual life, he notes that the meaning of such a life resides in continual questioning of the status quo. This questioning is not mere skepticism but is oriented by a vision of truth and justice that is still to be attained.

Socrates and Plato were problematizers of life, people who did not accept reality as it is given, but rather saw it as shaken—but the conclusion they drew from this was that some kind of peculiar, *other* life *is possible*; another direction of life, something like a *new ground*, and only here is it possible to gauge what is and what is not.

Finally, in "The Dangers of Technicization" Patočka offers a critique of an instrumental view of the world, highlighting how our technoscientific paradigm potentially distorts human meanings and contributes to destroying the planet we inhabit. The idea of sacrifice at the end of this essay challenges a narrow biologism, which sees the scope of life as a process of need and gratification. Sacrifice is presented as an assertion of meaning beyond the actual; as such, it resists the prevailing instrumental understanding of the human being as a "resource."

CHAPTER SIXTEEN

The Spiritual Foundations of Life in Our Time (1970)

Translated from the Czech by Alex Zucker

Does this title, "The Spiritual Foundations of Life in Our Time," make any sense? Should the foundations, the principles on which human life is built in our day and age, be "spiritual," that is, not material, not objective, but rather based in "spirit"? Is it not in fact one of the distinguishing features of the present day that everything vital in it has been shorn of the idealism that "spiritualizes" reality, i.e., that illusorily strips it of its solid, objective nature, leaving it to melt away on the one hand into imaginary demands, unfounded in any possibility for realization, and on the other into fictions and empty constructions of the mind? At one time perhaps these fictions and constructions had practical, ideologically active meaning, but today they no longer deceive anyone. If we speak of spiritual foundations, is that not tantamount to associating ourselves with what in our day survives only as a specter, a phantom of something that was once obsessive reality, though of course only seemingly objective?

We could neutralize this question by being modest, contenting ourselves with a conception of spiritual foundations that seeks simply a formula for the "spirit of our time." The "spirit of the time" may of course lie in objectivity, technicality, materiality. It is then only a question of the method used to determine this "spirit," this all-determining essence and form of our present day. There is much of the past in the present, just as ancient geological layers lie on the earth's surface. What is alive, what is dead in our present day? Clearly whatever is growing is alive, whatever has prospects, pushing out the old, the bygone and the decrepit. The question then is how to find what is new and dynamic. That requires a comparison with the previous era, with yesterday. But what an immense task it is to examine and analyze yesterday and today, to express a hypothesis about their basic determining framework, to verify it on the facts, and from there perhaps even dare an outlook for tomorrow! A task that would involve an entire methodology of contemporary history, as well as the main points of implementing that methodology. Needless to say, we cannot do anything here that would lead us too far astray from our own subject. We must ask our listeners to trust us to create such a conceptual framework and to base it on the critical reception of ideas voiced by others. In describing the basic features of this idea, perhaps too the opportunity will present itself for us to turn from "the spirit of the time," in the sense of a descriptive essence, to the discovery that this essence consists in a particular spiritual stance, a particular notion of what spirit is, its nature and its fundamental working and task; in this way we will try to move from a "modest" conception of the problem of spiritual foundations to a more demanding one. But let us now turn to the matter at hand.

Hypothetically, we can draw on the analyses of the English historian Geoffrey Barraclough, in his *Introduction to Contemporary History*.[1] The thesis is this: in the period after the Second World War, specifically in the 1960s, we enter a world substantially different from that of the past, a world prepared by yesterday but different from it, at least in the way the epoch of the so-called modern age, inaugurated by humanism, the Reformation, and the emergence of modern science, differs from the previous era. The basis for this change was the Industrial Revolution in Europe, beginning in the second third of the nineteenth century, a revolution that made Europe the sole proprietor of modern science and technology, and, as a result, of the power that enabled its unrivaled imperial expansion. Hand in hand with this went a demographic boom, the emergence of large urban and industrial centers, a modern mass industrial society. These facts forced a revision of existing political structures: mass democracy emerged, the party became the organ of political life, and the State a State of universal suffrage, a State of parties. Imperialism brought the question of the European balance of power to a global scale, and led to the powers of Europe dividing the world among themselves. Yet imperialism proved to be an insoluble problem: the European powers were incapable of actually ruling the world. Instead, their mutual rivalry and concerns about the future of their own power led them into a global conflict that greatly reinforced the pre-existing seeds of the era of dual superpowers that was to come, as well as the new world of post-imperialism. This same unresolved issue was brought to an end by the Second World War: during and after it, under pressure from the superpowers, and thanks to the shift of mass democracy and its organizational principles into the realm of emancipation, as well as brilliant campaigning by major political figures in the nations lagging behind, a post-imperial world emerged, Europeanized in form, but in terms of content a new, non-European world in which Europe ceased to play a decisive role, in terms of power and culture, and in which, besides the two superpowers, other demographic and political giants began to appear outside of Europe. Rather than the "Concert of Europe," it is the constellation of these countries, their demands and problems, that will determine the world of tomorrow. At the same time, the Industrial Revolution is accelerating, turning into a scientific and technical revolution. The structure of industrial society, too, is undergoing change, with the emergence of control technology, cybernetics, and automation, the revelation of the interior of the atom, the unleashing of forces enabling missions into space, and the construction of mechanisms for the precise regulation of their functioning. Meanwhile the atomic chess match hardens the positions of the superpowers and their ideologies into a state of mutual tension. Still, the new world, the world of regenerated nations, has a chance to resolve this spiritual futility, to eliminate the decadent culture of subjectivism that Europe has been drowning in since the start of the century; one hopes this new world will succeed in articulating the energetic will for life, which it is so full of, and in doing so also make room for art to express itself on those monumental achievements of science and technology that the European soul has not been able to find a positive way to relate to in our century.

This picture, optimistic for the emerging new world, but pessimistically colored from the standpoint of the old Europe, this demise of the West, observed with nothing but the historian's empirical eye, free of metaphysical speculation, demonstrates the defining features of today in its new level of technology (cybernetics, self-regulation, electronics, computers, the unleashing of enormous forces and mechanisms of unprecedented precision and accuracy), in its new possibilities for the biological and medical sciences, in the mass character of social and political life, in the entrance of massive new societal forces onto the historical stage as the existing European ones are sidelined. We can of course also see the encouraging role that Marxist-Leninist ideas must have played in the dialectic of the self-disintegration of imperial Europe and the emergence of new dominant social forces in the post-imperial and post-colonial era.

At times, Barraclough seems too harsh about the inability of today to express the world of technology through art. Let us look to the experience presented to us by the history of art, namely, that fine art has a special ability, not fully shared by other artistic disciplines, to express by direct, intuitive means the fundamental tendencies, the framework, of the "spirit" of the time; this is why historical periods are so often characterized by the stylistic hallmarks of fine art, in particular of architecture. One may dispute whether or not our time has its *own* style; the nineteenth century, for example, did not, instead living off its historical knowledge of other periods' styles; that was *its* style. But we need only enter the hall showing American painting from after 1945[2] to be confronted by a wholly different world than the one we considered up until recently to be the world of "modern" art. What we encounter here, exceptions aside, is not a deformation of given reality or a making visible of the invisible, but simply an expression of the tendencies of industrial supercivilization as it immediately presents itself to the eye, which absorbs merely the general intention—"technology, enormity, automation, control"—of this chaos, with the guiding principle shining through from the background. Advertising projected into the absolute, into deformed space, energy expressed with a spray of colors, the materialization of sunbeams, geometry in motion, humanity multiplied and distributed into the infinity of its variants, humanity as society, humanity as the mass, intersecting with space, with lines of force, mechanisms—what more could Barraclough want to be expressed by today's world of "cosmicism," of production that manages, gradates, and regulates itself, of mass society, of precision, of repeating the same in an indefinite number of copies?

Our author recalls how European intellectuals in the 1930s rejected this world even as it was being born. He recalls Toynbee, T. S. Eliot, and by the same right he might also recall Klages, Heidegger's *The Question Concerning Technology*,[3] and other expressions of this view. Today we are engulfed in this world, breathing, living, existing in it. And it is, as patently clear, an essentially material world, determined by material forces the likes of which are unprecedented, and likewise controlled with unprecedented precision. Similarly, the human race, massive and enormous, has a new, inorganic body. The planetary limbs and organs of planetary humankind reach all the way to earth's pale satellite. Needless to say, there are many who take delight in this. They may also find support for their enthusiasm in Heidegger's statement that the essence of technology is not itself technological or material. But the *immateriality* of its essence does not yet mean it is *spiritual*. The body of this epoch lies ready before us, a gigantic polyp, with all of us as its cells, determining us all far more than it can be determined by any of its suborganisms, despite its having no existence unto itself. The body is ready for action, but which way will this action turn, and what meaningful content will its movement bring into being?

It could be said that Barraclough's perspectives might still be surpassed in optimism if we consider what sort of transformation modern technology constitutes in the structure of human labor, of the fundamental ability we have to transform the given natural world into a human one, into self-objectification, materializing our humanity, projecting our interior into the exterior. Work up until now has been inextricably tied to the exploitation of the human organism as a physical force. This era brings the prospect of excluding this component ever closer to the point where its use will near zero. There is already increasing weight attached to technological intelligence in the ranks of the productively employed, and in the future the burden of the labor process will rest squarely on the technological intelligentsia. Accordingly, its numbers and volume are increasing as a proportion of the total workforce; in the last decade it exceeded the classical working class by more than 10 percent in the United States. The rising tertiary sector of the economy requires ever greater numbers of trained workers, colleges are spewing out an ever-greater number of graduates, and universities are exploding, breaking out in student revolt, a harbinger of structural change in a society that—for the first time in history—could be based on intellectual production and realize the interests of reason. The current stage may be chaotic, characterized by the collapse of traditional educational, political, and social structures. But beyond this collapse there is the possibility taking shape for a community of working people who will be able to value as a matter of their own self-interest the freedom of work without exploitation by the incompetent, the freedom of a spirit conscious of solidarity across every field of intellectual labor; a community of workers who promote the general interest as being both in their own interest as well as everyone else's. The intelligentsia as the decisive mass in the age of the masses: does this not offer hope in otherwise opaque times?

Thus we see the close connection between work, technology, and intellect as their capacities enter into a new relationship. Intellect as a primary productive force does not cease to be spiritual, even though as applied in the realm of technology it is specialized and focused on output. But this of course poses an entirely new *moral* problem, the problem of the consciousness of the intelligentsia as a whole, of its internal unity, its responsibility toward all of society: so that not only in terms of the content but also the form of its truth and its work, the intelligentsia become representative of the universal, of the community. How can this happen without a new understanding, a new spirit? Is not the intelligentsia in its specialized form so entrenched a representative of the old spirit, and so sealed off from the community, that it cannot be relied on to transcend itself and offer an understanding of the new problems?

The revolution in the sphere of labor, and the revolution of the intelligentsia as a mass, although by and large not currently felt to be positive phenomena, in fact suggest a highly positive potential, demonstrating what might be possible in the conditions of a growing society with scientific and technical tools at its disposal: to free humanity from the burden of physical labor and ensure a level of production sufficient to dispel the specter of poverty and hunger that looms over our overpopulated planet, where, in non-socialist countries, 15 percent of the population controls more than 60 percent of the world's capital; where the amenities of civilization increasingly provide for the bare necessities of life, but nothing more—either in terms of breadth or depth.

This immediately raises the prospect of yet another moral problem. Physical labor is not simply a negative, but has been such a significant weight on the overall structure of human life to date that we must ask whether freeing humanity from the burden of physical labor will cause the structure to lose equilibrium. It is a well-known thesis of numerous psychologists that work absorbs a great amount of energy that might be otherwise discharged in the form of interpersonal aggression. So human energy must be presented with new challenges; there is certainly no lack of them in this age of conquering space. The question is whether the energy unleashed as a result can be diverted into adequately prepared channels in time to avoid its being applied destructively—given that, from the perspective sketched by

Barraclough, it is clear: the rapid advancement of technoscience, and the revolutionizing of work and society, taking place amid a situation of plurality and a polarization of human social organization, are so far proceeding unevenly and in such a way that the benefits of wealth and power that flow from it are also distributed in a highly uneven manner. And it is not only uneven distribution and the underdevelopment of so many regions that pose problems. These newly awakening and newly forming enormous communities, the new masses of power, may be Europeanized in form, embracing European technology and organization. But internally, for the most part, they are foreign to and disapproving of Europe, of its traditions and its spiritual historical essence. For their part, Europe and its enormous scions, the United States and the Soviet Union, may be largely alienated from their own great traditions of antiquity and Christianity, but life in those places is at least based on spiritual ideas and themes developed by the dialectic of the decay of this essence. It is conceivable that Marxism-Leninism and its continued expansion, adapted to other conditions, will make its way into a great many of these countries that are united in opposition to today's *beati possidentes*.[4] But even then, its elaboration will certainly make use of domestic impulses and traditions, which these nations and communities are proud of, which they do not intend to give up, and which they believe they can continue to draw on and live from. This pluralism will not be merely formal, then, but nourished by the diversity of these communities' historical foundations. Mutual distrust and misunderstanding are highly likely to result; non-transparent, rationally incalculable factors will continue to assert themselves in the historical process, as they have up to now, and will stand in the way of humanity addressing its extremely sensitive problems in a rational and timely way in an age when it is under constant threat from the immense forces that are now at its disposal but also have the potential to destroy it. In a sense, this world will be more divided than the old European world, which had something of a common base, a common spiritual denominator, compared to which the rest of the world paled into insignificance, as a result of Europe's exclusive ownership of technological and economic power, so that Europe was the world—and in that sense was united. The wars showed that it was an illusory unity. Today, however, the explicit plurality of the various social giants is coming to the fore: Europe–USA (based on traditional Christianity), the USSR (Marxism-Leninism), the Arab Islamic world (Islam), Latin America (the Neolithic), Africa (likewise, but a different version), China (astrobiology, the cosmic), India (a more positive variant of the same). What common denominator can there be here? What can act as a bridge between these disparate premises of life, which in the foreseeable future will be fully equipped with power, technology, and organizational capability?

After all these considerations—from the optimism of Barraclough to realizing the problematic aspects of the picture that are foreign to the idea of a new enlightenment and hint at dangerous conflicts—we must now ask, however: Is Barraclough's picture of the new world a picture of the new "spiritual" situation overall ("spiritual" in the sense of "spirit of the time"), or is it merely the conclusion, the universalization of a spirit that was here already before? There is no disputing it is a new world in the sense of a new, universal, planetary, political power structure, which disposes of modern technology as the body with which it rules. But the question is whether there is a truly new spiritual element in all this enormity and universality, or if what comes to the fore is on the contrary the pluralism of the social giants, which may signify a phenomenon far more revolutionary and profound than any of us today realize.

How did the new situation that Barraclough so vividly describes come into being? Where are the roots of that dialectic by which the "European concert" is transformed into imperialism and by which imperialism digs its own grave, doing away with the "European concert"? There is no doubt that the expansion of the European concert into imperialism has its basis in the conception of State sovereignty. Philosophically, this conception was most deeply and thoroughly described (in such a way that the reality of nineteenth-century history confirms the theory) by Hegel: the State is the realization of the spirit, it is freedom on earth, absolute independence, an earthly God; it cannot recognize anything outside itself, all that has value, meaning, significance dwells within it, not outside of it. The State is the realization of a closed subject—not an individual subject, naturally, but a collective "spirit," an abstract subject of which the individuum is a concrete part. So *this* State concept rests on the basis of modern subjectivity, of the doctrine that reality is identical with the subject, and that the subject is free, i.e., closed to itself; reality does not lead it out of itself, but only deeper within. *This* concept, then, leads to imperialism and world conflagration, and Masaryk rightly viewed the First World War as an outcome of modern subjectivism. Kant-Hegel-Bismarck also rightly figure in his scheme of the "Prussiafication" of Germany, yet Masaryk's scheme is still one-sided, since of course it is not only a matter of Prussiafication. There was a parallel development in every European state toward an identical absolute sovereignty, but elsewhere for the most part it did not have the Prussian flavor of a synthesis of old-feudal and modern forms. This contradiction of absolutes in the plural is not accidental—it is a manifestation of the fact that despite all aspirations to unconditionality, independence, and self-containment, the subject cannot repudiate its essential contingency, its fragmentation into various individual and collective "personalities."

On the other hand, our modern technoscience also grows from a similar ground, that is, on the basis of a subjectivity that aspires to be self-confident, to control things, and above all itself, with the power to end all powers, and to that end it must secure its position in a world that has no other, independent meaning for it, but is sheer instrumentality, a reservoir of efficacy. This discovery of the world as a force is also correlative here to the concept of the spirit as absolute, free, i.e., self-contained, all-inclusive.

The modern world and its enormity, then, is the result of long-standing tendencies that were already burgeoning in the previous period, even if they did not yet have the role of exclusive principles, since allowance had to be made for a symbiosis with the earlier European foundation of Christianity, antiquity, and humanism. Subjectivity in its acute form came into effect only with the dialectical turn in the situation that knocked Europe out of the leading position it had held in the world up until then.

Now, the question is whether, in parallel with this overthrow of Europe's de facto leading role, the *principles* of the past must be overthrown as well. Whether the questions surfaced by the dialectic mentioned above require a revision of these principles and whether in fact this revision is already somewhere in some way in progress. Whether this revision can be detected in some of the problems being raised today, in the disappointing aspirations of the modern scientific and technical world to look to itself for solutions. And whether, somewhere in our lives, tendencies toward a new spirituality are appearing, in opposition to the closed soul—an isolated continent or besieged city—which served as the basis for development of the whole dialectic mentioned above.

Today, then, humanity stands with one foot planted on the ground of what used to be called utopia and is now more than a possibility. Technology is fulfilling our age-old dreams, which appear to be the primordial form of technology's actual products. What once sounded like the unfulfillable wish of myths and fairy tales is now a reality that still makes us dizzy but intoxicates us even more. On the other hand, however, the problems of modern mass societies arise, in the very same process and of equally superhuman enormity; overpopulation, malnutrition, misunderstandings, tensions, differences in mentality, problems which, again, can only be partially solved by rational-technical means. So it would be hasty to indulge with Barraclough in the optimism of a purely technical perspective on the new age in which humanity is beginning to live. Maybe that is why it will be an epoch of optimism, but hardly an epoch of happiness. Not only the individual, but whole traditional communities, which we have grown accustomed to thinking of as autonomous, will be bound to new, much more intensive and universal ties than ever before. The shadow of the giants will fall over every individual and smaller whole, a gentle rhythm, ever repeated in imperceptible variations, a subtle hatching fading into a shade of gray. Often it will require unprecedented discipline, or better put, obedience, docility, fitting in, and there will be many times when it is achieved automatically, before it is requested; it will become a matter of course, just as no one in the age of industrial production would think of making their own keys or shoes, or weaving their own fabrics. Tearing apart this world will require an effort as enormous as the world's dimensions and means. Immense powers seem to be inviting it to step into utopia; yet the impediments preventing this are no less enormous. The humanity of this era seems reminiscent of the chariot pulled by two winged horses in Plato's *Phaedrus*:

one horse races toward the outer ring of the heavens, giving us a glimpse of the ideas that can shine a light on the way forward, while the other races furiously into the abyss.[5]

Let us return for a moment to the utopian member of the pair. Within it we include technoscience and its impact on society, the restructuring of society's organization. All this seems to concern, in the first place, the means at the disposal of people today and in the future, what might be called the inorganic body of humanity. But the body of something that is alive is never a mere *res extensa*.[6] We have observed this already in the moral problems posed by the new form of human labor. We have seen it in the "utopian" nature of our technology, in the fact that it is a rational realization of myths. It seems there is a connection beginning to emerge between the rationality of means, the materiality of their results, and the spiritual motivation of these realizations. We could never realize what was originally a utopia if we did not dream of it. It is not only urgent needs that drive a person forward, but also our personal dreams, anchored in our most basic possibilities. What needs and dreams have in common is they relate to something I do not have, something I am lacking. We would never fly unless in the core of our being we had already been everywhere, unless we were beings who, being universal, having a relationship with the universe, were perpetually approaching everything. The means to realize this approach may be lacking; the moment we have the means, the approach appears as well. That does not yet mean that every *human* dream can be realized. But *all* human realizations are realizations of dreams. Dreams are the first step, the first representation of an originally empty intention, of a mere possibility showing up in the form of pure desire. We would never be able to realize anything if we did not live *ahead of* ourselves, if even in the present itself we were not already in the future, in possibilities that are as yet possibilities. If possibility is taken away from a person, the present ceases to exist for them as well. The given follows from the not-given. The not-given is its precondition.

And so even as what once seemed a utopia is realized, amid all the enthusiasm and the justified pride in humanity, the realizations of utopia are intermingled with shadow, a feeling of disappointment. In enriching ourselves, we grow poorer in terms of possibilities. In making the future the present, we live only in these presents.

This disappointment is particularly noticeable where utopian realization offers nothing but a surrogate. In realizing a utopia, new purposes are sought, new meaning, new goals—when what was once ahead of us is all of a sudden here, we need a new "ahead." Humans have a fundamental desire for "happiness" or "good fortune." However, good fortune, *túkhē*,[7] is something that fundamentally escapes our capture, that is never within our power, but rather has power over us. We cannot seize hold of fortune, we can only be accepted by it. In a sense, we exist only because we have the good fortune of being accepted. In a purely physical sense, human beings exist only by virtue of being *accepted* into the human community, and they long for acceptance wherever they live out in the open, unprotected—for acceptance by another being. In a totally different sphere, although closely related to it and also rooted in it, is the *pleasure* of acceptance, the pleasure of fulfillment. Modern psychology teaches that instinctive desire in every sphere is subject to the pleasure principle, and that in cases where it conflicts with the reality principle it is subject to repression, a forcing into the realm of the unconscious. The most important factor in repression is society, its structure and the demands of work placed on us by reality. As far back as the ancient myth of Gilgamesh, we learn that Gilgamesh forces the men to leave their women and build his city walls. It is now a seemingly obvious consequence of the theory of surplus society, a society that arises out of the new technology and the organization of class and production that come with it, that this society will not require such extensive repression, such strict sexual taboos, as societies of past civilizations did, including those that are capitalist. Asceticism will be replaced by new, richer needs, some believe, and life will be happier. It is beyond doubt that repression is on the retreat, that people are winning the right to do what they want with their bodies, their physical selves. Our bodies and our physical possession of things are indeed something we control and dispose of as we please. Yet what eludes this sexual utopia—no longer a utopia—is the sophistry of desire, which pretends to offer something it cannot. The only thing this false utopia has in common with true happiness [the happiness of love] is the pursuit of happiness. Yet in fact it is chasing only the shadow of happiness, so that all it succeeds in catching is the companion of happiness [sexual pleasure], believing it to be happiness itself. Hence the chase is in vain.

Another utopian task that seems to me no less problematic is the realization of human immortality. Immortality is of course an ancient human desire, and the empirical achievement of immortality is a problem humans have taken up since time immemorial, in art, magic, and today technology as well. Contemporary biologists, as we know, claim that the perpetual existence of living matter is achievable within the framework of our capabilities. Assuming it would be possible to bring about the conditions needed for unending human existence, the question is, would that not alter the fundamental structure of humanity, would it not actually result in the end of age-old problems? Is it not finitude, mortality, the mystery of nothingness and survival that have spurred such tremendous activity in the realm of the spirit, especially religion, throughout human history up to now? Are we not *homo religiosus* precisely because we are mortal? If it were possible to bring about human immortality in the laboratory, would that not be the end of all these realms of activity. Would that not mean, in practical terms, the definitive unmasking of the anthropomorphic nature of our concepts, which so many formerly went to such lengths to prove in the abstract? An attack on this root would thus be reserved for the present day's large biological institutes and laboratories, allowing humanity to enter into a permanently positive stage. In fact, there would not even need to be anything like total biological immortality, the task would be much simpler: what makes the phenomenon of death so insidious and mysterious is simply that it is not under our control, it besets us when and how it wants; it would suffice to solve several still pending methodological problems, which are on the way to being solved as it is, such as cancerous tumors, organ transplants, and the like, and prolong life in such a way that the will to live would fade away automatically—then death would cease to be such a fatal, insidious, uncontrollable phenomenon, crushing people with the realization that they know neither the day nor the time of its coming and that they are not its master in any way.

If we look at the prolongation of the human lifespan that accompanies the development of European civilization, in fact the trend appears to be that we are moving in the direction of "natural death," which we were not able to achieve earlier in history largely due to a lack of wherewithal. A visitor to old monasteries, which have records of the age of those buried there, is struck by the early age at which monks died, for example, in the twelfth and thirteenth centuries. Asceticism in those days was often a complete abstraction from life. Today for the most part we have the resources, so we should be able to solve even this great problem of human self-management, the problem of human control over humans. This would result in the human world being self-contained, becoming one that we control both in terms of quantity—through voluntary choice and birth control as well as eugenic procedures for the selection of offspring, which are now on the way—and quality, once we are able to influence hereditary endowments at will, and ultimately in terms of the course life takes and how it ends.

Yet the finitude of human life consists not in its factual course but in its *facticity*; not in the *reality* that it is ruptured from outside with no possible intervention or defense, but rather that this *can* happen at any time; not in the fact that its flow has an end, but in its *being toward an end*. Life is no less life toward an end by being excessively catered to, pampered, and kept safe. That only shifts the milestones. Its finitude lies precisely in that constant need for care and security. Life never ceases to be the life *ahead of us*, in advance of our own present, and ultimately at the last possibility, which cannot be outrun, where I stand face to face with nothingness. It goes without saying that life may carefully conceal this possibility from itself, and people may develop a technology for this concealing, a consensus of mutual relief. Yet the finitude will still be there, even in this escape, albeit in highly diluted and internally deadened form. It will remain in life, however dismissed or glossed over. At the present stage, things are such that comprehensive care, as Simone de Beauvoir for example describes in her book *Une mort très douce*,[8] may even sometimes lead to a situation where the natural *taedium vitae*, a disinterest in life due to its inner weakening, does not occur at all and the fatally ill abruptly find themselves faced with a situation where they are cruelly wrenched from life by the sudden removal of what had preserved it, so that the end is not very different from a death staring down the barrel of a gun.

Just as there is a substitution of pleasure for happiness in the relaxing of sexual taboos, in managed death there is a substitution of external closure for inner finitude. And that again presupposes a view of life from the exterior, as a series of moments, the problem being how to lengthen or shorten it. However, the problem is not only one of lengthening or shortening, nor is it even in death being something one can have or adopt as *one's own*, something one can agree to. The problem is in the primordial and humanly unavoidable condition of "living death in life," living as a finite being, because as humans we have no choice.

Nor in the present day is there any lack of thinkers attempting to show that life must be internally infinite. Husserl, in one remarkable text from his posthumous writings,[9] seeks to show that although human beings are of course finite and mortal, the foundation of humanity as such, which is constantly at work in us, a transcendental consciousness responsible for our experience, is infinite and immortal. According to Husserl, this follows from the phenomenon that there is no such thing as a first and last moment of life, that we are always retaining and protaining, that no part of this leaning forward burdened by the past may be excised. It may be conceivable that this consciousness will be forever darkened and veiled, that it will fall asleep for all eternity; but to fall asleep is not to perish, to vanish into an absolute nothing. In dying in fact we literally cloak ourselves in eternal sleep, and the fact that it is eternal is determined only by our worldly experience; phenomenologically speaking, neither reincarnation nor coming back to life in a purely internal personal world can be ruled out.

What is inconceivable is only complete disappearance. Pure passivity is not disappearance. To make his point, Husserl seized on the *inconceivability of death*. Death, extinction are things we cannot even conceive of. There is in fact no philosophical way to treat the subject of pure extinction. We can think of it in terms of change, although change presupposes the persistence of something in change, or in terms of a continuum of extinction, an infinitesimal dwindling away that never comes to a complete end; or we can conceive of it dialectically under the heading of "being and nothing are identical," but then nothing unavoidably transitions also into being, a good being even, no less than a being in nothing.[10] However, the experience of death—of being in oneself as well as in another—is perhaps testament to the fact that thinking is not an adequate approach to everything that is indisputably part of the world. Thinking is always object-oriented; when the object disappears, it is left facing a mystery it cannot solve. By contrast, the basic mood that makes us aware of our being in the world, of our being in it and having to carry the burden of our existence, because its origin, its beginning, is something we can never control, and because we are denied substantive, positive access to these things, just as we are denied access to our end, this mood keeps us feeling uncanny, eerie, sinister, and creates the feeling of an abyss in our lives. It is the abyss of nothingness, of true non-being. All it takes for it to be present and play a determining role is the fact that it cannot be eliminated, and in that sense this abyss of nothingness is the outer limit of our position.

It is not, however, a purely negative limit. In it lies our human freedom—being within the world, in the world, while at the same time in relation to it as a whole, which means to be freed of everything individual, of all the meaning of the world, and of all ties and relationships to ourselves. Here is the ultimate allowance, which is granted everyone, the possibility to withdraw from all interests and attachments in favor of the first and most fundamental. Here we know, and always will "know," that to be as a human means to be a *human individuum, individual, mortal, and everlastingly incomplete and one-sided*, and confronted with the fact that we are and must carry on the burden of our being, we cannot help but be preoccupied with our own being. Here, where we feel our own pure being because we have withdrawn from all biases toward individuals, we stand at the center, and yet face to face with the whole. Whereas all other life is always without a beginning, in contingent arrangements and roles, which may be this way or that, *here*, in the face of primordial contingency, faced with the bare fact of being, we are outside of any secondary contingencies. And only then do we have a chance of being captivated by the world in a genuine way, that is, in such a way that the note of the primordial situation never ceases to sound explicitly. The solemnity of it will be with us the rest of our lives. Solid ground has been found for ourselves, but that does not mean merely for circling around our own person, whose finitude we come to know in our living toward an end whose invitation we have understood and therefore accepted. The person is sacrificed either way: what matters now is simply to identify what is unique to me as a human being and to find out what it can be and what it ought to be expended on, what to devote myself to. Here it is revealed that a human being is not simply here, but is *sent*. Sent to everything and to all who do not have the privilege that is now acquired: the privilege of being captivated by the whole and by being, by this primordial interest that is the source of all clarity. A human being here changes into one who is sent into the world to bear witness to the truth, in order to testify to it with every act and every behavior, in order to help everything similar to them to find itself, in order to let people be what they are, in clarity and in truth, to offer oneself to things and beings alike as a ground for their development, rather than using them for profit and heedlessly exploiting them for one's own arbitrary interests.

It is only in light of this attitude that the meaning of several major attempts within contemporary thought at regaining *hope* is revealed to us. For a long time during and after the Second World War, Western countries were dominated by the idea of a heroism undaunted in the face of ruthless death in extreme and hopeless situations. Being toward an end was thus portrayed from a dramatic point of view, alas, in literature and theater alike. So attempts to turn attention away from this horror in favor of building support for the great tasks that speak to us based on the situation of our time, of our present-day actions, knowledge, and art, doubtless have positive value, even if at the same time we must recognize their limits. Philosophies and theologies of hope are emerging. The hope in them is not a mere *relief* from the horror and fear that are left in us by the perils of the times, but rather the very possibility of opening ourselves to the future. The discovery of the future is one of the most distinguishing, most important features of our time. Time has been a theme in human thought for ages, but a minor one; the momentousness of it could be felt in the backdrop to it provided by the major theme of eternity, timelessness, and everlastingness. Kant's thinking, and modern historicism developing in parallel with it, tore time out of this secondary, overshadowed position; but not until the late nineteenth century did time become the center of philosophical reflections, with the past dimension dominating, a subjective view of time as memory and reminiscence, of qualitative accumulation and the creative development that takes place in it; but that was just a prelude to today. Today we have, on the one hand, philosophies of the future as the fundamental, primordial dimension of time and temporality; on the other, attempts less philosophical, but no less characteristic of our time, at a scientific analysis of the future through the analysis of developmental trends, and we see how these estimates and the life in them are becoming themselves a powerful factor in the present. The discovery that the present is possible only because of the future has led to an intensification of interest in the future component in our current life.

The most important revelation connected with looking into the nature of time, however, seems to be the dawning conviction that time is not an environment in which the timeless, once-and-forever existing nature of things breaks up in our view, remaining in its essence, in its being, event-free. Not things as the isolated ultimate level of what is, but the nature of the universe to manifest, appear, and reveal itself in its possibilities is inexhaustible yet capable only of temporal, historical manifestation, revealing the whole every time, though always from just one side. The possibilities of manifestation cannot be adequately taken in, and therefore still less so exhausted by ontology or logic, even the most dialectical. At the very least, natural-scientific rationality is the ultimate instance of revealing what the universe is, since it itself is nothing but one particular form of the manifestation of the universe. Natural-scientific and technological rationality is the form of manifestation most closely associated with the idea of subjectivity as all-controlling, unleashing the powerful forces of the objective world and putting them at the service of this subjectivity whose expanding rule and power fundamentally know no bounds, so that ultimately it is superior to everything and closed in on itself.

Yet if the mystery of time does not lie in the fact that things which are in themselves determinable outside of or without regard to time, and therefore in some sense finished, develop in time, undergoing evolution, and thereby exhaust their possibilities, if time is not just the hourglass of the universe, then it cannot mean anything other than its resistance to any positive, substantive understanding. Time, then, is not only a mask of the essentially timeless, a mask that must be discarded in order for a disguised essence to be revealed, but on the contrary it is a mystery itself, it is what keeps the ultimate nature of things forever hidden while also being a fundamental condition for the possibility of its disclosure. Time is then also, in its whole nature and structure, distinct from a mere unspooling of events situated in linear dimensionality: on the contrary, it is a paradoxical joining of the ever-new, which is denied us before it appears in the present, and the always-the-same, which has forever eluded us. Time, in a sense, in revealing itself says always the same hidden thing, and yet its hiddenness cannot fail to manifest itself anew. The locked essence of the universe has within it the power to defy the efforts of the spirit that seeks to know, and it is this same power that determines the knowing spirit to such an extent that there cannot be even the first inkling of clarity about things and ourselves without it; this power is time. In a sense, then, one can say that through time we return to the supratemporal, assuming that by supratemporal we mean that which can never be located on a timeline, that which has no location in the one-dimensional unspooling where everything existing appears at some point. Thus time and its mystery are "supratemporal," whereas the one-dimensional diversity of moments is derived, secondary, abstract. Time in the sense of unspooling is only an illusion of finitude, which seeks to exhaust the universe in order to subordinate it and embody it with spirit; time in its essence is a mystery as the ultimate backdrop to every human attempt at an answer.

It would be wrong to interpret this doctrine of the riches of the universe as a claim of poverty, as the skeptical view that all our efforts to unlock the essence of the universe are in vain and that everything means the same thing and ends in the same frustration and absurdity. It does mean that every great human endeavor must revolve around *individual expression*, an individual style and expression of essentially the same mystery, which is the same only at the cost of showing itself in this substantial diversity. (Herder said already at the beginnings of the historically thinking era that each period has its center within itself, just as every sphere has a center of gravity, and the historical school spoke of immediacy to God.) However, it is not a process in which ultimately what is exposed is a great emptiness, darkness, and nothing, but on the contrary endless being. It may even require the ability to conceive of infinity in the first place, an infinity, all of whose objective forms, mathematical and philosophical, up to now have proven to be an attempt to cast as finite what cannot be cast as finite. The reason we cannot comprehend the universe is not because it is hopelessly absurd, and therefore poor, but because of its inexhaustible richness. Not because there is no key to it, but because all the keys are insufficient, in effect opening one aspect while locking the others, and there is no way to control this unlocking locking in such a way that we can talk about a single key that would render history itself and its inexhaustible creative destruction unnecessary.

Because this variant of cosmicism surpasses every cosmicism considered to be exhaustive, we cannot leave unremarked the phenomenon that many once believed to be the highest expression of cosmic openness attained by our time: the work of Teilhard de Chardin. One clearly feels here the impetus to transcend the traditions and ideological boundaries so characteristic of nineteenth-century Europe. At a time when specialized science, philosophical speculation, theological tradition, and the path of mysticism stood sharply at odds with one another, Teilhard's flight through the eons sought to show that at bottom they were one and the same. In this transcending of particularities, in this struggle against exclusive viewpoints on the one hand, and on the other, in the struggle against all human privacy, against the practical confinement of oneself to the reduced dimensions of personal interest, incapable of finding powerful inspiration and resonating in harmony with other beings, we can plainly see the significance of his work. But I do not know if his mystical views on the interblending and spiritualization of all that exists have much to offer us. For this culmination of his evolutionary perspective keenly demonstrates how he did not break free of the metaphysics of time that unavoidably apply to evolution, of the metaphysics of an ultimately supratemporal substrate, of the determination to offer a perspective that positively contains everything. Teilhard's example must be interpreted very cautiously if it truly has something to say to us on the great openness and absolute transcendence of self that he calls for and which today's world is in dire need of. As a tendency in the above sense, however, Teilhard is a perfect illustration of the spiritual direction of our time.

Allow me now to return to the tragic contradiction that I see as a consequence of the open perspective on the new tendencies shaping the era now unfolding, in which we have been given to live. There is a contradiction between, on the one hand, the vast potential of today's technological rationality, which requires unity, methodical planning, precision functioning, and a uniform outlook from a single standpoint, and on the other, the pluralism of the new giant societies, which regard these issues from a myriad of historical perspectives. This contradiction will lead to a future world that is the very opposite of idyllic. Technological rationality offers unprecedented means for the building of life as well as its destruction, but being itself merely instrumental, it cannot be expected to provide a solution. For that a new positivity bridging the gap is required, something purposeful, not just instrumental; non-instrumental purposefulness, however, is actually one way to define spirituality—a spiritual life lives by its goals, it exists of itself, not only en route. Of course we cannot determine what type of spirituality the future will actually choose. We have already voiced the hypothesis that this era will demand new and perhaps unprecedented displays of subservience from individuals and certain portions and segments of society. Humanity will continue to modify the conditions and form of its existence within the whole in a very radical way, but the determination and dependence of the individuum as such will at the same time and at the same pace continue to increase. There is a great danger of humanity losing its soul, not only under pressure from the vast historical masses, but also due to the promises of power and abundance that beckon in the age of technoscience. In our reflections here, we can only highlight the type of spirituality that seems as though it might be capable of playing the role of planetary soul to the new means that constitute the planetary body of humanity—a spirituality that contains the seeds of a possible solution to the question of how to reconcile a plurality of foundations in a positive way, without causing impoverishment and skepticism. The patience and steadiness required for this can only be exerted by one who has found their own center; in the words of Josef Čapek: a human being with a soul.[11] In this new planetary period of enormity we have entered into, humans will remain what they were before, existing beings who have not only an end, but because they have an end, also an eternal beginning. The existing being that does not close itself off, but whose motto is openness, will, let us hope, be capable of coping with the divisions whose pressure we can already feel, divisions today's humanity will increasingly have to address in the period we now live in.

A human being with a soul is one who has a sense of others, not only in terms of their neediness, of their blatant distress; a human being with a soul also has a sense of the essential mystery of all things. Not skeptical tolerance, which tends to result from indifference toward what it is that people depend on for their lives, but the realization that all our keys are not enough to unlock the treasures that await us could perhaps be a path to the mutual understanding of the plurality of historically established social giants, which represent something absolutely essential, drawn from the depths of existence, and which promise to be one of the main signatures of the epoch of history that we have clearly just entered.

Notes

1   Geoffrey Barraclough, *An Introduction to Contemporary History* (New York: Basic Books, 1964) (Ed.).

2   The traveling exhibition *American Painting After 1945: The Disappearance and Reappearance of the Image*, January–November 1969, Wallenstein Riding School, Prague. This exhibition included the main representatives of pop art: Andy Warhol, Robert Rauschenberg, Jasper Johns, James Rosenquist, and Roy Lichtenstein (Ed.).

3   Martin Heidegger, "Die Frage nach der Technik," in *Die Technik und die Kehre* (Pfullingen: Neske, 1962) (Ed.).

4   "blessed owners" (Ed.)

5   Plato, *Phaedrus*, 246–8 (Ed.).

6   In *Meditations*, Descartes divides the world into thinking subjects (*res cogitans*) and corporeal things (*res extensa*) (Ed.).

7   τύχη, fortune, good fortune, success.

8   Simone de Beauvoir, *Une mort très douce* (Paris: Gallimard, 1964) (Ed.).

9   Cf. Edmund Husserl, *Zur Phänomenologie der Intersubjectivität: Texte aus dem Nachlass. Zweiter Teil: 1921–1928.* Hrsg. von Iso Kern, 154ff., in *Husserliana*, vol. 14 (The Hague: Martinus Nijhoff, 1973) (Ed.).

10 Cf. the analyses by Eugen Fink in *Metaphysik und Tod* (Stuttgart: Kohlhammer Verlag, 1969).

11 See: Josef Čapek, "Kulhavý poutník" (Limping pilgrim), in *Spisy bratří Čapků* (Works of the Čapek brothers), vol. 37 (Prague: František Borový, 1936). See also page TK in this volume (Ed.).

CHAPTER SEVENTEEN

The Dangers of Technicization in Science according to E. Husserl, and the Essence of Technology as Danger according to M. Heidegger (Varna Lecture, 1973)[1]

Translated from the German by Erazim Kohák

I

There are philosophical topics that can occupy a thinker for years and still their deepest significance can become clear even to him only afterwards—though then they can cast a new light on all of his previous conceptual efforts. We encounter an instance of this in Edmund Husserl, whose long career as a thinker devoted to the foundations of philosophy as a rigorous science went full circle from an initial concern with the relation of dator intuition[2] to meaning isolated from intuition until it finally came upon the root of the crisis of the sciences in the draining away of meaning in fully formalized modern natural science, a crisis that in the end endangers not only science itself but all of our spiritual life and with it even our life itself. From their initial constitution, science and scientific philosophy represented an instance of life in truth and responsibility. Once they found themselves in a state of crisis, humankind lost the basis of a life based on insight.

Husserl's entire first work, *The Philosophy of Arithmetic*, revolves around the relation between genuine and non-genuine conceptions of number and around proving that arithmetic is an instrument reflecting our limited seeing ability, its goal being to substitute entailment for a direct grasp of multiplicities and their relations. If that is true, arithmetic would be based on the fact of the limited human grasp of the ground and would really be nothing more than a gigantic technical tool. The task of the philosophy of arithmetic would then be to bring us to a clear awareness of its foundations in direct intuition. The quest for discovering a justification of the claim of mathematical infinity in finite intuition—that is something that, for all the profound differences, links Husserl's first work with his unfinished late work about the crisis of the sciences. For what constitutes the sole ground of dator intuition—which is the ultimate recourse of all truth claims—is, in the late Husserl, precisely the finite world of our life, defying idealization. Between these two stages of Husserl's scholarly career, however, there lies the research in which one of the important themes that constitute the originality of phenomenological investigation is the relation between intention and its counterpart in seeing. Only so was it possible to develop the newly conceived investigation of reason which investigates degrees of evidence and their object corelates on a broader basis. In the course of this investigation, whose methodological apparatus and basic themes we need not explain here, it becomes evident that the meaning of higher-level objectivities such as judgments, multiplicities, theories, classes, stemming from our spontaneous mental activity, depends for the most part on operations with what is given; and in no case are these objects and objective contents as non-problematic as they are treated in scientific practice. Thus a theory guided by a will to radical clarity absolutely cannot approve of them on the basis of their theoretical and practical successes, since just the significance of such successes remains initially in darkness. We have even to say that these exceptional successes carry with them the danger that they will be accepted non-problematically and uncritically, for successes are most tangible in the realm of the application of mathematics to nature and just these applications give the impression that here we really find ourselves on the level of reality itself, with the directly given human context explained away for the most part as its "mere appearance."

Husserl then seeks to show by a rigorous investigation that modern science, animated by a will to universal rationality, develops a formal mathematics that makes possible first an arithmetization of geometry, then the indirect mathematization of qualitative contents and a project of precise causality: in the course of it, each step achieves an exact and universal determination of experiential givens, reflected in practice in precise predictability, but at the same time each step brings about a special draining away of meaning because the procedures used in dealing with formulas are of a formal nature. With that, such science becomes a *techne*, the art of a precise calculation of nature which would not be bad in itself, were it done fully consciously, if humans were aware, at each step, of just what they are doing, cloaking the primordially given world, subjective and unprecise, in an ideational garb which transposes it into a precise universe of truths for all and so makes it calculable. The erroneous impression that we are thereby also reaching truth and ultimate true being in itself arises because the fundamental tools of rationality, mathematical concepts and theories, were from the start of this process of rationalization taken over from an unquestioned tradition, technically evaluated while the question of their meaning and origin remained forgotten; therewith we leaped over the entire realm of the working rationality which constitutes the transition from our subjectively unprecise lifeworld, operating within a natural inductivity, to the objectifying idealizations and so to being the truth for all.

Accordingly, we need to seek the root of the spiritual crisis in the draining away and shift of meaning brought about by the inevitable but falsely interpreted technicization—and here what can help is a radicalization of rationality striving for direct insight, embodied in the new phenomenologically proceeding philosophy and especially in the philosophical discipline devoted to the tasks of our life and to those activities which aim and lead to rigorous science and rigorous induction.

Heidegger's assessment of the situation shares many particulars with Husserl's, for instance the stress on the technical traits in the foundations of modern natural science. However, we believe that it differs from Husserl's view fundamentally in that Heidegger takes the draining of meaning which he decries for an inevitable part of the new meaning of being, characteristic of our time. In Husserl, technicization is something negative, a certain *steresis*, a lack of meaning which can be in principle eliminated by greater attention to the observed continuities of meaning. A broader foundation of a new level, that of the effective transcendental subjectivity, could overcome this state of affairs. For Heidegger, things are otherwise. Precisely the technical procedures of certain and precise calculation belong to the modern way of uncovering being. A recourse to a putatively ultimate effective subjectivity as the final source of meaning inevitably transforms this source once more into a specific existent of its own kind, stripping it of the role of the originator of all meaning and the beginning of all clarity. A recourse to our lifeworld makes sense as a stage in the recourse to absolute subjectivity, but it is not radical enough to include in its field of vision that "within" man which is responsible for meaning for clarity and truth.

Thus Heidegger begins where Husserl's analysis ends, with the recognition that modern science has the character of a *techne*, yet science uncovers being precisely because it is a *techne*, in the very essence. It does so, to be sure, in a special manner, specifically, but unlocking the immediately given with respect to a certain utility, it transforms what it thus unlocks, assembles the product and places it again at our disposal for further use. This procedure does not simply bring our lifeworld into a relation to a universal level of formal generalities, but rather it is something that generates such a level for the sake of transforming and assuring a supply of materials; this procedure brings about even a transformation of our very lifeworld: it is being rebuilt and transformed in its factual state and meaning. The draining away of meaning, for instance, is here carried over from the sphere of meanings into the realm of reality itself. A process of universal uncovering is set in motion which will pass over nothing: both things and people receive their "meaning," that is, their place within the process. All and everyone is set to certain task, arranged for and placed on order. All and everyone becomes a mere resource available for possible and actual orders. With that not only the autonomous nature of things but even the objective nature of the objective begins to vanish—the relation to the self-presenting I from which we cannot derive the characteristic of "being-on-order." Thus apparently autonomous units are integrated into a vast network of relations in which they function rather than dwell, have an effect rather than repose, though in this sense they are: the very meaning of their being has been transformed.

Where, though, is any danger in all this? This great transformation, after all, can be viewed from its positive side. We have achieved greater transparency and manipulability of the world around us than ever before. For the first time in history, man has truly become universal, has become a planetary being. He can order virtually everything, at least as long as he can overlook that he himself, both as an individual and as the bearer of a certain role in a social context, now belongs among the resources that are "on order." We do not see the great danger in, as is often said, "technology enslaving man," as if we knew what man is, what his freedom and slavery mean. We discover the danger if we present for ourselves once more the Husserlian starting point of our reflections. Husserl saw the crisis of humankind in the contemporary man standing in danger of losing the dimension of a life in truth. For Heidegger, however, truth in the traditional sense—truth of judgments, as rightness—is dependent on a more basic truth which makes the truth of judgments possible by opening up a clearing in which what is can first appear. This clearing of appearance is not itself visible but enters in only in that which appears to us: it casts light but itself draws back because only so can it make possible the original opening up of truth without itself becoming one of the things that appear among others. Modern technology, however, is, as we have seen, an uncovering by its very essence, a process of veracity in the sense of making truth possible. At the same time, technology as an agent generating change shows itself to be historical by its very nature as every profound manifestation of the truth. It stands out, however, among all the various manifestations of truth by setting in motion a universal uncovering which has not even an indirect and objectified awareness and knowledge of the ground of the uncovering itself. For this uncovering, by its very conception of what is, closes itself up against all that claims to transcend its sphere. For nothing but just the calculable resources that are "on order" can penetrate the unitary network of technically uncovered reality, including all that can be objectively grounded, showing no lacunae.

And therein precisely lies the danger. The uncovering that prevails at the essential core of technology necessarily loses sight of uncovering itself, concealing the essential core of truth in an unfamiliar way and so closing man's access to what he himself is—a being capable of standing in an original relation to the truth. Among all the securing, calculating, and using of raw materials, that which makes all this possible is lost from view—man henceforth knows only individual, practical truths, not the truth.

If, though, we will but reflect philosophically on the reality that the technical world of supplies and orders arises and persists only on the basis of a certain mode of revealing, that in its essential core it *is* this way of revealing, we can glimpse a "saving" dimension: nothing shows as penetratingly the decisive power of original clarity, of the fundamental occurring of truth, as just the modern technology with its all-seizing and all-embracing network of orders and with its power of transforming meaning and so transforming things and people. And if, furthermore, we also glimpse the historical character of original truth, we cannot but grasp the hope that precisely this understanding of being, revealed at the essential core of technology, could be transformed once more, in such a way that the original clarity would turn again toward man and would speak to him. A mere possibility, however, will not solve the problem, and so Heidegger turns to reflect on the meaning of *techne* and so to the dimension of art.

Man, to be sure, cannot bring about something on the order of a fundamental transformation of the primordial clarity of understanding of being, since that clarity is no thing, since it lies abysmally below all interference and all manipulation and cannot be drawn, even minimally, into the sphere of what is "on order." We could thus have no recourse but to see the possibility of change, hoping and waiting—if the very fact that the original clarity has been denied us did not suggest to us how to seek a way out of the purely technical world free of otherworldly illusions and the arrogance of conceit.

The technical world is a world devoid of a metaphysics in the sense of a duplication of the world, in the sense of projecting the ground of the process of appearing upon the very limit of that which appears. That ground refuses to yield to us. Yet it is already present in the way it resists us. It is not present in philosophical reflection which uncovers only the possibility of its coming but can bring about no transformation of the understanding of being. It is not in art, or not only in art alone, since even though art provides a profound insight into being and offers consolation, it is hardly able to undertake a profound transformation of the original truth.

It is not man who, in modern technology, rules over nature, the earth, and the planets; rather, the essential core of technology, the primordial truth as it refuses to yield to us, is what rules over all that is. As refusing to yield: for it remains concealed in its rule. It is as if it "did not want" to be with us. With it there came to us a certain disfavor which we cannot deflect with any measure, through any effort at arranging ourselves in the domain of what is "on order."

Can we, however, understand this great upheaval which, historically, manifests itself in the readiness of ever so many to sacrifice themselves for the sake of a different, better world simply in terms of a will to arrange oneself within what is manageable, within our power and calculation? Is it not a misunderstanding to explain this upheaval with the help of the conceptual apparatus of the technical, as an anticipatory grasp of what is to be managed? Such a self-explanation surely comes easily: there is, after all, nothing beside the inner-worldly contents. And yet perhaps precisely here a transformation of our relation to what is primordial may be being prepared, because a sacrifice means precisely drawing back from the realm of what can be managed and ordered, and an explicit relation to that which, not being anything actual itself, serves as the ground of the appearing of all that is active and in that sense rules over all. Here Being already "presents" itself to us, not in a refusal but explicitly. To be sure, only a man capable of experiencing, in something so apparently negative, the coming of Being, only as he begins to sense that this lack opens access to what is richest, to that which bestows everything and presents all as gift to all, only then can he begin to experience this favor. And he who takes this path gives to the others not simply something that can be placed "on order," though he might attempt so to treat it, but rather, first of all, this glimpse of a reversal, a new primordial truth. Just perhaps, this reversal might also prove to provide a ground for a link with an earlier manifestation of that which saves, though, to be sure, this time that which saves is free of anything otherworldly and so of any metaphysical leftovers as well, and so remains also indebted to the technological world in this sense.

We shall seek to clarify this suggestion further in a special section to follow. Now, though, we need to ask just wherein consists on the one hand a certain agreement, and on the other the difference, between the two thinkers who called themselves and considered themselves phenomenologists (in Heidegger's case, at least for a time).

The focus of the agreements, it seems, is that technology represents deep and evident dangers that must be carefully differentiated, and that only such a differentiation will allow us to penetrate the problem itself. For while speaking of technology, our two thinkers pay no attention to its cultural consequences which are usually the topic of discussion, not permitting, in their ambiguity, a clear assessment of the overall situation. Quite the contrary, both focus on a central point in which the essential core of technology touches upon the essential core of man, and for both this point is *the relation of the human being to truth*, a relation of which man alone among all the beings we know is capable. In this respect both thinkers see the essential core of technology not as actually a disaster but still as a danger. Not technology as such but technology in its relation to that in man which is capable of truth represents a danger that needs to be blocked—technology itself need not be opposed, limited, or eliminated. We need also to note that, in Husserl, given the way he conceives of the topic of his work—as the crisis of the sciences—technology does not come to the fore in its full extent;

however, since for this thinker the crisis of science implies a crisis of humanity, it is clear that technology plays an important role, actually taking the initiative, in this crisis. Thus the difference between the two thinkers must lie in the realm of the conception of truth and of its relation to the essential core of man.

Still, before we turn to explicating the differences, we need to note one more agreement which will come in handy in presenting them. Both thinkers seek to reach a more original relation to the truth than the one at our disposal when we speak of the truth as of the rightness of a judgment.

Husserl seeks to base this more fundamental sense of truth, on which our worldly strivings are grounded, systematically on a specially purified transcendental consciousness which sees through all the "prejudices" of ordinary reality without sharing in them and which can see through them precisely because it does not. However, according to Husserl, our most basic prejudices have to do precisely with the being of objects and of our own objectified subjectivity. This subjectivity needs to be worked clear of this entanglement with the help of an abstention from judgment whose possibilities we had not suspected before. Thus the old thesis of the primacy of spiritual being (or better, of its precedence) is to be demonstrated in a new way.

For all the radical nature of Husserl's conception of consciousness, marked, in contrast with the traditional, by its breadth, attributing to consciousness not only the activity but also the passivity of a wide range of intentional achievements, we must nonetheless ask whether this conception of the fundamental role does not already contain a certain decision concerning the being of consciousness which grounds consciousness in a certain contemplative conception of faith, conceiving of the "faith in the world" as a "thesis" which, like any thesis, might not be a thematic judgment but is still a theoretical act. Along these lines we also need to ask whether the finitude of being human has its basis only in the theoretical sphere of belief (still inadequately analyzed) or, far more deeply, in the very being of this being, and whether we might not set out from a far more radical analysis of being human as an unlocking of a relation to the world. Is a relation to the world really something like a universal presupposition which can be suspended under certain circumstances, setting out of action even the trait of finitude, without affecting the essential core of the functioning of consciousness? Is it really possible to shift this way from a psychological to a transcendental consciousness so that, in spite of the change of the presupposition, perception would remain what it is and so would all other acts? Or does finitude penetrate the very content of our being so deeply that it constitutes the fundamental content of our being in all its moments and expressions? So conceived, Heidegger's phenomenology of finitude would represent a fundamental (negative) response to Husserl's idealistic conception of the phenomenological reduction. Henceforth we would need to make not a consciousness, characterized by the subject's relation to the object, but an understanding human existence, finite throughout, the starting point for phenomenological analyses.

From the fundamental difference we have described it is evident that the two thinkers, even though they both began with technology, inevitably present not only a different diagnosis of the crisis of humanity but a different therapy as well. For Husserl, the dominance of the technological, which he traces and analyzes as typical in science, means that dator perception, perceptual experience as the source of truth, is being pushed back into the background, something he then seeks to prevent by appropriate theoretical measures. For Heidegger, by contrast, the crisis is one of the very essential core of man which understands being and makes truth possible. Just like every theoretical inversion, this one, too, is rooted primarily in a certain transformation of being. For that reason the crisis is far more deeply rooted and can only be approached with far greater difficulty than by a radicalized reflection. In conceiving of the crisis as a crisis of being, there is a certain parallel between Heidegger and Marxism, even though Heidegger does not trace being human in its social objectification and does not tend to believe that it could be grasped and exhausted with the help of historical dialectics. Heidegger's conception of history, insofar as it exists at all, appears to us to revolve around the "rare and clear" decisive turns of history. Even though it often seems that in his thought history, and European history in particular, takes place in the realm of thought in which the event of "being's destiny" is being fulfilled, his starting point—human existence, understanding being—is in no way tied to this realm since understanding being takes place as much in the sphere of non-understanding as in that of explicit conceptual understanding, in the sphere of needs as well as in the sphere of spiritual creativity. In every such realm a certain more primordial relation to being and so a more primordial truth is possible: history, however, follows no "logic of being," either empirically observable or conceptually construable. However, because being itself is primordially finite but, equally primordially, has and must have a certain dimension of the hidden, history, following "the destiny of being," cannot be a gradual development. It can only be an ever-repeated rising out of fallenness, though that fallenness, characterized by a loss of primordial relation to the truth, might hide beneath the mask of progress, of enlightenment and power (which, however, does not mean that these phenomena are identical with it). It appears that it is such a rising, such a turn of history which is not dependent on arbitrary human will but also is not independent of grasping and accepting our own finitude, is what is at stake where our present technological world becomes genuinely a philosophical question.

II

Perhaps we could append the following comment to the foregoing.

How can that saving dimension become effectively a saving one, that is, how can it stand out of forgetting and manifest its power in history? It would seem that in a technically dominated world there exists no possibility for the essential core of technology to be understood in its inmost sense and become manifest. And yet there are certain phenomena of the technically dominated world which seem to pose the question of whether a basic transformation of man's relation to truth is not being prepared in them, a transformation which might lead from truth as correctness, which is all that the rule of technology requires, to a more primordial form of truth.

Because the technical age is one of calculable resources and their use which can be "on order," and because that age seeks to isolate and squeeze out of everything and everyone the utmost possible performance, it is also an age of an unaccustomed unfolding of power. The most powerful means of its escalation, however, proved to be contradiction, dissension, and conflict. In conflict it becomes especially clear that man as such is understood as dominant but is included as something that is "on order." Yet it is a fact nonetheless that countless people have willingly entered into such conflicts, offering themselves as instruments of the accumulation, escalation, and discharge of power, fully aware that thereby they either sacrifice themselves or are sacrificed in it. What does the sacrifice[3] mean here, and why are we speaking of sacrifice at all and not simply of resources, of their utilization and consumption?

The idea of sacrifice is mythico-religious in origin. Even there, where it has already been obscured and covered over by later motivations, there speaks in it the will to commit oneself, by self-abnegation and self-castration, to something higher and, as a result of a reciprocity so provoked, to bind that something higher to oneself and be assured of its power and favor. The paradoxical conception here is that man gains by a voluntary loss. We speak of parents sacrificing for a child and so for further continuation of their lifeline, of combatants sacrificing themselves for the preservation of the society and the State, and so forth. Within the meaning of the technological view of the world, however, there really are no distinctions in the order of being; rather, all hierarchy is arbitrarily subjective, and practically there are only quantitative differences of power. From this viewpoint, to continue speaking of sacrifices is an inconsistency and a prejudice.

In a sacrifice, however, the idea of a difference of order is contained in the true sense of the word. A religious sacrifice presupposes a difference of order between divine and non-divine being. A sacrifice for something or for someone presupposes the idea of a difference of order between human being and the being of things, and within the sphere of the human in turn possibilities of intensification or of failing of being. A person does not sacrifice something that is indifferent to him, something that does not concern him: a genuine sacrifice is always a sacrifice either in an absolute sense or in the sense of sacrificing that which intensifies our being, rendering it rich, content-full, fulfilled.

We are wont to speak of sacrifices of human lives exacted by a natural catastrophe, with an undertone of a distinction between human and inanimate being; likewise when economic losses are described as "sacrifices" exacted by a tornado, a feeling of this distinction lingers in the background. Conversely, we speak of someone having been sacrificed in cold blood when some member of the order of human beings is dealt with as something that a man possesses as an object and "sacrifices" in the interest of self-preservation or development. In short, speaking of sacrifice points to an entirely different understanding of being than the one exclusively attested by the technological age. If people have the feeling in their mind's eye that they or others sacrifice themselves or are sacrificed, they submit quite naturally to such a self-understanding—or, better, an understanding of the human mode of being.

The experience of a sacrifice, however, is now one of the most powerful experiences of our epoch, so powerful and definitive that humankind for the most part has not managed to come to terms with it and flees from it precisely into a technical understanding of being which promises to exclude this experience and for which there exists nothing like a sacrifice, only utilization of resources. Revolutionary and war-like conflicts of our century were born of and borne by the spirit of a technical domination of the world; but those who had to bear the cost were in no case a mere store of disposable resources, but something quite irreducible to that. That precisely comes to the fore when we speak of sacrifices.

Thus sacrifices represent a persistent presence of something that does not appear in the calculations of the technological world. In order to escape their reproach, the postwar period turned to technology, and that in a way which not only guarantees this forgetting but can actually intensify technologicization through conflicts, for while one part of the world has concentrated on increasing the possibilities of supply and so committed itself to the process of consumption, the other seeks to continue in conflict and so understands and utilizes technology differently but yields to it no less essentially; and since in this respect the two stand in a disharmonic and conflicting unity, the process of technological domination of the planet shows a constant increase.

This is not in any sense to deprecate the economic miracle of the postwar period or to overlook the social benefits which are a part of it and not comparable with anything that preceded it. However, we believe that we also must not overlook the fact that therein the "human" assumes a form which may be capable of increasing productivity and its consequences but is not capable of understanding it, and that sacrificial victims, wherever they appear, relate to us as beings who essentially care about the mode of their being.

Under these circumstances it may be important that there are people who have undertaken the repetition of the experience of the sacrificial victim, thereby prying it out of forgetting. Here it also seems most important that such repetition comes about remarkably frequently from those who are known as the protagonists of the technical world. On the one hand this makes it evident that in their case no metaphysico-mythological remnants are responsible for it, on the other hand that in their human experience of the world they have come up against a real limit of the technical.

The repetition of the experience of the sacrificial victim bears with it certain distinctive traits which are capable of making it continuous with a certain transformation of the relation to the truth.

The sacrificial victims of the wars that either were world revolutions or were linked with them, as well as the sacrificial victims of the technological age and of its stupendous possibilities, lived in the same naive experience of the sacrifice which does presuppose a certain understanding of the specifically human mode of being yet functions exclusively in the mode of a "preliminary" understanding. Human being in its distinctiveness does not therewith become in any way explicit. That functioning produces the sacrificial victim in a concrete, almost, so to speak, an objectified sense—a certain exchange of one entity for another. What stands out explicitly here are things which stand in a hierarchical ordering that appears not at all arbitrary to those who sacrifice themselves for them, but which do not allow the basis of their hierarchical ordering to become manifest.

The repetition of sacrifice presupposes a voluntary self-sacrifice, just as in the case of the naive sacrifice, but not only that. For if in this repetition the central point is the overcoming of the technical understanding of being which is the basis for the non-acknowledgement and vanity of sacrifice, then the naive stance with respect to sacrifice will no longer do at all. For that reason, in the case of the repeated sacrifice, that for which the sacrifice is made does not stand out concretely in the foreground. The entire mode of acting needs to be understood as a protest, not against individual concrete experiences but, in principle, against the understanding by which they are borne. From this perspective, the repeated sacrifice is something no longer concerned with any positive content. As in every radical sacrifice, the agent's own finitude is naturally in view here. Not, to be sure, as a topic of meditation or reflection, since that is not the point here, as much as the opening up of a certain stultified situation. Those who thus sacrifice themselves do not avoid finitude, nor do they seek admiration on that account. Without ignoring or making light of certain concrete historical social goals, they have another focus. In giving themselves for something, they dedicate themselves to that of which it cannot be said that it "is" something, or something objective. The sacrifice becomes meaningful as the making explicit of the authentic relation between the essential core of man and the ground of understanding which makes him human and which is radically finite, that is, which is no reason for being, no cause, no force. Out of just this situation stems the need for man to take the part of this ground and to commit himself for it, thereby, however, first winning his humanity in the true sense of the word. For, considered in itself, the ground of understanding is no force; it is, quite the contrary, something like a light or a clearing which makes manifestation possible. However, in man, whose being is essentially elevated by this ground, it does become a force and, as the essential core of technology shows, an immense and terrifying force, which, though, might be transformed into a saving one through sacrifice.

In this way, sacrifice acquires a remarkably radical and paradoxical form. It is not a sacrifice for something or for someone, even though in a certain sense it is a sacrifice for everything and for all. In a certain essential sense, it is a sacrifice for nothing, if thereby we mean that which is no existing particular.

Such an understanding of sacrifice might basically be considered that in which Christianity differs from those religions which conceived of the divine always as a power and a force, and of a sacrifice as the activity which places this power under an obligation. Christianity, as we might perhaps think, placed at the center a radical sacrifice in the sense of the interpretation suggested above and rested its cause on the maturity of the human being. The divine in the sense of the suprahuman, the suprahuman in the sense of turning away from ordinary everydayness, rests precisely in the radicalness of the sacrifice. Perhaps it is in this sense that we need to seek the fully ripened form of demythologized Christianity.

Whatever, though, might be the case in this respect, it seems to us that radical sacrifice is the experience of our time and of the time just passed, an experience which might lead to a transformation in the way we understand both life and the world—a transformation capable of bringing our outwardly rich yet essentially impoverished age to face itself, free of romantic underestimation, and thereby to surpass it.

Notes

1   "Die Gefahren der Technisierung in der Wissenschaft bei E. Husserl und das Wesen der Technik als Gefahr bei M. Heidegger," prepared in German for presentation at the 15th World Congress of Philosophy in Varna, Bulgaria, in September 1973, and in part presented there, but omitted from the *Acta* of the congress. A Czech version, "Nebezpeči technizace ve vědě u E. Husserla a bytostné jádro techniky jako nebezpeči u M. Heideggera," appeared in *Svědectví* (Paris) 16, no. 62 (1980): 262–72. The present translation is based on a comparison of the typescript of the German original on file in the Patočka Archive of Institut für die Wissenschaften vom Menschen with the Czech version.

2   The original presentive intuition, an intuition which gives, supplies, is the source of knowledge. See Dermot Moran, "Foreword to the New Edition," in Edmund Husserl, *Ideas: A General Introduction to Pure Phenomenology* (Milton Park: Routledge Classics, 2012) (Ed.).

3   Patočka takes advantage of the fact that in both Czech and German the same word (*obět'*, *Opfer*) is used to speak of a victim (as of an earthquake) and of a sacrifice (as a religious sacrifice). This enables him to claim that technologicization claims many victims/sacrifices. I have tried to suggest this by

resorting to the term *sacrificial victim*. However, Patočka's point does not depend on the pun but rather on the fact that even in the technological age so many people experience their own victimization as a sacrifice and the victimization of others as their "being sacrificed on the altar of Progress." As long as that is so, nihilism has not prevailed (Trans.).

CHAPTER EIGHTEEN

The Spiritual Person and the Intellectual (1975)

Translated from the Czech by Eric Manton[1]

What I would like to present to you today is not a continuation of the interpretations that I have already given here.[2] It is rather a reflection on what a spiritual person is and what an intellectual is, and the difference between them; on what the spiritual life is and culture is, and the difference between them; and on what the situation of the spiritual person is in the world—especially in *today's* world.

I think that today the term "spiritual person" does not sound very pleasant. It sounds spiritualist in some way and nowadays we tend to dislike such phrases. But does there exist a better expression for what I have in mind? Take it as a makeshift phrase of necessity. Anyone who has a better terminological proposal should kindly let me know.

It is very important to realize clearly that concealed within what is commonly called a person of intellect, a person of intelligence, an intellectual, there are two completely different things, which are nevertheless connected to each other, perhaps like a thing and its shadow and also—in the words of the person who first attempted to clarify this difference—like reality and its distorted image. This is because, on the one hand, we have the intellectual, the cultural actor or worker, and possibly the creator as a certain social reality, which we can objectively define and analyze—sociologically: this is a person who has a certain education, particular skills, some credentials perhaps, and on the basis of this they develop a specific activity from which they derive a livelihood. So they earn a living just like anybody else by performing some kind of activity—the way a cobbler earns a living making shoes, a worker by going to a factory; so, too, the writer makes their living by writing on paper, and what they create is printed, sold, bought, and enters into the economic sphere, etc. Naturally this is described in only very rough terms; of course, this means of livelihood has its own history and incorporation in other human activities . . .

And what about the other? This is not as simple and self-evident. It is not a matter that we can define externally by way of statements and observations that these people do this or that. The majority of these so-called spiritual people also write something on paper and pursue an activity like the others— like those who make a living through culture: externally it looks completely the same, there is no difference. They are writers like other writers, they are teachers like other teachers, they lecture like other lecturers, etc. Thus, in this respect, I would say, *we cannot distinguish between them*. That is precisely the problem we are faced with here. And yet there exists an absolutely profound difference. It was Plato who first noticed something of this sort: the terrible difference between a person like Socrates and a person like Protagoras or Hippias and all those other wonderful virtuosi who knew how to do so many things and who dazzled so wonderfully as teachers and as skillful moneymakers. Where does this difference lie?

Plato endeavored throughout his entire intellectual life to somehow define this difference. He dedicated his greatest efforts and the majority of his works to this endeavor, and the question remains as to whether he was successful, despite the fact that the dialogue containing the most deeply elaborated problematic of this duplicity—the *Sophist*—is a mature work of Plato's wisdom. This dialogue (all of you have no doubt read it or at least heard about it) shows how this other, the sophist—the person of intelligence, the intellectual, the cultural person—how difficult it is to grasp them, how they are always hidden. Always when we suppose that we have grasped them in some way, they are already somewhere else.

It is strange, isn't it? Plato sets out from the view that the figure of the spiritual person is clear and real, and that the sophist is someone who hides in the shadow of this bright figure. This is a slightly different point of departure from mine today: I am saying that the cultural person is something self-evident; they perform certain activities that can be externally stated, described, and defined—sociologically, economically, etc.—whereas the spiritual person, it seems to me, is a horrible problem.

Precisely because he was such a deeply spiritual person and this spirituality was close and obvious to him, Plato reversed this.

But let us return to our initial position. How can we shed light on what a spiritual person is? I shall try to proceed from the words of a great modern philosopher who attempted to define a certain type of spiritual life, namely philosophy, by saying: philosophy is a world inverted.[3]

In what sense is it inverted? In what sense does the philosopher invert the reality of other people, of those who are not—as I tried to say—spiritual?

The philosopher differs from others in that the world, for them, is not self-evident. We all live in a world that is given to us, that is open to us, and that we take as reality. This reality is something that is simply here and that we take as a matter of self-evidence to be a reliable base on which we can move without difficulty. Moreover, our life in the world is also self-evident. All of our learned reactions, all of the objects around us we have learned to name on the basis of the language we have accepted, all of the opinions we have from tradition, all of the ideas we have from school: so everything is, so to speak, prescribed for us, and whenever we show a little of our own initiative, we are also adhering to what is clear and self-evident to us. And most of the time, as long as we do not encounter any great difficulty or unpleasantness, that is enough; we do not need anything more. Life thus accepted does not encounter any obstacles.

It is rare to have experiences that show us that precisely this whole way of seeing the world as self-evident and received is something that *disappoints*, something exposed to negative outcomes; such experiences are rare, but in the end everyone encounters them in one form or another. We see that the people with whom we live together, act together, work together, think together, learn together, that precisely these people—even we ourselves—are inconsistent, that they are disunited, and that they live in contradiction; we see that they betray one another, that their life projects disappoint them, that they abandon their former beliefs. There are, however, even harsher experiences. There are experiences like the unexpected end of life, death; experiences of the collapse of entire societies. These are experiences that you all know from your childhood, or that those of us know who have been through these experiences several times during our lives. They all suddenly show that life, which looked so obvious, in reality is somehow problematic, that something is in disarray, that something is not in order. Our original attitude is that *it is in order*, that all of these minute unpleasantries, disagreements, and incongruities have no significance and that it is possible to get over them. For after all, the world at every moment says something to us: our actions are nothing other than an answer to the fact that the world says something to us; that things have meaning for us, that they challenge us to do something, and we answer them. And if we were to really, consistently follow this negative that suddenly makes itself heard, if we were to pursue it consistently, that would mean that nothing would say anything to us, and that nothing would challenge us to do something, to react or act in some way, and as a result we would remain in a vacuum, stuck in a kind of emptiness. It is not possible to live in that! And yet *here*, in this lies the beginning of spiritual life.

I have already mentioned Plato several times: Plato presents the origin of spiritual life in the figure of Socrates. And Socrates' spiritual life consists in his attempting to feel out, through conversing with other people, whether these people and *he himself* are capable—in the most diverse questions of life, the simplest as well as those more complicated—of maintaining unity within themselves; whether they are able to be consistent; whether that which they take as given is truly sufficient for the life that is identical with itself, in accord with itself; whether these people are truly what they believe themselves to be; and whether their supposedly united figure does not collapse in mere conversation. And the experience that Socrates has—the result he arrives at through quite simple methods, through a cleverness that is quite simple but does not avoid this problematicity—is that *nowhere* does he come across anything like a truly solid person capable of realizing their own identity. And Socrates himself does not pretend to be such a figure. He only wants it, he only goes toward it, he only strives for it. *He is only on a quest.* And that is the most important thing: the spiritual person is one who is, in a way, *on a quest.* One who knows about these negative experiences and never loses sight of them, unlike the common person, who seeks to forget them, who seeks to get past them by means of instinct, since life will work itself out one way or another; the common person can *already* bear this life somehow; they *already* have a cure for these problems. Whereas this is not true for the spiritual person: precisely the spiritual person exposes themselves *to these experiences*, and their life consists in being thus exposed.

To be thus exposed to the negative, to create a special life scheme, means in a certain sense a completely *new* life. While the usual life exists in presumed self-evidence and security and is directed towards such security, dismissing incongruities and negatives, the new life is lived from these negatives. And this means that everything has a different keynote, a different value than in this unfragmented, straightforward, and naive life.

I named the kind of life experiences that no one can avoid and that everyone seeks at first to somehow evade; but under these surface experiences there are, I would say, experiences that are in a certain sense deep. These are experiences that show something like the peculiarity, the strange wonderment of our situation—that *we are* at all and that *the world is*, that this *is not* self-evident, that there is something like an astonishing wonder, that things *appear* to us and that we ourselves are among them. This wonderment! It is "*divné*":[4] there is "*wonder*" contained in this word. We wonder: to wonder means not to accept anything as self-evident, to stand still, to stop oneself, not to go further in one's quest, to stop functioning. An obstacle. Such an immense obstacle over which we may stumble so that we will never return. And truly, to stumble over it means never to return.

When I wonder in this way—it is strange, isn't it? Materially the world is completely the same as before, there are the same things, the same surroundings, the same chairs and tables, people and stars, and nevertheless there is something here *completely* changed. No *new* thing has been discovered, no new reality; what has been discovered is not a *thing*, not a reality, but the fact that this everything *is*. But this "everything *is*" is not a thing.

This new manner of life consists, then, in our being able to live in such a way that we do not accept life simply, but rather we accept its *problematicity*. From this moment on, this is our base; it is that in which we live and breathe. This also means that, from this moment on, we cannot accept anything as a finished and given thing, we cannot rely on anything; everything we accepted as self-evident is not self-evident; everything we know is prejudice.

These are the several features I have attempted to put my finger on: not ignoring negative experiences, but on the contrary settling into them; problematizing the usual; creating a new life *possibility* from within this open sphere. To live not on firm ground, but rather on something that moves; to live in *unanchoredness*. You will object: what you say here may concern philosophy, but it does not touch upon everything we normally call a spiritual life—including in this not only art and religion but also active life, a life, let us say, of sacrifice, devotion, and responsibility, and perhaps something like the creation of social institutions, like law, etc. All this is spiritual life!

This objection is fully justified, but in all these areas (this can be proved, but I do not intend to elaborate on it here) there is the identical difference, the difference between, on the one hand, an activity that can be externally described, stated as a certain fact, and introduced into other factual contexts, and, on the other hand, the way people live and act who problematize in these areas.

To make this more concrete, I could cite the example of poetry: think of the poetry of Homer, commonly considered naive, seemingly unfragmented, and presenting a picture of life that is seemingly so clear and naive. However, in reality we know that Homer's epic is the embodiment of the immense experience of the post-Mycenaean era, which saw the decline of the age of heroes, and that all of this poetry is a reflection on the experience of the collapse of an epoch. And who can think about Homer without calling to mind the great theater at the end of *The Iliad*, the colossal scene toward the end where Achilles and Priam stand across from each other—these two who so thoroughly destroyed each other—and speak together in one such instant of human unanchoredness, when life is like a ceasefire between two battles, and in this moment each comes to know the other as the reality of what a human being is. And think about the figure of Achilles himself—a person who chooses precisely this short and glorious life! Something directed *against* the direction of usual life, something that belongs to the foundation of Greek political sentiment.

Or Dante, who sees life "here" through life "there"—our life, here, this life which we live in this unfragmentedness, *through* that life which he recognizes by making his pilgrimage to the *other* world.

Or Rilke, who lives in a continual exchange between this life and the other world—this life, which continually disappears somewhere and to which that *from whence* it came and *whither* it again departs continually speaks.

Essentially, all of philosophy is nothing other than the development of this problematicity as great thinkers have expressed and grasped it. The struggle to extract out of this problematicity something that emerges from it; to find a firm shore, but then again problematize that which emerges as a shore. This is the primal Greek wisdom expressed in the words "The thunderbolt steers all things":[5] the flash that reveals *the light of dawn* in the darkness but at the same time reveals *the darkness*—the emerging of entirety, but from out of the darkness that belongs to it and which this lightning only tears through, but does not overcome.

And then, in antiquity, where Socrates was the role model, Plato made an immense effort to deduce that which is found from the search itself; and in the course of this search, he sought to find a firm foundation, a new ground beneath his feet—in metaphysics. The discovery of the instability of the world around us leads Plato to see that on the basis of which the instability of things around me first opens up to me. He sees that there is no measure here. Later Plato says that the measure is real being. And this attempt to jump out of this search onto new, firm ground, then for millennia becomes a great model and at the same time a seduction.

This would mean describing the entire history of philosophy, even the whole history of human thought. This path of reflecting off from non-problematic reality; of searching, the effort to find new ground in searching itself; of problematizing that which is found; the path always again renewed; the path, in the end, leads to a certain discovery, but not to what philosophy had expected at the beginning. What philosophy found in the end was not new ground to stand on, but only a new way of dealing with the old ground.

What philosophy found at the beginning of the modern era we no longer call philosophy but rather science. This is the new certainty, if you like; a certainty that is the result of the philosophical search that results from spiritual activity, that offers something firm, that offers the possibility of mastering our life and the world around us, but in a special way—so that this negative now becomes the basis. In science we no longer have the experience of the *problematicity* of life and the *problematicity* of reality, but rather the experience of all meaning having been stripped away. What science provides—at least science as it has been conceived since the seventeenth century and the direction it has been moving in consistently ever since—is a reality truly stripped of all meaning. This is precisely why we can do whatever we want with it, and why it seems to us like nothing more than a standing reserve of forces. This is the result of *spiritual activity*, the result of long centuries of spiritual struggle. But this spiritual struggle goes on, and its results have been more and more negative for a long time. Nevertheless it is a life of the spirit, it is a path the spiritual person must travel, it cannot be avoided: sometimes it looks as if the result of the whole adventure of the spiritual life is that we find ourselves once again at the start, where this whole movement began: at the life that is given to us, which we cannot go beyond.

This is the cruelest situation for the spiritual person—this final resulting suspension, this final resulting skepticism, the disappointment in the attempts at searching thus far, which again and again appear empty and futile. Confronted with this situation, the spiritual life itself is understandably not enticing. It is as if it abandons itself, as if it devalues itself. It is neither accidental nor insubstantial that, after millennia of monumental effort, philosophy is ruled by something that could be called nihilism. That all this searching is the basis upon which spiritual life today develops and comes to the conclusion that life and the world are problematic, and that meaning as an answer to this question not only is not found, but *cannot* be found, that the final result is *nihil*: a self-negation, a self-denial.

How does it look when we confront the aspirations of the spiritual person with this situation, with the aspirations that they declared from the very beginning, that they imposed on the life of the community?

Socrates and Plato were problematizers of life, people who did not accept reality as it is given, but rather saw it as shaken—but the conclusion they drew from this was that some kind of peculiar, *other* life *is possible*; another direction of life, something like a *new ground*, and only here is it possible to gauge what is and what is not. They were so firmly convinced of this that they challenged this naive and banal reality in battle. We know how Plato defined the position of the spiritual person in the world and in society; one of the reasons we still read Plato's works, especially his work about the State, with such anticipation is that they contain the classically defined relationship of the spiritual person to the whole of society—to the society of that day, and we often still feel it to be quite relevant.

Plato says there are only three possible attitudes:

One is the path that Socrates took—to show people how things are in reality, to show them that the world is dark and problematic, that *we do not possess it*; but this means coming *into conflict* and going to one's death. The logic of this process is rigorously enacted in Plato.

The second possibility is the one that Plato chooses—internal emigration, withdrawal from the public, withdrawal from contact and conflict with the world (and mainly with the city) in the hope that, through philosophical searching, we will find something like a community of spiritual people that makes it possible for spiritual people to live and not to die.

And the third possibility is to become a sophist. There are no other possibilities.

You see—when we express it in this way—that there is something in this whose strength and relevance we feel still today. Of course, we do so with the assumption that we will not obtain the agreement of those who regard skepticism as the last word.

Philosophers like Socrates and Plato are not sophists, but rather real spiritual people searching and fighting with the greatest sincerity to prevent us from being deceived by illusions and inventing some illusory world of our own upon which we might ostensibly be able to stand firmly. That they are the ones who wanted to search most radically, of that, I think, there is no doubt. This is the challenge put forth by these philosophers, these great destroyers and great rebels who refused to let themselves become drunk on any illusions, who did not want to leave this problematicity—and this is what makes them spiritual and philosophical. This great challenge is truly relevant to the utmost degree.

But how is it possible that these philosophers, these spiritual people, have anything to say to us at all? How is it possible that they consider it appropriate to address us, that they consider it worthwhile? Each such address is a certain act, but each act has meaning only when it makes sense to do it, when something speaks to us, when some reality addresses us. But where nothing has any value or worth, it does not make sense even to speak. Is this not the inconsistency in the nihilism of those who deny instead of problematizing? Is the last word of problematizing negation? Or is problematizing fundamentally different from negation, more negative, in a way, than mere negation. And precisely because of this, does it not make a life program possible after all? Perhaps if we return to the beginning of this problematizing something will dawn on us.

We said that wherever we are struck by a strange sense of wonder at all that surrounds us, at that in which we are, in which we act and react, in reality there is no new thing being revealed to us, no new reality. Yet still *something* is revealed, which is not an absolute nothing, or which is mere nothing only from the point of view of the reality of things. Does this not suggest that there is something in the nature of reality—if we take it as a whole, that is, as a reality that reveals itself—that is in itself problematic, that is in itself a question, that is *darkness*. This is not a darkness that is only our subjective unfamiliarity, our subjective ignorance, but rather something that is a *precondition* for something to appear in the world at all. And precisely the fact that something appears in the world, that the world appears, this is the most fundamental fact of reality—of the reality that we live, the reality that is a phenomenon.

So although at this point we do not get any firm ground of some reality, it is revealed to us that this questioning is not only a subjective caprice on our part after all, that it is not only one attitude among many other possible attitudes, that it is not something arbitrary. Rather it is something founded on the deepest basis of our life, only *here* do we stand on our own ground— not there, where we initially supposed. And perhaps precisely *here* also lies the possibility for all those who are searching, and all those who presume to have found and those who show them that they have not found, and those who delight in once again having caught a glimpse of something—precisely here is the possibility for all of these in their disagreement to be able to agree on one fundamental level, i.e., on the level of the spiritual life.

Thus, in the spiritual life it is possible to find unity precisely *without firm ground*, and it is possible to overcome this absolute negativity, negative skepticism, negative nihilism without being dogmatic. In one respect, the present situation of the spiritual person admittedly looks, as I attempted to show, especially radically harsh. When we see, face to face with today's most radical thinkers, that it is as if the great spiritual acts of the past have disintegrated, and as though the spiritual life itself forced us to abandon and be skeptical of them (specifically, to abandon metaphysical questioning and metaphysical solutions), it seems to prove the opponents of spiritual life right. That is why we also see that the world and life of today is in reality, and with such a clear conscience, non-spiritual. On the one hand, the situation in the present era looks less hopeful and harsher than it has at any other time in history, but on the other hand, it can be said that certain moments exist that do not cast the contemporary situation in the worst light, several of which I shall mention here.

First, contemporary nihilism is itself developing in a certain way: today one can already speak of the history of contemporary nihilism. One author[6] distinguishes three phases in contemporary nihilism that, beginning with Nietzsche, gained ground as a certain thought construct. The author I have in mind discerns joyful, creative nihilism where an optimistic attitude is derived from the understanding that reality is completely nonsensical. Thus, it is possible to behave toward reality in whatever way we want and form it arbitrarily according to our will. This attitude—confronted with the impossibility of forming reality according to the will of anybody—changes into a nihilism of self-subordination to a particular objective power. I will not describe this in more detail, since you all know that these phenomena are exceedingly widespread; the entire history of recent decades, both world wars, and the periods between and since them are full of these phenomena.

Second, after the Second World War, there was talk of the nihilism of resignation, a nihilism that does not know what to do, that is not interested in any attitude, is absolutely unanchored, refuses every solution, and also refuses all help.

And the latest version resembles something like inner mental paralysis. It is also beginning to realize that all of nihilism up to now has not been radical enough, namely, that it itself lacks skepticism toward skepticism. However, it does not have enough strength to pull itself together in this attitude that is beginning to have something positive within it. Nevertheless, this skepticism toward skepticism, this possible suspension of absolute negation, is the result of consistently thinking through this thought, but this consistent thinking through means nothing other than the path back to the Socratic.

Another distinctive aspect of the present era (and it is no accident that it is in the present) is that element of our spiritual life, of our historical horizon, that possibly contributes most to the universal spread of nihilistic thoughts and moods, namely science, is beginning to discover in itself a skepticism toward the nihilistic concept of science, toward the concept of science as factological without any kind of meaning. We see this in the fact that even the most objective sciences, such as physics, are aware today of the limits of objectification. It is also noticeable in the penetration of structuralist tendencies, since structuralism everywhere means not only reasoning from the point of view of the whole, but also from the point of view of meaning. Structures are *meaningful* structures. Contemporary structuralism is not yet fully aware of the entire extent of this shift, which is being introduced to science through its influence. This structural shift first gains its full significance in connection with yet another important present-day phenomenon. This final motif is the discovery of the openness of human being. It was precisely this discovery that negated the concepts of beings and being that enabled the development of modern mathematical natural science, and consequently also of factological science and its concept of reality, which also encompasses the famous Cartesian dualism, i.e., the division of the world into subject and object. Human openness disputes the subject, disputes this duality, and enables a different view of phenomena, of the appearance of reality and the appearance of the world as a whole. Right now, all these phenomena are only a sort of twilight, indicating perhaps that midnight no longer rules.

One more thing comes to mind, however, which is that in effect everything in this cruel world we have experienced and are experiencing, the cruel world of two wars and terrible revolutions, of everything we see around us, is not comprehensible, I think, in any other way than this: that the people who exposed themselves to these terrible catastrophes did not succumb to them only passively, but went into Moloch's jaws for the most part voluntarily, even happily—this involved something like an awareness that this immediate life and world are not everything, that it is possible to sacrifice them, and that in this sacrifice it is possible to catch a glimpse of the thunderbolt in the darkness. This, I think, is what lies behind the horrors of our time.

If we have to deduce some sort of summation from all this, perhaps we could say that the spiritual person today has no reason for resignation. The spiritual person today can once again see possibilities. The spiritual person must cease to be afraid, and the basis for not being afraid lies precisely in that which they can glimpse.

The spiritual person who is capable of sacrifice, who is capable of *seeing* its significance and meaning—as I attempted to indicate—*cannot* be afraid. The spiritual person is not of course a politician and is not political in the usual sense of the word. They are not a party to the dispute that rules this world—but in a different way they are political, obviously, and cannot be apolitical because the *non-self-evident nature of reality* is precisely what they throw into the face of this society and all they find around them.

The conflict that Plato spoke about is a phenomenon. Here we return to what we said before about the relevance of *Politeia*. Life in this position is precisely what the positive powers of reality do not tolerate and do not want to see, what they cannot account for, and what they fight against with all their strength—it is something they cannot endure. And here the spiritual person must, of course, advocate their position. This does not mean engaging in propaganda. I simply either avow what I have indicated to be the program of the spiritual life, or not—either I am a spiritual person, or I am just a sophist, a pretender, and that is the usual culture and literature and the various ways that people make a living. But to pretend to be a spiritual person by saying that politics is unworthy of one's own spiritual activity, that it destroys and thwarts spiritual activity—this is the worst sophistry imaginable.

So these are the remarks I wanted to present to you today. I wanted to emphasize the difference between what is called culture (which is a kind of external fact—a sociological reality that is absolutely ambiguous if we look at it from the viewpoint that there exists such a thing as the attempt to live in truth) and what I called the spiritual life, which is something entirely different.

That is my basic thesis, and now we can debate it.

Notes

1   Transcribed from a tape recording by Ivan Chvatík (Ed.).

2   Patočka gave this lecture just after he presented the third seminar of the Heretical Essays, on April 11, 1975 (Ed.).

3   G. W. F. Hegel, *Werke*, vol. 2, *Jenaer Schriften, 1801–1807* (Frankfurt: Suhrkamp Verlag, 1969–71), 182 (Ed.).

4   This Czech word means "peculiar" or "strange." The root of the word is *div*, meaning "wonder." Patočka is showing the etymological relationship between wonder and what is regarded as strange (Ed.).

5   Heraclitus, Fragment B64 (Ed.).

6   Cf. Helmut von Gollwitzer and Wilhelm Weischedel, *Denken und Glauben* (Stuttgart: W. Kohlhammer Verlag, 1965), 268–74. Wilhelm Weischedel, *Der Gott der Philosophen*, vol. 2 (Munich: Nymphenburger Verlagshandlung, 1971), 165–82 (Ed.).

CHAPTER NINETEEN

An Outline of History (1975–6)

Translated from the German by Andrea Rehberg

History has not been the history of humankind from its very beginning. It only became so because Western history turned into European history, and European history expanded to become planetary history. Each of these steps was marked by catastrophes; and even in Western history there occurred the catastrophe of the *polis*.

The gradual expansion of the field of history had nothing inevitable about it. It was not a linear necessity, based on a law of development, be it that of the human spirit or of economic relations. It can only be understood from the inner shape of the respective historical periods. There was no inner necessity that drove the *polis* to overcome itself; the Roman *Civitas* (commonwealth of citizens) always had to be victorious in order for it to become the *Imperium* (empire), but then it was no longer a *polis*. If city-states chafed against such developments both externally and internally as much as was the case in Greece, the *polis* easily succumbed to an external attack which assimilated it into a new world empire. But the problem posed by the conception of political life remained: people did not return to their earlier state in which they had previously lived as a matter of course, to the political state of nature of a theocratic ruler's *oikos* (household). A kind of public space became indispensable. What was to be done for the community could no longer be accomplished simply by care for life and out of fear, but rather still required an ἀριστεία (excellence), as in the time of the mutual recognition between the citizens of the *polis*. But what was required there had already been partly prepared by philosophy, especially in its theories of the State, and partly it tried to express it in a new way. Both jurisprudence and theology were necessarily based on it, even if Christianity brought with it a new approach, different from that of philosophy, and which took God and the advent of God's kingdom as its point of departure. For this approach was itself understood as an answer to the insufficiency of the Greek approach.

What does this vacillation at the very outset of history mean? Did history actually come into being with the *polis*, as I claimed in the essay on the beginning of history?[1] What was it that raised history above the *polis* and led it further? What gives history its impulse again and again, and why is an impulse necessary again and again?

Perhaps the answer lies in the relation between the founding of the *polis* and philosophy. Undoubtedly, at the time of its emergence philosophy was a new possibility of human being. It is not only not contained but not even hinted at in myth or in poetry, not in craftsmanship or technical ability. There is in it a freedom of human being towards what is, that replaced the former integration and subordination. But such a freedom contained concrete possibilities, the foremost of which was perhaps that of the construction of a political public space, a space not for the necessities of life but for rising above them.

But such a political existence is always threatened not only from outside, but above all from within. Just as philosophy is threatened from the beginning by non-philosophy in the form of the truisms of the common understanding, truisms which in contact with philosophy lead to sophistry, so the political order too is threatened by the dangers of public opinion, by a lack of objectivity and by demagogy, by loss of tradition and exaggerated traditionalism. It is not merely external obstacles which free human action encounters, but above all those obstacles that arise out of this action itself and only take on a firm shape in the concrete situations of history.

Thus history turns into an arena of human being's inner struggle for genuineness and autonomy. Historical action becomes the combat against what proved to be the greatest danger in a situation that resulted from the inner and outer destructions of what had once been conquered, and it becomes the restoration of genuine possibility. But this possibility is never definitive and never unimperiled. What initially appears to be a way out and for a time path-breaking can soon be lost and prove to be an aberration when submitted to deeper probing. Success can be deceptive and can turn into a temptation that becomes fatal. On to this dangerous path history lured human being. Human being could, irrespective of its deepest possibilities, remain like other *animalia* in a state of life that always only circles around the biological. Or else, as the immense constructions of pre-historic peoples demonstrate, it could form a systematics of deliberate dependence, into which life weaves itself. History has hitherto put a temporary end to all that; it has, to use a famous quote, awakened human being from its dogmatic slumber. History has hitherto been the real practical proof of human freedom. We speak of a temporary end because after all it lies in the "nature" of history not to know anything final and not to be able to prove anything for the future.

Can one therefore speak of continuity in history when facticity is at home in it and facticity knows nothing final and is always in motion? Human being struggles and decides, but the fundamental possibilities must already be open to it. But it is these fundamental possibilities that are much more permanent than empires and other federations and real organizations. The *polis*, the *Civitas*, the *Imperium*, the holy empires have passed, while the Greek world wisdom's explorations and clarifications of being have not and still perdure in their re-formations albeit in altered form.

In the essay "On the Beginning of History," I tried to show that philosophical questions and the origins of political praxis are equiprimordial, but now the precedence of philosophy shows itself. For in philosophy being itself articulates itself, which conditions and opens up all factical possibilities of being human. On the other hand, philosophy does itself stand under the condition of a factical praxis: only when a stance of free independence has preceded it can philosophy come into being. Freedom towards beings is first practiced, and only then does it return to thought. The equiprimordiality is here that of beings and being. But just like in the above-mentioned difference, freedom itself would not be if there was no being to carry it out, so too it is in history: it is philosophy which first says what actually happened with and in political freedom, and nothing would have happened had it not been for philosophy.

But this means that there is and will be history only for as long as there are human beings who want not only "to live," but who are ready, especially in contrast to bare life, to establish and defend the foundations of a community of mutual recognition. What is being founded in this way is not the securing of life being eked out, but freedom, i.e., the possibilities that lie beyond the level of bare life. These possibilities are basically of two different kinds, namely the responsible care for others and an explicit relation to being, i.e., truth. In these relations, human being is neither someone who is ordered nor someone who consumes, but instead someone essentially constructing, founding, extending, and preserving a community, albeit, as already stated above, never without threat. It is the construction of a world that is being founded in an invisible region, but which has to be transposed into the visible and perduring in order to support human life and to give it the opportunity to be historical.

In this sense the Greek city-states were probably the first historical formations. But the question can certainly be raised as to whether Israel did not also present such a primordial cell of history. The question is of great importance because in the form of Christianity an offspring of the Israelite tradition intervened so powerfully in Western history that we can almost speak of an assimilation. Nevertheless, I do not think so because Christianity was initially without a world and world-denying in its eschatological hopes and could become historical itself only through entry into a world that was already historical.

The triumph of history becomes manifest in the eschatological message of the Gospel being used for the construction of a new public space which availed itself of Greek philosophy's concepts of being and without which it would have remained incomprehensible. The concept of transcendence, assumed by Christian theology as a matter of course and indispensable for the founding of the kingdom of God, was of Greek origin. But it is this transcendence which made a return to "the state of nature without a public space" impossible. The new theocracy, which gives human being a communal basis in the worship of God and in the conception of life as worship of God, is transcendentally grounded, with the exclusion of any possibility of a connection between human being and nature.

The Church's new public space, grounded in transcendence, was confronted by a new private sphere, not only as a new organization of production with a correspondingly altered conception of work, but also as a new domain of inner life with respect to the unique demand to make something of one's life and the infinite responsibility that is inextricably connected with it. The outward act was now accompanied by the inward act of conscience.

The *Imperium Romanum* found in the Constantinian transformation the long-desired solution to the problem of its alienated public space. But in the disintegration of the Western Empire and the weakening of the Eastern Empire, the space of the opposition between the *Civitas terrena* (earthly city) and the *Civitas Dei* (city of God) made itself felt. Under pressure from the Islamic version of a holy empire and with the inclusion of the anonymous traditions of the Germanic tribes there emerges a Western version, initially that of aristocratic Christianity. In it the potentialities of societal production without slave labor are first being made to count, an expansion, a new public space in the cities, a new clamor for recognition of the aristocracy: the foundations for society's process of leveling out were being laid, albeit a process that will be held back for a long time by the dominant understanding of the harmony of forces and powers.

Although the expansion of aristocratic Christianity founded and consolidated Europe, the true locus of action was from now on the sphere of inner life. It was the clergy, and especially the ascetics, the mystics, and the organizers of the Church, who now took humanity in hand, who instilled every directive in it, with whom lay every initiative. By virtue of this predominance over the earthly, a new spiritual space now imposed itself, which—despite all inner grappling of the soul in the uniqueness of its fate and in the uncertainty of its salvation—was filled by a fundamental attitude of faith. From this superior standpoint Church Christianity had to take from aristocratic Christianity its ostensible leadership. The Church had after all reached that miraculous point at which the uncertainties of the earthly sphere had been overcome.

*   *   *

Aristocratic Christianity by itself could not become an actualization of the *Sacrum Imperium* (Holy Empire). Even where it was a question of the external expansion of Europe, the reconquest of the Mediterranean world, and the repulsion of the East, Church Christianity maintained the initiative. The Church became Platonic: it became a spiritual power, not on an equal footing with worldly power, but superior to it, but not on the basis of knowledge, ἐπιστήμη (episteme), but because of faith, although this became dogmatic, i.e., Hellenized and Romanized. It became Hellenized because faith was no longer effective and organized as action, as message and as creed, but rather in the reflecting form of the λόγος, (logos) [word]. It became Romanized because on this basis a new community, a new reciprocal recognition, and an internally binding sovereign power came into being.

The *polis*, the *Imperium*, and the *Sacrum imperium* were altogether metaphysically grounded. Despite all their differences, both Plato's and Aristotle's attempts at founding a *polis* showed that it aimed towards the timeless and away from the given. But even the Church, as a spiritual empire, was designed in the same metaphysical way, albeit with an element of Roman will.

Both *polis* and *Civitas* as well as *Imperium* and Church offered human being a necessary space for the development of those great possibilities that lie beyond the bare necessities of life and that call into question the taken-for-granted nature of one's drifting through daily life.

The metaphysical approach of all the above-mentioned spaces showed that the metaphysical concept of being, which dated back centuries, still exerted, though concealed from them, a power which they could not deny themselves. On the other hand, it might also be supposed that in history there is something like the wholly metaphysically unredeemed, something that is foreign to the metaphysics of eternity, that only makes itself felt when the latter is expelled, something that cannot be completely suppressed and that strives to be thought in its own way. Christianity presented to the Greek element something to process that was and remained completely different and that accordingly showed itself initially in the form of negation and disturbance. Christianity, that impulse to expose oneself to the unique call that sounds once and for all and in each case for the individual, again and again broke through the shell of the established worldly and ecclesiastical organizations. For this reason nothing was more dangerous to temporal culture than this movement of reversal and return, which in the end had to break through the metaphysical, hierarchical structure of harmony in the direction of a laymen's Christianity which imposed on each Christian essentially the same responsibility for the Christian life and which did not recognize an expertise in being Christian since it did not recognize a more or less of it.

Church Christianity strengthened all tendencies towards territorial emancipation which had existed from the very beginning within the framework of the renewed Roman Empire (of the West), weakened the core of Europe, the Holy Empire, and when in the framework of this empire itself powerful bodies arose, it was the laymen's Christianity that became a centrifugal power. The Roman character of Church Christianity asserted itself in the tendency towards expansion, which the world powers also practiced in their own way, certain of the comprehensive sanctioning by the Church: after the Crusades the Western powers' push into the Baltic and beyond; in the West the Spanish *Reconquista* and as its continuation the Iberian expansion, which burst the boundary of the Old World to the South and West. It was the Roman character, the succession of the Roman Empire in a new guise, which founded the opening of Europe to the world and in which that leap on to the level of world domination and the global seizure of resources was also grounded, the leap that constituted the transition from European to planetary history, which, long in preparation and initiated as European world expansion, really only broke through after the catastrophes of Western Europe.

The emancipation of states, the leap into the world and the grab for the world's resources, the rebirth of *Romanitas* were all surely already prefigured in traditional metaphysics and metaphysical theology. But there was a trait in them that pointed ahead to a transformation of the metaphysical tradition. There was a hitherto unheard-of universalism and an unprecedented actualization of the will underway, which focused not so much on the realm of human matters (at least not exclusively on them), but on the realm of material things.

The discovery of the world and the conquest of the Western continent was an act of the *Romanitas* which had loosened the chains of Church Christianity. Another was the new conception of the sovereign state. Laymen's Christianity, on the other hand, by extending the Christian idea of Church service to all of life and especially to working life, in this way attained the same path, that of world domination. What both had in common pointed to a transformation of traditional metaphysics. The interiority of the soul and its struggle for salvation now became effective only indirectly and the world became the true drama of human striving for a genuine possibility.

A new form of metaphysics brought with it a new light that spread rapidly and that integrated the previous movements towards the world into a unity, for which it opened up new possibilities by means of explicitness. It brought with it a new concept of knowledge and cognition, directed towards the subject and its object and the construction of this object in a deliberate, methodical activity. While the earth dropped out of the center of the universe, the subject stepped into the center of being.

The humanity oriented towards this new light everywhere set itself new tasks, whose main feature was a hitherto unknown universality. While at the beginning of this movement people still admired the old science because of its impartiality and believed they should follow its example, they soon discovered that they could and should avoid the limitations of the ancients. People dropped the reduction of logic to genus and species relationships; they discovered a new logic in mathematics which had rid itself even of the old compartmentalization (into discrete and continuous quantities); they mathematized nature; movement and natural processes were approached from the standpoint of predictability and were mastered by means of the new mathematics. In this process the difference between the thus-defined specialized knowledge and the originally unified general science that was oriented towards a whole became evident, and there arose the reality and the idea of specialized science. Science was no longer, as in antiquity, an intellectual probing of what was somehow already known or believed to be known, it no longer moved in the common, natural lifeworld, but rather became the adventure of a reconstructing voyage of discovery. In a very short time a wealth of knowledge was being accumulated, which produced a feeling of superiority over the rest of the world and the whole of the past, and which soon made applications and technologies appear "naturally" as parallel phenomena.

A parallel of this was the new economy, which threw off the previous limitations, for example of a spatial kind, but above all the personal goal of the acquisition of wealth, and which became something autonomous. That which is was here conceived according to the model of science: an actively rational objectivity, determined by calculation, was conceived as that reality to which one had to conform in the same way as in science one finally integrated into nature reconstructed by the methodical will of science.

The modern national economy, with its emphasis on labor as the source of property and wealth, emerged from the observation of the economic process not so much in the manner of a natural process as rather of a natural scientific process. Through the amalgamation of labor and production it turned the positive Christian evaluation of labor, which was ascetic, into an optimistic one.

Already with the leap into the wide world, which brought the grab for the world's resources with it, the public power of the State becomes entangled in economic matters. At the time of the founding of the Anglo-Saxon colonies by religious dissidents striving for freedom, this leap became a heroic venture which was linked to the economic opening of an enormous continent. With astonishing speed a structure grew which was European in a certain sense, but in another was a negative copy of the motherland. Without sovereignty, but with self-imposed discipline, without injurious and exploitative privileges and differences in social status, there emerged a community that was largely leveled out, which soon became conscious of its difference from the Old World and which was tending towards complete separation from it. Only here did Europe produce something that was a real extension of its limits and not merely a territory exploited for the benefit of the European homeland, a territory that would have come into being as a result of the collapse of a pre-historic structure, as was the case with the former great empires of Central and South America, which collapsed hopelessly after contact with a small but more advanced group of invaders.

While Europe's drive into the world progressed this way in the West, in the East it came to an end. This was initially due to the weakening of its front because of the unrest which had arisen in the wake of an active formation of laymen's Christianity, soon followed by the great expansion of the Ottoman Empire into Europe. But soon, namely after the conquest of Constantinople, Europe had to contend with two powers which opposed its expansion to the East. In addition to the Ottoman Empire, Moscow became increasingly important as the heir to the Eastern Roman vision of a world empire.

Laymen's Christianity was the last word in the confrontation concerning the *Sacrum Imperium* but at the same time it caused the fundamental weakening of those structures which had emerged from the oldest phases of that motif: the Holy Roman Empire and the Roman Church. Laymen's Christianity could only have had a disintegrating effect on these two universal structures. Laymen's Christianity and Roman universalism confronted one another and once more people were dying for them, while already a new sun was rising which was beginning to cast shadows in another direction. Soon after the Thirty Years' War there stood a different Europe whose former worldly center had crumbled. In its stead modern centralized states supported by the military, by bureaucracy, and by economic power occupied the active human being. But the thinking human being was occupied by the supreme knowledge of natural science and the documented knowledge of historiography supported by critically examined sources.

Despite France's efforts to replace Europe's center of gravity, such centering of power no longer came into effect in Europe. The power structures were particular, and what remained of universality in Europe, the new spirit of science, was only indirectly connected with matters of state. This spirit, the spirit of the universal critique of the understanding, was now increasingly connected with the rationality pressing for leveling out in administrative matters and in the new economy. Laymen's Christianity, in conjunction with the complete absence of traditional social stratification, allowed a great leveled-out social structure to emerge in America, in which for the first time the possibility appeared of a political society of great magnitude without privileged individuals, groups, or classes. As was shown in a brilliant essay,[2] this was the origin of the modern "revolutionary" thinking and ideal. In Europe, such thinking largely had to oppose Christian traditions. The revolutionary stance had to bring about a particular attitude that was at first critical of the Christian tradition, then indifferent and finally hostile to it, and that had to embroil Europe in a crisis that was protracted and difficult to resolve.

For certain reasons, the problem of political freedom could not be resolved in Europe. It is true to say that it was recognized as a task and envisaged as the only possible aim in light of an actively willing subjectivity, and there was no lack of enthusiasm to experience extreme sacrifices for it. But the problem of recognition, the problem of political partnership, could not be resolved because the political sphere was not separate from the economic and social spheres, and action threw up increasingly complicated problems.

The inability to separate these spheres was, however, nothing other than the consequence of the fact that human being was seen and grasped abstractly, according to the subject-object schema: although as moral subjects people attained general recognition, this did not extend to political action. The political sphere itself, however, insofar as it was differentiated from the moral, was viewed from the economic perspective, and the economic sphere from the perspective of labor. Thus human being, insofar as it was able and willing to assume responsibility above the level of merely eking out a living, became either the subject of a good will or else a creature productive of wealth, whose emphasis lay in the economic sphere and whose goal therefore had to be economic emancipation.

Thus the human being of modern subjectivity, by striving for the solution to its basic problem, the problem of freedom and emancipation from the narrow confines of the universe of faith, and by pursuing genuineness and authenticity as distant lodestars, entangled itself in difficulties from which there was no escape under the reign of those interpretations whose origins lay at the source of scientific and philosophical modernity. In the political sphere since the end of the eighteenth century this human being wavered between the *Ancien Régime*, radical democracy with the threat of mob tyranny and rule by demagogues, military dictatorship, and compromise with the remains of the *Ancien Régime*. But after the radically democratic motif was conjoined with the social motif and the tendency towards upheaval and leveling out were exacerbated, the wavering turned into a movement which threatened the stability, and even the very existence, of what had hitherto been the center of history of the Europe which, as Hegel says,[3] had once been unified. In the modern human being there lurked inner dangers, which were inextricably connected with its entire external orientation, above all the danger of confusing the original reality of the world with its own works, to complement this all-too manipulable silent world with new idols (humanity, progress, historico-logical lawfulness), and amid all the hustle and bustle to neglect conscientious acts and everything connected with them—in short, the danger of becoming shallow.

In the meantime, the external danger too began to take on a more concrete complexion. Although in the East the pressure of the Ottoman Empire lessened, the whole Balkan peninsula, the motherland of the West, was being surrendered to it. Since the end of the seventeenth century, the colossus of Moscow began, with the help of a European-style bureaucratization and militarization, hard on the heels of which followed mechanization, to set in motion the Eastern Roman tendency towards the complete capture of all human affairs and at the same time systematically to realize together with it a pretension to supremacy vis-à-vis the West, a supremacy that was anchored in the original Eastern Roman tradition. The Western overseas empire, which from now on also formed an independent boundary, exerted a rather internal pressure: revolution, thanks in part to America's example and in the growing awareness that upheaval was the essence of modernity, turned into the problem and program of the most important parts of the continent. Hardly had they grown out of their peripheral position than the future heirs of Europe started to exert pressure on it and co-determine its fate.

The West and history had essentially grown out of the care for the soul, for that in human being which lies beyond the region of the mere eking out of life. Acts of conscience and the life devoted to "spirituality" were the sources from which history was nourished. Modernity's growing independence, which increasingly asserted itself in the general change in the Enlightenment's style of living and thinking, especially in the European West where the initiative of the new change lay, had to be perceived as a threat to what was most holy and most important, especially in those places where Christian spirituality had received a stronger impulse through the intensified participation of laymen and where it had long been elevated to the center of thought and action, in the disintegrating Holy Roman Empire and its later, most spirited new guises, above all in Prussia. There occurred the final attempt to counter enlightened externalization with a reminder of the inner life, the inner realm of the spirit, the spirit as divine, as that which alone is efficacious and real in nature and history. Based on the Kantian intensification of the enlightened approach to knowledge and action, and on the foundation of human freedom in the face of mechanistic nature, and following on from the preceding protests of sentimentalism and the independence of life, this movement had arrived at a historical system of spirit: at the same time a completion of the modern subjective turn and a preventative measure against its externalization. For spirit, as comprehending everything in itself and taking back everything into itself, is after all the most extreme interiority conceivable. At the same time, modern aesthetic culture was being constituted here, an attempt was being made to internalize even exteriority itself and to experience the reconciliation with reality in this sphere and in this way either to revive or to replace the diminishing warmth and intensity of the religious sphere. An awakening of the long-dormant artistic and intellectual activity followed the brilliant and vigorous beginnings and filled the entire following century in its wake, although it was soon overshadowed by the renewed approach of a much more sober and practically more successful Enlightenment. The success and the outcome of this memorable turn within the overall movement of modernity were determined both by its subjective starting point as by the growing consciousness of the inevitability of a modern world of objectivity. The opposition to modernity, which here often broke out passionately and denominationally, was basically an opposition within the same frame of interpretation, but more radical conclusions were being drawn from the subjective approach which dated back more than a hundred years.

The absolute spirit is perhaps the most consequential, but by no means the only way to conceive the objectivity of the subject as the essence of what is, and as soon as the basic tendency of the Enlightenment, with its hostility towards the Church, pushed itself once more into the forefront, there were formative influences at work which gave priority to objectivity, to nature externally and in the human being. Apart from that, the picture of the last century in Europe was characterized by the unsolved problems of the preceding one. It offered the picture of a riven particularity, for life retreated into separate regions and self-contained national states, in which ever greater and broader strata of society were being adversely affected, in that they were participating in a way of life and a kind of occupation which increasingly moved away from tradition. The national character of societies, which could only function through the active participation of as many people as possible (in modern production and administration), was accorded an increased importance. Europeans, who had hitherto been united by a common "culture" and by an international upper class, the aristocracy, now increasingly discovered that their differences were more important, and that there was basically no contemporary spirituality common to them. The political endeavors of the time also bore the stamp of this natural particularism, especially insofar as they had emancipation, the unresolved problem of freedom, as their theme. What characterized them *all*, nonetheless, did not characterize them *together*: science and technology, in essence the same, were accorded to individual states and nations in the form of their particular power and superiority. Only the workers' associations that cut across all these movements strove for something like supranational unity, although they attained this more as a program than as reality. But this brought even more disunity into the European picture.

In the meantime, the progress of the colossus of the Eastern periphery became more obvious and the last French attempt at a unification of the continent was thwarted with its help—which for a time gave it a previously unsuspected significance for the events of European history. Since then Europe had roused itself to a common action just once,[4] only to break up again into its particular entities; and the solutions to individual "European problems," such as the German or Italian, put no end to the disintegration of all former unities and their lifeless sediments.

Even that commonality which was guaranteed by the possession of power and technology, supported by a global economic organization and by commerce, and which represented such an immense superiority that the rest of the world could do nothing at all about it and was left helpless, turned out to be a disaster for the holders of this power due to their disputes. The unresolved nature of all problems (of freedom, nation, society), the general feeling of insecurity which resulted from it, the slow decay of the spiritual traditions under the overwhelming impact of the industrial world, in which the modern interpretation of the world showed itself, the work of scholars, who saw in industry and production, but also in the mind and its creations, in thought and poetry, merely the means of the maintenance of life—all this testified to an unease that was slowly increasing, to an inability to act, to an indecisiveness, which prevailed at the apex of the world at that time. For by virtue of its rational civilization and its monopoly, Europe at that time was *the world* and did not need either externally, as it believed, or intellectually to concern itself about others, not even about potential heirs. Although even at the time of the French Revolution people asked themselves who after all would advance to become the successor of this classical world, these were academic questions; and even when individual societies of the East were adopting European science and technology or the European organization of political parties, this did not seem to be detrimental to European hegemony. In reality, however, it was a significant step forward on the path towards planetary history.

The First World War, also, was the decisive step on this path. It was an apparent way out of an internal and external indecisiveness and irresolution that dominated Europe and humankind in this world of matured mass society. Nobody dared to put forward an affirmative principle. After all, the Central Powers in their striving for hegemony basically assumed the lack of a universal principle and tried to make up for this deficit with action, with the establishment of a de facto predominance. The rationale, however, was basically a biological one—life chances for those who (whether justified or not) considered themselves the ablest. Because of this, the opponents, who, at least in the beginning, also did not themselves have any universal idea, had the opportunity to establish something more superior merely by resisting. That which was hierarchical in the State and in the leadership was in clear contradiction with the biological rationale of the Central Powers' striving. Nationalism did not chime with the tradition on which the political decisions and their implementation were based. Although they would have had the option of making decisions according to their own insights, the Central Powers allowed themselves to be driven into war by fear; they hesitated with concessions and with ending the war until it was too late— and all of them allowed their entire industry worldwide to work towards the destruction of Europe's predominance and its prestige in the world. As a result of all of this, the non-Europeans' holding-on turned into pressure, Europe had to give up its monopoly of power and industry; the instability of European supremacy became evident.

Wilson's America was the only power in this conflict which at least pretended to follow an idea that did not stem from the sphere of arguments based on biological necessity, but instead belonged to the contents of laymen's Christianity: that of the emancipation of nations. But it was more than doubtful whether, in a Europe where the religious conditions for it were lacking, this idea could really take hold in the sense in which the citizens of the United States had understood it once upon a time and had based their own constitution upon it, i.e., whether the European concept of nation was not on the contrary all too biologically determined and thus essentially not emancipatory but rather stamped by instinct and a will to power and for that reason necessarily gave rise to new conflicts.

For this reason the Central Powers' attempt at European hegemony (and through it, world domination) was essentially different from the Napoleonic attempt at unification of the continent under France's leadership. For Napoleon's attempt could still be based upon the consciousness of a common European spirit and could be concerned with a universally European idea that was largely worldly but was nonetheless felt to be real: the idea of a universal empire, rejuvenated and enriched by the modern questions of emancipation. Despite concrete experiences, to the very end it had been possible to maintain the belief in the reality of this idea even among those nations that later denounced the abstract character of this view most passionately. Here, by contrast, from the very beginning armed force had to be used to "persuade," and it was not at all a matter of a commonality, but rather of their sovereign right and of securing their own future.

The war had broken out in an atmosphere of a particularism that set itself up as a generality, and it was widely perceived as the self-assertion of the will to power, and that meant, the generality disclosed by the war, that which really mattered to everyone was the furthering and enhancement of one's own life. Nationalism was thinking in terms of biology, the most easily understood topic, which was taken for granted by all participants. But one also thought in terms of biology on the part of the revolutionaries, who found in war the much-longed-for opportunity to deal a mortal blow to the traditional social order and who had at least succeeded in gaining complete control over the largest European empire [Russia]. Thus, although the Central Powers had been defeated and one of their empires had completely disappeared [the Austro-Hungarian Empire], this was not the only result that mattered. What mattered above all was that the original American objective, because of Wilson's disavowal of it, itself turned out not to be fundamental. Thus the world was left to instinctively biological conceptions in two different modifications which were nevertheless deeply akin in their hostility towards everything that transcended bare life. Modern "scientific socialism"—based on Marx's adoption of the identification of labor and production, which had been initiated by the English national economy, and which conceived the emancipation of human being as the emancipation through labor and at the same time from labor, i.e., the emancipation from bodily toil, but not in the end from the biological growth of an overpowering collective—thought just as much in terms of survival as did nationalism, which unambiguously declared itself for this origin in the racial theories which soon became popular. If a Europe abandoned to this idea was the most important result of the war, then in the end only the prospect of a new war could prove decisive. What in the first war was still relatively coyly veiled now, clearly expressed, came to the fore.

Quite a few of the best people in Germany consoled themselves over the defeat because at least a victory of the Russian bureaucracy had been averted. They thereby underestimated the success of the decisive renunciation of the war on the part of the Russian Revolution, which enormously increased the prestige of the Soviet Union among the European nations. Moreover, they underestimated the no less significant consequences of the modernization of the intellectual foundation of the Russian and Soviet leadership while it maintained its essentially anti-European character. In addition, the Soviet Union became the first example of how in the time of mass society such colossi could be administered and how previous states of emergency could become the norm.

The European nations' loss of prestige was greater than the reduction of their overseas holdings, but also more important. The non-European peoples were first dragged into the conflict as rather passive participants, but their striving for emancipation was thereby promoted, and due to European resources, organization, and technology, and historical and political knowledge of European origins, this striving for emancipation has become a part of history.

Thus in the interwar period what emerged convincingly was that hopes for a development in Europe, in the age of mass society and biological thinking, that would be the parallel of American democracy were illusory. Not laymen's Christianity but rather technology, organization, the massing of force to a concentrated strength proved to be in accordance with the current interpretation of the world; and when a biological-technological race-based nationalism, corresponding to this constellation and the opportunities it offered, had taken hold of the heart of Europe with its fury for revenge, nothing remained but to let oneself be rescued by the colossi, one of which, albeit in a theoretically more founded and more logically consistent manner, exhibited basically the same biological-technological faith and the same contempt for everything that had made history possible up to that point as the enemy that had finally been overpowered with the utmost effort.

The postwar period was distinguished by the fact that what remained of Europe's global assets, its global power, its economic dominance was but a mere fragment; that all of Central Europe fell under the sway of Soviet Russia and was thus separated from the rest of Europe; that the former powers expended their efforts on themselves and their own reconstruction, and sought to forget their own insignificance in restoration and never-before seen social achievements. American pressure was not only bearable for them but beneficial, their endeavors for a kind of independence were chaotic and impotent, not least because every easing towards one side necessarily meant getting into the grip of the other side.

In this atmosphere there now occurred a process which characterized the emergence of a post-European world. A decade after the war one had to observe that a post-European epoch had begun. Whole continents which previously were thought unworthy of attention rose up and intervened in history as states or empires, although not always with clear knowledge and purpose, but with the determination never again to allow a return to the former state of dependence. Although Japan was one of the defeated nations, the entrance of China more than compensated for this loss on the part of nations newly appearing on the world stage. Before long it was clear that this state would become one of Europe's successors, something that had previously never been considered when matters of succession had been pondered.

The planetary era was initiated and enabled by European technology and organization, in short, by Europe's rational civilization. Rational civilization itself was nothing other than the fruit of an interpretation of the world oriented towards the unfolding of life's power and force. Is it any wonder that precisely this had to lead to the collapse of Europe when the history-forming element in that part of the world from which history sprang, itself confessed to this negation of the historical element? Now, at the end of European history, are the non-European parts of humankind not justified, can they not be gratified to discard their previous kind of pre-historicality, namely the mythical, and to exchange it for a post-historical rationality? Did it not seem as if China had until now been a country dedicated to the functioning of biological survival and its cult, a country which owed its continued existence to the tenacious adherence to this element, to fertility and its cult? And did the pre-historical not seem to have been essentially alike everywhere, albeit with certain divergences, such as, for example, certain Buddhist developments seem to illustrate them?

From this point of view, is the planetary epoch then anything other than an *end of history*? But the paradox of a historical entry into the unhistorical does after all have its other side, which one has to take into account. Viewed from one very striking perspective, one could interpret this strange phenomenon as a deficiency of previous European spirituality: our philosophy, the most important element of our interpretation of the world, from which the chief possibilities of our historical existence are derived, is inadequate for the historical human being—it cannot grasp this human being, but instead it tarries in the contradiction of a concept of being that is only made possible by human being living *above* the level of mere life and yet that is only capable of grasping it as a living being.

Such a contradiction is by no means proof that one has to live differently, that the contradiction will be felt and consequently found to be unbearable. After all, one also resisted this through the substitution of philosophy by science (in the form of the fact-based sciences) and through a fast-paced technological development, followed everywhere by far-reaching social implementation. By now the consequences of this biological revolution are to some extent already apparent: the world as something like a highly industrialized China is no solution, but rather a problem from which one must find a way out. Admittedly, this is not an argument that can bring about a reversal: an impossibility does not lead to any new possibilities. Rational civilization's gauging of its own boundaries can only produce a review of the possibilities within its own framework, of a "religion" and a "culture" which are not authentic. All the same it is significant that such a review and such an unease exist—what dominates is uncertainty instead of a triumphant mood, and the peoples emancipated from Europe do not enter the new era via a triumphal arch. They come upon a largely depleted and plundered earth, of which they have not yet actually and exclusively taken possession, with the aim of exploiting and devastating it further themselves through mass extraction.

The emergence of a planetary era and of a history of humanity is as such only the completion of a process which was initiated a long time ago and which was inherent in the essence of rational civilization. But will the human being of the planetary epoch really be capable of living historically? What is needed is reflection, which is perhaps not to be accomplished by those who are now entering the historical arena, but by Europeans in the broad sense of the word. What is there, viewed spiritually, that is living on this earth? On what could one still base the faith, or rather, the hope for a life beyond the merely biological level? We have seen very few attempts really to undertake this. Historical reflection upon history has become very rare. Cultural morphologists in the manner of Spengler and Toynbee think unhistorically and essentially even biologistically. The Husserlian critique of rational civilization as oblivious to the lifeworld is profound, to be sure, but its proposal of a renewed metaphysics of spirit is abstract and without contact with the essence of the modern situation: how did we get, via mathematical physics, to the predominance of life and the biological perspective? Incidentally, a brilliant critic[5] surmised that Husserl's lifeworld was itself a concession by a fundamental rationalist to the mood of a time of the "cults of originality" and of life-philosophy. I do not believe that this is justified: Husserlian life and lived experience has nothing to do with the immediacy of the instincts in life-philosophy. But how then should the biologistic approaches of today be comprehended and overcome on the basis of his thought?

Notes

1   Jan Patočka, "The Beginning of History," in *Heretical Essays in the Philosophy of History*, trans. Erazim Kohák (Chicago: Open Court, 1996), 27–52 (Ed.).

2   Hannah Arendt, *On Revolution* (New York: Penguin, 1963) (Ed.).

3   G. W. F. Hegel, *Die Verfassung Deutschlands*, in *Werke*, vol. 1: *Frühe Schriften* (Frankfurt am Main, 1971), S. 478.

4   At the Congress of Vienna, 1814–15.

5   Theodor W. Adorno, *Metakritik der Erkenntnistheorie*, Gesammelte Schriften 5 (Frankfurt am Main, 1970), 28ff. (Ed.).

Postscript: Philosophy, Fate, and Sacrifice

Luděk Sekyra

Founder of the Sekyra Foundation

Translated from the Czech by Alex Zucker

Not many figures in twentieth-century Czech history can compete with the philosopher Jan Patočka. This extraordinary personality speaks to us through his philosophical work and his moral positions alike. His death after many hours of questioning by the secret police became a symbol for the birth of Charter 77, Czechoslovakia's largest dissident movement, which played a fundamental role in the fall of the Communist regime. Despite his age, the courageous philosopher admirably decided to take on the risk of serving as the platform's first spokesperson, a decision that ended in the ultimate sacrifice. The moral foundations of Charter 77 are perhaps best illustrated by Patočka's famous statement that "there are things worth suffering for" and that "they are what make life worth living." What this sentence conveys above all is an emphasis on fundamental human rights, on "living in truth," which is the core of "anti-" or "non-political" politics springing from values and the power of conscience. We later find these same ideas in concentrated form in the work of Václav Havel, on whom Patočka had a profound influence.

In his youth, the Czech philosopher was one of the most gifted pupils of Moravian native Edmund Husserl, the founder of phenomenology. This became the starting point of his lifelong philosophical journey. In his habilitation thesis, "The Natural World as a Philosophical Problem," Patočka developed and deepened Husserl's concept of the natural or lifeworld (*Lebenswelt*). Patočka, like his teacher—or Kant, Hegel, Heidegger, and, of course, Wittgenstein—sought to disclose the structure of the world: to grasp the world as a whole, not in the dualism of the natural and scientifically mediated mathematical world. This is the path that leads to the overcoming of fragmentation, to the renewal of life as a whole. How relevant in this age of social networks and filter bubbles with their algorithms sealing us off into virtual echo chambers. In this environment, there is a general lack of critical reflection and debate, resulting in fragmentation, an absence of reflection and respect for perspectives different from ours, and the canalization of our own attitudes.

For Patočka, philosophy is the bold path leading to the essence of things, which "a naive life seeks to avoid." His work is primarily anchored in the continental philosophical tradition, so we need not agree with his belief that phenomenology best describes the structure of our world. Some are on closer terms with analytic philosophy, such as the formal logic of Wittgenstein and Carnap; others subscribe to Kant's transcendental idealism. I myself am more convinced of the primacy of the moral structure of the world. Regardless, no one can deny the originality of Patočka's ideas and interpretations. His phenomenology is not merely existential, but always emphasizes the importance of understanding others, of consideration for them and coexistence with them.

What is amazing is the sheer breadth of his interests, always serious-minded and in many ways revealing. Among those we must mention are Greek philosophy, literature, and art, educational theory focused on the fundamental work of his compatriot and pedagogical genius John Amos Comenius, and, last but not least, the philosophy of history.

Though at his core a philosophical, apolitical person, Patočka's fate was shaped by political tumult: the traumatic experience of 1930s Berlin, the Nazi German occupation of Czechoslovakia, and the Communists' rise to power in 1948, after which he had to leave the university, although he returned for a brief spell in 1968 in connection with the Prague Spring. Subsequently, his public engagement was limited to the teaching of apartment seminars, which, however, shaped the character of Czech dissent in a substantial way. He also returned to Greek philosophy, developing his ideas about the historical role of the city, or *polis*, as a place of "care for the soul"—a source of unity in life, albeit born in battle, in struggle (*polemos*).

Socrates' thesis that "the unexamined life is not worth living" could serve as the motto for Patočka's thinking at the tail end of his philosophical journey. Life in Patočka's view is inextricably bound up with problematization, upheaval, and a resultant "solidarity of the shaken." What remains constant is the question of meaning and meaningfulness, and these fateful experiences lead him to the conviction that "the world is dark and problematic . . . *we do not possess it*; but this means coming *into conflict* and going to one's death" (see "The Spiritual Person and the Intellectual"). Intellectual insight must necessarily be accompanied by engagement, by concrete acts. The context of these reflections clarifies his lifelong admiration for the man of action Tomáš Garrigue Masaryk, Czechoslovakia's first president and the only philosopher to found a state.

Patočka sees the meaning of both history and individual life in the unifying message of the victim, a beacon of resistance for all those who hesitate, tolerate, and adapt in spite of disagreement. He invites us to undertake a fundamental reflection, to be brave enough not to fear the truth, a choice which may result in sacrifice. Most of us live within the confines of our comfort zones; it is urgent that we leave them—this is what I would refer to as "Patočka's appeal." It is the call to take a moral stance, to take action affirming the meaning of our own existence.

His multilayered philosophical legacy opens a broad space for interpretation and debate. Recall his reflections on the idea of the West, highlighting the benefit of the creative struggle between Czech elements and Western cultural influences, and emphasizing that we must be "more western than the West itself," a statement that may be applied to all of Central Europe, this unique space in between the West and Russia. Despite the often loud criticism of the West here, frequently chiming in with the West's own withering self-critique, I still feel that the people who inhabit this in-between space realize there is a substantially worse alternative, namely, the threat from the East.

Patočka's reflections on the universal character of European culture, the moral crisis of Europe, the post-European era, and supercivilization are similarly a source of unrelenting debate. Finally, his observations on freedom "as letting being be," not distorting it, in which he presages the current environmental crisis, are unjustly neglected. These inquiries of Patočka's are especially important for the international philosophical public, who in this volume of translated essays by the great Central European thinker have access to the best of the Czech philosophical tradition, knowledge of which remains rather marginal, particularly in the Anglo-American environment.

I am extremely pleased that our foundation—which has long supported the philosophy and work of Jan Patočka, and whose board includes direct students of his, such as the philosophers Daniel Kroupa and Martin Palouš, and the theologian Tomáš Halík—was able to be involved in the publication of this book.

LIST OF CONTRIBUTORS

David Charlston is an independent UK researcher, translator, and co-editor of *New Voices in Translation Studies*. He recently published *Translation and Hegel's Philosophy: A Transformative, Socio-narrative Approach to AV Miller's Cold-War Retranslations* (2020).

Ivan Chvatík is the co-director of the Center for Theoretical Study (CTS) an institute for advanced study at Charles University and the Czech Academy of Sciences. A former student of Jan Patočka, he was central in preserving and publishing his teacher's work—as well as critically interpreting it. In 1990 he established the Jan Patočka Archive as part of the Institute of Philosophy of the Czechoslovak Academy of Sciences; until 2020, he served as the director of this Archive, publishing the series of *Complete Works of Jan Patočka* (twenty volumes out of planned twenty-five). The Jan Patočka Archive has been part of the CTS since 1993.

Graham Henderson is a cultural entrepreneur based in the UK. He is best known for developing the arts organization Poet in the City and then serving as chief executive of the Rimbaud and Verlaine Foundation, an organization committed to promoting culture and championing a new funding model for the arts. His career has involved him in many other arts-related initiatives, including the development of a public art consultancy and the creation of an international arts network. He conceived the idea of the present volume, motivated in part by the privileged role that Jan Patočka attributes to the arts in human understanding and meaning.

Erin Plunkett teaches Philosophy and Religious Studies at the University of Hertfordshire, UK. Her work addresses questions of form in philosophy as well as phenomenological themes of world disclosure, subjectivity, and environment, and her book *A Philosophy of the Essay: Scepticism, Experience, and Style* (2018) takes up these themes.

Andrea Rehberg teaches Philosophy at Newcastle University, UK. Her area of expertise is post-Kantian European philosophy, especially nineteenth- and twentieth-century German and French thought, with emphasis on Kant, Nietzsche, Heidegger, and phenomenology. She is a member of the executive of the British Society for Phenomenology, the Society for European

Philosophy, the Friedrich Nietzsche Society, and the UK Society for Women in Philosophy.

Alex Zucker is an award-winning translator of Czech. His translations include novels by J. R. Pick, Petra Hůlová, Jáchym Topol, Magdaléna Platzová, Tomáš Zmeškal, Josef Jedlička, Heda Margolius Kovály, Patrik Ouředník, and Miloslava Holubová. He has also translated stories, plays, subtitles, young adult and children's books, song lyrics, essays, poems, and an opera. He is a winner of the American Literary Translators Association's National Translation Award and two English PEN Writing in Translation awards.

BIBLIOGRAPHY

This bibliography has been divided into four sections:
1.1: Patočka works in English translation
1.2: English secondary sources on Patočka
1.3: Other works cited in this volume
1.4: Selected bibliography of Patočka's works

1.1 Patočka Works in English Translation

Jan Patočka: Philosophy and Selected Writings. Translated and edited by Erazim Kohák with a biography by Erazim Kohák. Chicago and London: University of Chicago Press, 1989.

Heretical Essays in the Philosophy of History. Translated by Erazim Kohák, edited by James Dodd, preface by Paul Ricœur. Chicago: Open Court, 1996.

Body, Community, Language, World. Translated by Erazim Kohák, edited by James Dodd. Chicago: Open Court, 1998.

Plato and Europe. Translated by Petr Lom. Stanford, CA: Stanford University Press, 2002.

Living in Problematicity. Edited by Eric Manton, translated by Eric Manton and Erazim Kohák. Prague: OIKOYMENH, 2007.

The Natural World as a Philosophical Problem. Translated by Erika Abrams, edited by Ivan Chvatík and L'ubica Učnik. Evanston, IL: Northwestern University Press, 2016.

"Intellectuals and Opposition" and "Intellectuals and Opposition: Alternative End." Translated by Francesco Tava and Daniel Leufer. In *Thinking After Europe: Jan Patočka and Politics*, edited by Darian Meacham and Francesco Tava, 7–26. London: Rowman and Littlefield, 2016.

An Introduction to Husserl's Phenomenology. Translated by Erazim Kohák, edited by James Dodd. Chicago: Open Court, 2018.

"Husserl's Subjectivism and the Call for an Asubjective Phenomenology" and "Epochē and Reduction: Some Observations." Translated by Matt Bower, Ivan Chvatík, and Kenneth Maly. In *Asubjective Phenomenology: Jan Patočka's Project in the Broader Context of His Work*, edited by L'ubica Učník, Ivan Chvatík, and Anita Williams, 17–40, 41–52. Nordhausen: Traugott Bautz, 2019.

1.2 English Secondary Sources on Patočka

Edited Volumes and Special Journal Issues Dedicated to Patočka

Chvatík, Ivan and Erika Abrams, eds. *Jan Patočka and the Heritage of Phenomenology*. Dordrecht: Springer, 2011.

James, Petra and Jan Tlustý, eds. Special Issue on Jan Patočka, Aesthetics, and Literature. *Bohemia Litteraria* 23, no. 2 (2020).

Ludger Hagedorn and James Dodd, eds. Religion, War, and the Crisis of Modernity. A Special Issue Dedicated to the Philosophy of Jan Patočka. *The New Yearbook for Phenomenology and Phenomenological Philosophy* 14 (2015).

Special Issue on Myth, Philosophy, Art, and Science in Jan Patočka's Thought. *AUC Philosophica et Historica* 1 (2014).

Tava, Francesco and Darian Meacham, eds. *Thinking After Europe: Jan Patočka and Politics*. London: Rowman & Littlefield International, 2016.

Učník, Ľubica, Ivan Chvatík, and Anita Williams, eds. *Asubjective Phenomenology*: *Jan Patočka's Project in the Broader Context of His Work*. Nordhausen: Traugott Bautz, 2019.

Other Secondary Sources

Bolton, Jonathan. *Worlds of Dissent: Charter 77, the Plastic People of the Universe, and Czech Culture Under Communism*. Cambridge, MA: Harvard University Press, 2014.

Chvatík, Ivan. "Solidarity of the Shaken." *Telos* 94 (1993): 163–6.

Chytry, Josef. "On the 'Terror' of Polis Freedom: From M. Heidegger to J. Patočka and the Czech Velvet Revolution." In *Between Terror and Freedom: Philosophy, Politics, and Fiction Speak of Modernity*, edited by Frederik M. Dolan and Simona Goi, 119–72. London: Rowman and Littlefield, 2004.

Derrida, Jacques. *The Gift of Death*. Translated by David Wills. Chicago: University of Chicago Press, 1995.

de Warren, Nicolas. "Homecoming: Jan Patočka's Reflections on the First World War." In *Phenomenologies of Violence*, edited by Michael Staudigl, 219–23. Leiden and Boston: Brill, 2014.

Dodd, James. "Patočka and the metaphysics of sacrifice." *Studies in East European Thought*, doi: 10.1007/s11212-020-09391-1.

Findlay, Edward F. "Classical Ethics and Postmodern Critique: Political Philosophy in Václav Havel and Jan Patočka." *Review of Politics* 61, no. 3 (1999): 403–38.

Findlay, Edward F. *Caring for the Soul in a Postmodern Age: Politics and Phenomenology in the Thought of Jan Patočka*. Albany, NY: SUNY Press, 2002.

Forti, Simona. *New Demons: Rethinking Power and Evil Today*. Translated by Zakiya Hanafi. Stanford, CA: Stanford University Press, 2015.

Forti, Simona. "Parrhesia Between East and West: Foucault and Dissidence." In *The Government of Life: Foucault, Biopolitics, and Neoliberalism*, edited by Vanessa Lemm and Miguel Vatter, 187–207. New York: Fordham University Press, 2016.

Frei, Jan. "The hidden teacher: On Patočka's impact on today's Czech philosophy." *Studies in East European Thought* (2021), doi: 10.1007/s11212-020-09404-z.

Fried, Gregory. *Heidegger's Polemos: From Being to Politics*. New Haven, CT: Yale University Press, 2000.

Gubser, Michael D. *The Far Reaches: Phenomenology, Ethics, and Social Renewal in Central Europe*. Stanford, CA: Stanford University Press, 2014.

Hagedorn, Ludger. "Philosophical Dissident." *The New Presence* 4, no. 3 (2002): 24–6.

Halík, Tomáš: "Ego Dormio: A Meditation on the Night Path of Knowledge." Translated by Milan Pomichalek and Anna Mozga. In *Good-bye, Samizdat*, edited by Marketa Goetz-Stanikiewicz, with a foreword by Timothy Garton Ash, 275–84. Evanston, IL: Northwestern University Press, 1992.

Havel, Václav et al. *The Power of the Powerless: Citizens Against the State in Central-Eastern Europe*, edited by John Keane. London: Hutchinson, 1985.

Hejdánek, Ladislav. "Nothingness and Responsibility: The Problem of 'Negative Platonism' in Patočka's Philosophy." In *La Responsabilité/Responsibility*, edited by Petr Horák and Josef Zumr, 36–41. Prague: Filosofický ústav ČSAV, 1992.

Hubick, Joel. "Heretical Hindsight: Patočka's Phenomenology as Questioning Philosophy." *Journal of the British Society for Phenomenology* 49, no. 1 (2018): 36–54.

Jünger, Ernst. "Total Mobilization." In *The Heidegger Controversy: A Critical Reader*, edited by Richard Wolin, 119–39. Cambridge, MA: MIT Press, 1993.

Kearney, Richard. "Poetics and the Right to Resist: Patočka's Testimony." *International Journal of Philosophical Studies* 2, no. 1 (1994): 31–44.

Koci, Martin. "Sacrifice for nothing: The movement of kenosis in Jan Patočka's thought." *Modern Theology* 33, no. 4 (2017): 594–617.

Koci, Martin. *Thinking Faith After Christianity: A Theological Reading of Jan Patočka's Phenomenological Philosophy*. Albany, NY: SUNY Press, 2020.

Koci, Martin. "The World as a Theological Problem." *Journal for Continental Philosophy of Religion* 2 (2020): 22–46.

Kohák, Erazim. "The Crisis of Rationality and the 'Natural' World." *Review of Metaphysics* 40, no. 1 (1986): 79–106.

Kohák, Erazim. *Hearth and Horizon: Cultural Identity and Global Humanity in Czech Philosophy*. Prague: Filosofia, 2008.

Kouba, Petr. "The Phenomenology of Sacrifice in Marion, Patočka and Nancy." *Open Theology* 5 (2019): 377–85, doi: 10.1515/opth-2019-0027/html.

Landgrebe, Ludwig. "An Obituary by Ludwig Landgrebe." *Philosophy and Phenomenological Research* 38, no. 2 (1977): 287–90.

Lau, Kwok-Ying. "Jan Patočka: Critical Consciousness and Non-Eurocentric Philosopher of the Phenomenological Movement." *Studia Phaenomenologica* 7 (2007): 475–92.

Leufer, Daniel. "The wound which will not close: Jan Patočka's philosophy and the conditions of politicization." *Studies in East European Thought* 69 (2017): 29–44.

Lom, Petr. "East Meets West—Jan Patočka and Richard Rorty on Freedom." *Political Theory* 27, no. 4 (1999): 447–59.

Manton, Eric. "Patočka on Ideology and the Politics of Human Freedom." *Studia Phaenomenologica* 7 (2007): 465–74.

Manton, Eric. "Political Philosophy of a Non-Political Philosopher." In Jan Patočka, *Living in Problematicity*, translated and edited by Eric Manton, 70–9. Prague: OIKOYMENH, 2007.

Meacham, Darian and Francesco Tava. "Epochē and institution: The fundamental tension in Jan Patočka's phenomenology." *Studies in East European Thought*, https://link.springer.com/article/10.1007/s11212-020-09398-8.

Mensch, James. *Patočka's Asubjective Phenomenology: Toward a New Concept of Human Rights*. Würzburg: Köningshausen & Neumann, 2016.

Mensch, James. *Selfhood and Appearing: The Intertwining*. Studies in Contemporary Phenomenology, vol. 17. Leiden and Boston: Brill, 2018.

Moural, Josef. "Patočka and Heidegger in the 1930s and 1940s: History, Finitude and Socrates." In *Heidegger in Russia and Eastern Europe*, edited by Jeff Love, 117–36. London: Rowman & Littlefield International, 2017.

Moural, Josef. "The Question of the Core of Patočka's Work: Phenomenology, History of Philosophy, and Philosophy of History." In *Report of the Center for Theoretical Study Praha*. No place of publication/publisher, 1999.

Mout, Nicolette. "Consolation at Night: Jan Patočka and His Correspondence With Comeniologists." *Acta Comeniana* 27 (2013): 175–87.

Novák, Josef. "The Art of Sculpture: Jan Patočka's Concept of Incarnate Being." *Journal of the British Society for Phenomenology* 50, no. 3 (2019): 171–88.

Palouš, Martin. "Jan Patočka versus Václav Benda." Translated by Paul Wilson. In *Civic Freedom in Central Europe, Voices From Czechoslovakia*, edited by H. G. Skilling and Paul Wilson, 121–8. London: MacMillan, 1991.

Palouš, Martin. "Post-totalitarian Politics and European Philosophy." *Public Affairs Quarterly* 7, no. 2 (1993): 149–64.

Paparusso, Riccardo. "Salvation Without Redemption: Phenomenology of (Pre-) History in Patočka's Late Work." In *Shapes of Apocalypse: Arts and Philosophy in Slavic Thought*, edited by Andrea Oppo, 68–87. Boston: Academic Studies Press, 2013.

Paparusso, Riccardo. "The Ekstatic Animal in Jan Patočka's Phenomenology." *Interpretationes Studia Philosophica Europeanea* 1 (2017): 60–71.

Paparusso, Riccardo. "Jan Patočka." In *Routledge Handbook of Phenomenological Philosophy*, edited by Burt C. Hopkins, Claudio Maiolino, and Daniele De Santis, 573–81. London: Routledge, 2020.

Pavlík, Ján. "On Patočka's Conception of the 'Ideal Genesis' of Language." *E-LOGOS: Electronic Journal for Philosophy* (1993).

Porter, Theodore M. *Trust in Numbers: The Pursuit of Objectivity in Science and Public Life*. Princeton, NJ: Princeton University Press, 1996.

Prozorov, Sergei. "Foucault's Affirmative Biopolitics: Cynic Parrhesia and the Biopower of the Powerless." *Political Theory* (October 9, 2015): 1–23.

Ricoeur, Paul. Preface to the French edition of Jan Patočka's Heretical Essays. In Jan Patočka, *Heretical Essays in the Philosophy of History*, translated by Erazim Kohák, edited by James Dodd. Chicago: Open Court, 1996.

Ritter, Martin. "Patočka's Care of the Soul Reconsidered: Performing the Soul Through Movement." *Human Studies* 40 (2017): 233–47.

Ritter, Martin. "The Hubris of Transcendental Idealism: Understanding Patočka's Early Concept of the Lifeworld." *Journal of the British Society for Phenomenology* 49, no. 2 (2018): 171–81.

Ritter, Martin. *Into the World: The Movement of Jan Patočka's Philosophy*. Dordrecht: Springer, 2019.

Rorty, Richard. "The Seer of Prague: Influence of Czechoslovakian Philosopher Jan Patočka." *The New Republic* 205, no. 1 (1991): 35–9.

Schaller, Klaus: "Patočka's Interpretation of Comenius and its Significance for Present-Day Pedagogics." In Klaus Schaller, *Comenius 1992, Gesammelte Beiträge zur Comeniusforschung, Schriften zur Comeniusforschung, Veröffentlichungen der Comeniusforschungsstelle im Institut für Pädagogik der Ruhr-Universität Bochum*, vol. 22, 249–64. Sankt Augustin: Academia, 1992. Reprinted in *Science in Context* (Oxford) 6 (1993), 617–31.

Ševčík, Miloš. "A Testimony About Ontological Metaphor and the Expression of Problematic Meaning: Jan Patočka on the Relation between Myth and Literature." In *2nd International Akşit Göktürk Conference: Myths Revisited*, 172–83. Istanbul: Diltra, 2013.

Sohma, Shinichi. "Various Aspects of Openness and Its Potential According to J.A. Comenius." In *Gewalt sei ferne den Dingen! Contemporary Perspectives on the Works of John Amos Comenius*, edited by Goris Wouter, Meinert A. Meyer, and Vladimír Urbánek, 45–57. Dordrecht: Springer, 2016.

Suvák, Vladislav. "Patočka and Foucault: Taking Care of the Soul and Taking Care of the Self." *Journal of the British Society for Phenomenology* 50, no. 1 (2019): 19–36.

Tava, Francesco. "Jan Patočka and the Heritage of Phenomenology." *Journal of the British Society for Phenomenology* 45, no. 2 (2014): 180–5.

Tava, Francesco. *The Risk of Freedom: Ethics, Phenomenology and Politics in Jan Patočka*. Translated by Jane Ledlie. London: Rowman and Littlefield International, 2015.

Tava, Francesco. "The brave struggle: Jan Patočka on Europe's past and future." *Journal of the British Society for Phenomenology* 47, no. 3 (2016): 242–59.

Tucker, Aviezer. "Patočka's World Movement as Ultimate." *Central European Studies* 20 no. 2–3 (June–September 1997): 107–22.

Tucker, Aviezer. *The Philosophy and Politics of Czech Dissidence From Patočka to Havel*. Pittsburgh, PA: University of Pittsburgh Press, 2000.

Učník, Ľubica. "*Esse* or *Habere*: To be or to have: Patočka's Critique of Husserl and Heidegger." *Journal of the British Society for Phenomenology* 38, no. 3 (2007): 297–317.

Učník, Ľubica. "Human Existence: Patočka's Appropriation of Arendt." In *Selected Essays From Asia and Pacific: Phenomenology in Dialogue With East Asian Tradition*, edited by Chang-Chi Yu, 409–434. Bucharest: Zeta Books, 2010.

Učník, Ľubica. "The Allure and impossibility of an algorithmic future: A lesson from Patočka's supercivilisation." *Studies in East European Thought* (2021), doi:10.1007/s11212-020-09394-y.

Williams, Anita. "The Freedom of Thought: Patočka on Descartes and Husserl." *Journal of the British Society for Phenomenology* 50, no. 1 (2019): 37–49.

Williams, Anita. "The Meaning of the Mathematical." In *Asubjective Phenomenology: Jan Patočka's Project in the Broader Context of His Work*, edited by Ľubica Učník, Ivan Chvatík, and Anita Williams, 227–52. Nordhausen: Traugott Bautz, 2019.

1.3 Other Works Cited in this Volume

Arendt, Hannah. *The Human Condition*. 2nd edition. Chicago: University of Chicago Press, 2018.

Aristotle. *De Anima*. Translated by R. D. Hicks. New York: Arno Press, 1976.

Baeumler, Alfred. *Bildung und Gemeinschaft*. Berlin: Junker und Dünnhaupt, 1942.

Balázs, Trencsényi, Maciej Janowski, Monika Baar, Maria Falina, and Michal Kopecek, eds. *A History of Modern Political Thought in East Central Europe*: Volume 1: *Negotiating Modernity in the "Long Nineteenth Century."* Oxford: Oxford University Press, 2016.

Beneš, Josef. *Descartesova metoda ve vědách a ve filosofii*. Prague: Československá akademie věd, 1936.

Biemel, Walter. *Philosophische Analysen zur Kunstwerk der Gegenwart*. The Hague: Martinus Nijhoff, 1968.

Biemel, Walter. "Die Wahrheit der Metaphysik: Die Wahrheit der Kunst." In *Gesammelte Schriften*, vol. 2, 7–28. Stuttgart: Frommann-Holzboog, 1996.

Biemel, Walter. "Kunst und Übersetzung." In *Gesammelte Schriften*, vol. 2, 265–85. Stuttgart: Frommann-Holzboog, 1996.

Bradatan, Costica. *Dying for Ideas: The Dangerous Lives of Philosophers*. London: Bloomsbury, 2015.

Burtt, Edwin Arthur. *The Metaphysics of Sir Isaac Newton: An Essay on the Metaphysical Foundations of Modern Science*. New York: Columbia University Press, 1932.

Burtt, Edwin Arthur. *The Metaphysical Foundations of Modern Physical Science: A Historical and Critical Essay*. London: Kegan Paul; New York: Harcourt, Brace, 1924.

Čapek, Josef. "Tvořivá povaha moderní doby." *Volné směry* 17, no. 4–5 (1913): 112–30.

Čapek, Josef. *Kulhavý poutník: Co jsem na světě uviděl*. Prague: František Borový, 1936.

Čapek, Josef. "Co má člověk z umění a jiné úvahy." In *Výbor z článků z let 1911–1937*, 34–44. Prague: Výtvarný odbor Umělecké besedy, 1946.

Čapek, Josef. "O naději." In *Básně z koncentračního tábora*, 127. Prague: František Borový, 1946.

Čapek, Josef. "Před velikou cestou." In *Básně z koncentračního tábora*, 228. Prague: František Borový, 1946.

Čapek, Josef. "Ty, který . . ." In *Básně z koncentračního tábora*, 125. Prague: František Borový, 1946.

Čapek, Josef. *Psáno do mraků*. Prague: František Borový, 1947.

Čapek, Josef. *Moderní výtvarný výraz*. Edited by Miroslav Halík, 83–94. Prague: Academia, 1958.

Comenius, John Amos. *Theatrum universitatis rerum*. In *Opera omnia* 1, 95–181. Prague: Academia, 1969.

Cooper, John M., ed. *Plato: Complete Works*. Indianapolis: Hackett, 1997.

Costa de Beauregard, Olivier. *La notion de temps: équivalence avec l'espace*. Paris: Hermann, 1963.

de Cusa, Nicolai. *De docta ignorantia: Nicolai de Cusa Opera omnia*. Edited by Ernst Hoffman and Raymond Klibansky. Leipzig: Felix Meiner, 1932.

Descartes, René, *Oeuvres de Descartes*, vol. 10. Edited by Charles Adam and Paul Tannery. Paris: Léopold Cerf, 1913.

Diels, Hermann and Walther Kranz, eds. *Fragmente der Vorsokratiker*, vol. 1. Berlin: Weidmann, 1951.

Dodd, James. "Jan Patočka's Philosophical Legacy." In *The Oxford Handbook of the History of Phenomenology*, edited by Dan Zahavi, 396–411. Oxford: Oxford University Press, 2018.

Feuerbach, Ludwig. *Gedanken über Tod und Unsterblichkeit*. Nuremberg: Johann Adam Stein, 1830.

Forti, Simona. "Parrhesia Between East and West: Foucault and Dissidence." In *The Government of Life: Foucault, Biopolitics, and Neoliberalism*, edited by Vanessa Lemm and Miguel Vatter, 187–207. New York: Fordham University Press: 2016.

Funke, Gerhard. *Phänomenologie: Metaphysik oder Methode*. Bonn: Bouvier Verlag Herbert Grundmann, 1966.

Funke, Gerhard. *Phenomenology: Metaphysics or Method*. Translated by David J. Parent. Athens, OH: Ohio University Press, 1987.

Hegel, Georg Wilhelm Friedrich. *Phänomenologie des Geistes*, IV, A. In *Werke*, vol. 3. Frankfurt am Main: Suhrkamp, 1970.

Heidegger, Martin. *Sein und Zeit*. Tübingen: Max Niemeyer Verlag, 1927.
  English: *Being and Time*. Translated by Joan Stambaugh. Albany, NY: SUNY Press, 1996, 2010.

Heidegger, Martin. "Die Frage nach der Technik." In *Die Technik und die Kehre*, 5–36. Pfullingen: Neske, 1962.
  English: "The Question Concerning Technology." In *The Question Concerning Technology and Other Essays*, edited by William Lovitt, 3–35. New York: HarperPerennial, 1977.

Heidegger, Martin. *Grundprobleme der Phänomenologie*. Edited by Friedrich-Wilhelm von Hermann. Frankfurt am Main: Vittorio Klostermann, 1975.
  English: *Basic Problems of Phenomenology*. Translated by Albert Hofstadter. Bloomington: Indiana University Press, 1982.

Heidegger, Martin. "Was ist Metaphysik?" In *Gesamtausgabe*, vol. 9 of Wegmarken, 103–22. Frankfurt am Main: Vittorio Klostermann, 1976.
  English: "What Is Metaphysics?" In *Heidegger: Basic Writings*. 2nd edition, edited by David F. Krell, 89–110. New York: HarperCollins, 1993.

Heidegger, Martin. "Die Zeit des Weltbildes." In *Holzwege*. Frankfurt am Main: Vittorio Klostermann, 1977.
  English: "The Age of the World Picture." In *The Question Concerning Technology and Other Essays*, edited by William Lovitt, 115–54. New York: HarperPerennial, 1977.

Heidegger, Martin. "Only a God Can Save Us: The Spiegel Interview." In *Heidegger: The Man and the Thinker*, translated by William J. Richardson, 45–67. Piscataway, NJ: Transaction Publishers, 1981.

Heidegger, Martin. *Reden und andere Zeugnisse eines Lebensweges (1910–1976)*. Edited by Hermann Heidegger. Frankfurt am Main: Vittorio Klostermann, 2000.

Hesiod. *Theogony*.

Horace. *Odes* III, 1, 1.

Hrdlička, Josef. "Druhý čas Máje." *Souvislosti* 14, no. 4 (2003): 162–201.

Husserl, Edmund. "Die Philosophie als strenge Wissenschaft." *Logos* 1 (1910–11): 289–341. Reprinted in vol. 25 of *Husserliana*: Aufsätze und Vorträge (1911–21), edited by Thomas Nenon and H. R. Sepp. The Hague: Martinus Nijhoff, 1987.

Husserl, Edmund. *Die Krisis der europäischen Wissenschaften und die transzendentale Phaenomenologie*. In *Philosophia. Philosophorum nostri temporis vox universa* (Belgrade), edited by Arthur Liebert, 1, no. 1 (1936).

Husserl, Edmund. *Cartesianische Meditationen und Pariser Vorträge*. Vol. 1 of *Husserliana*, edited by Stephan Strasser. The Hague: Martinus Nijhoff, 1950. English: *Cartesian Meditations*, translated by Dorion Cairns. The Hague: Martinus Nijhoff, 1960.

Husserl, Edmund. *Die Krisis der europäischen Wissenschaften und die transzendentale Phänomenologie. Eine Einleitung in die phänomenologische Philosophie*. Vol. 6 of *Husserliana*, edited by Walter Biemel. The Hague: Martinus Nijhoff, 1954.
English: *Crisis of the European Sciences*. Translated by David Carr. Evanston, IL: Northwestern University Press, 1970.

Husserl, Edmund. *Phenomenology and the Crisis of Philosophy*. Translated by Quentin Lauer. New York: Harper Torchbooks, 1965.

Husserl, Edmund. "Philosophy as Rigorous Science." In *Phenomenology and the Crisis of Philosophy*. Translated by Quentin Lauer. New York: Harper and Row, 1965.

Husserl, Edmund. *Die Idee der Phänomenologie: Fünf Vorlesungen. Husserliana 2*, reprint of the second edition, edited by Walter Biemel. The Hague: Martinus Nijhoff, 1973.

Husserl, Edmund. *Ideen zu einer reinen Phänomenologie und phänomenologischen Philosophie. Erstes Buch: Allgemeine Einführung in die reine Phänomenologie*, edited by Karl Schuhmann. The Hague: Martinus Nijhoff, 1976.
English: *Ideas Pertaining to a Pure Phenomenology and to a Phenomenological Philosophy. First Book: General Introduction to a Pure Phenomenology*. Translated by Fred Kersten. The Hague: Martinus Nijhoff, 1983.

Husserl, Edmund. *Logische Untersuchungen. Vol 2:1: Untersuchungen zur Phänomenologie und Theorie der Erkenntnis*. Vol. 19/1 of *Husserliana*, edited by Ursula Panzer. The Hague: Martinus Nijhoff, 1984.
English: *Logical Investigations*, vol. 2. Translated by John Niemeyer Findlay, edited by Dermot Moran. 2nd edition. London: Routledge, 2001.

Ingarden, Roman. *Das Literarische Kunstwerk: Eine Untersuchung aus dem Grenzgebiet der Ontologie, Logik und Literaturwissenschaft*. Halle: Max Niemeyer, 1931.

Jaspers, Karl. *Psychologie der Weltanschauungen*. Berlin: Julius Springer, 1919.

Josl, Jan. "The End of Art and Patočka's Philosophy of Art." *Horizon Studies in Phenomenology* 5, no. 1 (2016): 232–46.

Kafka, Franz. "Der Bau." In *Gesammelte Schriften*, vol. 5, edited by Max Brod, 172ff. New York: Schocken Books, 1946.

Kähler, S. A.. *Wilhelm von Humboldt und der Staat*. Munich and Berlin: R. Oldenbourg, 1927.

Kant, Immanuel. *Kritik der reinen Vernunft*. Hamburg: Felix Meiner, 1967.
English: *Critique of Pure Reason*. Edited and translated by Paul Guyer and Allen W. Wood. Cambridge: Cambridge University Press, 1998.

Kant, Immanuel. *Prolegomena to Any Future Metaphysics That Will Be Able to Come Forward as Science*. Edited and translated by Gary Hatfield. Cambridge: Cambridge University Press, 2004.

Koyré, Alexandre. *From the Closed World to the Infinite Universe*. Baltimore, MD: Johns Hopkins University Press, 1957.

Kožmín, Zdeněk. "Modely interpretace: Patočkovské vyhlidky." *Studia philosophica* 51, no. B49 (2001): 190–1.

Králík, Oldřich. "Máchova věrnost zemi." In *Platnosti slova: Studie a kritiky,* edited by Jiří Opelik and Jan Schneider, 401–2. Olomouc: Periplum, 2001.

Kranz, Walther. *Die Fragmente der Vorsokratiker,* vol. 1. Berlin: Weidmann, 1951.

Leibniz, Gottfried Wilhelm. *Discours de métaphysique* (1686), § XIII.

Mácha, K. H. *Dílo Karla Hynka Máchy,* vols 1–3. Prague: František Krčma, 1928–9.

Mácha, K. H. *Spisy K. H. Máchy,* vols 1–3. Prague: Karel Janský, Karel Dvořák and Rudolf Skřeček, 1959, 1961, 1972.

Mácha, K. H. "Budoucí vlast'" (The Future Homeland). In *Dílo,* vol. 1, 145; *Spisy,* vol. 1, 180.

Mácha, K. H. "Columbus." In *Dílo,* vol. 1, 62–6; *Spisy,* vol. 1, 296–300.

Mácha, K. H. "Die Führer durchs Leben" (The Leaders Through Life). In *Dílo,* vol. 1, 53; *Spisy,* vol. 1, 285.

Mácha, K. H. "Dodatky k literárním zápisníkům—autografy" (Addenda to literary notebooks—handwritten manuscripts). In *Dílo,* vol. 3, 326; *Spisy,* vol. 3, 251.

Mácha, K. H. "Duše nesmrtelná . . ." (Immortal Soul . . .). In *Dílo,* vol. 1, 249; *Spisy,* vol. 1, 222.

Mácha, K. H. "Glaube, Hoffnung, Liebe, Vertrauen" (Faith, Hope, Love, Trust). In *Dílo,* vol. 1, 51ff.; *Spisy,* vol. 1, 283ff.

Mácha, K. H. "Královič" (The Crown Prince). In *Dílo,* vol. 1, 154ff.; *Spisy,* vol. 1, 115ff.

Mácha, K. H. "Máj" (May). In *Dílo,* vol. 1, 28; *Spisy,* vol. 1, 32.

Mácha, K. H. "Návrat" (The Return). In *Dílo,* vol. 2, 143–8; *Spisy,* vol. 2, 123–6.

Mácha, K. H. "Noc" (Night). In *Dílo,* vol. 1, 150; Spisy, vol. 1, 203.

Mácha, K. H. "Pouť krkonošská" (Krkonoše Pilgrimage). In *Dílo,* vol. 2, 163ff.; *Spisy,* vol. 2, 114ff.

Mácha, K. H. "Večer na Bezdězu" (Evening at Bezděz). In *Dílo,* vol. 2, 167, 168; *Spisy,* vol. 2, 133, 134.

Mácha, K. H. "Vzor krásy" (The Form of Beauty). In *Dílo,* vol. 1, 148; *Spisy,* vol. 1, 120.

Mallarmé, Stéphane. *Œuvres complètes.* Paris: Gallimard/Bibliothèque de la Pléiade, 1945.

Masaryk, T. G. *Blaise Pascal, jeho život a filosofie.* Prague: Jan Otto, 1883.

Meacham, Darian. "Biologism and Supercivilisation." In *Thinking After Europe: Jan Patočka and Politics,* edited by Francesco Tava and Darian Meacham, 95–116. London: Rowman and Littlefield, 2016.

Meacham, Darian and Francesco Tava, eds. *Thinking After Europe: Jan Patočka and Politics.* London: Rowman and Littlefield, 2016.

Meinecke, Friedrich. *Die Entstehung des Historismus,* vols 1–2. Munich and Berlin: R. Oldenbourg, 1936.

Michelson, Albert A. and Edward W. Morley. "On the Relative Motion of the Earth and the Luminiferous Ether." *American Journal of Science* 34, no. 203 (November 1887): 333–45.

Plunkett, Erin. "'New Human Possibilities' in Patočka's Philosophy of Literature." *Bohemica litteraria* 23, no. 2 (2020): 69–80.

Patočka, Jan. "Několik poznámek k důkazům boží jsoucnosti u Tomáše Akvinského" (A few remarks on the proofs of God's existence in Thomas Aquinas). *Česká mysl* 29, no. 3–4 (1933): 138–48.

Patočka, Jan. "Dějepis filosofie a její jednota" (The history of philosophy and its unity). *Česká mysl* 36, nos 2 and 3 (1942): 58–72, 97–114.

Patočka, Jan. "Time, Eternity, and Temporality in the Work of K. H. Mácha." In *Realita slova Máchova,* edited by Růžena Grebeníčková and Oldřich Králík, 183–207. Prague: Československý spisovatel, 1967.

Patočka, Jan. "*Epochē* und Reduktion: Einige Bemerkungen." In *Bewusst sein: Gerhard Funke zu eigen,* edited by A. J. Bucher, Hermann Drüe, and Thomas Mulvany Seebohm, 76–85. Bonn: Bouvier Verlag Herbert Grundmann, 1975.

Patočka, Jan. *Body, Community, Language and World.* Translated by Erazim Kohák, edited by James Dodd. Chicago: Open Court, 1998.

Patočka, Jan. "Sixth Essay: Wars of the Twentieth Century and the Twentieth Century as War." In *Heretical Essays in the Philosophy of History*, translated by Erazim Kohák, edited by James Dodd, 119–37. Chicago: Open Court, 1999.

Patočka, Jan. *Aristote, ses devanciers, ses successeurs.* Translated by Erika Abrams. Paris: J. Vrin, 2011.

Patočka, Jan. "What is Phenomenology?" Translated by Hayden Kee. In *Husserl: German Perspectives*, edited by John J. Drummond and Otfried Höffe, 84–109. New York: Fordham University Press, 2019.

Ricœur, Paul. "Jan Patočka, le philosophe—résistant." *Le Monde*, March 19, 1977.

Ruyer, Raymond. *La conscience et le corps.* Paris: Félix Alcan, 1937.

Scheler, Max. *Versuche zu einer Soziologie des Wissens.* Munich and Leipzig: Druncker & Humbolt, 1924.

Ševčík, Miloš. "Dominant science and influential art: Jan Patočka on relations between art and science." *AUC Philosophica et Historica* 1 (2014): 73–84.

Sombart, Werner. *Deutscher Sozialismus.* Berlin and Charlottenburg: Buchholz und Weisswange, 1934.

Soyfer, Valery N. *Rudá biologie: pseudověda v SSSR.* Translated by Klára Hladilová. Stilus: Brno, 2005.
>   Russian: Валерий Сойфер, *Красная биология: Псевдонаука в СССР*. 2nd edition. Flinta: Moskva, 1998.

Stalin, Joseph V. *Marxism and Problems of Linguistics.* Moscow: Foreign Languages Publishing House, 1955.

Tlustý, Jan. "Contemplating literature with Jan Patočka: phenomenology as an inspiration for literary studies." *Bohemica litteraria* 23, no. 2 (2020): 81–98.

Whitehead, Alfred North. *Science and the Modern World.* New York: Macmillan Company, 1925.

Zouhar, Jan. "Patočkovy máchovské studie." *Filosofický časopis* 45, no. 5 (1997): 909–16.

1.4 Selected Bibliography of Patočka's Works

1928/1 "Francouzská filozofie" (French philosophy). *Česká mysl* 24, no. 6 (1928): 564–5.

1929/2 "Listy o francouzské filozofii, I–III" (Letters on French philosophy, I–III). *Česká mysl* 25, nos 4 and 5 (1929): 294–300, 401–6; *Česká mysl* 26, no. 1 (1930): 40–56.

1930/1 "Současný stav francouzské etiky" (Contemporary French ethics). In *Přítomný stav etiky*, edited by J. B. Kozák, 109–17. Prague: Dědictví Komenského, 1930.

1931/1 "Pojem evidence a jeho význam pro noetiku" (The concept of evidence and its significance for epistemology). PhD diss., Charles University, Prague, 1931.

1932/1 "Die tschechische Philosophie seit 1918" (Czech philosophy since 1918). *Prager Rundschau* 2, no. 1 (1932): 4–24.

1932/2 "Bericht über die tschechische Literatur zur gesamten Geschichte der Philosophie (von 1922 bis 1931)" (Report on Czech literature covering the entire history of philosophy (from 1922 to 1931)). *Archiv für Geschichte der Philosophie* 41, no. 1–2 (1932): 293–312.

1933/2 "Platonism a politika" (Platonism and politics). *Česká mysl* 29, no. 3–4 (1933), 236–8.

    English: "Platonism and Politics." Translated by Eric Manton. *Report of Center for Theoretical Study*, no. CTS–96–09 (1996): 1–4. Reprinted in *Living in Problematicity*, translated by Eric Manton, 13–17. Prague: OIKOYMENH, 2007.

1934/1 "Metafysika ve XX. století" (Metaphysics in the twentieth century). In *Dvacáté století, co dalo lidstvu*, vol. 7: Z duševní dílny lidstva, 7–24. Prague: Vladimír Orel, 1934.

1934/2 "Několik poznámek k pojmům dějin a dějepisu" (A few remarks on the concepts of history and historiography). *Řád* 2, no. 3 (1934–5): 148–56.

    French: "Quelques remarques sur les concepts d'histoire et d'historiographie." Translated by Erika Abrams. *Conférencen* 14 (spring 2002): 227–45. Reprinted in Jan Patočka, *L'Europe après l'Europe*, 139–53. Lagrasse: Verdier, 2007.

    German: "Zum Begriff der Geschichte und der Geschichtsschreibung." Translated by Thomas Kletečka. In *Ketzerische Essais zur Philosophie der Geschichte und ergänzende Schriften*, edited by Klaus Nellen and Jiří Němec with an introduction by Paul Ricœur, 318–30. Stuttgart: Klett-Cotta, 1988.

1934/6 "Osmý mezinárodní filosofický kongres v Praze (2.—7. 9. 1934)" (Eighth international congress of philosophy in Prague (2–7 September 1934)). *Nové školy* 8, no. 2–3 (1934): 49–58.

    German: Partial translation: "Achter Internationaler Kongreß für Philosophie in Prag." Translated by Ludger Hagedorn. In *Jan Patočka. Texte—Dokumente—Bibliographie*, 176–87. Prague: OIKOYMENH and Freiburg/Munich: Karl Alber, 1999.

1935/1 "Několik poznámek o pojmu 'světových dějin'" (A few remarks on the concept of "world history"). *Česká mysl* 31, no. 2 (1935): 86–96.

    French: "Quelques remarques sur le concept d''histoire univerzelle'." Translated by Erika Abrams. In Jan Patočka, *L'Europe après l'Europe*, 155–71. Lagrasse: Verdier, 2007.

    German: "Zum Begriff der Weltgeschichte." Translated by Jana Stárková. In *Ketzerische Essais zur Philosophie der Geschichte und ergänzende Schriften*, edited by Klaus Nellen and Jiří Němec with an introduction by Paul Ricœur, 331–45. Stuttgart: Klett-Cotta, 1988.

1935/3 "Pražský filosofický kroužek" (The Prague philosophy circle). *Česká mysl* 31, no. 2 (1935): 123–6.

French: "Le cercle philosophique de Prague." Translated by Erika Abrams. *Cahiers philosophiques* 50 (1992): 37–40.

German: "Der Prager Philosophische Kreis." Translated by Ludger Hagedorn. In *Jan Patočka: Texte—Dokumente—Bibliographie*, 201–9. Prague: OIKOYMENH and Freiburg and Munich: Karl Alber, 1999.

1936/1 *Přirozený svět jako filosofický problém* (The natural world as a philosophical problem). Prague: Ústřední nakladatelství a knihkupectví učitelstva československého, 1936.

English: "The Natural World as a Philosophical Problem." Translated by Erika Abrams. In Jan Patočka, *The Natural World as a Philosophical Problem*, edited by Ivan Chvatík and Ľubica Učnik, 1–114. Evanston, IL: Northwestern University Press, 2016.

French: "Le monde naturel comme problème philosophique." Translated by Jaromír Daněk and Henri Declève, 1–167. New afterword: "Postface de l'auteur au 'Monde naturel comme problème philosophique,'" 168–81. In *Le monde naturel comme problème philosophique*. Phaenomenologica, vol. 68. The Hague: Martinus Nijhoff, 1976. New translation: *Le monde naturel comme problème philosophique*. Translated by Erika Abrams. Paris: Librairie Philosophique J. Vrin, 2016.

German: "Die natürliche Welt als philosophisches Problem." Translated by Eliška and Ralph Melville. In *Die natürliche Welt als philosophisches Problem*, edited by Klaus Nellen and Jiří Němec with an introduction by Ludwig Landgrebe, 23–179. Stuttgart: Klett-Cotta, 1990.

Polish: "Świat naturalny jako problem filozoficzny." Translated by Juliusz Zychowicz. In *Świat naturalny a fenomenologia*, 5–139. Cracow: Papieska akademia teologiczna, 1987.

1936/2 "Masarykovo a Husserlovo pojetí duševní krise evropského lidstva" (Masaryk's and Husserl's conception of the spiritual crisis of European humanity). *Kvart* 3, no. 2 (1936): 91–102.

English: "Spiritual Crisis of European Humanity in Husserl and Masaryk." Translated by Erazim Kohák. In *On Masaryk: Texts in English and German*, edited by Josef Novák, 97–109. Amsterdam: Rodopi, 1988. Reprinted under the title "Masaryk's and Husserl's Conception of the Spiritual Crisis of European Humanity," in *Jan Patočka: Philosophy and Selected Writings*, edited by Erazim Kohák, 145–55. Chicago: University of Chicago Press, 1989.

French: "La conception de la crise spirituelle de l'humanité européenne chez Masaryk et chez Husserl." Translated by Erika Abrams. In *La crise du sens I: Comte, Masaryk, Husserl*, 19–37. Brussels: Ousia, 1985.

German: "Masaryks und Husserls Auffassung der geistigen Krise der europäischen Menschheit." Translated by Dan Adler. In Jan Patočka, *Die Bewegung der menschlichen Existenz*, edited by Klaus Nellen, Jiří Němec, and Ilja Šrubař with an introduction by Ilja Šrubař, 455–69. Stuttgart: Klett-Cotta, 1991.

1936/3 "Der Geist und die zwei Grundschichten der Intentionalität." *Philosophia* (Belgrade) 1, no. 1 (1936): 67–76.

French: "L'esprit et les deux couches fondamentales de l'intentionnalité." Translated with notes by Erika Abrams. *Cahiers philosophiques* 50 (1992): 27–36.

1936/6 "Kapitoly ze současné filosofie" (Chapters in contemporary philosophy). *Kvart* 3, no. 3 (1936): 175–88.

1937/1 "Význam pojmu pravdy pro Rádlovu diskusi s positivismem" (The significance of the concept of truth in Rádl's debate with positivism). *Česká mysl* 33, no. 1–2 (1937): 40–54.

1937/5 "Existe-t-il un canon définitif de la vie philosophique?" (Is there such a thing as a definitive canon of philosophical life?). In *Travaux du IXe Congrès international de philosophie* (Congrès Descartes, Paris, 1.–6. 8. 1937), vol. 10: La valeur. Les normes et la réalité. Ire Partie, edited by Raymond Bayer, 186–9. Paris: Hermann, 1937.

1938/1 "Myšlenka vzdělanosti a její dnešní aktuálnost" (The idea of education and its relevance today). *Kritický měsíčník* 1, no. 6 (1938): 241–53.

    French: "L'idée de la culture et son actualité aujourd'hui." Translated by Erika Abrams. In Jan Patočka, *L'idée de l'Europe en Bohême*, edited by Erika Abrams, 175–94. Grenoble: Jérôme Millon, 1991.

    German: "Die Idee der Bildung und ihre heutige Aktualität." Translated by Ilja and Věra Šrubař. In *Schriften zur tschechischen Kultur und Geschichte*, edited by Klaus Nellen, Petr Pithart, and Miloš Pojar, 3–18. Stuttgart: Klett-Cotta, 1992.

1938/2 "O spolupráci filosofie a vědy" (On the cooperation between philosophy and science). *Česká mysl* 34, no. 3–4 (1938): 196–209.

1938/5 "Úvaha o porážce" (A reflection on defeat). *Kritický měsíčník* 1, no. 8 (1938): 380ff.

    English: "Reflection on Defeat." Translated by Eric Manton. In *Living in Problematicity*, 29–31. Prague: OIKOYMENH, 2007.

1939/1 *Česká vzdělanost v Evropě* (Czech Culture in Europe). Prague: Václav Petr, 1939.

    English: Partial translation under the title "European Culture." Translated by Paul Wilson. *Cross Currents* 3 (1984): 3–6.

    French: "La culture tchèque en Europe." Translated by Erika Abrams. In Jan Patočka, *L'idée de l'Europe en Bohême*, edited by Erika Abrams, 133–73. Grenoble: Jérôme Millon, 1991.

    German: "Die tschechische Bildung in Europa." Translated by Ilja a Věra Šrubař. In *Kunst und Zeit: Kulturphilosophischen Schriften*, edited by Klaus Nellen and Ilja Šrubař with an introduction by Walter Biemel, 351–86. Stuttgart: Klett-Cotta, 1987.

1939/2 "Životní rovnováha a životní amplituda" (Life balance and life amplitude). *Kritický měsíčník* 2, no. 3 (1939): 101–6.

    English: "Life in Balance, Life in Amplitude." Translated by Eric Manton. In *Living in Problematicity*, 32–42. Prague: OIKOYMENH, 2007.

    French: "Equilibre et amplitude dans la vie." Translated by Erika Abrams. In Jan Patočka, *Liberté et sacrifice*, edited by Erika Abrams, 27–39. Grenoble: Jérôme Millon, 1990.

    Hungarian: "Az élet egyensúlya és amplitúdója." Translated by István Németh. In *Mi a cseh?*, edited by Ivan Chvatík with a foreword by Petr Pithart and an afterword by Mihály Vajda, 27–36. Pozsony and Bratislava: Kalligram, 1996.

    German: "Leben im Gleichgewicht, Leben in der Amplitude." Translated by Ludger Hagedorn. In *Jan Patočka: Texte—Dokumente—Bibliographie*, 91–102. Prague: OIKOYMENH and Freiburg and Munich: Karl Alber, 1999.

Spanish: "Vida en eguilibrio y vida en la amplitud." Translated by Iván Ortega Rodríguez. In Jan Patočka, *Libertad y sacrificio*, 33–45. Salamanca: Ediciones Sígueme, 2007.

1939/4 "Husserl—Bibliographie" (Husserl: a bibliography). *Revue internationale de philosophie* 1, no. 2 (1939): 374–97.

1940/1 "O filosofii dějin" (On the philosophy of history). *Kritický měsíčník* 3, no. 5–6 (1940): 217–23.

    French: "Sur la philosophie de l'histoire." Translated by Erika Abrams. In Jan Patočka, *L'Europe après l'Europe*, 173–86. Lagrasse: Verdier, 2007.

    German: "Zur Philosophie der Geschichte." Translated by Ludger Hagedorn. In *Andere Wege in die Moderne: Studien zur europäischen Ideengeschichte von der Renaissance bis zur Romantik*, 81–91. Würzburg: Königshausen & Neumann; Prague: OIKOYMENH, 2006.

1941/2 "O nový pohled na Komenského" (A new look at Comenius). *Kritický měsíčník* 4, no. 5–6 (1941): 222–31.

    German: "Ein neuer Blick auf Comenius." Translated by Ludger Hagedorn. In *Andere Wege in die Moderne: Studien zur europäischen Ideengeschichte von der Renaissance bis zur Romantik*, 295–306. Würzburg: Königshausen & Neumann; Prague: OIKOYMENH, 2006.

1941/5 "J. G. Herder a jeho filosofie humanity" (J. G. Herder and his philosophy of humanity). In J. G. Herder, *Vývoj lidskosti,* trans. Jan Patočka, 451–63. Prague: Jan Laichter, 1941.

    French: "J. G. Herder et sa philosophie de l'humanité." Translated by Erika Abrams. In *Lumières et romantisme: Annales de l'Institut de Philosophie de l'Université de Bruxelles*, edited by Gilbert Hottois, 17–26. Paris: J. Vrin, 1989.

    German: "Johann Gottfried Herder und seine Philosophie der Humanität." Translated by Ludger Hagedorn. In *Andere Wege in die Moderne: Studien zur europäischen Ideengeschichte von der Renaissance bis zur Romantik*, 409–19. Würzburg: Königshausen & Neumann; Prague: OIKOYMENH, 2006.

1942/1 "Dvojí rozum a příroda v německém osvícenství. Herderovská studie" (Dual reason and nature in the German enlightenment. A Herderian study). *Svazky úvah a studií*, vol. 70. Prague: Václav Petr, 1942.

    English: "Two Senses of Reason and Nature in the German Enlightenment: A Herderian Study." Translated by Erazim Kohák. In *Jan Patočka: Philosophy and Selected Writings*, edited by Erazim Kohák, 157–74. Chicago: University of Chicago Press, 1989.

    German: "Zweierlei Vernunft und Natur in der deutschen Auklärung." Translated by Ludger Hagedorn. In *Andere Wege in die Moderne: Studien zur europäischen Ideengeschichte von der Renaissance bis zur Romantik*, 387–407. Würzburg: Königshausen & Neumann; Prague: OIKOYMENH, 2006.

1942/2 "Světový názor, obraz světa, filosofie" (World view, world picture, philosophy). *Kritický měsíčník* 5, no. 3 (1942): 79–87.

1942/4 "Dějepis filosofie a její jednota" (The history of philosophy and its unity). *Česká mysl* 36, nos 2 and 3 (1942): 58–72 and 97–114.

1944/1 *Symbol země u K. H. Máchy* (The symbol of the earth in K. H. Mácha). Prague: Václav Petr, 1944.

French: "Le symbole de la terre chez Karel Hynek Mácha." Translated by Erika Abrams. In Jan Patočka, *L'écrivain, son "objet,"* edited by Erika Abrams, 195–231. Paris: P.O.L., 1990; 2nd edition: Paris: Presses Pocket, 1992.

German: "Das Symbol der Erde bei Karel Hynek Mácha." Translated by Ilja and Věra Šrubař. In *Kunst und Zeit: Kulturphilosophischen Schriften*, edited by Klaus Nellen and Ilja Šrubař with an introduction by Walter Biemel, 387–410. Stuttgart: Klett-Cotta, 1987.

1946/1 *Praesokratovská filosofie* (Pre-Socratic philosophy). Prague: Akční výbor posluchačů filosofie na Karlově universitě, 1946.

1946/3 "Masaryk včera a dnes" (Masaryk yesterday and today). *Naše doba* 52, no. 7 (1946): 302–11.

French: "Masaryk hier et aujourd'hui." Translated by Erika Abrams. In *La crise du sens I: Comte, Masaryk, Husserl*, 46–62. Brussels: Ousia, 1985.

German: "Masaryk gestern und heute." Translated by Pavel Ambros. In *Schriften zur tschechischen Kultur und Geschichte*, edited by Klaus Nellen, Petr Pithart, and Miloš Pojar, 245–57. Stuttgart: Klett-Cotta, 1992.

1946/4 "Ideologie a život v ideji" (Ideology and life in the idea). *Kritický měsíčník* 7, no. 1–2 (1946): 8–14.

English: "Ideology and Life in the Idea." Translated by Eric Manton. In *Living in Problematicity*, 43–50. Prague: OIKOYMENH, 2007.

French: "L'idéologie et la vie dans l'idée." Translated by Erika Abrams. *Critique* (Paris) 43, no. 483–4 (1987): 813–20.

German: "Ideologie und Leben in der Idee." Translated by Ilja Šrubař. In *Ketzerische Essais zur Philosophie der Geschichte und ergänzende Schriften*, edited by Klaus Nellen and Jiří Němec with an introduction by Paul Ricœur, 379–88. Stuttgart: Klett-Cotta, 1988.

Spanish: "La ideología y la vida en la idea." Translated by Iván Ortega Rodríguez. In Jan Patočka, *Libertad y sacrificio*, 44–56. Salamanca: Ediciones Sígueme, 2007.

1947/1 "Sokrates" (Socrates). Prague: Spolek posluchačů filosofie, 1947.

French: *Socrate*. Translated by Erika Abrams. Fribourg: Academic Press Fribourg Suisse, 2017.

Italian: "Socrate." Translated by Martin Cajthaml. In Jan Patočka, *Socrate, testo ceco a fronte*. Santarcangelo di Romagna: Rusconi, 1999. 2nd edition: *Socrate, testo ceco a fronte*. Milan: Bompiani, 2003.

Persian: Partial translation under the title *Soghrat: Agahi az jahl*. Selected and translated by Mahmoud Ebadian. Teheran: Hermes, 1999.

1948/1 *Platon* (Plato). Prague: Karlova universita, 1948.

1948/3 "La philosophie en Tchécoslovaquie et son orientation actuelle" (Philosophy in Czechoslovakia and its current orientation). *Les études philosophiques*, new series, 3, no. 1 (1948): 63–74.

Czech: "Filosofie v Československu a její současná orientace." Translated by Filip Karfík. In Jan Patočka, *Češi I*, 706–18. Prague: OIKOYMENH, 2006.

1949/1 *Aristoteles* (Aristotle). Prague: Karlova universita, 1949.

1949/3 "Remarques sur le problème de Socrate" (Remarks on the problem of Socrates). *Revue philosophique de la France et de l' étranger* 74, no. 4–6 (1949): 186–213.

1950/1 "Josef Čapek: myslitel" (Josef Čapek: thinker). Lecture delivered to Čapek Brothers' Society in commemoration of the fifth anniversary of Josef Čapek's death in a concentration camp, Prague, March 22, 1950. An expanded and modified version of this paper was given at the Society of the Čapek Brothers on March 25, 1953 under the title "Ethos a tragika cesty Kulhavého poutníka" (Ethos and the Tragedy of the Lame Pilgrim's Journey). This second version was published in the magazine *Tvář* 1 no. 9–10 (1964) under the title "Kulhavý poutník Josef Čapek" and is translated in this volume.

1952/1 "Čas, mythus, víra" (Time, myth, faith). *Křesťanská revue* 19, no. 3–4 (1952): 112–16.

    English: "Time, Myth, Faith." Translated by Ludger Hagedorn. In *The New Yearbook for Phenomenology and Phenomenological Philosophy: Volume 14, Special Issue: The Philosophy of Jan Patočka*, edited by Ludger Hagedorn and James Dodd, 3–12. Routledge: London, 2015.

    Bulgarian: "Vremje, mit, vjara." Translated by Margarita Kostadinova. *Jezik i literatura* (Sofia) 49, no. 3 (1994): 14–17.

    French: "Le temps, le mythe, la foi." Translated by Erika Abrams. In Jan Patočka, *L'art et le temps*, edited and translated by Erika Abrams, 27–46. Paris: P.O.L., 1990.

    German: "Zeit, Mythos und Glaube." Translated by Ilja and Věra Šrubař. In *Kunst und Zeit: Kulturphilosophischen Schriften*, edited by Klaus Nellen and Ilja Šrubař with an introduction by Walter Biemel, 70–84. Stuttgart: Klett-Cotta, 1987.

1952/3 "Jan Amos Komenský" (John Amos Comenius). *Přednášky Čs. společnosti pro šíření politických a vědeckých znalostí, ústřední sekce: Pedagogika—psychologie* 1 (1952).

1953/1 "Dvojí filosofování mladého Komenského" (The dual philosophizing of the young Comenius). *Křesťanská revue* 20, no. 8–10. Theological supplement no. 4–5 (1953): 123–33.

1953/2 "Aristotelova filosofická přírodověda" (Aristotle's philosophical natural science). *Vesmír* 32, no. 3 (1953): 102–5.

1953/3 "První kritikové aristotelismu" (The first critics of Aristotelianism). *Vesmír* 32, no. 7 (1953): 254–6.

    German: "Die ersten Kritiker der Aristotelismus." Translated by Ludger Hagedorn. In *Andere Wege in die Moderne: Studien zur europäischen Ideengeschichte von der Renaissance bis zur Romantik*, 211–23. Würzburg: Königshausen & Neumann; Prague: OIKOYMENH, 2006.

1953/4 "Rozklad Aristotelovy dynamiky a předehra moderního mechanismu" (The decline of Aristotle's dynamics and the prologue to modern mechanism). *Vesmír* 32, no. 8 (1953): 285–7.

    German: "Zerfall der Aristotelischen Dynamik und Vorspiel des modernen mechanistischen Weltbildes." Translated by Ludger Hagedorn. In *Andere Wege in die Moderne: Studien zur europäischen Ideengeschichte von der Renaissance bis zur Romantik*, 225–35. Würzburg: Königshausen & Neumann; Prague: OIKOYMENH, 2006.

1953/5 "Mezihra na prahu moderní vědy: Cusanus a Komenský" (Interlude on the threshold of modern science: Cusanus and Comenius). *Vesmír* 32, no. 9 (1953): 322–5.

1954/1 "Cusanus a Komenský" (Cusanus and Comenius). *Pedagogika* 4, no. 7 (1954): 508–23.

1954/2 "Galileo Galilei a konec starověkého kosmu" (Galileo and the end of the ancient cosmos). *Vesmír* 33, no. 1 (1954): 27–9.

German: "Galileo Galilei und das Ende des antiken Kosmos." Translated by
Sandra Lehmann. In *Andere Wege in die Moderne: Studien zur europäischen
Ideengeschichte von der Renaissance bis zur Romantik*, 245–56. Würzburg:
Königshausen & Neumann; Prague: OIKOYMENH, 2006.

1956/1 "Filosofie dějin v Palackého Krásovědě" (The philosophy of history in
Palacký's Aesthetics). *Křesťanská revue* 23, no. 3 (1956): 86–91.

German: "Die Geschichtsphilosophie in Palackýs 'Wissenschaft vom Schönen.'"
Translated by Pavel Ambros. In *Schriften zur tschechischen Kultur und
Geschichte*, edited by Klaus Nellen, Petr Pithart, and Miloš Pojar, 199–210.
Stuttgart: Klett-Cotta, 1992.

1956/2 "Idea božnosti v Palackého Krásovědě" (The idea of sacredness in Palacký's
Aesthetics). *Křesťanská revue* 23, no. 4 (1956): 118–23.

German: "Die Idee des Göttlichen in Palackýs 'Wissenschaft vom Schönen'."
Translated by Pavel Ambros. In *Schriften zur tschechischen Kultur und
Geschichte*, edited by Klaus Nellen, Petr Pithart, and Miloš Pojar, 211–22.
Stuttgart: Klett-Cotta, 1992.

1956/3 "Komenský a hlavní filosofické myšlenky 17. století" (Comenius and the
main philosophical ideas of the 17th century). *Vesmír* 35, no. 10 (1956): 346–50.

1956/4 "Bacon Verulamský a Komenského Didaktika" (Bacon of Verulam and
Comenius's Didactics). *Pedagogika* 6, no. 2 (1956): 207–12.

German: "Francis Bacon und die Didaktik des Comenius." Translated by Ludger
Hagedorn. In *Andere Wege in die Moderne: Studien zur europäischen
Ideengeschichte von der Renaissance bis zur Romantik*, 321–9. Würzburg:
Königshausen & Neumann; Prague: OIKOYMENH, 2006.

1956/5 "Náčrt Komenského díla ve světle nových objevů" (A sketch of Comenius's
work in the light of new discoveries). *Pedagogika* 6, no. 4 (1956): 411–26.

1957/2 "Základní filosofické myšlenky J. A. Komenského v souvislosti se základy
jeho soustavného vychovatelství" (The basic philosophical ideas of J. A.
Comenius in relation to the fundaments of his systematic pedagogy). In Jaromír
Kopecký, Jiří Kyrášek, and Jan Patočka, *J. A. Komenský. Nástin života a díla*,
93–128. Prague: Státní pedagogické nakladatelství, 1957.

1957/3 "Některé z dnešních úkolů bádání o Komenském" (Some of the present-
day tasks for research on Comenius). *Archiv pro bádání o životě a díle J. A.
Komenského* 16, no. 1 (1957): 18–25.

1957/4 "Filosofické základy Komenského pedagogiky" (The philosophical
foundations of Comenius's pedagogy). *Pedagogika* 7, no. 2 (1957): 137–77.

1958/1 "O Hegelově pojetí zkušenosti" (On Hegel's conception of experience).
Křesťanská revue 25, no. 6. Theological supplement 3 (1958): 73–7.

1958/2 "Bolzanovo místo v dějinách filosofie" (Bolzano's place in the history of
philosophy). In *Filosofie v dějinách českého národa: Protokol celostátní
konference o dějinách české filosofie v Liblicích ve dnech 14.–17. 4. 1958*, edited
by Jiřina PopelováOtáhalová and Karel Kosík, 111–23. Prague: Československá
akademie věd, 1958.

German: "Bolzanos Platz in der Philosophiegeschichte." Translated by Ludger
Hagedorn. In *Andere Wege in die Moderne: Studien zur europäischen
Ideengeschichte von der Renaissance bis zur Romantik*, 445–64. Würzburg:
Königshausen & Neumann; Prague: OIKOYMENH, 2006.

Polish: "Bolzano a problem teorii nauki." Translated by Tadeusz Kroński. *Studia
filozoficzne* (Warsaw) 6, no. 9 (1958): 170–86.

1959/1 "L'état présent des études coméniennes" (The present state of Comenius studies). In *Historica I*, 197–240. Prague: Československá akademie věd, 1959.

1960/1 "Vývoj pedagogického myšlení Komenského ve všenápravném období" (The development of Comenius's thinking in his panorthotic period). *Archiv pro bádání o životě a díle J. A. Komenského* 19, no. 1 (1960): 166–184. Special supplement: Nationum conciliatarum provisoris memoriae: Materialen einer komeniologischen Konferenz, Prague, September 1957.

1961/1 "L'idée d'espace depuis Aristote jusqu'à Leibniz" (The idea of space, from Aristotle to Leibniz). *Sborník prací filosofické fakulty Brněnské university, Řada uměnovědná* 10, no. 5 (1961): 23–41.

1961/2 "Cesta světla—předosvícenská brána k osvícenským ideálům" (The way of light: pre-Enlightenment gateway to Enlightenment ideals). In *J. A. Komenský: Cesta světla dosud vyhledaná a i nadále vyhledávaná—Via lucis vestigata et vestiganda*, edited, translated, and afterword by Jaromír Kopecký, Jiří Kyrášek, Jan Patočka, and Jiřina PopelováOtáhalová, 287–307. Prague: Státní pedagogické nakladatelství, 1961.

1961/3 "O významu Francise Bacona z Verulamu" (On the significance of Francis Bacon of Verulam). *Vesmír* 40, nos 5 and 6 (1961): 152–5 and 186–8.

1962/1 "Z osudů Komenského Opus grande" (The fortunes of Comenius's Opus grande). *Křesťanská revue* 29, no. 4. Theological supplement 2 (1962): 59–64.

1963/1 "J.-J. Rousseau" (Jean-Jacques Rousseau). *Acta Universitatis Carolinae: Philosophica et historica* 2 (1963): 59–67.

German: "Jean-Jacques Rousseau." Translated by Sandra Lehmann. In *Andere Wege in die Moderne: Studien zur europäischen Ideengeschichte von der Renaissance bis zur Romantik*, 353–64. Würzburg: Königshausen & Neumann; Prague: OIKOYMENH, 2006.

1963/2 "Bernard Bolzano." In *Antologie z dějin československé filosofie*, vol. 1, edited by Robert Kalivoda and Josef Zumr, 365–73. Prague: Nakladatelství ČSAV, 1963.

1964/1 "Aristoteles, jeho předchůdci a dědicové" (Aristotle, his predecessors and his heirs). In Jan Patočka, *Studie z dějin filosofie od Aristotela k Hegelovi*. Prague: Nakladatelství ČSAV, 1964.

1964/4 "Zur Entwicklung der ästhetischen Auffassung Hegels" (On the development of Hegel's aesthetic conception). In *Hegel-Jahrbuch*, edited by Wilhelm Raimund Beyer, 49–59. Meisenheim am Glan: Anton Hain, 1964.

1965/1 "Die Lehre von der Vergangenheit der Kunst" (The theory of the past character of art). In *Beispiele: Festschrift für E. Fink zum 60. Geburtstag*, edited by Ludwig Landgrebe, 46–61. The Hague: Martinus Nijhoff, 1965.

French: "La théorie de l'art comme chose du passé." Translated by Erika Abrams. In Jan Patočka, *L'art et le temps*, edited and translated by Erika Abrams, 305–43. Paris: P.O.L., 1990.

Hungarian: "A művészet múlttá válásának tana." Translated by Mária Hegyessy. *Gond* (Budapest), no. 13–14 (1997): 21–33.

1965/2 "O Burckhardtově pojetí renesance" (On Burckhardt's conception of the Renaissance). *Dějiny a současnost* 7, nos 4 and 5 (1965): 4–8 and 23–7.

French: "La conception de la Renaissance chez Burckhardt." Translated by Erika Abrams. In Jan Patočka, *L'art et le temps*, edited and translated by Erika Abrams, 104–27. Paris: P.O.L., 1990.

German: "Zu Burckhardts Auffassung der Renaissance." Translated by Ilja and Věra Šrubař. In *Kunst und Zeit: Kulturphilosophischen Schriften*, edited by Klaus Nellen and Ilja Šrubař with an introduction by Walter Biemel, 157–74. Stuttgart: Klett-Cotta, 1987.

1965/6 "Úvod do Husserlovy fenomenologie" (An introduction to Husserl's phenomenology). *Filosofický časopis* 13, nos. 5 and 6 (1965): 693–701 and 821–49; *Filosofický časopis* 14, nos. 1, 3, 5 (1966): 1–21, 289–305, 569–89.

English: *An Introduction to Husserl's Phenomenology*. Translated by Erazim Kohák. Edited with an introduction by James Dodd. Chicago: Open Court, 1996.

French: *Introduction à la phénoménologie de Husserl*. Translated by Erika Abrams. Grenoble: Jérôme Millon, 1992.

Italian: "La fenomenologia come filosofia e il suo rapporto con le tendenze storiche della metafisica." In Jan Patočka, *Che cos'è la fenomenologia? Movimento, mondo, corpo*. Verona: Edizioni Fondazione Centro Studi Campostrini, 2009.

German: "Einführung in die Phänomenologie Husserls." Translated by Peter Sacher. In Jan Patočka, *Die Bewegung der menschlichen Existenz*, edited by Klaus Nellen, Jiří Němec, and Ilja Šrubař with an introduction by Ilja Šrubař, 144–62. Stuttgart: Klett-Cotta, 1991.

1965/7 "K prehistorii vědy o pohybu: svět, země, nebe a pohyb lidského života" (On the prehistory of the science of movement: World, earth, heaven, and the movement of human life). *Tvář* 2, no. 10 (1965): 1–5.

English: "On the Prehistory of the Science of Movement: World, Earth, Heaven and the Movement of Human Life." Translated by Erika Abrams. In *Dis-orientations: Philosophy, Literature and the Lost Grounds of Modernity*, 65–73. London and New York: Rowman & Littlefield International, 2014.

French: "Notes sur la préhistoire de la science du mouvement: le monde, la terre, le ciel et le mouvement de la vie humaine." Translated by Erika Abrams. In Jan Patočka, *Le monde naturel et le mouvement de l'existence humaine*, edited by Erika Abrams, 3–12. Dordrecht: Kluwer Academic Publishers, 1988.

Italian: "Per una preistoria della scienza del movimento: il mondo, la terra, il cielo e il movimento della vita umana." Translated by Gianlorenzo Pacini, revised by Alessandra Pantano, 63–75. In Jan Patočka, *Che cos'è la fenomenologia? Movimento, mondo, corpo*. Verona: Edizioni Fondazione Centro Studi Campostrini, 2009.

German: "Zur Vorgeschichte der Wissenschaft von der Bewegung: Welt, Erde, Himmel und die Bewegung des menschlichen Lebens." Translated by Simona Löwenstein. In Jan Patočka, *Die Bewegung der menschlichen Existenz*, edited by Klaus Nellen, Jiří Němec, and Ilja Šrubař with an introduction by Ilja Šrubař, 132–43. Stuttgart: Klett-Cotta, 1991.

Spanish: "Notas sobre la prehistoria de la ciencia del movimiento: el mundo, la tierra, el cielo y el movimiento de la vida humna." Translated from the French by Diana H. Maffía. *Intentum: Cuadernos de gnoseología* (Buenos Aires) 2 (1996): 21–37.

1965/9 "K vývoji Hegelových estetických názorů" (On the development of Hegel's aesthetic views). *Filosofický časopis* 13, no. 2 (1965): 382–6.

1966/1 "Komenského názory a pansofické literární plány od spisů útěšných ke 'Všeobecné poradě'" (Comenius's views and pansophic literary plans, from his consoling writings to the "General Council"). In *Orbis scriptus: Festschrift für D. Čyževskij zum 70. Geburtstag*, edited by Dietrich Gerhardt, Wiktor Weintraub, and Hans-Jürgen zum Winkel, 593–620. Munich: Wilhelm Fink, 1966.

1967/1 "Čas, věčnost a časovost v Máchově díle" (Time, eternity, and temporality in the work of Mácha). In Jan Patočka, *Realita slova Máchova*, edited by Růžena Grebeníčková and Oldřich Králík, 183–207. Prague: Československý spisovatel, 1967.

    French: "Temps, éternité et temporalité dans l'oeuvre de Mácha." Translated by Erika Abrams. In Jan Patočka, *L'écrivain, son "objet"*, edited by Erika Abrams, 232–82. Paris: P.O.L., 1990. (Translation also includes, under the title Annexe, a new variant of part III of the essay.) 2nd edition: Paris: Presses Pocket, 1992.

    Hungarian: "Az idő, az örökkévalóság és az időbeliség Mácha műveiben." Translated by Róbert Kiss Szemán. In *Mi a cseh?*, edited by Ivan Chvatík with a foreword by Petr Pithart and an afterword by Mihály Vajda, 111–38. Pozsony/Bratislava: Kalligram, 1996.

    German: "Zeit, Ewigkeit und Zeitlichkeit in Máchas Werk." Translated by Frank Boldt. In *Kunst und Zeit: Kulturphilosophischen Schriften*, edited by Klaus Nellen and Ilja Šrubař with an introduction by Walter Biemel, 411–43. Stuttgart: Klett-Cotta, 1987.

1967/2 "Prirodzený svet a fenomenológia" (The natural world and phenomenology). Translated by Ján Bodnár. In Jan Patočka, *Existencializmus a fenomenológia*, edited by Ján Bodnár, 27–71. Bratislava: Obzor, 1967.

1967/5 "Roman Ingarden. Pokus charakteristiky filosofické osobnosti a díla" (Roman Ingarden. An attempted characterization of the person and his work). In Roman Ingarden, *O poznávání literárního díla*, 261–76. Prague: Československý spisovatel, 1967.

    German: "Roman Ingarden. Persönlichkeit und Werk." Translated by Ludger Hagedorn. In *Jan Patočka: Texte—Dokumente—Bibliographie*, 314–34. Prague: OIKOYMENH and Freiburg and Munich: Karl Alber, 1999.

1967/6 "Slova a věci: Rozbor antropologiocké epochy evropského myšlení v 'Archeologii' Michela Foucaulta (Words and things: An analysis of the anthropological epoch of European thinking in Michel Foucault's "Archeology"). *Světová literatura* 12, no. 6 (1967): 229–34.

    German: "'Die Wörter und die Dinge': Eine Analyse der anthropologischen Epoche des europäischen Denkens in Michel Foucaults 'Archäologie'." Translated by E. H. Plattner. In *Kunst und Zeit: Kulturphilosophischen Schriften*, edited by Klaus Nellen and Ilja Šrubař with an introduction by Walter Biemel, 542–55. Stuttgart: Klett-Cotta, 1987.

1968/3 "Husserlův pojem názoru a prafenomén jazyka" (Husserl's concept of intuition and the ur-phenomenon of language). *Slovo a slovesnost* 29, no. 1 (1968): 17–22.

    German: "Husserls Anschauungsbegriff und das Urphänomen der Sprache." Translated by Susanna Roth. In Jan Patočka, *Die Bewegung der menschlichen Existenz*, edited by Klaus Nellen, Jiří Němec, and Ilja Šrubař with an introduction by Ilja Šrubař, 535–44. Stuttgart: Klett-Cotta, 1991.

1968/4 "O principu vědeckého svědomí" (On the principle of scientific conscience). *Literární listy* 1, no. 18 (1968): 3.
  English: "On the Principle of Scientific Conscience." Translated by Karel Kovanda. *Telos* 18 (1973–4): 158–61.
  Italian: "I principi della coscienza scientifica." In *La scienza assediata: Libertà della ricerca scientifica nell'Europa dell'Est*, 11–15. Venice: Marsilio, 1977. Previous translation: "Del principio della morale scientifica." Translated by Gianlorenzo Pacini. In *Il senso dell'oggi in Cecoslovacchia*, 21–6. Milan: Lampugnani Nigri, 1970.
  Hungarian: "A tudományos lelkiismeret elve." Translated by István Németh. In *A jelenkor értelme. Kilenc fejezet egyetemes és cseh problémákról*, 30–6. Bratislava: Kalligram, 1999.
  German: "Das Prinzip des Gewissens in der Wissenschaft." Translated by Dorothea Neumärker. In *Nachrichten aus der ČSSR*, edited by Josef Škvorecký, 85–90. Frankfurt am Main: Suhrkamp, 1968.
  Spanish: "Acerca del principio de la conciencia científica." Translated by Fernando de Valenzuela. In *Los intelectuales ante la nueva sociedad*, 41–7. Madrid: AKAL, 1976.
1968/5 "L'art et le temps." In *Kunst und Erziehung: Bericht über den 18. Kongreß der INSEA, Praha 1966*, 105–13. Prague: Státní pedagogické nakladatelství, 1968. Presented at 18th INSEA (International Society for Education Through Art) World Congress, Prague, August 4, 1966.
  Hungarian: "Művészet és idő." Translated by V. Horváth Károly. *Gond* (Budapest), no. 13–14 (1997): 34–48.
  German: "Kunst und Zeit." Translated by Frank Boldt. *Postylla Bohemica* (Bremen) 4, no. 13–14 (1976): 3–26. New translation: "Kunst und Zeit. Erziehung zum Kunstverständnis in unserer Zeit." Translated by Ilja and Věra Šrubař. In *Kunst und Zeit: Kulturphilosophischen Schriften*, edited by Klaus Nellen and Ilja Šrubař with an introduction by Walter Biemel, 49–69. Stuttgart: Klett-Cotta, 1987.
1968/6 "Die Kritik des psychologischen Objektivismus und das Problem der phänomenologischen Psychologie bei Sartre und Merleau-Ponty" (The critique of psychological objectivism and the problem of phenomenological psychology in Sartre and Merleau-Ponty). In *Akten des XIV. Internationalen Kongresses für Philosophie, Wien, 2.—9. September 1968*, vol. 2, 175–84. Vienna: Herder, 1968.
  French: "La critique de l'objectivisme et le problème de la psychologie phénoménologique chez Sartre et Merleau-Ponty." Translated from the German by Gudrun and Youri Boisselet and Philippe Merlier. *Les Temps Modernes* 55, no. 608 (2000): 223–34.
1968/7 "Max Scheler: Pokus celkové charakteristiky" (Max Scheler: An attempt at an overall characterization). Foreword to Max Scheler, *Místo člověka v kosmu* (*Die Stellung des Menschen im Kosmos*. Translated by Anna Jourisová, 5–41. Munich: Nymphenburger Verlagshandlung, 1928; Prague: Academia, 1968. Reprinted in Jan Patočka, *Fenomenologické spisy II*, 561–97. Prague: OIKOYMENH, 2009.
  German: "Max Scheler: Versuch einer Gesamtcharakteristik." Translated by Ludger Hagedorn. In *Jan Patočka: Texte—Dokumente—Bibliographie*, 338–382. Prague: OIKOYMENH and Freiburg/Munich: Karl Alber, 1999.

1968/8 "Profesor L. Landgrebe a jeho Filosofie přítomnosti" (Professor L.
    Landgrebe and his Philosophy of the present). In Ludwig Landgrebe, *Filosofie
    přítomnosti*, 5–10. Prague: Academia, 1968.
    German: "Ludwig Landgrebe und seine 'Philosophie der Gegenwart'."
        Translated by Ludger Hagedorn. In *Jan Patočka: Texte—Dokumente—
        Bibliographie*, 390–6. Prague: OIKOYMENH and Freiburg and Munich:
        Karl Alber, 1999.
1968/9 "Husserlova fenomenologie, fenomenologická filosofie a 'Karteziánské
    meditace'" (Husserl's phenomenology, phenomenological philosophy, and the
    "Cartesian meditations"). In Edmund Husserl, *Karteziánské meditace*,
    translated by Marie Bayerová, 161–90. Prague: Svoboda, 1968.
    French: "La phénoménologie, la philosophie phénoménologique et les
        Méditations cartésiennes de Husserl." Translated by Erika Abrams. In Jan
        Patočka, *Qu'est-ce que la phénoménologie?*, edited by Erika Abrams,
        149–88. Grenoble: Jérôme Millon, 1988.
    German: "Husserls Phänomenologie, die phänomenologische Philosophie und
        die 'Cartesianischen Meditationen'." Translated by Peter Sacher. In Jan
        Patočka, *Die Bewegung der menschlichen Existenz*, edited by Klaus Nellen,
        Jiří Němec, and Ilja Šrubař with an introduction by Ilja Šrubař, 163–81.
        Stuttgart: Klett-Cotta, 1991.
1968/13 "Reflexions sur la relation entre science et morale traditionelle"
    (Reflections on the relation between science and traditional morality). *Journées
    d'études* 58 (November 1968): 109–17.
1969/1 "Dilema v našem národním programu: Jungmann a Bolzano" (The dilemma
    in our national program: Jungmann and Bolzano). *Divadlo* 20, no. 1 (1969): 1–8.
    Italian: "Il dilemma del nostro programma nazionale: Jungmann e Bolzano."
        Translated by Gianlorenzo Pacini. In *Il senso dell'oggi in Cecoslovacchia*,
        77–92. Milan: Lampugnani Nigri, 1970.
    Hungarian: "Nemzeti programunk dilemmája: Jungmann és Bolzano."
        Translated by István Németh. In *A jelenkor értelme: Kilenc fejezet egyetemes
        és cseh problémákról*, 96–114. Bratislava: Kalligram, 1999.
    German: "Das Dilemma in unserem Nationalprogramm: Jungmann und
        Bolzano." Translated by Pavel Ambros. In *Schriften zur tschechischen Kultur
        und Geschichte*, edited by Klaus Nellen, Petr Pithart, and Miloš Pojar,
        223–36. Stuttgart: Klett-Cotta, 1992.
1969/2 *O smysl dneška: Devět kapitol o problémech světových i českých* (On the
    meaning of today: Nine chapters on world and Czech problems). Afterword by
    Josef Zumr. Prague: Mladá fronta, 1969.
    Italian: "Il senso dell'oggi in Cecoslovacchia." Translated by Gianlorenzo Pacini.
        Milan: Lampugnani Nigri, 1970.
    Hungarian: *A jelenkor értelme: Kilenc fejezet egyetemes és cseh problémákról*.
        Translated by István Németh. Bratislava: Kalligram, 1999.
    Spanish: Partial translation: *Los intelectuales ante la nueva sociedad*. Translated
        by Fernando de Valenzuela, foreword by Carlos París. Madrid: AKAL, 1976.
1969/11 "Filosofie českých dějin" (Philosophy of Czech history). *Sociologický
    časopis* 5, no. 5 (1969): 457–72.
    French: "La philosophie de l'histoire tchèque." Translated by Erika Abrams. In
        Jan Patočka, *L'idée de l'Europe en Bohême*, edited by Erika Abrams, 115–32.
        Grenoble: Jérôme Millon, 1991.

German: "Die Philosophie der tschechischen Geschichte." Translated by
Gerhart Höfflin. *Postylla Bohemica* (Bremen) 1, no. 1 (1972): 8–18.
Reprinted in *Schriften zur tschechischen Kultur und Geschichte*, edited by
Klaus Nellen, Petr Pithart, and Miloš Pojar, 107–21. Stuttgart: Klett-Cotta,
1992.

1970/2 "O filosofii J. A. Komenského" (On the philosophy of J. A. Comenius).
Slavia 39, no. 4 (1970): 489–511.
German: "Die Philosophie der Erziehung des J. A. Comenius." Paderborn:
Ferdinand Schöningh, 1971.

1970/3 "Comenius und die offene Seele" (Comenius and the open soul). In *Jan
Amos Komenský: Wirkung eines Werkes nach drei Jahrhunderten*, edited by
Klaus Schaller, 61–74. Heidelberg: Quelle & Meyer, 1970.
French: "Comenius et l'âme ouverte." Translated by Erika Abrams. In Jan
Patočka, *L'écrivain, son "objet,"* edited by Erika Abrams, 101–27. Paris:
P.O.L., 1990. 2nd edition: Paris: Presses Pocket, 1992.
Italian: "Comenio e l'anima aperta." Translated by Martin Švehlík. *Vita e
pensiero* (Milan) 74, no. 3 (1991): 126–40.
Hungarian: "Comenius és a nyitott lélek." Translated by István Németh. In *Mi a
cseh?*, edited by Ivan Chvatík with a foreword by Petr Pithart and an
afterword by Mihály Vajda, 139–53. Pozsony and Bratislava: Kalligram,
1996.

1970/4 "Betrachtungen über die 'Pambiblia' des J. A. Comenius" (Reflections on
the "Pambiblia" of J. A. Comenius). *Pädagogische Rundschau* 24, no. 12 (1970):
887–902.

1970/5 "De la relation entre la science et la morale traditionelle" (On the relation
between science and traditional morality). *Revue Universitaire de Science
Morale* (Geneva) 15 (1970): 141–50.

1970/6 "Der Subjektivismus der Husserlschen und die Möglichkeit einer
'asubjektiven' Phänomenologie" (Husserlian subjectivism and the possibility of
an "asubjective" phenomenology). In *Philosophische Perspektiven, ein Jahrbuch*,
vol. 2, edited by Rudolph Berlinger and Eugen Fink, 317–34. Frankfurt am
Main: Vittorio Klostermann, 1970.
Chinese: Translated by KwokYing Lau. In 面对实事本身： 现象学经典文学 (To
the Things Themselves: Selected Classical Essays in Phenomenology), edited
by Ni Liangkang, 690–709. Beijing: Eastern Press, 2000.
French: "Le subjectivisme de la phénoménologie husserlienne et la possibilité
d'une phénoménologie 'asubjective'." Translated by Erika Abrams. In Jan
Patočka, *Qu'est-ce que la phénoménologie?*, edited by Erika Abrams,
189–215. Grenoble: Jérôme Millon, 1988.
Italian: "Il soggettivismo della fenomenologia husserliana e la possibilità di una
fenomenologia 'asoggettiva'." Translated by Giuseppe Di Salvatore. In Jan
Patočka, *Che cos'è la fenomenologia? Movimento, mondo, corpo*, 261–83.
Verona: Edizioni Fondazione Centro Studi Campostrini, 2009.
Hungarian: "A Husserli fenomenológia szubjektivizmusa és egy 'aszubjektív'
fenomonelógia Lehetősége." Translated by Balázs Mezei. *Gond* (Budapest)
13–14 (1997): 100–15.
Portuguese: "O subjectivismo da fenomenologia husserliana e a possibilidade
de uma fenomenologia 'assubjectiva'." Translated by Pedro M. S. Alves.
Phainomenon (Lisbon) 4 (2002): 149–65.

Spanish: "El subjetivismo de la fenomenología husserliana y la posibilidad de una fenomenología 'asubjetiva'." Translated by Teresa Padilla. In Jan Patočka, *El movimiento de la existencia humana*, 93–112. Madrid: Ediciones Encuentro, 2004.

1970/7 "Heidegger vom anderen Ufer" (Heidegger from the other bank). In *Durchblicke: M. Heidegger zum 80. Geburtstag*, edited by Vittorio Klostermann, 394–411. Frankfurt am Main: Vittorio Klostermann, 1970.

Polish: "Heidegger z drugiegi brzegu." Translated by Wojciech Patyna. *Aletheia* (Warsaw) 4, no. 1 (1990): 216–24.

Serbian: "Hajdeger s druge obale." Translated by Dragan Stojanović. In *Rani Hajdeger: Recepcija i kritika "Bivstva i vremena,"* edited by Dragan Stojanović and Danilo Basta, 113–30. Belgrade: Vuk Karadžić, 1979.

1970/8 "Ivanov." Program notes, Anton Chekhov, *Ivanov*, directed by Otomar Krejča, Divadlo za branou, Prague, 1970.

French: "Ivanov." Translated by Erika Abrams. In Jan Patočka, *L'écrivain, son "objet,"* edited by Erika Abrams, 150–60. Paris: P.O.L., 1990.

1970/9 *Přirozený svět jako filosofický problém* (The natural world as a philosophical problem). 2nd edition, Prague: Československý spisovatel, 1970.

Contents: Přirozený svět jako filosofický problém (The natural world as a philosophical problem), 7–153; "Přirozený svět" v meditaci svého autora po třiatřiceti letech ("The natural world" meditated on by its author after thirty-three years), 155–234.

English: "'The Natural World' Remeditated Thirty-Three Years Later." Translated by Erika Abrams. In Jan Patočka, *The Natural World as a Philosophical Problem*, edited by Ivan Chvatík and L'ubica Učnik, 115–80. Evanston, IL: Northwestern University Press, 2016.

French: "Méditation sur 'Le Monde naturel comme problème philosophique'." Translated by Erika Abrams. In Jan Patočka, *Le monde naturel et le mouvement de l'existence humaine*, edited by Erika Abrams, 50–124. Dordrecht: Kluwer Academic Publishers, 1988.

Hungarian: "A szerző utószava: 'A természetes világ nimt filozófiai probléma' cseh kiadásához." Translated by Edit Rózsahegyi. *Gond* (Budapest) 13–14 (1997): 116–78.

German: "Nachwort des Autors zur tschechischen Neuausgabe (1970)." Translated by Simona Löwenstein with Klaus Nellen. In *Die natürliche Welt als philosophisches Problem*, edited by Klaus Nellen and Jiří Němec with an introduction by Ludwig Landgrebe, 181–269. Stuttgart: Klett-Cotta, 1990.

1970/11 "Duchovní základy života v naší době" (The spiritual foundations of life in our time). *Křesťanská revue* 37, nos. 1 and 2 (1970): 12–15 and 33–40.

French: "Les fondements spirituels de la vie contemporaine." Translated by Erika Abrams. *Études phénoménologiques* (Brussels) 1 (1985): 65–94.

German: "Die geistigen Grundlagen des Lebens in unserer Zeit." Translated by Ilja Šrubař. In *Ketzerische Essais zur Philosophie der Geschichte und ergänzende Schriften*, edited by Klaus Nellen and Jiří Němec with an introduction by Paul Ricœur, 353–78. Stuttgart: Klett-Cotta, 1988.

Serbian: "Duhovni temelji života u našem vremenu." Translated by Tihana Hamović. In *Izbor iz filosofskih spisa*, edited by Časlav D. Koprivica, 45–67. Novi Sad: Akademska knjiga, 2013.

Spanish: "Los fondamentos spirituales de la vida contemporánea." Translated by Iván Ortega Rodríguez. In Jan Patočka, *Libertad y sacrificio*, 221–48. Salamanca: Ediciones Sígueme, 2007.

1970/13 *Il senso dell'oggi in Cecoslovacchia* (The meaning of today in Czechoslovakia). Translated by Gianlorenzo Pacini, foreword by Josef Zumr. Milan: Lampugnani Nigri, 1970.

1971/1 *Die Philosophie der Erziehung des J. A. Comenius* (J. A. Comenius's philosophy of education). Paderborn: Ferdinand Schöningh, 1971.

1971/2 "Der Subjektivismus der Husserlschen und die Forderung einer asubjektiven Phänomenologie" (Husserlian subjectivism and the call for an asubjective phenomenology). *Sborník prací filosofické fakulty Brněnské university, Řada uměnovědná* 19–20, no. 14–15 (1971): 11–26. Reprinted in Jan Patočka, *Die Bewegung der menschlichen Existenz*, edited by Klaus Nellen, Jiří Němec, and Ilja Šrubař with an introduction by Ilja Šrubař, 286–309. Stuttgart: Klett-Cotta, 1991. 2nd reprint in *Edmund Husserl: Critical Assessments of Leading Philosophers, vol. I: Circumscriptions: Classic essays on Husserl's phenomenology*, edited by Rudolf Bernet, Donn Welton, Gina Zavota, 278–97. London: Routledge, 2005.

English: "Husserl's Subjectivism and the Call for an Asubjective Phenomenology." Translated by Matt Bower, Ivan Chvatík, and Kenneth Maly. In *Asubjective Phenomenology: Jan Patočka's Project in the Broader Context of His Work*, edited by L'ubica Učník, Ivan Chvatík, and Anita Williams, 17–40. Nordhausen: Verlag Traugott Bautz, 2015.

French: "Le subjectivisme de la phénoménologie husserlienne et l'exigence d'une phénoménologie asubjective." Translated by Erika Abrams. In Jan Patočka, *Qu'est-ce que la phénoménologie?*, edited by Erika Abrams, 217–48. Grenoble: Jérôme Millon, 1988.

Italian: "Il soggettivismo della fenomenologia husserliana e l'esigenza di una fenomenologia asoggettiva." Translated by Giuseppe Di Salvatore. In Jan Patočka, *Che cos'è la fenomenologia? Movimento, mondo, corpo*, 285–311. Verona: Edizioni Fondazione Centro Studi Campostrini, 2009.

Portuguese: "O subjectivismo da fenomenologia husserliana e a exigência de uma fenomenologia asubjectiva." Translated by Pedro M. S. Alves. *Phainomenon* (Lisbon) 4 (2002): 127–48.

Spanish: "El subjetivismo de la fenomenología husserliana y la exigencia de una fenomenología 'asubjetiva'." Translated by Teresa Padilla. In Jan Patočka, *El movimiento de la existencia humana*, 113–35. Madrid: Ediciones Encuentro, 2004.

1971/3 "Pravda mýtu v Sofoklových dramatech o Labdakovcích" (The truth of myth in Sophocles' Labdacian dramas). Program notes, Sophocles, *Oedipus Rex, Antigone*, Divadlo za branou, Prague, 1971.

French: "La vérité du mythe dans les drames de Sophocle sur les Labdacides." Translated by Erika Abrams. In Jan Patočka, *L'écrivain, son "objet,"* edited by Erika Abrams, 30–42. Paris: P.O.L., 1990.

German: "Die Wahrheit des Mythos in Sophokles' Labdakiden-Dramen." Translated by Ilja and Věra Šrubař. In *Kunst und Zeit. Kulturphilosophischen Schriften*, edited by Klaus Nellen and Ilja Šrubař with an introduction by Walter Biemel, 106–15. Stuttgart: Klett-Cotta, 1987.

1971/4 "Německá duchovnost Beethovenovy doby" (German spirituality in Beethoven's day). *Hudební rozhledy* 24, no. 1 (1971): 30–8.

French: "La spiritualité allemande de l'époque de Beethoven." Translated by Erika Abrams. In Jan Patočka, *L'art et le temps*, edited and translated by Erika Abrams, 142–76. Paris: P.O.L., 1990.

German: "Die Geistige Epoche Beethovens." Translated by Ludger Hagedorn. In *Andere Wege in die Moderne. Studien zur europäischen Ideengeschichte von der Renaissance bis zur Romantik*, 421–43. Würzburg: Königshausen & Neumann; Prague: OIKOYMENH, 2006.

1972/1 "La philosophie de la crise des sciences d'après E. Husserl et sa conception d'une phénoménologie du 'monde de la vie'" (The philosophy of the crisis of the sciences according to E. Husserl and his conception of a phenomenology of the "lifeworld"). *Archiwum Historii Filozofii i Myśli Społecznej* (Warsaw) 18, edited by Andrzej Walicki (1972): 3–18.

English: "Edmund Husserl's Philosophy of the Crisis of the Sciences and His Conception of a Phenomenology of the 'Life World'." Translated by Erazim Kohák. In *Jan Patočka: Philosophy and Selected Writings*, edited by Erazim Kohák, 223–38. Chicago: University of Chicago Press, 1989.

Italian: "La filosofia della crisi delle scienze secondo Edmund Husserl e la sua concezione di una fenomenologia del 'mondo della vita'." Translated by Alessandra Pantano. In Jan Patočka, *Il mondo naturale e la fenomenologia*, 127–48. Milan: Mimesis, 2003.

German: "Die Philosophie der Krisis der Wissenschaften nach Edmund Husserl und sein Verständnis einer Phänomenologie der Lebenswelt." Translated by Klaus Nellen. In Jan Patočka, *Die Bewegung der menschlichen Existenz*, edited by Klaus Nellen, Jiří Němec, and Ilja Šrubař with an introduction by Ilja Šrubař, 310–29. Stuttgart: Klett-Cotta, 1991.

Polish: "Filozofia kryzysu nauki według E. Husserla i jego koncepcja fenomenologii 'świata życia'." Translated by Juliusz Zychowicz. In *Świat naturalny a fenomenologia*, 140–57. Cracow: Papieska akademia teologiczna, 1987. Reprinted under the title "Filozofia kryzysu nauki według Edmunda Husserla i jego koncepcja fenomenologii 'świata przeżywanego'" in *Świat przeżywany: Fenomenologia i nauki społeczne*, edited by Zdzisław Krasnodębski and Klaus Nellen, 25–47. Warsaw: PIW, 1993.

Spanish: "La filosofía de la crisis de las sciencias según Edmund Husserl y su concepción de una fenomenología del mundo de la vida." Translated by Jesús María Ayuso. In Jan Patočka, *El movimiento de la existencia humana*, 137–55. Madrid: Ediciones Encuentro, 2004.

1972/2 "Weltganzes und Menschenwelt: Bemerkungen zu einem zeitgenössischen kosmologischen Ansatz" (The world as a whole and the human world: Observations toward a contemporary cosmological approach). In *Weltaspekte der Philosophie: Festschrift für R. Berlinger*, edited by Werner Beierwaltes and Wiebke Schrader, 243–50. Amsterdam: Rodopi, 1972.

French: "Le tout du monde et le monde de l'homme." Translated by Erika Abrams. In Jan Patočka, *Le monde naturel et le mouvement de l'existence humaine*, edited by Erika Abrams, 265–72. Dordrecht: Kluwer Academic Publishers, 1988.

Italian: "Intero del mondo e mondo dell'uomo: Osservazioni per un inizio di cosmologia contemporanea." Translated by Alessandra Pantano. In Jan

Patočka, *Il mondo naturale e la fenomenologia*, 149–58. Milan: Mimesis, 2003.

    Spanish: "Universo y mundo del hombre: Observaciones a un planteamiento cosmológico contemporáneo." Translated by Teresa Padilla. In Jan Patočka, *El movimiento de la existencia humana*, 85–92. Madrid: Ediciones Encuentro, 2004

1972/3 "Zur ältesten Systematik der Seelenlehre" (Toward the oldest system of the doctrine of the soul). In *Phänomenologie heute: Festschrift für L. Landgrebe*, edited by Walter Biemel, 122–37. The Hague: Martinus Nijhoff, 1972. Reprinted in *Péče o duši*, vol. 3, 103–18. Prague: OIKOYMENH, 1988. Reprinted again in *Ketzerische Essais zur Philosophie der Geschichte und ergänzende Schriften*, edited by Klaus Nellen and Jiří Němec with an introduction by Paul Ricœur, 288–303. Stuttgart: Klett-Cotta, 1988.

1972/4 "Zu Roman Ingardens Ontologie des malerischen Kunstwerks" (On Roman Ingarden's ontology of the pictorial work of art). *Philosophische Perspektiven* (Frankfurt am Main) 4, edited by Rudolph Berlinger and Eugen Fink (1972): 117–25.

1973/3 "Stabilisierung der Wissenschaft und Bildung: Auguste Comte" (Stabilizing science and education: Auguste Comte). In Theodor Ballauff and Klaus Schaller, *Pädagogik: Eine Geschichte der Bildung und Erzihung*, vol. 3, 487–98. Freiburg and Munich: Karl Alber, 1973.

1975/1 *Kacířské eseje o filosofii dějin* (Heretical essays on the philosophy of history). Prague: Edice Petlice, vol. 49 (samizdat), 1975.

    English: *Heretical Essays in the Philosophy of History*. Translated by Erazim Kohák, edited by James Dodd, foreword by Paul Ricœur. Chicago: Open Court, 1996.

    Bulgarian: *Eretični eseta za filosofija na istorijata*. Translated by Valentin Trajanov, afterword by Filip Karfík. Sofia: Valentin Trajanov, 1994.

    French: *Essais hérétiques sur la philosophie de l'histoire*. Translated by Erika Abrams, foreword by Paul Ricœur, afterword by Roman Jakobson. Lagrasse: Verdier, 1981. 2nd edition: Lagrasse: Verdier, 1988. 3rd (revised) edition: Lagrasse: Verdier, 1999. 4th (revised) edition: Lagrasse: Verdier, 2007.

    Italian: *Saggi eretici sulla filosofia della storia*. Translated by Gianlorenzo Pacini, foreword by Václav Bělohradský. Bologna: CSEO, 1981.

    Japanese: *Rekishi tetsugaku ni tsuite no itanteki ronkō*. Translated by Tatsuo Ishikawa. Tokyo: Misuzu Shobō, 2007.

    Lithuanian: *Eretiški esė apie istorijos filosofiją*. Translated by Almis Grybauskas. Vilnius: Regnum fondas, 2002.

    Hungarian: "Eretnek esszék a történelem filozófiájáról." Translated by István Németh and Róbert Kiss Szemán. In *Mi a cseh?*, edited by Ivan Chvatík with a foreword by Petr Pithart and an afterword by Mihály Vajda, 254–379. Pozsony/Bratislava: Kalligram, 1996.

    German: "Ketzerische Essais zur Philosophie der Geschichte." Translated by Joachim Bruss and Peter Sacher. In *Ketzerische Essais zur Philosophie der Geschichte und ergänzende Schriften*, 21–164. Stuttgart: Klett-Cotta, 1988. New translation: *Ketzerische Essais zur Philosophie der Geschichte. Mit Texten von Paul Ricœr und Jacques Derrida*. Translated by Sandra Lehman with an afterword by Hans Rainer Sepp, edited by Jan-Patočka-Archiv des Institut für Wissenschaften vom Menschen (Vienna). Berlin: Suhrkamp, 2010.

Norwegian: "Kjetterske studier i historiens filosofi." Translated by Milada Blekastad. In *Kjetterske studier i historiens filosofi*, edited by Asbjoern Aarnes and E. A. Wyller, 15–186. Oslo: Tanum-Norli, 1979. (Includes Patočka essay 1975–8, "Vlastní glosy ke Kacířským esejům" (Own glosses on the Heretical essays), 187–207.)

Polish: *Eseje heretyckie z filozofii historii*. Translated by Juliusz Zychowicz. Warsaw: Bibliotéka Aletheia (samizdat), 1988. 2nd (revised) edition: Warsaw: Aletheia, 1998.

Romanian: *Eseuri eretice despre filosofia istoriei*. Translated with an introduction by Anca Irina Ionescu. Bucharest: Editura Herald, 2016.

Russian: *Jereticheskie esse o filosofiyi istoriyi*. Translated by Pavel Prylutski. Minsk: I. P. Logvinov, 2008.

Slovenian: *Krivoverski eseji o filozofiji zgodovine*. Translated with an afterword by Frane Jerman. Ljubljana: Cankarjeva založba, 1997.

Serbian: *Jeretički eseji o filosofiji povesti*. Translated by Tihana Hamović. In *Izbor iz filosofskih spisa*, edited by Časlav D. Koprivica, 69–202. Novi Sad: Akademska knjiga, 2013.

Spanish: *Ensayos heréticos sobre la filosofía de la historia seguido de glosas*. Translated by Alberto Clavería, foreword by Paul Ricœur. Barcelona: Península, 1988. New translation: *Ensayos heréticos sobre filosofía de la historia*. Translated by Iván Ortega Rodríguez. Madrid: Ediciones Encuentro, 2016.

Swedish: *Kätterska essäer om historiens filosofi*. Translated with an afterword by Leo Kramár. Gothenburg: Daidalos, 2006. (Includes Patočka essay 1975–8, "Vlastní glosy ke Kacířským esejům" (Own glosses on the Heretical essays), 187–202; and 1990 foreword by Ivan Dubský, 7–20.)

Ukrainian: "Jeretychni ese pro filosofiyu istoriyi." Translated by Halyna Syvachenko and Ihor Melnychenko. In Jan Patočka, *Jeretychni ese pro filosofiyu istoriyi*, 203–369. Kyiv: Vydavnyctvo Solomiji Pavlychko "Osnovy," 2001.

1975/9 "Epochē und Reduktion. Einige Bemerkungen" (Epochē and reduction. Some remarks). In *Bewusst sein: Gerhard Funke zu eigen*, edited by A. J. Bucher, Hermann Drüe, and Thomas Mulvany Seebohm, 76–85. Bonn: Bouvier Verlag Herbert Grundmann, 1975.

English: "Epochē and Reduction: Some Observations." Translated by Matt Bower, Ivan Chvatík, and Kenneth Maly. In *Asubjective Phenomenology: Jan Patočka's Project in the Broader Context of His Work*, edited by Ľubica Učník, Ivan Chvatík, and Anita Williams, 41–52. Nordhausen: Verlag Traugott Bautz, 2015.

French: "Epochē et réduction." Translated by Erika Abrams. In Jan Patočka, *Qu'est-ce que la phénoménologie?*, edited by Erika Abrams, 249–61. Grenoble: Jérôme Millon, 1988.

Italian: "Epochē e riduzione." Translated by Alessandra Pantano. *Aut aut* 299–300 (2000): 142–51.

Spanish: "Epojé y reducción." Translated by Teresa Padilla. In Jan Patočka, *El movimiento de la existencia humana*, 241–50. Madrid: Ediciones Encuentro, 2004.

1976/1 *Los intelectuales ante la nueva sociedad* (Intellectuals in the face of a new society). Translated by Fernando de Valenzuela with a foreword by Carlos París. Madrid: AKAL, 1976.

1976/2 "Erinnerungen an Husserl" (Memories of Husserl). In *Die Welt des Menschen—Die Welt der Philosophie: Festschrift für Jan Patočka*, edited by Walter Biemel, vii–xix. The Hague: Martinus Nijhoff, 1976.
Spanish: "Recuerdos de Husserl." Translated by Augustín Serrano de Haro. *Devenires* (Morelia, Mexico) 6 (2002): 9–22.

1976/3 *Le monde naturel comme problème philosophique*. Translated by Jaromír Daněk and Henri Declève. The Hague: Martinus Nijhoff, 1976. (With a new afterword by the author in French, viz. 1976/4.)

1976/5 "Roman Jakobsons phänomenologischer Strukturalismus" (Roman Jakobson's phenomenological structuralism). *Tijdschrift voor filosofie* 38, no. 1 (1976): 129–35. (Review of Elmar Holenstein, *R. Jakobsons phänomenologischer Strukturalismus*. Frankfurt am Main: Suhrkamp, 1975.) Reprinted in *Jan Patočka: Texte—Dokumente—Bibliographie*, 409–18. Prague: OIKOYMENH and Freiburg and Munich: Karl Alber, 1999.

1976/6 "Karteziánství a fenomenologie" (Cartesianism and phenomenology). In *Karlu Kosíkovi k padesátinám*, 1–51. Prague: samizdat, 1976.
English: "Cartesianism and Phenomenology." Translated by Erazim Kohák. In *Jan Patočka: Philosophy and Selected Writings*, ed. Erazim Kohák, 285–326. Chicago: University of Chicago Press, 1989.
French: "Cartésianisme et phénoménologie." Translated by Erika Abrams. In Jan Patočka, *Le monde naturel et le mouvement de l'existence humaine*, edited by Erika Abrams, 180–226. Dordrecht: Kluwer Academic Publishers, 1988.
German: "Cartesianismus und Phänomenologie," translated by Věra Koubová, revised by Klaus Nellen. In Jan Patočka, *Die Bewegung der menschlichen Existenz*, edited by Klaus Nellen, Jiří Němec, and Ilja Šrubař with an introduction by Ilja Šrubař, 360–414. Stuttgart: Klett-Cotta, 1991.
Spanish: "Cartesianismo y fenomenología." Translated by Teresa Padilla. In Jan Patočka, *El movimiento de la existencia humana*, 187–240. Madrid: Ediciones Encuentro, 2004

1977/1 *Dvě studie o Masarykovi* (Two studies of Masaryk). Prague: samizdat, 1977.
French: "Deux études sur Masaryk." Translated by Erika Abrams. In *La crise du sens I: Comte, Masaryk, Husserl*, 95–216. Brussels: Ousia, 1985.
Italian: "Due studi su Masaryk." Translated by Riccardo Paparusso. In *Jan Patočka: Due studi su Masaryk*, 59–160. Rome: Editrice Apes, 2014.

INDEX